The Cultural Roots of American I

The Cultural Roots of American Islamicism explores the heritage of how Americans have long pressed orientalist images of Islam into service to globalize the authority of domestic cultural power. By delving deeply into rich and interdisciplinary archives of expression from the seventeenth to nineteenth centuries, the book examines how Muslim history and practices provided a contentious global horizon that Americans engaged to orient the direction of their national project, the morality of their social institutions, and the contours of their romantic imaginations. Early Americans first viewed the Islamic world as an antichristian and despotic threat but progressively revised these images into a resource for fashioning more comparative and cosmopolitan alternatives. Readers will better understand how long-held habits of intercultural perception have shaped present impasses between the United States and the Muslim world.

Timothy Marr is assistant professor in the Curriculum in American Studies at the University of North Carolina at Chapel Hill, where he teaches seminars on cultural memory, captivity, tobacco, birth and death, and mating and marriage. He originally became interested in the subject of this book while teaching Herman Melville's *Moby-Dick* in Pakistan in the late 1980s. He is the coeditor of *Ungraspable Phantom: Essays on* Moby-Dick.

This book is published in association with the American Antiquarian Society (AAS), in Worcester, Massachusetts, which supported the author's research and writing through a Mellon Post-Dissertation Fellowship, funded by a grant to the AAS by the Andrew W. Mellon Foundation.

The Cultural Roots
of American Islamicism

TIMOTHY MARR

University of North Carolina at Chapel Hill

CAMBRIDGE
UNIVERSITY PRESS

CAMBRIDGE UNIVERSITY PRESS
Cambridge, New York, Melbourne, Madrid, Cape Town, Singapore, São Paulo

Cambridge University Press
40 West 20th Street, New York, NY 10011-4211, USA

www.cambridge.org
Information on this title: www.cambridge.org/9780521852937

First published 2006

Printed in the United States of America

A catalog record for this publication is available from the British Library.

Library of Congress Cataloging in Publication Data

Marr, Timothy, 1960–
The cultural roots of American Islamicism / Timothy Marr.
p.   cm.
Includes bibliographical references and index.
ISBN 0-521-85293-5
1. United States – Civilization – 1783–1865.   2. Islam – Public opinion – History.
3. Orientalism – United States – History.   4. Islamic countries – Foreign public opinion,
American.   5. Public opinion – United States – History.   6. Islam and politics – United States –
History.   7. Islamic countries – Relations – United States.   8. United States – Relations –
Islamic countries.   9. Religion and sociology – United States – History.   10. United States –
Intellectual life – 1783–1865.   I. Title.
E164.M37   2006
909'.09767 – dc22   2005022675

ISBN-13   978-0-521-85293-7 hardback
ISBN-10   0-521-85293-5 hardback

ISBN-13   978-0-521-61807-6 paperback
ISBN-10   0-521-61807-X paperback

for Paula

for Paula

Contents

	Figures	*page*	ix
	Acknowledgments		xi
	Imagining Ishmael: Introducing American Islamicism		1
1.	Islamicism and Counterdespotism in Early National Cultural Expression		20
2.	"Drying Up the Euphrates": Muslims, Millennialism, and Early American Missionary Enterprise		82
3.	Antebellum Islamicism and the Transnational Crusade of Antislavery and Temperance Reform		134
4.	"Turkey Is in Our Midst": Mormonism as an American "Islam"		185
5.	American Ishmael: Herman Melville's Literary Islamicism		219
6.	Turning Turk: The Gendered Pageantry of Mid-Nineteenth-Century Islamicism		262
	Index		299

Figures

0.1   John Smith's Bashing of the Bashaw of Nalbrits from the
True Travels (1630).   *page* 4

1.1   Valentine Verax, "The Allied Despots. Or The Friendship of
Britain for America" (20 February 1794).   32

1.2   *An Affecting History of the Captivity and Sufferings of Mrs. Mary
Velnet* (Boston 1804).   48

1.3   M. Corne, "Triumphant Return of the American Squadron
under Com. Bainbridge from the Mediterranean 1815,"
The Naval Temple (Boston 1816).   63

1.4   *An Attempt to Analyse the Automation Chess Player of Mr. De
Kempelin* (London: Booth, 1821).   73

1.5   Detail from the 1808 Naval Monument (Tripoli Monument) on
the grounds of the U.S. Naval Academy in Annapolis, Maryland.   80

2.1   "The Apocalyptic Scorpion-Locust," *Horae Apocalyticae; or, A
Commentary on the Apocalypse* (London 1844).   96

2.2   Section of *A Chronological Chart of the Visions of Daniel and John*
(Boston c. 1843).   101

2.3   Illustration of "Afghaun" as one of the "Kings of the East" of
Revelation 16:12.   112

3.1   Frontispiece from Lyman Cobb, *The Evil Tendencies of Corporal
Punishment as a Means of Moral Discipline* (New York: Mark H.
Newman, 1847).   137

3.2   "The Turks are a grave people" from the book for children *People
of Different Countries* (New York 1837).   169

4.1   Illustrations from *Boadicea; The Mormon Wife. Life Scenes in Utah*
(1855).   211

5.1   Herman Melville's Turkish Slippers.   220

6.1   Portrait of Nicholas Boylston by John Singleton Copley (1767).   263

6.2   Portrait of Amos Lawrence by Chester Harding (1845).   264

6.3   Iranistan, P. T. Barnum's "Oriental Villa" in Bridgeport,
Connecticut.   266

6.4   Portrait of Bayard Taylor by Edward Hicks (1855).   269

6.5   Advertisement card for the Boston-built clipper ship *Akbar*.   271

6.6   Hiram Powers, "The Greek Slave" (1847).   275

6.7   Amelia Bloomer in Turkish Trousers, *The Water-Cure Journal* 12
      (October 1851), 96.   284
6.8   Zouave Soldiers in Company G, 114th Pennsylvania Infantry,
      Petersburg, Virginia, August 1864.   290
6.9   Winslow Homer, *Zouave*.   291
6.10 Ira Aldridge as Shakespeare's Aaron in *Titus Andronicus*.
      Frontispiece from *The Anglo-African Magazine* 2 (January 1860). 295

Acknowledgments

My experiences teaching for three years at Lahore American School in the late 1980s opened my eyes to Islamic cultures and to the kindness of Muslims. It was there, teaching *Moby-Dick* to a talented group of Pakistani students, that the ideas for this book originated. That extended time living in South Asia also helped me begin to understand cultural distortions in the ways that Islam is represented and interpreted in American situations. The significance of these patterns has dramatically increased during the international struggles over terrorism following 9/11. It is my hope that this book will contribute to a fuller analysis of the impasses between Americans and global Muslims and in some small way help to create new avenues of intercultural understanding. I have been sustained throughout my work on this book by the vision of Bahá'u'lláh that the earth is one common homeland consisting of a single human family sharing a diverse world culture.

The book would not be possible without all the institutional support I have received throughout the years, for which I wish to express my profound gratitude. Living on the campus of Milton Academy until I was eighteen provided me with a dynamic incubator for my intellectual and social development. Williams College allowed me the latitude to grow experientially as well as intellectually. Stanford University helped me learn the skills of seeing a classroom as a space for social exploration. Westover School provided my family with a warm environment to study and raise children during my doctoral research. The American Studies program at Yale University was a wonderful place to engage in the learning and research that launched this study. My thoughts were stimulated by many colleagues and professors during my years studying in New Haven. Special thanks to Jon Butler, David Brion Davis, and Richard Brodhead for their encouragement of my ideas and to Alan Trachtenberg for his unflinching support at every stage. I have also benefited greatly from conversations and collaborations with friends in the Melville Society, at the American Antiquarian Society, at Western Connecticut State University, and at the University of North Carolina. Special gratitude to my colleagues in the Curriculum in American Studies in Chapel Hill for their encouragement and support of my growth as a scholar and teacher.

My research was enabled by fellowships and research support generously administered by the National Endowment for the Humanities (with special gratitude to Giles Gunn); Yale University; the Pew Program in Religion and

American History (now the Center for Religion and American Life at Yale); the American Antiquarian Society (for a Paul Mellon Post-Dissertation Fellowship and a Kate B. and Hall J. Peterson Fellowship); Wildacres Retreat; and the College of Arts and Sciences, The Institute for Arts and the Humanities, and the University Research Council at the University of North Carolina at Chapel Hill. I am very grateful to those individuals and foundations who generously funded these irreplaceable opportunities.

My research was enabled and fostered by the dedicated labor of the staff and librarians who serve at these universities and institutions and to those who kindly read and commented on versions of my work: thank you.

Most integral to the growth and completion of this book have been the members of my immediate family. My parents, Ginny and Lefty, gave me the gift of feeling at home while at school and trusted me with the confidence to seek truth independently. My children – Dylan, Carey, Lucy, and Ginya – have expanded the dimensions of my life by keeping my feet on the ground while giving me fresh horizons to contemplate and precious emotions to feel. Paula has journeyed with me every step of the way even while walking her own path of teaching and service. I am deeply happy for her love and support without which none of these words would be here.

The Cultural Roots of American Islamicism

Imagining Ishmael:
Introducing American Islamicism

In April of 1997, a coalition of sixteen American Muslim organizations petitioned the U.S. Supreme Court to have a larger-than-life representation of the Prophet Muhammad sandblasted off the north wall overlooking the nation's central legal chamber. The Muslim groups took offense at the ivory marble statue that depicts a robed and bearded Muhammad with a curved sword in one hand and the Qur'an in the other. Part of the original Beaux-Arts architecture designed in the early 1930s by Adolph A. Weinman, the statue stands between Charlemagne and Justinian as one of eighteen great law givers of history. The presence of the frieze in such an official location, the Muslim leaders maintained, demonstrated insensitivity to Islamic prohibitions against displaying images of the Prophet, and the scimitar perpetuated stereotypes about Muslims as "intolerant conquerors." Deeply committed to removing the statue, they offered to pay the expenses for an appropriate replacement. Chief Justice William Rehnquist, however, rejected their request. He claimed that the figure represented an honor rather than a form of idol worship and that the sword was a general symbol of justice. He also noted that any alterations in the frieze would not only destroy the artistic integrity of the whole, but also violate a 1949 statute against the removal of statues from the Court's property. While he agreed with the literature handed out to visitors to the Bench that the "figure is a well-intentioned attempt by the sculptor to honor Muhammad," he nonetheless also agreed with the Muslim protesters that "it bears no resemblance to Muhammad."[1]

This ivory marble Muhammad and Rehnquist's defense of it are but recent examples of the ways in which U.S. Americans have long appropriated Islam as a resource for the definition of national culture. Rather than promote a better understanding of the religion of Islam or the interests of Muslims themselves, Americans have long pressed orientalist images of Islam into domestic service as a means to globalize the authority of the cultural power of the United States. On one level, the presence of the statue demonstrates the need to acknowledge Islam as an important world phenomenon as well as the desire to incorporate its exotic power within national

---

[1] Tamara Jones and Michael O'Sullivan, "Supreme Court Frieze Brings Objection; Depiction of Muhammad in 66-Year-Old Sculpture Offends Muslim Groups," *The Washington Post* (8 March 1997); Joan Biskupic, "From Two Friezes, Great Figures of Legal History Gaze upon the Supreme Court Bench," *The Washington Post* (11 March 1998).

genealogies. But the Supreme Court's refusal to act on this 1997 petition dramatizes the crucial injustice of the terms of inclusion. Recognition of Islam in the United States has been arbitrated largely by Americans from Judeo-Christian backgrounds who remain, for the most part, uninformed about and even antagonistic toward the ethos of Islamic belief. The statue in the Supreme Court monumentalizes Islam not as a major world religion (an act of veneration that would contravene the First Amendment) but rather as an outmoded system of juridical violence whose authority has been arrogated and superseded by American legal power. Indeed, in spite of the justified intent to honor Muhammad, the paradoxical logic of Rehnquist's defense of the statue demonstrates what Edward Said has noted in his influential *Orientalism* (1978) as "the almost total absence of any cultural position making it possible either to identify with or dispassionately to discuss the Arabs or Islam."[2]

Islam has figured in the fashioning of North American cultural definitions since as far back as the first years of European settlement. Inaugurating instances in colonial British America can be seen through brief biographical sketches of the Virginian leader John Smith and the Quaker preacher Mary Fisher. The adventures in Muslim lands of these radically disparate individuals and the contrasting deployments of their intercultural interactions intimate the dynamic cultural work performed by even momentary encounters with Islamic difference. Early American negotiations with the Islamic world were epitomized by the journeys of Smith and Fisher and the ways their adventures were constituted into legendary performances that embodied gendered models of intercultural heroism.

John Smith gained experience and credentials fighting Turks in Ottoman Europe well before he ventured across the Atlantic and he prided himself as a hearty crusader against the Muslims.[3] After successfully launching incendiary devices against the Turkish armies in Hungary, for example, he reveled that "the lamentable noise of the miserable slaughtered Turkes was most wonderfull to heare."[4] *The True Travels*, one of the first secular autobiographies published in the West, describes how Smith vanquished three Turkish warriors during combative dueling in Wallachia in 1602, a feat for

---

[2] Edward Said, *Orientalism* (New York: Random House, 1978), 26–7.

[3] Smith's accounts of fighting the Turks were long considered an extravagant fabrication. However, twentieth-century reevaluation of Smith's adventures has proven him to be so reliable about these experiences that he is viewed as "an authority on Hungarian history." Laura Polanyi Striker and Bradford Smith, "The Rehabilitation of Captain John Smith," *The Journal of Southern History* 28 (November 1962): 477. Philip L. Barbour, the editor of the works of John Smith, claimed: "Let it only be said that nothing John Smith wrote has yet been found to be a lie." *Three Worlds of Captain John Smith* (Boston: Houghton Mifflin, 1964), xi.

[4] Philip L. Barbour, ed., *The Complete Works of Captain John Smith, 1580–1631*, 3 vols. (Chapel Hill: University of North Carolina Press, 1986), 3: 116.

which he was granted a coat of arms portraying three Turks' heads. Smith afterwards became "a prey to the cruel devouring Turke" and was sold into slavery to a genteel Muslim woman. She became enamored with Smith and sent the twenty-two-year-old infidel to her brother in Tartary to learn the arts befitting a gentleman. Intolerant of his thralldom to this Bashaw of Nalbrits, Smith "beat out [his] braines with his threshing bat," assumed the Bashaw's clothes, and escaped back to Christendom, eventually making his way to Virginia. Smith's experience in the Islamic orient prefigured his attitudes toward the people and places of America and foreshadowed his celebrated experiences with Pocahontas. When Smith anchored in 1614 off the peninsula in northern Massachusetts now known as Cape Ann, he named it Tragabigzanda after the Muslim lady who saved him and called three other coastal islands there the Three Turks. His distinctive cross-cultural experiences reveal how old world patterns of disdaining "others" were imported into new world spaces as a strategy to situate the strangeness of cultural difference. His narrative also demonstrates how control over the "infidel," often through violence, was constitutive of both Christian identity and noble masculinity. Smith's coat of arms, whose shield depicts the turbaned heads of the three Turks, appears in the corner of one of the earliest maps of "ould Virginia," which has the scrolled motto "Vincere est Vivere" – "To conquer is to live."

Unlike the belligerent Smith who plundered his way through Islamic lands, Mary Fisher, an intrepid proponent of Quakerism, ventured to the eastern Mediterranean in 1658 on a mission to preach the gospel to the Sultan of Turkey. Fisher was one of the first Friends to visit Boston where in 1656 the Puritans stripped and jailed her and burned her books. Exiled from New England, she turned her attentions to the Islamic world where she traveled to negotiate a singular audience with Sultan Mehmed IV in Adrianople. Her courage in testifying Christ's truth to the "Great Turk" rendered her anecdotal exploits into a legend narrated in many versions throughout the early American period, including George Bancroft's *History of the United States*.[5] Her faith and fortitude provided a model of Christian witness that exposed the noble receptivity of the Sultan and thus the power of female religious testimony and the potential for evangelizing Muslim peoples. Although Smith and Fisher engaged Islam for different purposes, and although narratives of their encounters functioned distinctly in American

[5] *History of the Colonization of the United States*, 15th ed., 3 vols. (Boston: Little, Brown, and Co., 1855), 1: 452. Among these are two long poems that elaborate the drama of her visit: *Mary Fisher; or, the Quaker Maiden and the Grand Turk* (Philadelphia: Joseph Kite, 1840) and "Visit of Mary Fisher to the Sultan Mohammed IV. At Adrianople, 1658," in "Ruth Plumley," *Lays of Quakerdom, Reprinted from The Knickerbocker of 1853–54–55* (Philadelphia: The Biddle Press, 1855), 17–36. "Mary Fisher," in *American National Biography*, 24 vols. (New York: Oxford University Press, 1999), 8: 15–6. See also Nathaniel Hawthorne's short story "The Gentle Boy" in *Twice-told Tales* (1837).

FIGURE 0.1. In the first image, John Smith is led into captivity to the Bashaw of Nalbrits by a"Drub-man" (interpreter); in the second, Smith effects his escape by bashing the Bashaw to death with a club. These images are panels seven and nine from an nine-panel illustration in *The True Travels, Adventures, and Observations of Captaine Iohn Smith, in Europe, Asia, Affrica, and America, from Anno Domini 1593 to 1629* (London, 1630). Panels four, five, and six feature representations of Smith subduing three Turks in jousting combat on horses, feats for which he was granted a shield with three Turks' heads on his coat of arms.

cultural history, they demonstrate how early encounters with Islam and its territories, while seemingly outside the province of early American studies, must be seen as a wider horizon that informed the invention of cosmopolitan gender roles as well as critical discourses about ethnic difference, societal behaviors, and the relevance of American cultural production to the concerns of the wider world.

Many Americans incorporated the pre-Christian heritage of the orient – including Judaism – as part of the ancient civilizations that paved the way for Christianity and were then superseded by its claims. The rise of Islam as an independent religion after Christianity and its power and persistence as a diverse and far-flung civilization created an intractable conundrum whose difference has both troubled and fascinated Americans of every generation. Unwilling to view Islam as a legitimate religious dispensation, Westerners from as far back as the Crusades have imagined it as a post-Christian provocation to which they have responded by devising an archive of ideological fictions aimed at defusing the heretical rivalry of what Edward Said has called its "*original* cultural effrontery."[6]

---

[6] Said, *Orientalism*, 260.

The religious core of such a distant challenge has resonated powerfully within American cultural expression and still sounds loudly today. *The Cultural Roots of American Islamicism* documents distinctive aspects of the deep and dynamic domestic heritage of Islamic orientalism through the mid-nineteenth century. It unpacks the history and surprisingly vital diversity of selected instances when Americans interpellated orientalized images of Islam to articulate local knowledges and situations within a global context. In so doing it offers a critical history of cultural imagination that illuminates a more planetary perspective to a period of American Studies too often confined within concerns of the nation alone. The examination of the contours and careers of how Islam was represented within early and antebellum American cultural expression – in such varied forms as political theory, fictional imagination, religious belief, reform movements, and artistic creativity – reveals new insights into the transcontinental formulation of national conventions and aspirations. Historical and rhetorical encounters with Muslim places and practices provided an intercultural dimension of comparison that fostered a latitude for contesting a more global relevance for American agendas. It explores how views of Islam, even when misunderstood and kept at a distance, were transmuted within the alembic of American imaginations into cultural resources that citizens deployed in diverse ways to define, influence, revise, transform, and attempt to universalize the insularity of the national imaginary.

American Islamicism demonstrates that engaging with the Islamic orient has been a prominent interactive horizon throughout American history. It maintains that better understanding of the ways that Americans have imagined Islam in the past is essential if the dangerous disjunctures of the twenty-first century are to be surmounted. Interpreting instances of early American encounter with elements of the Islamic world exposes the habits of misperception and strategies of distortion that continue to hinder better relations between Muslims and non-Muslim Americans. The attacks of 11 September 2001, and the ensuing wars on terrorism and extremism are only the latest and most dramatic events to expand the global significance of Islam in the imaginations of Americans. The twentieth-century process of decolonization, including the breakup of the Soviet Union, helped to create a United Nations with almost one third of its members made up of states with predominately Muslim populations. The Middle East became increasingly important to the international interests of the United States during the Cold War because of its supply of oil and the challenge of pan-Arab nationalism. It has remained central because of the continuing spread of indigenous opposition to American power, including the United States' support of Israel, by such groups as Al Qaeda, Hamas, and the Iraqi insurgency. This increasing importance of Islam in world affairs has been propelled by recent wars in Iraq, Afghanistan, and Kuwait and by continuing struggles in such long-standing areas of civil strife as Algeria, Sudan, Israel/Palestine, Lebanon,

Cyprus, the Balkans, Chechnya, Kashmir, Thailand, and the Philippines. Moreover, traditional definitions of national identities in Europe and North America have been challenged by the increasing political influence of large numbers of recent Muslim immigrants who now reside in these countries. At the beginning of new the millennium, more than six million Muslims comprise the largest minority group in Europe, Africa is evenly divided between Muslims and Christians, and in the United States the followers of Islam – almost half of whom are African Americans – outnumber the nation's Jewish population.

This increasing global presence has provoked an important cultural struggle in the United States over how Americans should best understand the cultures of Islam. One popular strain in this struggle has revived the long-lasting orientalist heritage, examined in this book, of vilifying the religion of Islam. This response emphasizes the need to contain the jihad of a "Green Peril" that has replaced the Soviet Union as the civilization that clashes most contentiously with the political and religious destiny of the republic. Another strain seeks to understand Islam more fully and provide more space for Muslims at the table of American pluralism. Politicians eager to avoid further alienation of the world's Muslims, including those in their constituencies, have publicly proclaimed the importance of Muslim mosques, imams, and holy days and lauded Islam as one of the world's great faiths with a civilizing tradition of peace-making that "fundamentalists" are seeking to destroy. Such liberal efforts are evidence of the emergent trend of viewing Islam as part of a larger Abrahamic faith or covenant – an important attempt to broaden the inclusivity of a Judeo-Christian tradition that was itself invented in the twentieth century.

The historical engagement of white Protestant Americans with Islam has been tremendously complex and varied, and this is apparent even in the names that have been ascribed to Muslims in the United States. Americans did not commonly use the term "Islam" before the twentieth century; rather, they called the religion "Mahometanism" or "Mohammedanism," itself an orientalist designation that gave undue centrality to the place of the Messenger Muhammad in the faith of Islam. Muslims were most commonly known as "Turks" in the eighteenth and nineteenth centuries, although there were a variety of other protoethnic designations based on geography, including "Moors," "Persians," "Tartars," and "Malays." Other Muslims, especially the "Arabs" and "Bedouins," were also known in early America as "Ishmaelites" because Muhammad claimed descent from Abraham through Ishmael, his first son, who was born to Hagar, Abraham's bond servant. The most important religious festival in the Islamic calendar, 'Id al-Adha, commemorates Abraham's willingness to sacrifice Ishmael (Ismail) (in contrast to the biblical story of Isaac), and the pair are responsible for the construction of the Kaaba around which all Muslims circumambulate during the pilgrimage in Mecca. Ishmael is denied this primacy in the Book of

Genesis where he is deprived of his birthright after Sarah gave birth to Isaac through whom the Mosaic and Christian covenant has descended. Although Ishmael is promised in the Bible that his descendents would multiply and produce great nations, he is nevertheless cast out with his mother to wander in the desert. The United States is at a crossroads in its engagement with Islam, and the outcome depends on whether the figurative Ishmael remains a exiled wanderer in the desert whose "hands are against all men," or whether, following the lead of Herman Melville who made Ishmael the narrator of *Moby-Dick* (1850), he is naturalized as a symbolic agent of American diversity in the Abrahamic tradition.

Such attempts at patriarchal and biblical inclusion, however, may remain just another imperial appropriation of Islamic difference unless they enable a more engaged dialogue between non-Muslim Americans and diverse believers in Islam about the character of their faiths and the contingencies of their cultures. An essential step in moving beyond present impasses between the United States and the Islamic world is to analyze and understand more fully the complex historical legacy of orientalism that early Americans adopted from Europe and then developed within the specific matrices of their own cultural imaginations. In the eighteenth and nineteenth centuries, leading Americans converted the religion of Islam into a resource for universalizing American power. In so doing, they forestalled deeper conversations with Muslims themselves and thereby created one of the greatest and lasting impediments to understanding Islam on its own terms. This tradition of Islamic orientalism that was elaborated in the place of dialogical understanding accumulated its own long and varied genealogy and generated deformed patterns of intercultural perception that were – and often still are – replicated with considerable complexity and versatility.

Even though today there are active American Muslim organizations and others willing to challenge unjust representations of Islam, the powerful historical templates that preceded and prefigured the mass inmigration of Muslims still shape in some ways the contours of how Islam is perceived and received within the United States. As a form of imaginative colonization, the heritage of Islamic orientalism has left conceptual traces and patterns of intercultural assessment that can be as established and as difficult to alter as the ravages of physical imperialism. While orientalist rhetoric acknowledges the existence of Islam and therefore broadens cultural boundaries, its employment can also authorize cultural imperialism by arrogantly translating Islamic belief and practice into a domestic polemic that serves and underscores insular agendas.

However much American orientalist discourse may attempt to represent the *topos* of the Islamic world, it is ultimately a complex configuration of cultural ideologies that reveals more about the constitution of American imaginations than it does about the character of Muslim beliefs. This study therefore highlights the lowercase term *islamicism* to clearly register this variance between orientalist codes and Islamic faith. On a basic level, then, islamicism is merely a short form for Islamic orientalism, which confines the enormous geographical expanse of orientalism to its Muslim boundaries and constituents and its ancient dimension to its post-Islamic chronology. But it is also a useful counterpoint to the notion of *islamism*, which Western social scientists and policy makers have applied since the 1980s to describe the political agendas and ideologies of Muslims committed to establishing states that enforce social programs run on strict Qur'anic injunctions. Islamicism has discursive parallels with islamism in that both tend to essentialize Islam in ways that often prevent critical analysis of the diversity of Muslim peoples, the contingency of their cultures, and the complexities of their beliefs. Islamicism thus can validate distorted conceptions of Islam that islamists may use to justify more vigorous (and violent) challenges to what they see as the corrupt injustices of Western cultural imperialism.

This study of islamicism, nevertheless, focuses neither on affirming understandings of Islamic belief nor on analyzing islamist political action – both ventures within the academic province of Middle Eastern and Islamic Studies. It rather articulates the cultural connotations given to Islamic belief and behaviors by early Americans who ignored or rejected the religious claims of Islam. Islamicist idioms are best conceived as a transnational discourse referencing Islamic history and Muslim practices whose source lies neither in the Qur'an nor in Islamic theology but rather in the cultural imaginations of non-Muslims.[7] Islamicism constituted for many Americans what Pierre Bourdieu has called a "disposition" – an internalized and often unconscious structure of symbolic power that interpreted Muslim beliefs and behaviors in ways that habitually "misrecognized" the self-interest inherent in such a project.[8] The concept of a disposition is especially useful to the examination of islamicist practices because the term also suggests the dislocation of Islam from the latitudes of its historical expression and its transposition within performative moments of domestic cultural generation. Images of Islam have long provided elements of the integral process of constituting the worldly import of American situations. This book analyzes instances of islamicist cultural rhetoric as revealing transnational expressions that helped to define the broader contours of how early Americans from the white Protestant elite tried to find their home in the world.

---

[7] It is important to note, however, that the term "islamist" is itself an islamicist construction, in that it has been ascribed by Western scholars to certain Muslims and did not emerge as a category of self-affiliation. The intention of replacing "Islamic" with "islamist" was a genuine attempt to distinguish between Islamic religious practice and the political agenda of Muslims seeking to increase Islam's societal role, often with the goal of forming an Islamic state.

[8] Pierre Bourdieu, *The Logic of Practice* (Stanford, CA: Stanford University Press, 1990), 53. The concept of "disposition" bears some similarity to what Edward W. Said calls in *Orientalism* the "enunciative capacities" elicited by a "latent orientalism" (221–2) and in *Culture and Imperialism* "a structure of attitude and reference" (New York: Alfred Knopf, 1991), xxiii.

Islamicism remains, for the most part, a mirage for allowing a deeper understanding of the ethos of Muslim belief, but it nevertheless has provided a powerful reservoir of global rhetoric and imagery that Americans have regularly appropriated to authorize and to criticize cultural constructions of national mission, religious faith, moral behaviors, ethnic identity, and gender performance. The chapters of this book recover examples of how the cultural resources of orientalized Islam figured frequently within diverse and contrasting American archives from the colonial era through the middle of the nineteenth century. This study demonstrates that islamicism, as a practice of the *domestic* figuration of the foreign, constitutes a multivalent and largely unexamined dimension of transcultural definition that a variety of Americans have consistently focused upon to orient – quite literally – the direction of their national project, the morality of their social institutions, the shape of their romantic imaginations, and other important aspects of cultural work and play. Many Americans drew upon orientalist conventions to deal with the intractable difference of Islam in an attempt to counteract its threat as a contending ethos. Islamicist imaginations transformed the alien threat of Islamic difference into indigenous cultural capital that worked in complex ways to universalize American practices. These imaginary compensations provided rhetorical resources that other citizens exploited to share in the exoticism of oriental Islam by domesticating its alterity as a resource of significant power for globalizing their own cultural enterprises. As a constituent element of the hybridity of American cultural identities, therefore, islamicism needs to be seen as part of the long and variegated process through which Americans from the United States have aspired to build a global and historical status as a progressive civilization.

The place of the Islamic world in the cultural consciousnesses of Americans from the seventeenth through the nineteenth centuries was more prominent than today's citizens and scholars have previously supposed. This was in part because the Ottoman (or Turkish) Empire, the political center of the first orient to be encountered by Westerners moving east, was still a formidable political reality in world affairs – even if its power rested more on its past grandeur than on its declining contemporary clout. Indeed, the Ottoman Empire was losing territory and military power at a corresponding rate to the expansion of the size and power of the United States. American Protestant agents sought to establish their republican system and moral culture, linked in many minds with a clear sense of political destiny and religious mission, as one fit to replace (even if only symbolically) the decadent and outmoded Turks, whom many viewed as a despotic and satanic opposition. Moreover, this focus on a distant empire projected an exotic stage at once older and beyond the Europe from which the United States had declared its independence. This transcendence of an increasingly partisan and divided transatlantic heritage, combined with the general absence of Muslims within domestic political constituencies, rendered the Islamic world a global matrix for imagining more universal fantasies of nationalist enterprise. By countering a primary contender of Christian millennialism and republican government, the rhetorical resources of islamicism projected a global difference against which U.S. citizens of various domestic denominations and parties could distinguish a common but diversified national ethnos.

The recurrent cultural images of Islam circulating during the colonial period and inherited and enhanced by Americans in the early national period frequently stood in opposition to many qualities that citizens of the United States affirmed in their own bid for moral legitimacy as an emerging civilization. While Islam signified antichristian imposture, America promised Christian purity; while Islam meant barbaric despotism, America cherished enlightened democracy. In the minds of many Americans, Islam produced immoderate sensuality rather than public chastity, easy indolence rather than hard work, and irrational fatalism rather than progressive reform. This clean oppositional dualism attests to the mythical dimension of orientalism as a strategy of positioning the worldly relevance of American civilizational aspirations. The first two chapters of this book demonstrate how islamicist constructions of despotism and antichristianity in a wide variety of cultural expressions formed an inherent part of the process of reinventing republicanism and projecting Christian millennialism. Chapter 1 examines an interdisciplinary array of early national cultural expression that explores the conjunctures between "foreign" policy with Muslim leaders and islamicist constructions of despotism as an antirepublican political category. Chapter 2 investigates how Islam was figured within the powerful intellectual tradition of biblical eschatology and how this prophetic discourse affected the views and success of the first Protestant missionaries to Muslim lands. Some of the salient power of islamicism in early American cultural history emerged from the concurrence of Enlightenment and religious worldviews in inventing a common yet removed oriental opposition that bridged the gap that often separated republican liberty and redemptive Christianity, the two strongest strands of the imagined national mission.

American Islamicism demonstrates how this ideological opposition between the United States and the Islamic world was complicated and qualified by the application of islamicist dimensions to various domestic situations and through proliferating moments of intercultural contact. In its oppositional form, the Islamic world served as a distant mirror of foreign alterity that revealed and embodied anti-American models deployed to caution citizens about their excesses and remind them of the worldly importance of their enterprises. This book also explores the intricate interplay between three other valences of islamicism (which I call domestic, comparative, and romantic) to elaborate its vibrant dynamism as a dislocating global presence within the cultural politics of the early United States. A diversity of Americans appropriated these rhetorical resources within domestic discursive situations to articulate a complex variety of cultural work and play in a broad range of different ideological registers. A primary strategy of many Protestant reformers was to domesticate islamicist opposition in order to "infidelize" the practices of domestic communities within the United States whose ideologies were suspect and whose behaviors transgressed conventional bonds of communal virtue. This process of transposing negative islamicist notions onto American situations I call *domestic orientalism*.

Islamicist discourse served as a vital source of cultural imagination, however, because it did not remain confined within ideological processes of "othering" that imagined Islam as the idealized antithesis of domestic situations. It also constituted a hybrid resource for globalizing American expressions and performances. The changing power relationships between the United States as a developing market economy and Ottoman Turkey as a decaying empire enabled new opportunities for transcultural engagement that qualified traditional notions of the threatening depravity of Islam. The actual encounter of Americans with complex Muslim cultures checked and challenged the disposition to view Islam as cruel, sensual, idle, and fatalistic, giving rise to the modality I call *comparative orientalism*. For example, when Bostonian George Barrell traveled to the Mediterranean coastal city of Smyrna in 1819, he was pleasantly surprised to find the inhabitants of Turkey not full of the "thousand dangers" that prejudice had "instilled in his mind," but instead "all the virtues possessed by Christians, with but few of their vices."[9] In the midst of the bloody struggle of Greeks for independence from the Ottoman Empire, the *New York Mirror* reprinted excerpts from a 1795 travel narrative of Donald Campbell, who argued that the character of the Turks had been "grossly misinterpreted." Challenging the "involuntary" impulse to associate the Turk with "blood and murder," the excerpts contend that "there exist not a people in the civilized world whose real history and genuine state is so little known as that of the Turks; and the worst of it is, that not one misrepresentation, not one single mistake has fallen on the generous, charitable side; but all without exception tend to represent the Turk in the most degraded and detestable point of view."[10] Such comparative realizations provided contrasting images of Islam that placed ideological uses of islamicism in critical relief.

---

[9] [George Barrell] *Letters from Asia; Written by a Gentleman of Boston, to His Friend in That Place* (New York: A. T. Goodrich, 1819), 10. William Shaler, who served as the American Consul in Algiers, wrote in his memoirs about his similar impressions that North African Muslims "differ very much from the general opinion" and stated that "I have found them civil, courteous and humane. Neither have I ever remarked any thing in the character of these people that discovers extraordinary bigotry, fanaticism, or hatred of those who profess a different religion." William Shaler, *Sketches of Algiers Political, Historical, and Civil* (Boston: Cummings, Hilliard & Co., 1824), 55.

[10] *New York Mirror* 1 (1824): 23, 27, 182–3, 214–5; from Donald Campbell, *A Journey over Land to India, Partly by a Route Never Gone by Any European* (Philadelphia: T. Dobson, 1797), 170, 176–7. The book was originally printed in London in 1795 and in other American editions in New York (1798, 1801) and Philadelphia (1807). Donald Campbell was the pen-Name of an English journalist named Stephen Cutter Carpenter who emigrated to South Carolina in 1803, became an important editor, and later authored a biography of Thomas Jefferson.

Opportunities for the development of American familiarity with Islamic cultures increased during the 1830s as a result of the changing geopolitics of the Mediterranean region. The defeat of the Turkish Navy at Navarino in 1827 (combined with the massacre of the Ottoman army of the Janissaries a year earlier), the colonization of Algeria by the French in 1830, and the signing of commercial treaty between the United States and Turkey that same year removed many of the obstacles that had prevented a larger number of Americans from visiting the eastern Mediterranean. The accessibility of the Levant to Western visitors was also supported by the introduction of steamship service between Mediterranean ports, the opening of tourist hotels, and the publication of emerging genres of books establishing sightseeing routes, charting sacred geography, and narrating more engaged patterns of perceiving Near Eastern life. The growing number of travelers included those associated with missionary, military, and merchant enterprises, as well as a variety of tourists ranging from vacationing college presidents to drifting adventurers seeking the romance of authorship and the therapy of new biological and moral climates. The publication of their letters and narratives dispersed a somewhat more realistic portrayal of the practices of Ottoman life, which helped to instigate a slow reassessment of derogatory stereotypes of the Turk. While some observers merely sought out and confirmed the traditional perversities of orientalized Islam, other visitors took notice of Islamic cultural behaviors that were superior, even in terms of conventions of Christian virtue, to those practiced daily in the United States. In fact, Americans traveling in the Near East experienced a society that, although it was politically weak, had been more successful in averting some of the social problems most pressing on antebellum Americans, problems arising from xenophobia, drunkenness, exploitation, racism, and sectarianism.

The progressive growth of this comparative dimension of orientalism provided revisionist views of Islam that even offered cosmopolitan models of cultural comportment not available within the traditions of Euroamerican heritage. The reduction of the threat posed by the Ottoman Empire, especially after 1830, recharged the Islamic world more as a focus of desire and less than as a locus of repulsion. An early example of the dynamic transactions of comparative orientalism is a short book review by Lydia Maria Child called "A Few Words about Turkey," which was published in 1833 in a journal she edited called *Juvenile Miscellany*. Child had just read Dr. James E. De Kay's travel narrative *Sketches of Turkey* published by J. and J. Harper of New York and was surprised by what she learned. "We are apt to say 'as wicked as a Turk,' 'as cruel as a Turk,' &c.," she claimed, "but the author...resided in Turkey nearly a year [and] gives an account of the habits and manners of that country, which in many respects may well make us blush for our own." The bulk of the review then cites instances of Turkish virtue taken from the pages of De Kay, such as their honesty, hospitality, kind treatment of animals, temperance, cleanliness, and respect for the dead. Lydia Maria Child assails the vain habit of Americans who speak disparagingly of other cultures and takes a progressive position of encouraging her young readers and by extension "all the civilized world" to "imitate the Turks."[11] Child's review registers how reformers relayed revisionist assessments of Islamic behavior – derived from intercultural encounters of travelers – into the milieu of antebellum culture, where they became tactical resources in the effort to reform improper American behaviors.

Since these new engagements consisted mainly of perfunctory visits to Muslim cultures whose attraction remained a source of exotic difference, comparative islamicism ran the risk of engendering the inverse habit of romanticizing Islam. The negative tradition of islamicism had long been conditioned by the counterstrain of romantic exoticism, which arose from the imaginative opulence of the hugely popular *The One Thousand and One Nights* (known as *The Arabian Nights' Entertainments*), a book as important as the Qur'an for its influence on Western attitudes toward Islam, whose volumes were available in the colonies for much of the eighteenth century and published in the United States beginning in the 1790s.[12] *Romantic Islamicism* figured Islamic lands as one of the world's more desirably exotic locales by drawing upon a mélange of images arising from biblical notions of Eastern opulence, the fantastic supernaturalism of oriental tales, legends of Muslim chivalry, and images of indolent patriarchs enjoying captivating harems. Many antebellum Americans increasingly emphasized this reemergent valence of romantic islamicism – one that privileged qualities of gallant hospitality and sensual enjoyment – because it enabled them to absorb Muslim difference as an emblem of their own cosmopolitanism. By domesticating the liberatory energies associated with a romanticized Islam, this modality of mid-nineteenth-century islamicism capitalized upon exotic alterity to symbolize the universality of American cultural power and therefore increase the allure of domestic cultural and material productions.

The final four chapters of this book address several fields of these comparative negotiations in mid-nineteenth-century cultural expression in ways that Edward Said called "contrapuntal." Chapter 3 charts the islamicist dimensions of the antislavery and temperance movements by examining the ways that these practices were marked as Islamic irruptions in order to elicit domestic reform. These oppositional strategies were countered by new intelligence from travelers in the eastern Mediterranean that found Turkey

[11] Lydia Maria Child, "A Few Words about Turkey," *Juvenile Miscellany* 4 (January and February 1833): 310–1. Her article reviews James E. De Kay, *Sketches of Turkey in 1831 and 1832* (New York: J. and J. Harper, 1833).

[12] Early American editions of *The Arabian Nights* include (Philadelphia: H & P. Rice, 1794); (Norwich, CT: Thomas Hubbard, 1796); and (Dover, NH: Samuel Bragg, 1797).

to be a society with traditions of emancipation and sobriety that Americans were unable to adopt but nevertheless deployed to register a different dimension of cultural criticism. An analysis of polemic and expression by critics who figured the emergent Mormon church – and its theological, military, and marital excesses – as a replication of oriental Islam in the American West makes up the theme of Chapter 4. Islamicism was a common resource for literary imagination, and Chapter 5 unfolds a case study of how Herman Melville transgressively adapted its latitudinarian energies throughout his career as a creative author. The final chapter examines material manifestations of gendered islamicism in the form of paintings and sculpture as well as the popular dress fads of the Turkish bloomer trouser and the Zouave military uniform to demonstrate the increased prominence of its romantic valences by the time of the Civil War.

These examples demonstrate *American Islamicism*'s concurrence with the discovery of Edward Said that orientalist notions "responded more to the culture that produced them than to its putative object" and agree with the philosophical observations of Paul Ricoeur (and Emmanuel Levinas) that "the Other is not only the counterpart of the Same but belongs to the intimate constitution of its sense."[13] Its investigation of islamicism transposes onto American situations the contentions of scholars since Said that orientalism's discursive power was refracted, discontinuous, multivalent, and contested rather than consistently hegemonic. "Orientalism facilitates the inscription of many different kinds of differences as oriental otherness," Lisa Lowe explains, "and the use of oriental figures at one moment may be distinct from their use in another historical period, in another set of texts, or even at another moment in the same body of work."[14] This "heterotopical" heritage of islamicism enabled it to serve as a compelling process of cultural imagination in which multiple images were deployed in different ways both to serve a variety of distinct agendas and to define a diversity of domestic situations. Which modalities of these representations were privileged at any given historical conjuncture – whether they demonized Islam as the enemy of American aspirations, for example, or romanticized it as an exotic horizon for expanding the global repertoire of domestic expression – depended not only on changing evaluations of the Muslim world but more importantly on the ideological contingencies of situated rhetorical and expressive performances. Although early American islamicism did not emerge from the practices of a group of Muslim settlers within the United States, it nevertheless served as a useful "situational," "symbolic," or "fictive ethnicity" for defining the international contours of cultural positions

---

[13] Paul Ricoeur, *Oneself as Another*, trans. Kathleen Blamey (Chicago: University of Chicago Press, 1992), 329.

[14] Lisa Lowe, *Critical Terrains: French and British Orientalisms* (Ithaca, NY: Cornell University Press, 1991), 8.

construed as American.[15] Islamicism's protean and heterogeneous coordinates provided a potent means both of distinguishing a collective sense of commonality defined against an alien contender and of expanding the insularity of domestic concerns onto a global stage.

Both the presence and the importance of the pre-twentieth-century tradition of islamicism in the United States have been underexamined by academic scholarship. Central works on American contacts with Asia, including Frederick Carpenter's *Emerson and Asia*, Arthur Christy's *The Orient in American Transcendentalism*, Carl T. Jackson's *The Oriental Religions and American Thought*, and Arthur Versluis's *American Transcendentalism and Asian Religions* have for the most part disregard Islam and focused predominately on the refraction of Buddhist and Hindu concepts in American thought.[16] Many scholars who have studied Western representations of Islam have neglected their presence in eighteenth and nineteenth-century United States. When Fred Halliday asserts in *Islam and the Myth of Confrontation* (1996): "In the American case almost the only images of Muslims available until the 1960s were in films – Valentino as Sheikh of Araby [sic] [and] Palestinian terrorists in [Leon Uris's] *Exodus*," he exemplifies this ahistorical neglect of the depth and diversity of early American views of Islam and Muslims and is thus unable to argue how such a heritage provides important precedents for understanding the ways that islamicism established itself as a primary vehicle for trying to comprehend Islam. Nevertheless Halliday does argue that what he calls "anti-Muslimism" is comprised of "cultural residues and themes" whose "revival, reformulation, and redeployment" need to be explained in contemporary contexts. This book delves into the roots of these residues and themes by exposing their cultural roots and exploring their ramifications in earlier historical contexts within the United States.[17]

Three studies of early American engagement with the Islamic orient were published in the 1990s, and this study deepens and expands these works. In 1991, Fuad Sha'ban described the "intense involvement" and "emotional and intellectual attachment" of early Americans to the Muslim world in

---

[15] Jonathan Y. Okamura, "Situational Ethnicity," *Ethnic and Racial Studies* 4 (October 1981): 452–65; Herbert Gans, "Symbolic Ethnicity: The Future of Ethnic Groups and Cultures in America," *Ethnic and Racial Studies* 2 (1979): 9–17; Étienne Balibar, "The Nation Form," in Balibar and Immanuel Wallerstein, *Race, Nation, Class* (London: Verso, 1991), 96–100. Frank Shuffleton has noted the performative nature of early American ethnicity by noting that it "is not a constant but an index of a cultural group's continually changing self-understanding in the face of shifting relations to the larger world." *A Mixed Race: Ethnicity in Early America* (New York: Oxford University Press, 1993), 8.

[16] Frederick Ives Carpenter, *Emerson and Asia* (Cambridge, MA: Harvard University Press, 1930); Arthur Christy, *The Orient in American Transcendentalism: A Study of Emerson, Thoreau, and Alcott* (New York: Columbia University Press, 1932); Carl T. Jackson, *The Oriental Religions and American Thought: Nineteenth-Century Explorations* (Westport, CT: Greenwood, 1981); and Arthur Versluis, *American Transcendentalism and Asian Religions* (New York: Oxford University Press, 1993).

[17] Fred Halliday, *Islam and the Myth of Confrontation: Religion and Politics in the Middle East* (London, New York: I. B. Taurus, 1996), 160.

his *Islam and Arabs in Early American Thought*. Robert Allison's *The Crescent Obscured* examines the diplomatic and cultural interactions of the United States in the Mediterranean before 1815, finding the Muslim world to be "a remarkably useful rhetorical device." Allison acknowledges the strategic distortion inherent in islamicism when he pointed out that "Americans who used the Muslim world as a reference point for their own society were not concerned with historical truth or with an accurate description of Islam, but rather with this description's political convenience."[18] In *U.S. Orientalisms*, Malini Johar Schueller powerfully suggests how the imperial aspirations of the early nation were both articulated through and challenged by the cultural aesthetics of orientalism, claiming that the United States was "dependent on the Oriental qualities it sought to (control and) dissociate itself from."[19] Her book's focus on a broader temporal and spatial oriental imagry – including manifestations of orientalism that she calls "Egyptological" and "Indic" – has the effect, however, of diffusing the special challenges that Muslim cultures posed for early citizens. *American Islamicism* extends this scholarship by examining a more diverse and culturally embedded archive of images, artifacts, and situations through which Muslim practices were conveniently figured within an array of early American discourses and performances through the Civil War. By inquiring inductively into how the Islamic world served to internationalize early American cultural politics, this book provides an archival recovery of interdisciplinary idioms of engagement that helped to shape historical encounters with Muslim peoples as well as abiding constructions of American worldliness.

Most recently, historians and political scientists have focused on the importance of the Islamic orient to the international negotiations of American cultural power after World War II. In *American Orientalism: The United States and the Middle East Since 1945*, Douglas Little examines the "complex and sometimes inconsistent attitudes and interests" that have characterized the postwar foreign policy of the United States in its diplomatic relations with the Middle East. While he includes a cursory examination of the roots of anti-Islamic sentiment before the twentieth century, the chronological scope of his study restricts his analysis of the dynamics of the "earlier cultural assumptions and racial stereotypes" that were "converted . . . into an irresistible intellectual shorthand" that underlayed and authorized postwar policies of the United States.[20] Melani McAlister's *Epic Encounters: Culture, Media, and U.S. Interests in the Middle East, 1945–2000* is an excellent study

---

[18] Fuad Sha'ban, *Islam and Arabs in Early American Thought* (Durham, NC.: The Acorn Press, 1991), 199, 195; Robert J. Allison, *The Crescent Obscured: The United States and the Muslim World, 1776–1815* (New York: Oxford University Press, 1995), 59.

[19] Malini Johar Schueller, *U.S. Orientalisms: Race, Nation, and Gender in Literature, 1790–1890* (Ann Arbor: University of Michigan Press, 1998), 3.

[20] Douglas Little, *American Orientalism: The United States and the Middle East Since 1945* (Chapel Hill: The University of North Carolina Press, 2002), 3, 10.

that emphasizes the centrality of cultural practices and representations of the Middle East in the construction of multicultural American identities and postwar U.S. nationalism. *Epic Encounters* reveals many "unexpected convergences" and "uncoordinated conjunctures" between domestic cultural production and the ways that shifting "moral geographies" of the Middle East served as a "mobile sign" for globally situating and fashioning various popular, gendered, and racialized representations.[21]

By examining the uses of islamicism in the formation of domestic cultural identities and projects within the United States before its ascendency to global power, and even before the invention of the "Middle East," this book traces some of the earlier genealogies of what McAlister calls this "cultural logic." In so doing, it directly challenges Edward Said's contention that nineteenth-century Americans never made an "imaginative investment" in the orient because they were preoccupied in large part with the settlement of the West.[22] *American Islamicism* shows that a wide assortment of Americans engaged the Islamic world well before Muslims voluntarily migrated to the United States in the twentieth century. It demonstrates how the Islamic orient with its history and cultural expressions provided a diverse Eastern frontier that served as a vibrant field of transnational definition for a variety of early Americans seeking destinies less manifest and more global than that sought by pioneers in the territories to the west. Protestant Anglo-Americans adapted and invented a variety of notions and positions – as they did for Native Americans on the western frontier – through which they tried to counter, co-opt, or contain differences they were unable to comprehend through dialogical cross-cultural understanding.

Some of the most creative studies on Islam in the United States have come from scholars who have examined the role of Islam among slave communities and in African American cultural studies. The reconstructive illumination of the experiences of enslaved African American Muslims is one area of recent scholarship that acknowledges the sociological presence of Islam in early American cultural history. Allan Austin's *African Muslims in Antebellum America* has been augmented by transatlantic and hemispheric studies by Sylviane Diouf and Michael Gomez that demonstrate how the religious beliefs and practices of Muslim West Africans enslaved throughout the Americas served as a versatile cultural resource that assisted them to survive and even challenge the conditions of their bondage.[23] Although the horrors of slavery

---

[21] Melani McAlister, *Epic Encounters: Culture, Media, and U.S. Interests in the Middle East, 1945–2000* (Berkeley: University of California Press, 2001), 40, 276, 269, 42.

[22] Said, *Orientalism*, 290.

[23] Allan D. Austin (New York: Garland, 1984; condensed as *African Muslims in Antebellum America* [New York: Routledge, 1997]); see also "Islamic Identities in Africans in North America in the Days of Slavery, 1731–1865," *Islam et Societes au Sud du Sahara* 7 (1993): 205–19; Sylviane A. Diouf, *Servants of Allah: African Muslims Enslaved in the Americas* (New York: New York University Press, 1998); Richard Brent Turner, "Muslims in a Strange Land: African Muslim Slaves in America," in *Islam*

largely prevented the transmission of Muslim practices across generational lines, Islam has been readopted by many twentieth-century African Americans as a powerful resource that expresses not only religious faith but also symbolizes an African cultural heritage with a tradition of resistance to the indignities of racism. Although *American Islamicism* does not directly address this dimension of early American islamicism, the ways that African American Muslims negotiated their faith in different forms of Islam within a variety of historical situations remains an area for future work in this field.

Early American islamicism diverged from the transatlantic patterns of orientalism out of which it developed because it was, prior to the United States' military administration of the Muslim Moros of the Philippines at the turn of the twentieth century, a cultural imagination ungrounded in a colonial bureaucracy. Although Americans drew imagery from the inter-cultural encounters of missionary, diplomatic, military, and touristic enter-prises, islamicism played a freer and more symbolic role in shaping how Americans situated their popular and material expressions in more global terms. Unchecked by the models of Muslims in their midst, early Americans employed the difference of Islam to both frame and extend the boundaries of their own cultural enterprises. These dimensions dramatize the larger thesis of this book that the discourse of islamicism tried to contain the global challenge of Islam by converting its difference into a domestic resource, which, when diversely deployed, also helped to universalize national experiences as globally relevant phenomena.

Although this study assumes a traditionally nationalist framework in tem-poral terms by beginning with national independence and concluding with the era of the Civil War, it challenges the blinkered sovereignty of both national and religious exclusivity by dramatizing the fact that even tradi-tions of exceptionalism are dependent on more worldly comparative def-initions. This book also privileges the interdisciplinary variety of cultural sources over the diversity of American peoples, and therefore emphasizes the productions of the white Protestant elite of the eastern seaboard in formulating national culture. Nevertheless, this examination of the cultural processes of islamicism not only illuminates how these Americans tried to make sense of Islam as a global phenomenon but also broadens and enriches inquiries into more established categories of critical analysis. *The Cultural Roots of American Islamicism* opens a new dimension of critical study that was deployed by other groups and can be applied to other populations

---

in the African-American Experience (Bloomington: Indiana University Press, 1997), 11–46; Michael A. Gomez, "Muslims in Early America," *Journal of Southern History* 60 (1994): 671–709, and *Black Crescent: The Experience and Legacy of African Muslims in the Americas* (New York: Cambridge University Press, 2005). For a helpful bibliography of scholarship on Muslims in American slave communities, see Brent Singleton, "The Umma Slowly Bled: A Select Bibliography of Enslaved African Muslims in the Americas and the Caribbean," *Journal of Muslim Minority Affairs* 22 (2002): 401–12.

and moments throughout the Americas. Although seemingly peripheral to hemispheric cultural politics, the field of islamicism lays out a more global horizon that informed (and was conflated with) more established ideological formations ascribed to regional, racial, and religious minorities. Americans of Native, African, Hispanic, Catholic, and Jewish descent were often orientalized in overlapping attempts to define subordinate cultural positions. For example, the ethnic mélange of New Orleans makes it a revealing embodiment of a "domestic orient" that the critical discourse of islamicism could help to interpret from dynamic and innovatively transnational perspectives. The term "American" is used in this study to represent the territories that were consolidated within the United States nation-state. There is clearly a broader hemispheric story to American islamicism that addresses the ramifications of the reality that Spain's colonization of what came to be called the Americas began in the same year that its Muslim Moors – after helping to fashion the shape of Spanish society and culture – were exiled from the Iberian peninsula. This study also focuses primarily on Near Eastern Muslim cultures in North Africa and western Asia but understands that there are important insights to gained from examining how alternative islamicist perspectives were generated from contact with other Islamic societies in Africa and South/Southeast Asia. It is hoped that by introducing the ideological terrain of American islamicism, this book will help stimulate further research into these fertile and fascinating conjunctions.

Across the national mall from the statue of Muhammad in the Supreme Court, 190 feet up on the east wall of the obelisk of the Washington Memorial, is a five-foot stone with exquisitely carved turrets, floral decorations, and Arabic inscriptions on blue shields. A gift from Sultan Abdul-Mejid I – the Ottoman sovereign who would openly support the Union in the Civil War then looming in the future – the stone arrived from Turkey on the schooner *Arctic* in May of 1854. The inclusion of this stone into the tallest monument dedicated for the first president for whom the capital is named symbolizes the vision of this book: to reveal the hidden details of how Islamic difference has been naturalized into a constituent part of the formation and celebration of early national cultural production.[24] A fuller understanding of the hybrid history of American islamicism and its complex, diverse, and abiding patterns of transcultural appropriation provides a necessary perspective on twenty-first-century dispositions toward Islam that too often still pit it as the oppositional mirror of everything American.

---

[24] See image and National Park Service record at "Washington Monument Memorial Stones" at *http://www.nps.gov/wamo/memstone_563.htm*

Chapter 1

Islamicism and Counterdespotism in Early National Cultural Expression

When Thomas Jefferson accused King George III in the Declaration of Independence of scheming to reduce Americans "under absolute Despotism," he spoke from a political tradition that identified the purest form of despotism as that held by the Ottoman Sultan over his supposedly powerless subjects. Jefferson's first draft of the Declaration had gone further by charging the "CHRISTIAN King of Great Britain" with coresponsibility for the slave trade, which he called a "piratical warfare" that was "the opprobrium of INFIDEL powers."[1] The Ottoman Empire remained a global power in the late eighteenth century, and it represented a repressive political system at odds with the republicanism finding new form in the evolving government of the United States. Patriots used islamicist images of Muhammad and the excesses of contemporary Sultans as useful models to dramatize the injustice of British exploitation of their dependent colonies. The condemnation of King George in the Declaration presented his power as an unmanly aberration that privileged the will of the individual over the egalitarian ideal of a just commonwealth. For the only laws a despot felt compelled to contract, according to eighteenth-century political theory, were those that followed the whims of his own profane inclinations. This image corresponded with the tradition of islamicism that focused on Muhammad's usurpation of religious privilege and emphasized how he had imposed Islam upon his followers through a combination of violent threats and sensual promises. Independence-minded Americans attempted to transform the image of their lawful king into a usurping tyrant by depicting King George as a sultanic despot surrounded by his cruel minions.

After the new nation freed itself from British control, its citizens still had to face the specter of despotism as an internal and external threat to nascent republican rule. While some Americans of the new nation conceived of Islam as an antichristian dispensation, a cultural genealogy that will be analyzed in the next chapter, many others drew deeply upon the Enlightenment's equation of Islamic government with systematic despotism. Indeed many early Americans believed what the *New Haven Gazette*

---

[1] Julian P. Boyd, ed., *The Papers of Thomas Jefferson*. 26 vols. (Princeton, NJ: Princeton University Press, 1950), 1: 426.

reported in 1788: that "The faith of Mahomet, wherever it is established, is unified with despotic power."[2] The world of Islam was geographically removed from political struggles in North America; nevertheless, it played a significant role in early national thought and culture because orientalist constructions of tyranny and despotism formed an integral part of the process of reinventing republicanism. To establish their new nation firmly on democratic grounds, worldly Americans had to demonstrate their distance from, and superiority over, the despotic excesses of the old world.

For a half-century after the end of the American Revolution, aggressive acts by Muslims in North Africa, Greece, and even Eastern Asia presented actual threats to American sailors and traders as well as emblematic affronts to national ideals. The Islamic orient was conceived by many Americans as a vicious realm of inhumane bondage, unstable tyranny, illicit sensuality, and selfish luxury that symbolized the dangerous forces that threatened their fledgling political rights and freedoms. The orientalist construction of Islam as a cultural enemy, maligned as both antidemocratic and antichristian, served as an important oppositional icon in terms of which Americans of diverse denominational, ethnic, and partisan persuasions united in defining republican identities from the nation's founding through the Jacksonian era.

Muslim ascendancy in the Mediterranean, and elsewhere in Africa and Asia, challenged American global aspirations for expanding its blend of democratic principles and Christian values. Cultural negotiations of islamicist despotism comprised a key but critically neglected part of the symbolic construction and consolidation of early American nationalism. By exploring conjunctures of political philosophy, foreign policy, gender roles, and a broad variety of cultural expressions – ranging from literary genres to visual and material artifacts – this chapter reveals ways that the Islamic orient served as a useful global field against (and in terms of) which different Americans measured and performed the transnational relevance of their republican project. Islamicism thus constituted an important cultural resource that new nationals adapted and developed to dramatize more fully the forceful viability of democratic government and the desire of many to influence the political regeneration of corrupt systems of global power.

Early American citizens were prevented from acting on their aspirations to spread their nation's influence through the wider world for a variety of reasons, including the weakness of federal power, the peripherality of national geography, and the constricted domain of secular education. Despite the limited powers of their new federal government, Americans refused to capitulate before the historical reputation of the terror of Turkish despotism.

---

[2] "Difference on the Effects of Mahomedanism and Christianity on Human Happiness," *The New Haven Gazette and the Connecticut Magazine* 3 (1 May 1788).

Taking advantage of the weakening of Muslim control in the Mediterranean Sea, early national leaders eventually focused on the Islamic orient as a theater of military operations through which they projected and performed a renaissance of the virtue and valor of their revolution. "We ought to begin a naval power if we mean to carry on our own commerce," wrote Thomas Jefferson in 1785, "Can we begin it on a more honorable occasion, or with a weaker foe?"[3] Americans in the early republic were engaged in a series of conflicts with the Islamic world – negotiating with Algiers between 1785 and 1815, fighting in the Tripolitan War of 1801–5, supporting the Greeks during their War of Independence from 1821–2, and retaliating against Malays in Sumatra in 1831 – and each of these served as sites for testing their continuing devotion to ideals of liberty. During the early years of the republic, Americans imagined the Muslim despot in many different political guises: as not only the Turkish tyrant, but also the Barbary pirate, the Algerine spy, and the treacherous Malay – all offspring of the original corruption that Westerners believed that Muhammad had propagated through the introduction of Islam. Americans frequently portrayed sultans, deys, beys, and bashaws (or pashas) as both deluded infidels and renegades from the "sacred liberty" that many Americans enshrined at the core of their sense of national purpose.[4] The perverse excesses of the male Islamic despot – in both the public and private realms – symbolized a social order whose power was regulated neither by the people nor the influence of pure religion but rather one in which the virtue of liberty had degenerated into the vice of passionate license.

Central to the cultural work of islamicism was the positing of new gender roles that modeled for the nation a type of active citizenship in which private skill and pleasure were enlisted as both vitalizing and critical sources of collective patriotic resolve. With the birth of the U.S. Navy during the wars with Barbary, a powerful vehicle emerged to generate legends of male celebrity that rehabilitated American honor after the indignities of the nation's early weaknesses. As Americans equipped themselves with these inventive resources of national power, the specter of oriental despotism transformed from being a threatening danger to republican virtue to a useful opposition whose powerfully transgressive energies – including that of reason itself – were defused and then rechanneled into the construction of a stable national power capable of protecting and furthering its interests. Events in the Muslim Mediterranean (and in the broader Islamic orient) enabled worldly-minded Americans to affirm upon a global stage – through both historical and rhetorical means – the humanity of their own cultural

---

[3] Jefferson to James Monroe, 11 November 1784, Bernard Mayo, ed., *Jefferson Himself: The Personal Narrative of a Many-Sided American* (Charlottesville: University Press of Virginia, 1942), 116.

[4] Nathan Hatch, *The Sacred Cause of Liberty: Republican Thought and the Millennium in Revolutionary New England* (New Haven, CT: Yale University Press, 1977).

practices, the relevance of their new political system, and the heroism of
their men and women.

MONTESQUIEU AND AMERICAN COUNTERDESPOTISM

Enlightenment political thinkers characterized Islamic government as an
ideal type of despotism in ways that formed one of the fundamental under-
pinnings of the development of islamicism in Europe and America. As early
as the sixteenth century, Jean Bodin had labeled the Ottoman Empire as
a despotic government in which the Grand Seignior owned all individuals
and property in his realm. French critics of the monarchy criticized King
Louis XIV by comparing his reign to the despotism of oriental kings. Denis
Diderot, for example, described Turkey as "a herd of animals joined only
by habit, prodded by the law of the stick, and led by an absolute master according to his whim."[5] But it was Charles de Secondat, Baron De
Montesquieu who most fully popularized the rhetorical appeal of oriental despotism as the great opposition to republican modes of government.
Montesquieu's *The Spirit of the Laws* (1748) was the most comprehensive
eighteenth-century treatise on politics, and it painted a palpable picture of
Islamic government as a despotic system that enslaved its subjects under
an empire of fear and passion.[6] Turkish scholar Asli Çirakman has noted
that Montesquieu's categorical alliance of despotism with Ottoman government produced a "landmark verdict" with a "long-term influence" on how
Europeans and Americans observed Turkey.[7] The Enlightenment characterization of Islam as despotism played a key role in figuring the global relevance

[5] Denis Diderot, "Encyclopédie," *Political Writings*, trans. and eds. John Hope Mason and Robert Wokler
(Cambridge: Cambridge University Press, 1992), 10.

[6] Montesquieu, *The Spirit of the Laws*, trans. and eds. Anne Cohler et al. (1749; Cambridge: Cambridge University Press, 1989); Nicholas Antoine Boulanger, *The Origin and Progress of Despotism in the
Oriental and Other Empires of Africa, Europe, and America* (London, 1764). See also Madeleine Dobie,
Foreign Bodies: Gender, Language, and Culture in French Orientalism (Stanford, CA: Stanford Univer-
sity Press, 2001); Roger Boesche, "Fearing Monarchs and Merchants: Montesquieu's Two Theories
of Despotism," *The Western Political Quarterly* 43 (December 1990): 741–61; Melvin Richter, *The
Political Theory of Montesquieu* (Cambridge: Cambridge University Press, 1977); and David Carrithers,
"Montesquieu, Jefferson and the Fundamentals of Eighteenth-Century Republican Theory," *The
French-American Review* 6 (Fall 1982): 160–88. A statistical evaluation of the influence of European
thinkers on late eighteenth-century American political thought (based on how many times a given
author was cited, quoted, or paraphrased) came to the conclusion that "If there was one man read
and reacted to by American political writers of all factions during the stages of the founding era, it
was probably not Locke but Montesquieu," whom the study found "almost without peer during the
founding era for prominence." Donald S. Lutz, "The Relative Influence of European Writers on
Late Eighteenth-Century American Political Thought," *American Political Science Review* 78 (1984):
189–97.

[7] Asli Çirakman, *From the "Terror of the World" to the "Sick Man of Europe": European Images of Ottoman
Empire from the Sixteenth Century to the Nineteenth* (New York: Peter Lang, 2002), 109, 125.

of revolutionary and republican rhetoric during the nation's emergence and consolidation.

Montesquieu featured despotism as one of the three major types of political government along with republicanism and monarchy. Although Americans were most interested in Montesquieu's observations on the nature of republican government – especially the separation of political powers and the need for civic virtue – they could best understand these concepts in dialectic relation to the despotism that appeared with their absence. There were no checks and balances in a despotic system. All powers were "united in the person of the sultan," creating a uniform system of arbitrary power that Montesquieu found "atrocious" and "monstrous." The complete power held by the despot caused him to lose interest in the affairs of the state and retreat into the luxuries of the harem, necessitating the appointment of a vizier and a personal guard to protect him from the army that administered his realms. The motivating principle in despotism was not the virtue or honor found respectively in republican and monarchical systems, but rather it was fear itself, which – when perpetuated through violence – served to squelch any ambition or aspiration in the subjects of the realm. Justice in such a system was not a duty of upholding laws but rather a project of propagating terror, and it was administered quickly as a violent expression of the will of the despot who "glories in scorning life" and whose strength consisted in being able to take it away. In short, Montesquieu portrayed despotism as a system of ignorance where even the tyrant was a slave to his own inordinate passions: "he does not have to deliberate, to doubt, or to reason; he only has to want." The citizenry under despotic governments was so servile that Montesquieu can only compare them to beasts. "Men are all equal in republican governments ... because they are everything," Montesquieu asserts, but they are equal in despotic governments "because they are nothing."[8]

The characteristic flaw of the system of oriental despotism was its purported lack of any intermediate civil or political institutions capable of contravening the despot's will to power. Without a rich fabric of legal precedent, social interaction, cultural expression, and religious tradition that could instill independent consciences in its citizens and check the power of its leaders, despotic societies seemed doomed to remain mired in slavery. Bryan S. Turner has described this deficiency of civil society in Islam as "an essential feature of orientalist discourse."[9] Imagining Islamic society as "a system of absences," however, expressed most fully Westerner's own lack of comprehension of the social realities of Eastern cultures.[10] As a key

---

[8] Montesquieu, *Spirit of the Laws*, 157, 27, 75.

[9] Bryan S. Turner, "Orientalism and the Problem of Civil Society in Islam," in *Orientalism, Islam, and Islamists*, eds. Asaf Hussain et al. (Brattleboro, VT: Amana Books, 1984), 27.

[10] In actuality, Islamic societies had highly developed bureaucracies whose operations were not accessible to the European travelers whose sources provided the instances of authority for Montesquieu's

expression of islamicism, then, notions of oriental despotism inflated the despot's emblematic power, creating in the process a moral vacuum that Westerners used to bolster their sense of cultural superiority and ultimately to justify the colonization of Muslim territories in North Africa, the Middle East, South Asia, and the East Indies.

Orientalist constructions of despotism such as Montesquieu's helped to consolidate early American views of Islamic government as a systematic and oppositional model of the excesses to be avoided in chartering a new political system. American revolutionaries harnessed this discourse in the service of their fight for independence. American political thinkers figured Muslim societies as being infested with a host of behaviors associated with public vice – not only political tyranny, but also ambition, corruption, covetousness, ostentation, sensuality, and cruelty – all dangers fatal to the viability of a virtuous republic. Even after the United States rid itself of the institution of monarchy, the specter of despotism could arise in its midst if citizens became tyrannized by such vices. Some Americans in the early republic feared that if they allowed themselves to be seduced by the privileges of luxury they would fall into a despotism maintained not by the fearful dictates of a sultan or king but rather one propagated by their own immoderate desires and devotion to idols of fashion. If this developed, the rising nation would devolve into an "empire of passion" that would extend European decadence and reenact the licentious barbarism associated with Asia and Africa and the natural wilderness that surrounded them to the West.

Islamicist propaganda helped to motivate the spirit of independence by rallying diverse groups to the American cause and creating a new American civil society that contested the very Englishness of British rule. "Turkish policy" had long been employed as a model and metaphor for tyrannical power, and this designation thrived in the revolutionary period.[11] A folk song sung by Regulators during the Battle of Alamance in 1771, for instance, figured the Governor's militia as "Turkish bashaws [who] bear absolute sway."[12] Revolutionary political propaganda gained its charge by satirizing unpopular Massachusetts governors Francis Bernard and Thomas

---

classifications. Abraham Hyacinthe Anquetil-Duperron's 1778 book *Legislation Orientale* began questioning Montesquieu's ahistorical use of despotism. The fact that it was never a totalitarian system is intimated at various points in Montesquieu's own analysis. See David Young, "Montesquieu's View of Despotism and His Own Use of Travel Literature," *Review of Politics* 40 (1978): 392–405.

[11] An earlier attack on an emissary of the King as a cruel Bashaw can be seen in the case of Francis Nicholson, the Governor of Virginia at the turn of the seventeenth century, whose arbitrary edicts and despotic arrogance raised deep resentments. See Robert Beverly, *The History and Present State of Virginia*, ed. Louis B. Wright (1705; Chapel Hill: University of North Carolina Press, 1947), 90–1, 107, 256. Thanks to Matthew Dennis for bringing this to my attention.

[12] Arthur Palmer Hudson, "Songs of the Regulators," *William and Mary Quarterly* 4 (1947): 483. Rebelling students at Harvard in 1768 accused the administration of being Turks. Sheldon S. Cohen, "The Turkish Tyranny," *New England Quarterly* 47 (1974): 564–83.

Hutchinson as provincial "bashaws" bowing to immoral British tyranny.[13] "There was, first and foremost, the example of the Turks," noted historian Bernard Bailyn, "whose rulers – cruel, sensuous 'bashaws in their little divans' – were legendary, ideal types of despots who reigned unchecked by right or law or in any sense the consent of the people; their power rested on the swords of their vicious janissaries, the worst of standing armies."[14] By portraying British government over the colonies as a form of bondage equivalent to or worse than Turkish tyranny, patriots effectively encouraged Americans of both the political and religious righteousness of their revolution. One patriot protested British autocracy in 1774 by lashing out: "what greater power has the sovereign at Constantinople, over a province in the East, than the Sovereign at London now has over a province in the West!"[15]

EARLY AMERICANS, THE BARBARY COAST, AND
THE HUMILIATION OF THE ALGERINE CRISIS

While American patriots read about Islamic government and imagined their own political practices as diametrically opposed to those of the Ottoman Sultan, the Americans who initially encountered actual Muslims did so in the Nearer East of the Mediterranean Sea. The first American visitors to Muslim lands were sailors, traders, diplomats, and military officers who interacted with the societies along the Mediterranean littoral, most of which washed up on territories whose inhabitants professed the religion of Islam. After skirting the coast of the Empire of Morocco and passing through the straits at Gibraltar, American ships en route to ports in the eastern Mediterranean were never far from the North African regencies of Algiers, Tunis, and Tripoli – collectively known as the Barbary States – whose coastal terrain stretched for over two thousand miles along the southern shore of the sea. These states, once integrated into the Ottoman Empire itself, were by the late eighteenth century connected with the Sublime Porte only through the Turkish soldiers and settlers in their midst, and through

---

[13] Benjamin Church, *An Address to a Provincial Bashaw* (Boston, 1769). In *The Adulateur*, Mercy Otis Warren's allegorical drama of revolutionary Massachusetts, Thomas Hutchinson is a Julius Caesar figure called Rapatio who is attended to by Gripeall, Captain Bashaw and Bagshot, Aga of the Janizaries (Boston, 1773). Fifteen years later in her *Observations on the New Constitution*, Warren attacked the idea of a standing army by charging that "freedom revolts at the idea, when the Divan, or the Despot, may draw out his dragoons to suppress the murmurs of a few" (Boston, 1788), 8. Figuring colonial magistrates as bashaws was also expressed in the popular *Cato's Letters*. See David L. Jacobson, ed., *The English Libertarian Heritage* (Indianapolis, IN: Bobbs Merrill, 1965), 101.

[14] *Pamphlets of the American Revolution, 1750–1776*, Vol. 1, 1750–1765 (Cambridge, MA: Belknap Press of Harvard University Press, 1965), 43, 44 n. 8.

[15] William Henry Drayton, *A Letter from Freeman of South Carolina* (Charleston, 1774), 8.

the Sultan's religious sovereignty as the Caliph of Sunni Islam.[16] In the early decades of the new nation, direct commerce was opened with the Ottoman ports of Smyrna and Gallipoli for the trading of such Levantine goods as raisins, figs, carpets, and opium.[17]

North Africa symbolized to Americans a compound of political tyranny and antichristian darkness, a potent mixture that lent credence to the view that inhabitants of Barbary were truly barbarians. Part of this heritage was a result of the narrative disposition placed on the history of the southern Mediterranean by the powerful focus of Western education on the Bible and classical literature. Egypt's biblical heritage as enslavers of the Hebrews and the hegemony of Carthage in opposition to the Greeks and Romans initiated North Africa's reputation as land of dark tyranny. Successes in the spread of Christ's teachings in Africa, such as the trumpeted exploits of St. Anthony, had been largely erased by Arab advancement and later Ottoman control. In the same year as Columbus's sighting of the western hemisphere, the *reconquista* of Spain repopulated North Africa with Moors who resented their expulsion, producing the germs for future clashes. Even its geography, which consisted of a narrow coastal region harboring a huge unexplored continent with deserted interiors, stoked imaginations of monstrous semihuman inhabitants, or at least peoples whose alien religiosity, dark skins, and purported lack of civilization produced rationales for their enslavement.

Both Americans and Europeans faced difficulties conceiving of the complex status of Barbary States, and such confusion arose partly from the changing coordinates of cartographical imagination. Being the closest location for early American encounters with Muslims, Barbary's emergent autonomy from the Ottoman Empire (and distinction from what would later be called the Near East) rendered it a peripheral space that nevertheless embodied the despotic powers associated with Islam. Once considered an integral part of a Mediterranean culture, Barbary had by the eighteenth century been "Africanized" and relegated to the status of North Africa.[18] The more useful notion of the *maghreb*, a word meaning west in Arabic, better acknowledges the cultural connection of African Muslims with the Islamic world, but it ironically underlines its cartographical liminality. American geographical works of the 1790s painted North Africa's interior as a "savage desert" where even "lions, tygers [sic], buffaloes, wild boars, and porcupines ... are not the least amiable inhabitants." The wretchedness of

---

[16] For background on North African history, see John B. Wolf, *The Barbary Coast: Algiers under the Turks, 1500 to 1830* (New York: Norton, 1979).

[17] Up until the War of 1812, the United States still required the support of the British Levant Company to pay lower customs duties. S. E. Morison, "Forcing the Dardanelles in 1810, with Some Account of the Early Levant Trade of Massachusetts," *The New England Quarterly* 1 (April 1928): 208–25.

[18] Ann Thomson, *Barbary and Enlightenment: European Attitudes towards the Maghreb in the 18th Century* (Leiden, New York: Brill, 1987).

the natives was measured by the fact that "a Turk [is] the most respectable title in that country."[19] Even the "atmosphere" of North Africa was described as being "fraught with the most detestable depravity in human nature," while its proximity to Europe increased the virulent ferocity of "Mahometan antipathy."[20]

North Africa's reputation for tyranny was enhanced and animated by the practice of plundering European trade and capturing Christian sailors unless tribute or until ransom were paid to its leaders, who were renowned as despots in charge of pirates and renegades. The ranks of rowing galleys that had once captured Miguel de Cervantes had since been replaced by light sailing craft that enabled the privateers to sail out of the Mediterranean and attack European ships and Atlantic coasts, and even threaten the shores of North America.[21] From the earliest days of the settlement of British America, colonial ship captains had to be wary of the approach of North African xebecs and corsairs (from the Latin word *cursarius* for plunder).[22] As early as 1615, John Smith mentioned that one of the Virginia Company's ships returning to Spain with a cargo of fish was taken by the "Turks."[23] Between 1609 and 1616, Barbary corsairs captured no less than 466 English ships. Five years after the *Mayflower* arrived in New England, corsairs from the Moroccan port of Sallee ventured into the British Channel and took two Plymouth ships. That such a fate might have worried the Puritans during their exodus to New England is clear by the fact that by 1637 between four and five thousand British subjects had been carried into

---

[19] In 1794, the publisher Mathew Carey brought out two editions of his *Short Account of Algiers* in Philadelphia. A third edition of the book, doubled in expansion, was published in New York by Evert Duyckinck in 1805. Quotations are taken from the second edition (Brooklyn, NY: Thos. Kirk, 1800), 2.

[20] *An Historical and Geographical Account of Algiers* by James Wilson Stevens was first published in Philadelphia in 1797. The quotation is from second edition published in Brooklyn in 1800, p. iii.

[21] For the background of Barbary "piracy," see Sir Godfrey Fisher, *Barbary Legend: War, Trade, and Piracy in North Africa, 1415–1830* (Oxford: Clarendon Press, 1957).

[22] For accounts of early Americans being captured by North African ships see James G. Lydon, "Barbary Pirates and Colonial New Yorkers," *The New York Historical Society Quarterly* 45 (1961): 281–9; "White Slavery in the Barbary States," in The *Works of Charles Sumner*, 15 vols. (Boston: Lee and Shepard, 1870–83), 1: 432–4; Lotfi Ben Rejeb, "'To the Shore of Tripoli': The Impact of Barbary on Early American Nationalism" (Ph.D. diss., Indiana University, 1982), 57–9; Lotfi Ben Rejeb, "America's Captive Freemen in North Africa: The Comparative Method in Abolitionist Persuasion," *Slavery & Abolition* 9 (1988): 60–1; Robert Allison, *The Crescent Obscured: The United States and the Muslim World, 1776–1815* (New York: Oxford University Press, 1995), 110–1; Glenn Tucker, *Dawn like Thunder: The Barbary Wars and the Birth of the U.S. Navy* (Indianapolis, IN: Bobbs-Merrill, 1963), 60; and Émile DuPuy, *Américains & Barbaresques, 1776–1824* (Paris: R. Roger et F. Chernoviz, 1910).

[23] "New England's Trials" (1622) in Philip L. Barbour, ed., *The Complete Works of John Smith*. 3 vols. (Chapel Hill: University of North Carolina Press, 1986), 1: 426 and 2: 439; Lydon, "Barbary Pirates," 281; George Louis Beer, *The Origins of the British Colonial System, 1578–1600* (Gloucester, MA: Peter Smith, 1959), 319.

captivity, prompting an English raid on Sallee.[24] Massachusetts traders felt endangered enough to petition in 1644 for protection at sea, and ships were commissioned to pursue the pirates, resulting in a full-day action between American colonials and Algerian gunships that James Fenimore Cooper has called "the first regular naval combat in which any American vessel is known to have been engaged."[25] In the late seventeenth century, many American traders were unwilling to stop in England to pick up protective licenses allowing them to sail in the Mediterranean, and as a result many ships were taken and their crews enslaved "under the Power of the Infidell."[26] Colonial leaders such as the Puritan divine Cotton Mather and New York Governor Lord Cornbury (Edward Hyde) were among the many individuals who helped to raise charitable funds for the redemption of captives held in Sallee.[27]

This situation stabilized under the British mercantile system during most of the eighteenth century through treaties made with the deys, beys, and pashas of North Africa to whom the English government paid annual tributes for the privilege of trading in the Mediterranean. Passes were allowed to be issued in American ports (while many others were forged) whose perforations indicated that Britain was current in their payments. Although colonial American traders had been prohibited by the Acts of Trade from importing directly from Asia, they engaged in carrying such commodities as fish, grains, rice, and lumber between British and Mediterranean ports.

With the triumph of American independence, however, the new nation was faced with a significant foreign policy dilemma. When British ports in the West Indies closed to American commerce, alternative markets such as

---

[24] Nabil Matar, "England and Mediterreanean Captivity, 1577–1704," in *Piracy, Slavery, and Redemption: Barbary Captivity Narratives from Early Modern England* (New York: Columbia University Press, 2001), 1–52; *Turks, Moors, and Englishmen in the Age of Discovery* (New York: Columbia University Press, 1999); and *Islam in Britain, 1558–1685* (Cambridge and New York: Cambridge University Press, 1998). Linda Colley, *Captives: Britain, Empire and the World, 1600–1850* (London: Jonathan Cape, 2002).

[25] Sidney Perley, *The History of Salem, Massachusetts*, 3 vols. (Salem, MA: 1924–8), 2: 350. James Fenimore Cooper, *History of the Navy of the United States*. 2 vols. (Philadelphia: Lea and Blanchard, 1839), 1: 46–7.

[26] See the broadside issued by Benjamin Fletcher, "Captain General and Governour in Chief of the Province[s] of New York [and] Pennsylvania [etc.]" soliciting contributions to redeem Christians of New York City from Slavery in Morocco (New York, 1693). For a brief account of the captivity of Seth Southall, the King's appointed Governor to the Carolinas, see Fuad Sha'ban, *Islam and Arabs in Early American Thought* (Durham, NC: Acorn Press, 1991), 65–6.

[27] Lydon, "Barbary Pirates," 281–9. The first Barbary captivity narrative from America, written in 1687, told an allegorical story of redemption describing how Joshua Gee's faith in divine protection enabled him to survive capsize, capture, and cruelty in North Africa. See Paul Baepler, "The Barbary Captivity Narrative in Early America," *Early American Literature* 30 (1995): 95–120 for a reading and contextual analysis of Joshua Gee's *Narrative*, which was first published by the Wadsworth Atheneum in Hartford, Connecticut in 1943.

those in the Mediterranean and Eastern Asia assumed even more economic importance. The presence of American merchant vessels in the Mediterranean put them within striking range of North African privateers who may have been encouraged by Britain to capture these ships because the United States, now independent, was no longer shielded by treaties with North African regents. In 1785, two years after the Treaty of Paris which formally concluded the American Revolution, Algerian corsairs were emboldened by a recent treaty with Spain to sail out of the Straits of Gibraltar and capture two American trading vessels. These ships, the *Maria* and the *Dauphin*, with their combined crew of twenty-one, were taken into Algiers where ten would languish in captivity for more than a decade, seven would die from disease, and four others would be privately ransomed. The crisis was complicated by the fact the Algerians were confused about the wealth of the United States. On the one hand, the Dey of Algiers was influenced to expect and demand heavier ransom because of American success in defeating the British, the legendary riches of Spanish America, and stipends provided to the captives.[28] On the other hand, the U.S. government did not wish to appear to possess wealth than it was incapable of collecting and thereby entice the Algerians to capture more American sailors. As a result, the situation reached a stalemate. That more ships were not taken by Algiers in the next eight years was due to the practice of carrying counterfeit passports, the relocation of Barbary's corsairs to aid the Sultan in his war with Russia, and the convoying of American ships by the Portuguese.[29]

Widespread popular attention would not be paid to the plight of these Algerine captives until after North Africans again sailed out from the Straits of Gibraltar in 1793 and rounded up nine more American ships between October 8 and 23, to which two more ships were added in late November, raising the total number of American captives to nearly 120. The renewed activity of these "pirates" precipitated a two-month embargo on American shipping that raised marine insurance rates and inflated the cost of living. There was a huge public response to these indignities and discomforts and Americans launched efforts throughout the states to aid the captured seamen. Concerned citizens formed societies and committees, solicited charitable collections, staged benefit performances at theaters, and beseeched the federal government to act swiftly and end the national shame by freeing

---

[28] Henry G. Barnby, *The Prisoners of Algiers: An Account of the Forgotten American-Algerian War, 1785–97* (London: Oxford University Press, 1966), 133, 189. L. B. Wright and J. H. Macleod, *The First Americans in North Africa* (Princeton, NJ: Princeton University Press, 1945). Richard B. Parker, *Uncle Sam in Barbary: A Diplomatic History* (Gainesville: University Press of Florida, 2004). Frank Lambert, *The Barbary Wars: American Independence in the Atlantic World* (New York: Hill and Wang, 2005). See also Gary Edward Wilson, "American Prisoners in the Barbary Nations, 1784–1816" (Ph.D. diss., University of North Texas, 1979).

[29] Raymond F. Aube, "Worlds Apart: The Roots of America's Diplomatic Failures in Other Cultures – The Barbary Coast in the Early Nineteenth Century" (Ph.D. diss., New York University, 1986), 41.

its seamen and protecting American commerce.[30] One Connecticut man urged George Washington to institute a national contribution to ransom the prisoners, saying "I have lately traveled throughout the N England States Vermont &c. The Generale topick was the times but principally the Sufferings of our Citizens among the Algerines."[31] Since the capture of these ships coincided with the Royal Navy's seizure of hundreds of American merchant ships trading in the French West Indies, Americans blamed Britain for encouraging these Algerian depredations to preserve their own commerce in the Mediterranean.

This perceived complicity between British and Ottoman despotism is graphically represented in a Philadelphia engraving dated 20 February 1794 titled "The Allied Despots. Or The Friendship of Britain for America" (Fig. 1.1).[32] In this print, the monarch King George educates Sultan Mustapha about the utility of extralegal violence to the maintenance of authority. The despotic familiarity or "cousinhood" between the monarch and the sultan is demonstrated by their shared knowing glances as well as the similarity of their robes and regal headdresses. Four violent scenarios in the foreground allege the global reach of their collusive despotism following the Treaty of 1783 that ended the Revolutionary War. The scene of Native Americans butchering women and an infant with hatchets depicts the American anger with the British failure to abandon forts in the nation's northwest, and the looted merchandise with the names of merchants from New York and Philadelphia indicates American vessels and property illegally seized in the French West Indies. The islamicist representation in the front right scene depicts the captives held in North Africa. The black standard of piracy aboard the ship refers to the resumption of North African depredations on American shipping in 1793, events that caused Mathew Carey to call the Algerines "the African emissaries of England."[33] The sequence of dictatorial authority is clearly drawn as it devolves from the king to the sultan to the Dey who himself holds a whip to force his officials to inflict punishment on five bound and starving captives who are naked from the waist

---

[30] For a discussion of the domestic reaction to these captures see Gary E. Wilson, "American Hostages in Moslem Nations, 1784–1796, The Public Response," *Journal of the Early Republic* 2 (Spring 1982): 133–7; and Harley Harris Bartlett, "American Captives in Barbary," *Michigan Alumnus Quarterly Review* 61 (Spring 1959): 238–54.

[31] This anonymous letter to George Washington dated 4 April 1794 is quoted in Wilson, "American Hostages," 134–5.

[32] See print in E. McSherry Fowble, ed., *Two Centuries of Prints in America, 1680–1880* (Charlottesville: University of Virginia Press, 1987), 464–5. The engraver's lack of real familiarity with Turkey and the allegorical aim of his image is indicated by his naming of the Sultan: Mustapha III's reign had ended with his death twenty years earlier and the next Mustapha was a fifteen-year-old who only held power briefly in 1807–8. The man with the whip being pointed to by George's scepter is William Pitt ["Billy"] who suspended the right of habeus corpus, which led to arrests for sedition during the British war with France that had been declared one year earlier.

[33] Carey, *Short Account of Algiers* (Philadelphia, 1794), 45.

FIGURE I.I. Valentine Verax, *The Allied Despots. Or The Friendship of Britain for America* (20 February 1794). The commentary in script reads: "The Imperial George instructeth his good Ally & Cousin Mustapha, in the misteries of regal policy – Sheweth him as a proof of their efficacy, how Billy manageth John Bull – Relateth with Delight the depradations which his allies the Savages by his instigation make on the sons of Liberty – Exorteth him to annoy them by Sea, as implacably, as the Savages do by Land – Which Mustapha performeth – Then sheweth his Royal preceptor how prompt a pupil he is." Courtesy Winterthur Museum, Museum Purchase.

up. The presence of a distressed woman with her breasts exposed – despite the fact that there were no female Americans held in Algiers – signalizes the print's emotive intent to raise indignation about the fate of liberty and the shameful effects of inaction. The engraver's pseudonym "Valentine Verax" suggests that he was using his print "to speak the truth" about the need for a more vigorous republican response to these transatlantic indignities.

The languishing of American captives in Algiers accentuated the weakness of the new Constitution, raised important ethical issues about the direction and effectiveness of foreign policy, and eventually led to what historian Henry Barnby called "the forgotten American war with Algeria."[34]

---

[34] Barnby, *The Prisoners of Algiers*. See Syed Zainul Abedin, "In Defense of Freedom: American's First Foreign War, A New Look at United States–Barbary Relations, 1776–1815" (Ph.D. diss., University

The two options open to Americans (after hopes for European mediation failed) were either to carry on the historic policy of offering tribute and gifts to the Barbary regencies to ensure safe passage, or to build a naval fleet capable of retaliating with force if American rights continued to be transgressed. Both options required large amounts of public revenue difficult to raise in a new nation whose citizens were viscerally opposed to taxation. The crisis raised key issues about the exercise of early American political power. To what degree was the new federal government responsible for the fate of private citizens outside its domains? How could it be appropriate for a republic founded on notions of the sacredness of freedom from tyranny to pay tribute to Muslim despots? How could an adequate navy be funded, built, and maintained without appearing to endanger the freedom of a people skeptical of any centralized power? These questions highlighted the difficulties that precluded any vigorous and principled solution to the lingering problem of Americans held captive in Algiers, a disgrace that led one poet to lament "the sleeping vigour of his country's arm."[35]

The crisis was eventually forestalled by the signing of a treaty that freed the remaining captives on 12 July 1796. But the resolution had come at a humiliating cost: Americans were required to pay cash for ransom, to give expensive consular gifts with the arrival of each new official, and to deliver to the dey an annual tribute of specie and military provisions – a pattern of tribute that would persist through the War of 1812. Such humiliation was symbolically registered by the delivery of a handsome thirty-six-gun frigate – one of the early ships commissioned by naval appropriations ironically christened as the *Crescent* – as a gift to the Dey's daughter, one of several new ships delivered into Algerian control. When Commodore William Bainbridge delivered the annual tribute to Algiers in 1800 in the first U.S. naval ship to enter the Mediterranean, the Dey, under threat of force, commandeered the *George Washington* (in the year after the first president's death) to deliver his own ambassadorial suite of two hundred individuals and gifts – including lions, tigers, antelopes and parrots – to the Sultan in Constantinople. Submitting to the Dey's despotic decree, Bainbridge was forced to undergo "mortifying degradations" and replace the American flag with the Algerine standard before setting sail. Such national humiliation was compounded when the *George Washington* arrived in the Turkish capital, the first ship from the United States to enter the waters of the Bosphorus, and the Sultan's officers not only failed to recognize the American flag (that had

---

of Pennsylvania, 1975); Michael L. S. Kitzen, *Tripoli and the United States at War: A History of American Relations with the Barbary States, 1785–1805* (Jefferson, NC: McFarland, 1993).

[35] John Blair Linn, "The American Captive: An Elegy," *Miscellaneous Works, Prose and Poetical* (New York: Thomas Greenleaf, 1795), 141.

been restored during the journey), but many were not even aware of the existence of the United States.[36]

ENGENDERING AN IMPERIALISM OF VIRTUE: ALGERINES AND EARLY AMERICAN LITERARY IMAGINATION

As members of a post-colonial state with anti-imperial origins, United States citizens of the early republic did not seek to impose colonial bureaucracy on lands beyond what was considered national territory. Such an enterprise was largely confined to the acquisition (sometimes by violence and subterfuge that manifested its own despotic energies) of the continental lands lying west of the original states. In the international field, Americans tried to counter despotism through a cultural form of imperialism that emphasized the "benevolence" and morality of republican virtues and democratic institutions. Instead of supplying the ostensibly absent civil structures through the installation of a colonial regime, early Americans celebrated the example of their own civil society and the vitality of an emergent public sphere, which modeled republican virtue through a complex variety of organizations and cultural expressions, as the nation's most visible triumph over despotism. Various social and political institutions – such as a constitutional form of government, an egalitarian family, a free press, a public theater, voluntary philanthropic associations, commercial entrepreneurship, and eventually a regulated national navy – helped to comprise a spirited civil society of democracy whose cultural expression spelled defeat for despotism both inside and outside the United States. The vanquishing of oriental enemies in the early republic through the flourishing of republican example – first through imaginative fantasy, then eventually through naval might – signalized the success of democracy in deposing despotism as its political contender.

New citizens felt embarrassed by American submission to Muslim masters and viewed the affronts of captivity and tribute as an emasculating form of punishment for the weaknesses of the nation. Writers actively compensated for this diplomatic disgrace and their lack of actual global power by projecting fictional representations of national triumph over Algerine despotism. Most notably, in the years before the development of a capable navy, the cultural power of the United States was expressed through the dramatic creativity of literary imagination that preserved visions of the global relevance of both democracy and Christianity at a time when the new nation and its foreign policy seemed itself captive to dissension and disunity. The publication of a chorus of voices through the nation's print media embodied Noah

---

[36] Thomas Harris, *Life and Services of Commodore Bainbridge* (Philadelphia: Carey, Lea & Blanchard, 1837), 44; *Naval Documents Related to the United States Wars with the Barbary Powers*, 6 vols. (Washington, DC: GPO, 1939–44), 1: 375–81, 384–90, 398–401.

Webster's truism that "information is fatal to despotism" and enfranchised the cultural strength of American democracy by announcing the ability of a republic of letters to shout down the univocal domination of the despot.[37]

The democratic vibrancy of the civil society of the new republic had a fictional counterpart in the cultural imaginary, which was expressed through a multiplicity of generic forms ranging from tales, poems, plays, memoirs, letters, and political commentary. The cultural work and play of early American islamicism is revealed by interpreting this imaginative production as a means of understanding the shifting political struggles in the Muslim Mediterranean from 1785 to 1831. Islamicist "intelligence" was most creatively produced through four transatlantic genres of fictional imagination – the oriental tale, the Muslim spy narrative, the Barbary captivity narrative, and dramatic plays set in the Islamic Mediterranean – each of which provided vehicles of enculturation that educated Americans about the global relevance of their republican mission. Recuperating this tradition of early national expression reveals vital forms of transcultural imagination through which the triumphs of American values were projected into the wider world. Examining the interplay between literary production and "foreign" policy exposes the struggles of early national women and men to align their own cultural models of political allegiance and gender performance with their national aspirations to influence the course of world history.

Among the works that reveal the ideological versatility of islamicism as a cultural discourse are three examples of epistolary spy narratives penned by putative Muslims as well as the two fictional works of Barbary captivity most widely read today: Susanna Haswell Rowson's play *Slaves in Algiers* (1794) and Royall Tyler's narrative *The Algerine Captive* (1797). These publications and performances demonstrate how the emergence of a vital public sphere fostered the cultural construction of national strength even in the midst of moments of historical weakness. Central to this imaginary conquest of oriental tyranny was what I call an "imperialism of virtue" that dramatized the democratic vigor of American gender performance that celebrated the fortitude of female virtue and the viability of male valor in the face of global challenges. The rhetorical (and later historical) deposition of despotism proved to be a powerful cultural field for addressing anxieties about the relevance of an emergent republican culture whose global authority was as yet tenuous because it remained both peripheral to and preyed upon by the hegemonic systems of the old world.

By projecting domestic political agency through moral dramas set in (or symbolized by) extravagant and exotic climes, islamicist narration enabled the expression of both a deep cultural critique and a universal global fantasy

---

37 Webster, *On the Education of Youth in America* (Boston, 1782), 66. Quoted in Michael Warner, *The Letters of the Republic: Publication and the Public Sphere in Eighteenth-Century America* (Cambridge, MA: Harvard University Press, 1990), 124.

that compensated for the failures of foreign policy. Oriental tales served as secular counterparts to scripture in which fictional imagination performed the didactic function of moral exhortation. The oriental tale aimed to morally cleanse images of the east from libidinous desires of sensual excess by sublimating its thrills into a moral economy of national virtue. Dramatic scripts set in Barbary displaced scenes of oriental humiliation onto domestic stages, stimulating an agency for patriotism that effectively deposed the despot's will to power. The Muslim spy narrative genre deployed the cosmopolitan universalism of the Enlightenment so that readers might learn wisdom from the alien perspective of foreign cultural traditions (or at least satirize their own parochial pretensions). Shipwreck and captivity narratives set in Muslim lands often narrated how citizens of the United States could generate strength even out of the jaws of disaster by embodying in their experience and narration the persistence and survival of national character. By diffusing these sentiments through overlapping expressive genres in the early republic, the multivocal power of islamicism provided a form of literary diplomacy through which readers and citizens were able to negotiate the global dimensions of social responsibility and national mission.

Hundreds of oriental tales peppered the American periodical lore of the late eighteenth century, leading literary historian David S. Reynolds to claim that they constituted "the first body of religious fiction in America."[38] By transferring moral instruction from the dry didacticism of the sermon to the more exciting regimes of the moral tale, authors of these narratives coopted the potential subversiveness of private reading and enlisted its stimulus as a source for upholding public morality. These oriental tales most frequently took the form of moral apologues in which ambitious or unhappy Easterners learned lessons of resignation to the divine will, sometimes with the supernatural assistance of genii (from the Arabic word *djinn*, often confused with "genius"). Situating these tales in exotic oriental realms incorporated a global purview in which local cultural issues could be addressed as universal concerns. One writer's admiration for the Eastern fable was premised on its ability to insinuate moral messages into moments of idleness, claiming that the genre "borrows the garments of instruction from the wardrobe of pleasure."[39] Orientalist narration stimulated the expression of a sublime moral idealism through which Americans harnessed potentially transgressive desires for liberty and transmuted their energies into the process of national formation. A secular counterpart to

---

[38] David S. Reynolds, *Faith in Fiction: The Emergence of Religious Literature in America* (Cambridge, MA: Harvard University Press, 1981), 37. The best study of this genre remains Mukhtar Ali Isani's unpublished 1962 dissertation from Princeton, "The Oriental Tale in America through 1865: A Study in American Fiction."

[39] *The Emerald* 2 (21 March 1807): 140.

the eschatological millennialism that will be examined in the next chapter, islamicist fiction fantasized the capacity of democratic principles to entertain the world by instructing it in decency. Oriental narratives provided American audiences with the confirmation that underneath the apparently despotic behavior of threatening aliens there lived incipient democrats who could and would be converted by free expression, honest love, and benevolent works. Literary production, however fantastic, was thus an important cultural enterprise of counterdespotism, one that served to prophesy the triumph of democracy. As Michael Warner has argued, publication itself was "a political condition of utterance," and fictional work could accomplish utopian missions that actual American behavior in the world seemed unable to effect: the neutralization of the despot, the naturalization of the alien, and the conversion of the infidel, and thereby defuse the challenging excesses of islamicist difference that threatened the regulation of the republic.[40]

Soon after Algiers declared war on the United States in 1785, three strangers were detained in Virginia under the suspicion of Governor Patrick Henry that they might be spies sent from the Dey of Algiers. After an interrogation that revealed only some documents in Hebrew, they were deported in 1786.[41] This early incident documents American fears that the forces of old world tyranny, embodied both by the Barbary States doing the bidding of Britain and a supposed semitic collusion between Jews and Arabs, were conspiring to undermine the new republic under the Articles of Confederation.[42] *The Algerine Spy in Pennsylvania*, one of the earliest American full-length fictional productions when it was published in 1787, was the first of several American narratives that featured fictional Muslim spies in America.[43] These literary productions employed the traveler's observation that "all truth is but a variation of prejudice" as a liberating vehicle of cultural criticism. The vogue was established in England with the publication of Giovanni Marana's *Letters Writ by a Turkish Spy* in 1687, whose popularity gave rise to two other influential eighteenth-century examples: Montesquieu's *Persian Letters* (1722) and Oliver Goldsmith's *The Citizen of the World* (1762). These texts published letters ostensibly written by oriental narrators back to confidants in the East that reveal a paradoxical combination of philosophical impartiality and naive prejudice. By satirizing the savage

---

[40] Warner, *Letters of the Republic*, 8.   [41] Allison, *Crescent Obscured*, 3–4.

[42] In 1797, after the close of the Algerian War, Royall Tyler's novel, *The Algerine Captive*, was still disseminating rumors that Jewish/Algerian spies had been sent to the United States and were involved in a conspiracy to inflate the ransom demanded for American Captives ed. Jack B. Moore (Gainesville, FL: Scholars' Facsimiles & Reprints, 1967), 181.

[43] [Peter Markoe], *The Algerine Spy in Pennsylvania; or, Letters Written by a Native of Algiers on the Affairs of the United States of America, from the Close of the Year 1783 to the Meeting of the Convention* (Philadelphia: Prichard and Hall, 1787).

conventions of civilization, they also aimed to liberate a critical consciousness in their readers that could foster a more cosmopolitan form of cultural
engagement.

The Algerine Spy in Pennsylvania consists of a series of twenty-four fictional
letters written by sixty-year-old Mehemet from Europe and the United
States to his friend Solyman in Algiers. Both are members of the court
of Osman, the despotic Dey of Algiers. The Dey has given Mehemet the
"weighty commission" of assessing the strengths of the United States and, by
"separat[ing] the specious from the solid," developing a plan to subvert the
new nation. Mehemet's presence in the republic is ultimately an allegory of
the weaknesses of the government under the Articles of Confederation. The
years that the spy operates in the United States, 1783–7, are the exact years
during which the first national government faced not only dangers of foreign aggression like that inflicted by Algiers but also internal dissensions that
threatened the very survival of the new republic. Upon his arrival in 1783,
Mehemet finds "unsuspecting" citizens "unconscious of danger" and hur-
ried by business that prevents their notice of the swarthy spy in their midst.[44]
By publishing the spy's epistolary intelligence, Markoe enables his readers to
expose the specter of Mehemet's subversion. "While the despotic Orient is
indeed the Other held up for us to see," commented Alain Grosrichard,
"it is also the one that regards us, in every sense of that word."[45] *The
Algerine Spy in Pennsylvania* serves as what he calls an "endoscopic fantasy"
that counteracts antirepublican threats by subduing the challenge of alien
difference.

Mehemet's most imaginative proposal is to take advantage of Rhode
Island's obstinacy in ceding the right to tax to the federal government by
transforming it into an "Ottoman Malta on the coasts of America" (he
assumes Rhode Island is indeed an island). His plan involves the bribery
of Daniel Shays by gold delivered by a huge Ottoman fleet consisting of
"about one hundred thousand spahis and janizzaries" commanded by a
Bashaw of Three Tails. The rebellious Rhode Islanders would pay for their
protection by "tribute to the sultan in [a] certain number of virgins," which
would be augmented by plundering the coasts of the continent and carrying "young men and maidens triumphantly . . . into captivity."[46] Although
such a proposal is made to exemplify the hot-headed bigotry of the islamicist

---

[44] [Markoe], *Algerine Spy*, 13–14, 63, 68–9.

[45] Alain Grosrichard, *The Sultan's Court: European Fantasies of the East*. trans. Liz Heron (New York:
Verso, 1998), 23–4. For critical mention of *The Algerine Spy*, see Lotfi Ben Rejeb, "Observing
the Birth of a Nation: The Oriental Spy/Observer Genre and Nation Making in Early American
Literature," in *The United States & the Middle East: Cultural Encounters*. eds. Abbas Amanat and Magnus
T. Bernhardsson (New Haven, CT: The Yale Center for International and Area Studies, 2002), 253–
89; and Jennifer Margulis, "Spies, Pirates, and White Slaves: Encounters with the Algerines in Three
Early American Novels," *The Eighteenth-Century Novel* 1 (2001): 1–36.

[46] [Markoe], *Algerine Spy*, 104–6.

mentality, it does reflect American fears of Muslim power in the nation's early years. (The "translator" mentions that dating Mehemet's letters is "unnecessary" because "the principal facts mentioned in them are so notorious and recent."[47]) The fact that John Jay admonished New Yorkers in 1787 that if they refused to ratify the new Constitution, "Algerians could be on the American coast and enslave its citizens who have not a single sloop of war" reveals that use of such propaganda was not as absurd as it may appear.[48] Mehemet himself, in a cooler moment, acknowledges that the other American states would never concede to abandoning Rhode Island, their "unprincipled sister," nor would its wealth be capable of feeding a "sufficient garrison."[49] The official report of Mehemet's mission reveals similar intelligence: The United States is "too strong to be conquered, and too weak to think of conquering others." It is this impermeability of American independence that frustrates the despotic designs of the Dey, and ultimately converts Mehemet into a loyal American citizen. Indeed the presence of the Algerine spy in Pennsylvania persists only as long as the crisis of federalism itself. The moment that the Constitution is ratified, Mehemet is betrayed by his enemies and chooses instead the "united blessings of FREEDOM and CHRISTIANITY" offered by life in America.[50]

Mehemet's conversion to democracy and Christianity is a result of his disillusionment with the despotic practices of his homeland as well as his discovery of the democratic principles of freedom of speech and consent of the governed. He comes to understand Montesquieu's observation about a despot's power being premised on his use of inferior tyrants to gratify his own passion. Such insights lead Mehemet to reassess his status in Algiers, where even to be a wealthy citizen is little different than being a slave. In one early letter, he actually apologizes to his "illustrious masters," begging them to overlook the "weakness and incapacity of their slave." Such subjugation reaches its culmination at the end of the book when Mehemet learns that the Dey, reacting to rumors, has branded him a traitor. This despot, having confiscated all his property (including slaves), sells them to Achmet, a villainous European renegade. The text confirms how the immoral duplicity of Algerine behavior has squelched Mehemet's positive traits – such as

---

47 [Markoe], *Algerine Spy*, ix.

48 17 April 1788, *Pamphlets on the Constitution of the United States*. ed. Paul L. Ford (Brooklyn, 1888), 76, cited in Aube, *Worlds Apart*, 43. For example, the *New Haven Gazette* reprinted a story published in Charleston, South Carolina, in which a captain swore an oath that he heard a British mate recount the story of his ship being detained off Barbados by three armed Algerian vessels that were searching for American plunder. 1 (11 May 1786): 95.

49 [Markoe], *Algerine Spy*, 114. John Adams likewise rejected the notion that Americans coasts were endangered by "African pyrates [sic]" by writing to a friend "we are in no more danger [of that] than the Emperor of China is." John Adams to Thomas Hollis, 11 June 1790, quoted in Aube, *Worlds Apart*, 44.

50 [Markoe], *Algerine Spy*, 96, 129.

his taste, prudence, temperance, and economy – even as it dramatizes how these very characteristics are fostered through his exposure to American society. These redemptive traits are necessary to entice the reader to entertain the naturalization of the spy as a fellow American at the close of the book.[51]

Central to this transformation is Mehemet's repentance for his misguided use of sexual authority. At the outset of his mission, Mehemet is rebuked by French women who speak directly to him: "Strange thought I that the man, who, in his haram [sic], inspired awe and even terror, should in his turn be awed into silence, and shrink from the eye of female observation!" This miniature revolution later assumes a broader canvas when Mehemet's ruin deprives him of his family. Mehemet had been attracted to his wife Fatima because she was a woman "with whom silence is wisdom and reserve is virtue." But he woefully misinterprets the nature of this reserve: It was not a sign of love, but rather her "natural timidity" in recognizing that as his slave she could not refuse his advances. With the exception of his letters, Mehemet neglects his family by ignoring Fatima's complaints about his "cruel and intolerable absence" and even blames her for placing her maternal affections for their son above her own devotion to him. However the death of this son extinguishes Fatima's commitment to Mehemet and frees her to transfer her allegiance to Alvarez, a captive Spanish gardener. Their love emboldens them to abscond to Europe where Fatima converts to Catholicism, changes her name to Maria, and embraces legal Christian marriage, a series of acts that seals Mehemet's fate by seemingly confirming his treason to the Dey.[52] Mehemet's redemption is only complete when he uses the wealth he prudently protected to purchase a farm in Pennsylvania that he offers to the new couple. Mehemet's unnatural relation is cleansed by his determination to view her as neither a wife nor a slave, but democratically as a sister. That Fatima is Mehemet's only mentioned wife preserves him from the taint of polygamy, although she is only saved from such a fate by an orientalist assumption that their marriage was never legitimate in the first place. Markoe's narrative thus emasculates Mehemet's threatening virility (no doubt a reason why the spy is a sexagenarian) as part of the process of transforming him from an advance scout of despotism into a chaste and benevolent American citizen.

The Algerine Spy in Pennsylvania dramatizes how literary expression served as a form of imaginative alchemy through which the standard of America's democratic and millennial mission could be raised even in the time of crisis. The book symbolically enacts a multiple conversion through which Islam bows to Christian truths, despotism dissolves into democracy, and ethnic differences are assimilated into national character. The reform of Mehemet's

---

[51] [Markoe], *Algerine Spy*, 108, 95, 116, 121.   [52] [Markoe], *Algerine Spy*, 32, 35, 124.

family and its reconstitution on farms in Pennsylvania implants a microcosmic model of a multicultural democracy that accepts Catholics, Africans, and even former lechers, infidels, and spies if they are willing to adopt American practices and pursue lives of reformed virtue. It is perhaps for this reason that the "translator" urges that Mehemet's letters be printed "for the good of the United States."[53]

Naturalizing the Algerine spy demonstrated a vision of an inclusive American democracy. However, such a symbolic triumph was unable to challenge the powers of despotic egoism in Algiers itself. To be effective, the imperialism of virtue also had to imagine the conquest of the despots themselves on their own infidel turf. The Algerine diplomatic crisis openly exposed the inability of the United States to achieve this end in practice. In the place of direct retribution, American publishers printed a variety of narratives that fantasized the capacity of female virtue and fortitude to challenge and ultimately redeem the perceived immoralities of Islam.

A 1790 story from *The Massachusetts Magazine* by one "Sabena" elucidates the projective strength of this fantasy. *Louisa: A Novel* tells of the abduction of a woman from the shore of her British estate by Algerine villains. Far from being a chronicle of woe, however, the story celebrates the triumph of patient female virtue over all that might stand in her path. Louisa's prodigious fortitude functions throughout the tale as a redeeming force that eventually converts the political despotism and sensuality of Algiers itself into a realm of romantic righteousness. While held in captivity in Algiers, Louisa refuses to submit to the licentiousness of the Sultan Osmen. Such a resistance empowers her to transform his harem from a space of transgression into a forum where Osmen's good qualities are refined through the dignity of educated conversation. The key moment that precipitates the despot's abandonment of sensuality and slavery occurs when the Englishwoman Louisa praises George Washington as the epitome of democratic male honor in the very year he assumed the presidency. "I love, revere, and esteem their [America's] illustrious chief," Louisa attests, "He is . . . brave, gentle, and generous; he is prudent, valiant, and discreet; he is a faithful friend, the best of husbands, and the parent of all around him." Louisa's affirmation of Washington projects an American desire for British validation of their new government. Osmen, wishing to emulate this "godlike man," emancipates his slaves (in ironic contrast to the real Washington) – an act that frees him to merit the hand of a chaste Greek maiden who adored him but could never properly express her love while she was his slave. Osmen graciously provides the means for the happy return of Louisa to a life of generous simplicity in England. Algiers itself is transformed into an orientalized paradise by the fact that other freed slaves "preferring a connection with the smiling beauties of the east, were settled in some of Osmen's country seats, with every convenience of life."[54]

Fictional enterprises such as Mehemet's democratic conversion and Louisa's moral conquest helped to domesticate foreign affairs by communicating their concerns through the accessible form of family drama. An idealized equality of devoted love between two consensual citizens became the surest foundation for a virtuous republic and signalzed the moral blessings of democracy. Early American fiction provides countless examples of how orphanhood, bachelorhood, coquetry, widowhood, and spinsterhood became figured as extramarital categories of moral crisis that challenged the virtuous integrity of the family. "Marriage was the republic in miniature," explains the historian Jan Lewis, "it was chaste, disinterested, and free from the exercise of arbitrary power."[55] While Mehemet sacrificed the privilege of marriage in atonement for his past abuses, Louisa earns her status as the humble wife of a noble and wealthy man, himself a former slave of Osmen, by her virtuous negotiation of the dangerous waters between being a daughter and becoming a wife. The benevolent family served as the emblematic microcosm of the republic and the site where democratic virtues were established and propagated within the social fabric.[56]

If an emergent domesticity was celebrated as the matrix of virtue in a democracy, however, the seraglio (or harem) served as the seedbed of despotism. Enlightenment thought frequently figured the harem as the domain of sexual dissipation in which lawless passions disrupted the social process of moral home building – a space into which men withdrew from public virtue to relish unrestrained vice. Early American islamicist narratives clearly delineate how the excesses of despotic government stemmed from its lack of a stable moral family. According to many reports, beautiful women (often from the Caucasus) were made available for the Ottoman harem because their parents sold them with the hope that such service to the sultan would be advantageous to their daughters. Americans believed that despotic systems prevented the basis for egalitarian love between men and women. The possibilities of democracy were stifled in the home, and potential citizens remained slaves of leaders who were themselves the sons of slaves. Women in such a system were exempted from the requirement of useful education. Relegated to the status of private providers of sensual delights, they languished as objects of luxury, unable and unwilling to check their master's advances. In *The Spirit of the Laws*, Montesquieu perceived that the source

---

[54] [Sabena], "Louisa: A Novel," *The Massachusetts Magazine* 2 (1790): 78–82, 147–51.

[55] Jan Lewis, "The Republican Wife: Virtue and Seduction in the Early Republic," *William and Mary Quarterly* 44 (October 1987): 709–10.

[56] See Jay Fliegelman, *Prodigals and Pilgrims: The American Revolution against Patriarchal Authority, 1750–1800* (Cambridge: Cambridge University Press, 1982).

of despotic power was the patriarchal command that princes leveled over the heads of their wives and argued "Everything comes down to reconciling the political and civil government with domestic government."[57] The whole structure of democratic society therefore ran the risk of devolving into despotism if women learned to value unproductive idleness, petty display, and sensual pleasure over their roles as domestic economists, models of virtue, and "republican mothers." Cautionary tales of the 1790s (among them Hannah Webster Foster's epistolary novel *The Coquette*) dramatized how an American woman's submission to the advances of a rake signified the encroachment of despotism on democratic society by disrupting the virtue of moral marriage and thereby domesticating the practices of the harem.

The sensual slavery of the seraglio thus served as a metaphoric site for staging criticism of female education in the new republic. Without useful instruction in virtuous public behavior, American women ran the risk of an orientalized slavery that rendered them into sexual instruments incapable of instilling proper morals in their own children. Enlightenment notions about the domestic servitude of women was expressed in "An Occasional Letter on the Female Sex," a 1775 essay sometimes attributed to its editor Thomas Paine that has been called "one of the earliest pleas for the emancipation of women published in America."[58] Its author likens the fate of all women to those under an oriental oppression that forces them to submit to their masters with a feigned affection that deprives them of all virtue and happiness. The islamicism of Mary Wollstonecraft's writings, published first in the United States in 1792, excoriates the infidel libertinism that denied women their souls by confirming their status as mere playthings of male leisure. To her the "mussulman's creed" and its "true style" positions women as subordinate beings and "not as part of the human species."[59] In perpetuating female obsessions with fashion and emphasizing their "docile blind obedience" to men, Western cultural education creates beings fit for the seraglio rather than for republicanism. With female agency relegated to the realm of sexual power, women exercise an "illicit sway" over men that Wollstonecraft compares with the control that Turkish bashaws exert over their subjects. If the rights of women to pursue reason and respect are not vindicated, Wollstonecraft argued, they assume the soulless status that she believes Islam grants to women. Such a despotism, she argues, "kills virtue and genius in the bud" and, like the dreaded sandstorm called the *simoom*,

[57] Montesquieu, *Spirit of the Laws*, 60.

[58] *The Complete Writings of Thomas Paine*, ed. Philip S. Foner, 2 vols. (New York: Citadel Press, 1969), 2: 34–8. See Frank Smith, "The Authorship of 'An Occasional Letter on the Female Sex,'" *American Literature* 2 (November 1930): 277–80.

[59] *The Works of Mary Wollstonecraft*, eds. Janet Todd and Marilyn Butler, 7 vols. (New York: New York University Press, 1989); "Vindication of the Rights of Men" (1790), 5: 45; "Vindication of the Rights of Women" (1792), 5: 73.

threatens the West "with that destructive blast which desolates Turkey, and renders the men, as well as the soil, unfruitful."[60]

When orientalist dogma set up Muslim women as soulless slaves serving a perverse economy of voluptuousness, it conversely empowered the women of the West by highlighting their comparative agency. The symbolic resurrection of women as moral authorities within oriental spaces thereby became one of the most direct and direst threats to a despotic system. Writers recognized this revolutionary potential of a woman with a mind and soul of her own. The role that democratic women could play when projected into the Eastern seraglio, as had Louisa, was to reject a patriarchal dominance that reduced them to a life of sensuality, and to stand instead as revolutionary examples of how virtue might seduce despotism toward democracy. The fortitude of independent women emasculated the authority of the Muslim autocrat, either by showing indifference to his masculine privilege or, more actively, by directing her civic virtue and narrative power to redeem his selfish vice. Even the devotion to Islam of Muslim women depicted in early American islamicist fiction, such as that of Fatima in *The Algerine Spy in Pennsylvania*, was largely a portrayal of their submission to the despot's will. When this spell was broken, often by the charm of Western female courage, they are revealed to be the virtuous Christian democrats their composers wish them to be. Orientalist fiction thus served as a fruitful public stage upon which transnational fantasies about the social equality of women and the conversion of Muslims were simultaneously engendered and rehearsed.

An influential example of the persuasive power of female literary expression (as well as the powerful prototype for the genre of the oriental tale) is found in the tales told by Scheherezade in the *One Thousand and One Nights*. Many an early American child was charmed by the supernatural adventures and opulent extravagance of the Arabian Nights. The frame of the stories features two tyrannical brothers who butcher their wives after they catch them in unfaithful debauchery with their slaves. In retribution for the perfidiousness of female desire, the brothers decide that each will marry a new virgin each day, enjoy the night with her, and then kill her the next morning – and then repeat the ritual again and again. After three years of such carnage, their kingdoms are barely capable of perpetuating themselves. The force that is eventually able to stay this cruel despotism is Scheherezade (Shahrazad), the daughter of the Vizir, whose narrative skill beguiles her master with long, diverse, intricate, and often supernatural stories that are so enticing that Shahriyar invariably preserves her life in order to hear the continuation of the story. This pattern of commutation goes on for 1,001 nights until Scheherezade's inexhaustible and erotic

---

[60] Wollstonecraft, "Vindication of the Rights of Women," 5: 76, 88, 113.

literary power ultimately saves the kingdom from its horrible reign of gyno-cide.[61] After the despot witnesses the three sons whom Scheherezade had borne during the telling of the tales, he acknowledges her as a queen – an act that reconstitutes a stable family structure, redeeming both the brutal violence of the fraternal despots and the sensuality of their former wives.

Scheherezade's saga displays how the power of female ingenuity elevated the despot out of his sensual appetites toward more civilized behaviors. Such a cultural conversion is accomplished through the capacity of fiction to present a multiplicity of voices and perspectives that confound the despot's totalitarian will, a power that effectively democratized his authority. Narrative power served as an imaginary alembic for transmuting the erotic desire and brutal masculinity associated with the harem into the sublimity of a moral civilization embodied in the republican family. The vacuum of female agency in islamicist constructions of despotism provided a space for the expansion of Western women's influence over the domestic family into both the public sphere of cultural expression and the transnational field of imperial virtue. Islamicist fiction employed the enticements of oriental exoticism to charge the resources of private desire and then to channel these energies into constituting a vital political imagination of an emergent national community.

PICARESQUE PORNOGRAPHY AND IMPERIAL VICE

Imaginative fiction, however, could be a risky sort of surrogate scripture or sermon, as shown by the fact that Sheherezade's nightly tales function also as foreplay to sexual acts. As if to recognize the moral dangers of its own form of expression, a common theme of oriental tales was the need to moderate ambition and resign oneself to the dictates of providence. A review of a Western sequel to the *Arabian Nights*, for example, admitted that although supernatural fiction might "awaken curiosity, which otherwise might continue dormant," its ultimate effect might be to accustom "the mind rather to wonder than to inquire."[62] If orientalist fiction attempted to employ some of the libidinal charge of Eastern eroticism to entice the reader more pleasurably toward standard morals, this liberatory energy to "wonder" could also deliver a dangerous challenge to orthodox cultural beliefs. By unloosing expression to include actual scenes of heroic lovers ignoring the

---

[61] Shahriyar lists the qualities of Scheherezade that attract him: She is "pure, holy, chaste, tender, unassailable, ingenious, subtle, eloquent, discreet, smiling, and wise." *The Book of the Thousand Nights and the One Night*, ed. Powys Mathers, trans. J. C. Mardrus, 4 vols. (New York: St. Martin's Press, 1972), 4: 532.

[62] "Arabian Tales," *American Monthly Review* 2 (1795), 80.

restraints of their oppressive social systems, a subversive model that blurred the line between independence and impudence was established. As David S. Reynolds has noted, "The oriental tale permitted a freedom of doctrinal expression and satire that was available in expository prose only at the risk of the writer's reputation."[63] Islamicist fiction, because of its latitudinarian imagination, thus sometimes embodied the very form of licentiousness that it was designed to regulate.

The immediate model for Markoe's *The Algerine Spy in Pennsylvania* was in fact Montesquieu's *Persian Letters* of 1722, an epistolary novel of Persians satirizing Parisian practices to their ostensibly oriental audiences. The seraglio of Montesquieu's Usbek (similar to Markoe's Mehemet) is over-thrown by his wives whose revolt symbolizes the illusory nature of despotic autocracy. Montesquieu's cipher for revolutionary liberty is the unsatified libido of the female slave who refuses to accept sexual sacrifice to her master as the fullest possible expression of love and virtue. Roxana is able to stage a revolution in the seraglio by choosing her own interracial lover and thereby subverting Usbek's control. But unlike Fatima, Louisa, or even Scheherezade, Roxana's revolution also overturns the imperialism of virtue because her sexual excess remains dangerously uncontained by patriarchal control and serves indeed as the emancipatory force that topples Usbek's hegemony.[64]

To some male readers, the uncontrollable liberty of female sexuality threatened as much as it titillated, and they feared the fate of the unmanned Usbek. To reassert male sexual control, some early national orientalist narratives featured picaros who coopted female bodies *à la Turque* as a subversive celebration of their own masculine power. The narrator of *The Wanderings of William* from 1801 actively renders the reader into an accomplice of his imperial vice by explicitly relishing William's salacious romp around the world. In the first chapter William seduces a fifteen-year-old Muslim girl named Zorayda who drowns herself in the sea after he moves on to his next conquest. The open immorality of the American tars in this tale is acclaimed by one Jack Holiday, William's classmate at Columbia College, who claims "I would turn Infidel, Mussulman, Mahometan, to enjoy the bliss of a smile."[65] The *Narrative of the Captivity of John Vandike*, published in the same year, likewise applauds and relishes the adventures of an Algerine interlude as a profligate form of wooing disguised as exotic chivalry. The transgressive romance of this narrative is intimated when a woman exclaims

---

[63] Reynolds, *Faith in Fiction*, 19.

[64] Montesquieu, *Spirit of the Laws*, Book 16; *Persian Letters*, trans. C. J. Betts (Boston: Penguin Books, 1973), Letters 26, 156, 161.

[65] David John, *The Wanderings of William; or, The Inconstancy of Youth* (Philadelphia: R. T. Rawle, 1801), 22.

"I could almost be willing to be taken by the Algerines myself, if it would make me so lovely!"[66]

That these narratives denied the female captive any agency of her own with which to express her freedom is epitomized by the most widely published early Barbary captivity narrative: a story called the *History of the Captivity and Sufferings of Mrs. Maria Martin*, which was published a dozen times between 1800 and 1828 in various versions as far west as Ohio.[67] Paul Baepler has noted that "the demand for 'true' African captivity tales, particularly accounts of women in peril, outstripped their availability."[68] The attraction of this fabricated story can be explained by its gothic emphasis on the despot's power to inflict terror, torture, and rape on his female subjects. Similar to Mary Rowlandson's narrative of her captivity among the Pequots of Massachusetts, Maria is held against her will in an alien culture and only endures her horrific ordeal by seeing the hand of providence in whatever releases come her way. While Rowlandson asserts her will, negotiates advantages for herself, and maintains her virtue, however, Maria Martin always survives through her complete submission to any male she encounters. Even the agency she evinces in retelling her tale (if indeed it was written by a woman at all) is spent only in the recapitulation of her own victimage. Maria's submission enables her to survive and merit the sympathy of all readers, but this very virtue dooms her to a continuous confession of her captive state. Maria Martin's vulnerable body – both fleshly and textual – is thus one that circulates symbolically as a cipher for the transcultural supremacy of male authority. In one version of the narrative, an illustration portrays her as barebreasted and in chains (Fig. 1.2). Indeed an early reader commented inside the cover of an edition now held by the American Antiquarian Society: "To be kept in this room – the privy so Susanna won't get it!!!" This comment reveals how the circulation and seclusion of the book itself replicated the captivity of its narrator and rendered the reader into a surrogate despot. Maria Martin's narrative defuses the libidinal feminism of Montesquieu's Roxana by propagating male desire in an oriental setting and then sublimating its energies as a voyeuristic resource for sustaining the transnational authority of patriarchy.

---

[66] John Vandike, *Narrative of the Captivity of John Vandike, Who was Taken by the Algerines in 1791* (Leominster, MA: Chapman Whitcomb, 1801), 22. An earlier version was published in Hanover, New Hampshire, in 1799.

[67] The resonance of this palimpsestic text can been seen by the fact that various versions were published at various localities in New England as well as in New York, Trenton, Philadelphia, and as far west as St. Clairsville, Ohio, and that in some of these editions the narrator was known instead as Lucinda Martin, Mary Gerard, and Mary Velnet who have different nationalities and are tortured either in Algiers or Tripoli.

[68] Paul Baepler, "Introduction," *White Slaves, African Masters: An Anthology of American Barbary Captivity Narratives* (Chicago: University of Chicago Press, 1999), 11.

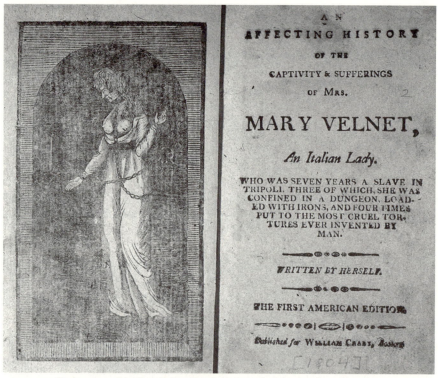

FIGURE 1.2. Barbary captivity literature offered the latitude for expressing licentious adventures that could not be represented within domestic situations involving Americans. Frontispiece and Title Page, *An Affecting History of the Captivity and Sufferings of Mrs. Mary Velnet* (Boston: William Crary, 1804). Courtesy American Antiquarian Society.

These narratives engaged with islamicism by deploying its suspect latitudes as global screens for fantasies of male desire that could not be openly enacted in domestic situations. The picaresque imagination of these stories borrowed the illicit freedoms enjoyed by the despot and redeployed them to universalize male domestic power. The Islamic orient served in this way as a transcontinental horizon into which men might expand the provincial power of their gender by coopting the cosmopolitan challenge of Muslim masculinity as a global cultural contender.

FEMALE ISLAMICISM AND THE IMPERIALISM OF VIRTUE

Most islamicist fiction in the early United States, however, did not exploit the transgressive infidelity of men but rather worked to transmute the unregulated freedom of sexual desire into virtuous female action, often in the service of patriotic ends. The historian Ruth Bloch has noted that during the 1780s and 1790s "a significantly separate image of female public spirit began to appear" in which wives and mothers were not only "increasingly presented as indispensable and active promoters of patriotism in men" but also "idealized as the source . . . of civic virtue itself."[69] For example, Penelope Aubin's narrative *The Noble Slaves*, recounting Spanish captives held in Algiers in 1708, was reprinted in the United States five times between 1797 and 1814 and furnishes didactic examples of the heroic power of females who courageously refuse to consent to the "Turkish policy" of the "odious Mahometan" and thereby both tranform her captors and inspire her readers.[70] The imperialism of virtue enabled women to be moral revolutionaries in Muslim contexts as long as they remained politically and sexually conservative models at home. The European ancestry of many of these heroines likewise conditioned the radical potential of American liberty while preserving the nation from their taint of transgression at the same time that it universalized its cultural power.

The imperialism of virtue in the early republic was most clearly dramatized by spectacles of female power in stage performances that transmuted the potential licentiousness of the theatre into a classroom of patriotic virtue. The stage, as Joseph Schöpp has noted, served as "an efficacious educational space in which new configurations would help articulate and transmit new political ideas."[71] Several British plays, some staged transatlantically to raise funds for the release of the American captives held in North Africa, provided models of how female liberty could thwart the power of Islamic despots by just saying no to their lascivious advances. As the oriental tale often did for the act of reading, female action on the public stage transformed the passive experience of spectatorial pleasure into a performance of civic progress. John Brown's 1755 play *Barbarossa* expresses the collective theme of this genre in the motto: "No Tyrant's threat can awe the free-born Soul,/ That greatly dares to Die." Brown's play, reprinted and staged frequently in North America during the years of the Algerian conflict, parallels the demise of an earlier Algerine tyrant with the rise of his daughter to power.[72] Charles Dibdin's

---

[69] Ruth Bloch, "The Gendered Meanings of Virtue in Revolutionary America," *Signs* 13 (1987): 46. See also Rosemarie Zagarri, "Morals, Manners, and the Republican Mother," *American Quarterly* 44 (June 1992): 192–215.

[70] Penelope Aubin, *The Noble Slaves, Being an Entertaining History of the Surprising Adventures and Remarkable Deliverances from Algerine Slavery of Several Spanish Noblemen* (Danbury, CT: Douglas and Nichols, 1797; New Haven, CT: George Bunce, 1798; New York: John Tiebout, 1800; New York: Evert Duyckinck, 1806, 1814).

[71] Joseph C. Schöpp, "Liberty's Sons and Daughters: Susanna Haswell Rowson's and Royall Tyler's Algerine Captives," *Early America Re-Explored: New Readings in Colonial, Early National, and Antebellum Culture*, eds. Klaus H. Schmidt and Fritz Fleischmann (New York: Peter Lang, 2000), 294.

[72] John Brown, *Barbarossa* (London, 1755; Boston, 1794; New York, 1809), quote is from Boston edition, p. 17.

comic opera of 1776 named *The Seraglio* features an English heroine named Lydia who resists the advances of the Algerian Bashaw Abdallah and uses "the Torment of disappointed Love" to overturn his despotism. As a result of her instruction in "the Duties of Humanity" the Bashaw is inspired to dismiss his courtiers, free his slaves, and merit the real love of a beautiful captive named Elmira. By converting from "rough tyrannic Rules" to "Reason's Precepts," Abdallah's despotic heart is democratized with a suffusion of moral sensitivity, leading him to usher a millennial reign into Algiers.[73] The Sultan in Isaac Bickerstaffe's play of that name (subtitled "A Peep into the Seraglio") is accustomed to flattery from "mere caressing machines" and not the sincerity of a bold and independent woman. The vivacious candor of Roxalana overturns the Ottoman Empire and the Sultan capitulates. "It is enough – my scruples are at an end," he confesses while losing syntactic control, "my prejudices, like clouds before the rising sun, vanish before the lights of your superior reason – my love is no longer a foible – you are worthy of empire."[74]

The performance of such British dramas before American audiences provided fresh female models who demonstrated the revolutionary agency of conventional gender roles when projected onto and performed upon an international stage. Susanna Haswell Rowson's 1794 play *Slaves in Algiers* borrows from this tradition to create the strongest American example of the power of the national fantasy of female virtue to convert patriarchal despotism, be it oriental or domestic, into a democratic regime of marriage and order. Rowson, herself a recent immigrant from Britain, writes the play as her symbolic act of naturalization. Subtitled *A Struggle for Freedom*, the play dramatizes how a divided American family, symbolizing both political inaction and the rift between the United States and Britain, is reunited in Algiers where they regain their collective virtue and are able to depose the Algerian system of fear, cruelty, and licentiousness. The potential eroticism of liberty is sublimated in the play to the social level of patriotic devotion premised on the equality of the sexes. The play ends by invoking an idealized imperialism of virtue where a feminized "Eagle" is called upon to "spread her benign influence thro' every nation, until with the dove and olive-branch, [it] waves high, the acknowledged standard of the world."[75]

---

[73] Charles Dibdin, *The Seraglio: A Comic Opera* (London, 1776), 15, 30, 31–2.

[74] Isaac Bickerstaffe, *The Sultan* (1775; Georgetown, DC: William Rind, 1810; New York: D. Longworth, 1812). Quotation from 1810 edition, 7, 33. The play was performed in New York during 1794–5 and again during the Algerian captivity crisis in 1796, this time rewritten by John Hodgkinson as *The American Captive* (no copy extant). George C. D. Odell, *Annals of the New York Stage*, 15 vols. (New York: Columbia University Press, 1927–49), I: 353, 381–2, 404, 425.

[75] Mrs. [Susanna Haswell] Rowson, *Slaves in Algiers; or, A Struggle for Freedom* (Philadelphia: Wrigley and Berriman, 1794), 72. The play has been republished by Jennifer Margulis and Karen M. Poremski (Acton, MA: Copley Pub. Group, 2000). See also Elizabeth Maddock Dillon, "*Slaves in Algiers*: Race, Republican Genealogies, and the Global Stage," *American Literary History* 16 (2004): 407–36.

In Rowson's play, Islam and Muslims symbolize all that impedes this American mission of benevolent universalism. A prologue to the play demonizes the Muslim as nothing more than an avaricious pirate whose "idol, is his pilfer'd gold," an untutored barbarian who is incapable of virtue because he was "untaught to feel for, what he never felt." In the play, Rowson frequently figures Algiers as "the land of captivity" not only because Americans are involuntarily held there but also because the Dey himself is a slave "to rude ungoverned passion; to pride, to avarice and lawless love." Muslim manhood in the play is portrayed through the burlesque metonymies of their comically ugly appendages such as their "tremendous whiskers, . . . long, hooked nose[s], . . . [and] great beetle brows." The cruelty of the North African despot named Muley Moloc is symbolized by the "fear of his huge scymetar," a fear that is comically deflated by rendering the impotency of his excessive phallicism.[76]

Male despotism in the play is most fully emasculated, however, by the power of female virtue. All the single women of the play – including the Muslim ones – espouse Christian values and desire American husbands. The Moriscan tart Fetnah clearly prefers "a young, handsome, good humoured Christian, to an old, ugly, illnatured Turk." An American captive female announces goddess-like, that "never shall Olivia, daughter of Columbia, and a Christian, tarnish her name by apostasy, or live the slave of a despotic tyrant." The women's courage and resourcefulness make them the leaders of the revolt against captivity, and they frequently conspire to demonstrate their superiority to men. Rejecting male protection, Fetnah affirms that "in the cause of love or friendship, a woman can face danger with as much spirit, and as little fear, as the bravest man." The source of this female virtue rests in their indifference to the prerogatives of male power and in their capacity to forgive instead of desiring vengeance. *Slaves in Algiers* is thus not only a drama of American valor vanquishing oriental despotism, it also celebrates the primary role that the power of female virtue plays in moralizing such a transformation, thereby justifying the cultural imperialism of republicanism.[77]

Rowson's play is ultimately one about women's liberation from male dominance, Muslim or otherwise, and the generation of a transgendered national character. She not only writes the play, she also acts in it, and even

---

[76] Rowson, *Slaves in Algiers*, 1, 41, 60, 7, 6.

[77] Rowson, *Slaves in Algiers*, 40, 68, 47. In a closet drama from 1818 modeled on Rowson's play, captivity in Algiers serves as "a purgatory for Christians" whose ordeals teach three young women to uphold the value of Southern virtue. By juxtaposing the incipient vices of the young Carolinians with Algerine custom, the author displays the dangers and temptations that follow upon any postponement of their betrothals. "The Young Carolinians, or, Americans in Algiers: a Play in Five Acts," in *Essays Religious, Moral, Dramatic & Poetical Addressed to Youth and Published for a Benevolent Purpose by a Lady* [variously attributed to Maria Pinckney and Mrs. Pogson Smith] (Charleston, SC: A. E. Miller, 1818), 58–111.

comes out on stage alone to read an epilogue in some of the performances. In doing so she takes on the air of humility, apologizing that her "confined education" limited her capacity for classical rhetoric and allusion, and claiming that such a bold publicity makes her "almost terrif'd to death." The evaporation of such fears before the liberality of her audience replicates the plot of the play itself. Once liberated from her "fear" of being on stage alone, she delivers a revolutionary manifesto of female power, by announcing directly to the audience: "Women were born for universal sway,/ Men to adore, be silent, and obey." By extending the fictional revolution she portrays in Algiers to the political situation of her actual American audience, Rowson liberates herself from her own script and relishes her Scheherezade-like power of holding "in silken chains – the lordly tyrant man."[78] That such a vision of female liberty was unsettling to men can be seen by the fact that Rowson's play elicited sharp criticism from Anglophile critic William Cobbett, writing as Peter Porcupine, who imagined the result of such a revolution being the presence of pregnant women in the House of Representatives.[79]

By figuring the muse of the new nation as a feminized Columbia conscripting others into its cause of liberty, writers like Rowson propagated a benevolent imperialism of virtue in dealing with the Barbary challenge. The goal of such a vision was to cleanse libidinous desires of sensual excess by sublimating its thrills into a moral economy of national virtue. In the realm of literary diplomacy, tyrants had no power to silence the voice of the writer; rather, fiction interdicted the despot's domination through the flourishing of its own expression. Literary islamicism effectively disempowered even the mightiest of Eastern potentates by appropriating his agency and denying him any dialogical discretion. Muslim males depicted in early American literary productions were doomed to remain puppets of occidental fantasy: either unregenerate tyrants who delight in their own cruelty; misguided men susceptible to the moral charm of virtuous women; or, in a valence that developed more fully in the antebellum period (and in later chapters of this book), romantic representatives of exotic cosmopolitanism. Early islamicist literature performed an imperialism of virtue that deflated the challenge of despotism by satirizing excessive male power as an unstable burlesque. Writers deposed the despot's authority by allegorizing the agency of female liberty, rendering it so firmly freed from the conflated status of slavery and sensuality as to embody the moral revolution of republicanism.

---

[78] Rowson, *Slaves in Algiers*, 73. *Slaves in Algiers* seems influenced directly from Bickerstaffe's *The Sultan* in which Roxalana argues that "Men were born for no other purpose under heaven but to amuse us" (10). At the close of a Dublin performance of "The Sultan," the actress playing Roxalana comes on stage to speak an Epilogue also in the false attitude of "trembling" with fear (122–3).

[79] "A Kick for a Bite" (Philadelphia: Thomas Bradford, 1795) in David A. Wilson, ed., *Peter Porcupine in America: Pamphlets on Republicanism and Revolution* (Ithaca, NY: Cornell University Press, 1994), 131.

THE SCHOOLS OF DESPOTISM: BARBARY CAPTIVITY
AND COMPARATIVE CRITIQUE

The imaginative efficacy of female virtue was conjured during the Algerian war as a direct consequence of the failure of the nation's males – its voting citizens – to redeem its captives. The prevalence of triumphant fantasies compensated for the actual impotence of the captives to affect their own release and the reluctance of the nation to fund their ransoms. For the thirty-five years following the Algerine crisis, however, American men rallied in many ways to redeem their lost honor, one that had relegated the vanquishing of despots to the imagined agency of women. Both narrative authority and military action became celebrated cultural sites for refurbishing the masculine heroism of the early Republic: American males also drew on philosophical notions of Islamic reason to criticize the excesses of religious dogmatism. A corollary response of male writers was to deflate the legendary power of Islamic leaders and coopt their energies as resources for American manhood. The growing power of the Navy and the quality of its ships, reflective of the increasing strength of the nation, provided the most prominent (and long-lasting) source for deposing the despot and defusing his challenge to democracy.

Among the captives released to return to the United States were some who chose to celebrate their survival by voicing their ordeals in autobiographical narratives. These narratives of captivity testified to the maturing of the American males in the "schools of despotism," highlighting their eagerness to entertain the challenges of the wider world, their invincible spirit in the face of extreme hardship, and their capacity to parlay these experiences into a public form of expression that reestablished their claims to republican citizenship. This genre of islamicist expression overturned the shame of slavery by publicizing the narrator's triumphant resumption of his own expressive autonomy as symbolic proof of the viability of American independence. The publication of captivity narratives symbolized the nation's courage in surviving shameful indignity, its ability to manufacture cultural strength out of perilous distress, and its ingenuity in engendering national sympathy as a resource for counteracting the weakness of its foreign policy. Situating these transnational dramas in the Islamic African littoral also produced a transnational space from which to criticize practices bound by the shores of the nation, especially the practice of slavery in a society dedicated to propositions of liberty (see Chapter 3). Barbary captivity narratives layed out an Eastern frontier from whose comparative latitudes Americans could critically measure the nation's commitment to its ideals.

John Foss claimed to be an "illiterate mariner," but the resident of Newburyport, Massachusetts, was nevertheless encouraged by his friends to publish a journal of his "Captivity and Sufferings" in Algiers. His account presents information about the geography and culture of Algiers as well as intimates the "horrors of unspeakable slavery" he experienced at "the hands of merciless Mahometans . . . whose tenderest mercies towards the Christian captives, are the most extreme cruelties."[80] Foss's narrative celebrates the survival of these unfortunate captives as a symbol of the national devotion to "the sweets of Liberty." Nevertheless, his ordeal also charts his shameful inability to challenge the humiliations that his captors heaped upon him in the form of chains and a rough surplice that reminded him of a woman's petticoat. Foss's agency is relegated to the performance of his own narrative voice and its publication after his return as a free man. Foss relates an anecdote, repeated in other narratives, of a tyrannical taskmaster in the quarries named Sherief who fell and was dashed to death on the rocks below immediately after an American captive muttered, "God, grant you may die, the first time you offer to abuse another man." Similar to how this "Godless wretch" was "swept away by the devout breath of a suffering Christian," Foss's own account of the survival of his ordeal among the Algerines expresses the triumph of liberty over despotism by celebrating the survival of his democratic voice as a symbol of the power of a nation that refused to allow its sailors to languish in suffering enslavement.

The most famous of the North African narratives was William Riley's frequently reprinted account of his shocking experience surviving six months of captivity after his ship the *Commerce* wrecked on the coast of Morocco in 1815. Riley's story demonstrates how North Africa still posed dangers even after the end of the active capture of American ships. His narrative was a five-hundred-page testimony to his "unparalleled sufferings" and providential rescue that was designed to justify the use of public funds for his ransom, to help rescue and provide for the destitute families of the rest of his crew, to reveal ethnographic and geographical information about the coast and interior of Africa, and to criticize the domestic enslavement of Africans. Riley's courage and fortitude made him into an American celebrity whose voice announced the viability of the new nation through a combination of divine providence, public sympathy, and individual pluck.[81]

---

[80] John Foss, *A Journal of the Captivity and Suffering of John Foss; Several Years a Prisoner at Algiers* (Newburyport, MA: Angier March, 1798), excerpts reprinted in Baepler, *White Slaves,* 95, 73, 81. In a similar way, *The Affecting Narrative of the Captivity and Sufferings of Thomas Nicholson* tells of six years of degrading captivity in Algiers during which time he was forced to submit to the Dey by licking the dust before him, by carrying heavy rocks on his back up the sides of a craggy quarry, and by wearing a heavy chain around his neck for two years. (Boston: G. Walker, 1816; Boston: N. Coverly, 1818). See also William Ray, *Horrors of Slavery; or the American Tars in Tripoli* (Troy, NY: Oliver Lyon, 1808); James R. Lewis, "Savages of the Sea: Barbary Captivity and Images of Muslims in the Early Republic," *Journal of American Culture* 13 (1990): 75–84; and Paul Baepler, "The Barbary Captivity Narrative in American Culture," *Early American Literature* 39 (2004): 217–46.

[81] William Riley, *An Authentic Narrative of the Loss of the Brig* Commerce, *Wrecked on the Western Coast of Africa, in the Month of August, 1815* (New York: T. and W. Mercein, 1817). Riley's fame led his son to publish in 1851 a sequel, about his life after returning to the United States, that was frequently reprinted during the antebellum period. On the influence of Riley's Narrative, see Allison, *Crescent*

The very publication of these white slave narratives celebrated the persistent ability of citizens to surmount slavery and reestablish the political condition of liberty. By subjecting their former captivity to narrative expression, they purged themselves of the shame of their prior powerlessness and became agents of national survival and critical proponents of a more proactive response to the troubling larger issues surrounding African slavery.

The most intriguing and accomplished of these narratives, Royall Tyler's fictional narrative of 1797 called *The Algerine Captive*, was among the first American literary works to be published in England. The book federalizes the different generic registers of the picaresque autobiography, the captivity tale, and the travel narrative to dramatize how the comparative experience of Algerian despotism taught its New England-born narrator a fuller appreciation of the virtues of liberty and the importance of national unity. Tyler communicates this contrast through the novel's diptych form that juxtaposes his narrator's ideological servitude to his impractical classical education while free in America with his critical liberation from some of these parochial notions as a result of his captivity in Algiers. This central paradox is reflected by the irrepressibility of his American name, Updike Underhill, and by the title by which he is known in Algiers – the "learned slave." Part of the ambiguity of Underhill's hybrid cosmopolitanism can thus be seen in the fact that the provincialism of his cultural education in America continues to coexist with the wiser elements that he derives from the privilege of his experience, which he calls "those kinder virtues which schools and colleges often fail to teach." *The Algerine Captive* thus relates the experience of one of the first American "innocents abroad" and the work is a compelling narrative of political complexity that charts the emergence of a critical transnational consciousness from the comparative perspective of Algerine space.[82]

Obscured, 207–25. See also Judah Paddock, *A Narrative of the Shipwreck of the Ship* Oswego, *on the Coast of South Barbary, and of the Sufferings of the Master and the Crew While in Bondage among the Arabs* (New York: Collins & Co., 1818); and Archibald Robbins, *A Journal, Comprising an Account of the Loss of the Brig* Commerce (Hartford, CT: Silas Andrus, 1818).

[82] Royall Tyler, *The Algerine Captive; or, the Life and Adventures of Doctor Updike Underhill, Six Years a Prisoner among the Algerines*, 2 vols. (London: G. and J. Robinson, 1802) reprinted in facsimile edition edited by Jack Moore (Gainesville, FL: Scholars' Facsimiles & Reprints, 1967), 2: 18. *The Algerine Captive* was first published in Walpole, New Hampshire, in 1796 and was one of the rare early American novels to be reprinted in England. After a fire destroyed most of the copies of this British edition, the novel was serialized in thirteen installments in the *Ladies' Magazine* in 1804. Its ongoing currency during the Barbary wars is shown by its republication in Hartford in 1816 and by the fact that Tyler himself was working on a revision of the book in the years before his death in 1826. See G. Thomas Tanselle, *Royall Tyler* (Cambridge, MA: Harvard University Press, 1967), 140–8. Critical appraisals of Tyler's book include John Engell, "Narrative Irony and National Character in Royall Tyler's *The Algerine Captive*," *Studies in American Fiction* 17 (1989): 19–32; Larry R. Dennis, "Legitimizing the Novel: Royall Tyler's *The Algerine Captive*," *Early American Literature* 9 (1974): 71–80; Cathy N. and Arnold E. Davidson, "Royall Tyler's *The Algerine Captive*: A Study in Contrasts,"

This ambivalence is clearly revealed through Tyler's imagined engagement with Muslims and Islamic practices during Underhill's experience in North Africa and the Near East. One of the goals of Tyler's narrative is "to observe the customs, habits, and manners of a people of whom so much is said but so little known at home," a goal that is challenged by its fictional nature. Tyler's enslavement of Underhill requires the reader to undergo the imaginative experience of passing in Muslim Africa and this situation confirms some islamicist prescriptions of Muslim depravity. From the moment he first encounters his North African captors, Underhill discovers behaviors that affirm his designation of Algerians as "the ferocious race." He suffers the humiliating degradations at the hands of his Muslim masters related in other narratives. He licks the dust before the Dey; places his cruel master's foot on his own neck; and receives a whipping from a malicious overseer. Such dehumanizing cruelty reaches its apogee in the "horrid spectacle" he is forced to be a witness of the impaling alive of a slave who had attempted an escape. Tyler upholds islamicist views when five different times he labels Algiers a despotism and finds Islam to be a "detestably ridiculous" faith built "on stubble."[83]

Despite this strategy of confirming many islamicist stereotypes, Tyler also employs his lawyerly logic to demythologize other orientalist notions of Islam. This mode reveals another register of islamicism in the early republic, namely the way that Islam's monotheistic disdain for idols offered a global reservoir of rationalism that challenged the emotionalism and exclusivity of evangelical Christianity. Underhill interrogates the boundaries of islamicist dogma by examining Muslim behavior with "reason's law" based upon the recognition that God is "the common parent of the great family of the universe, who hath made of one flesh and one blood all nations of the earth." His broad humanism renders it impossible for Tyler to write of Algiers merely as a land of slavery; instead, he repositions Algerine captivity as an ideological location for reflecting on the universal conditions of cultural bondage, or how, as Malini Johar Schueller has noted, "the ideology of the virtuous empire is both deformed and reappropriated."[84] Updike rises above "natal prejudices" about Islam's depravity and argues that if either Christian or Muslim "would follow the obvious dictates of his own scripture, he would cease to hate, abominate, and destroy the other." For Tyler's narrator finds the "ferocious race" also to be an "extraordinary people" who exemplify alternatives not available within Euroamerican

---

Ariel 7 (1976): 53–67; Cathy N. Davidson, "*Reading The Algerine Captive,*" in *Revolution and the Word* (New York: Oxford University Press, 1986), 192–211; and the previously cited articles by Schöpp and Margulis.

[83] Tyler, *The Algerine Captive,* 2: 64, 33.

[84] Malini Johar Schueller, *U.S. Orientalisms: Race, Nation, and Gender in Literature, 1790–1890* (Ann Arbor: University of Michigan Press, 1998), 53.

models. Some of the myths that Underhill subverts are those that highlight Islam's hypocrisy, polygamy, and cruelty. He only encounters one Muslim who drinks and discovers that most males content themselves with only one wife. He discovers that arranged marriages, while distasteful, do not necessarily destroy love and liberty. (Tyler's judicious balancing is evident when he asserts "an Algerine courtship would be as disagreeable to a hale New England youth as a common bundling [the practice of unmarried individuals sharing a bed] would be disgusting to a Mussulman.") He finds Islam to be a sincere "principle in life" to which most Muslims are honestly devoted, and comparative Muslim practices enable Underhill to criticize such weaknesses of Christian cultures as sectarianism, drinking, gambling, and greed. In fact, he blames the persistence of Barbary plundering (as did Thomas Jefferson) on the nationalistic jealousies and avarice of Christian nations that prevented any collective resolve aimed at terminating the depredations. At times, Underhill's charity toward Islam is openly expressed, such as when he argues that the rapacious behavior of the Algerines is not based upon any religious teaching and claims that Qur'anic verses "ever exhibited the purest morality and the sublimest conceptions of the deity."[85]

It is Underhill's encounter with the Mollah, a Muslim teacher who was formerly a Christian from Antioch, that most fully symbolizes his ambivalent encounter with Islam. The Mollah challenges the captive's Christian faith by arguing that it is based on no better rational grounds than his faith in Islam and that it may simply be another expression of cultural prejudice. The Mollah's curious mixture of devious reasoning and compassionate humanitarianism baffles Underhill, who had originally sought out the interview as a means of escaping a sentence of hard labor. Underhill calls the Mollah's suave manner an "insidious attack" and is unable to trust the Mollah's genuine "candor and gentleness." At the end of Underhill's five-day interview with the Mollah, he is "abashed by his assurance and almost confounded by his sophistry" to the point where he willingly "resumed [his] slave's attire, and sought safety in my former servitude."[86]

In fact, it is Underhill's encounter with the civility of the Mollah – one that develops into friendship – that saves him from despair, and possibly even death. This is first evident by the healing nature of the bathing and anointing (with the Balm of Mecca) that he receives upon arrival at the college, a process that literally allows him to shed his old skin of servitude and be reborn with new skin "as fair as a child's of six months old." This resurrecting relationship is even more evident in Underhill's second encounter with the Mollah that follows his physical and psychological breakdown after his return to harsh menial labor. Underhill enters the infirmary "resigned to die" but, as a result of the Mollah's care and concern, leaves "again attached to life."

[85] Tyler, *Algerine Captive*, 1: 169; 2: 145, 124, 142–3.   [86] Tyler, *Algerine Captive*, 2: 53.

"Though I abominated his faith," Underhill confesses, "I was charmed with the man," explaining how "his very smile exhilarated my spirits and infused health." After his healing, he is purchased by the director of the hospital who benignly allows him to practice medicine. For the rest of the time he is in Algiers (and during his pilgrimage to Mecca), he has more professional renown and remuneration than he ever earned while free in the United States. He even claims that he would have chosen to remain in Algiers "for a few years" if he could have been assured of returning to America, a situation that reflects both the undeveloped state of medicine in North Africa and the extent of Algerian generosity to a man who was, from their perspective, an infidel and a slave.[87]

The fact that the Mollah's intellectual justification of Islam is much more polished than Updike's defense of his own faith opened Tyler up to much criticism about being soft on Christianity. "The author too feebly defends that religion which he professes to revere," claimed one journal; another found Underhill's faith to be "the effect rather of obstinacy than of conviction."[88] Tyler retrospectively defended his book by arguing in the third person that

> He never thought that in adopting the liberality of the good Sale, the translator of the Koran he was even jeopardizing the truths of Christianity: for the Author considered then, and now considers, that, after exhibiting Islamism in its best light, the Mahometan imposture will be obvious to those who compare the language, the dogmatic fables, the monstrous absurdities of the Koran, with the sublime doctrines, morals and language of the Gospel Dispensation.[89]

Underhill's reliance upon his liberal Muslim mentor and his ambivalent equation of Christian tradition as itself a form of servitude represents a rare cultural moment when the possibility of rational dialogue existed within American involvement with Mediterranean Muslims. It comprised part of a larger gesture, consonant with the vogue of Deism and Freemasonry and the emergence of Unitarianism, that viewed Muslim belief in monotheism and its prohibitions against any iconic idolatry as a contentious challenge to the excesses of Christian denominationalism. James Turner has claimed that at the end of the eighteenth century, Islam was being characteristically employed by Deists "as a stick with which to beat the orthodox."[90] Indeed the Treaty of Peace and Friendship signed by Congress in 1796 with

---

[87] Tyler, *Algerine Captive*, 2: 37–9, 71–2, 76.

[88] "Retrospective Review," *The Monthly Anthology* 9 (November 1810), 346, in Allison, *Crescent Obscured*, 94; Tanselle, *Royall Tyler*, 172; *Monthly Review* 42 (September 1803): 86–93.

[89] Tyler wrote these lines in his proposed preface to his *Memoir*, 99–100, cited in Tanselle, *Royall Tyler*, 268, n29.

[90] James Turner, *Without God, without Creed: The Origins of Unbelief in America* (Baltimore: The Johns Hopkins University Press, 1985), 153. See also Gerald R. McDermott, "Edwards and Islam: The Deist Connection," *Jonathan Edwards's Writings: Text, Context, Interpretation*, ed. Stephen J. Stein

Tripoli acknowledged the benign nature of Islam as its eleventh article, a statement that has caused much debate and controversy over the years about the religious foundations of national character.

> As the government of the United States of America is not in any sense founded on the Christian Religion, – as it has in itself no character of enmity against the laws, religion or tranquility of Musselmen, – and as the said States never have entered into any war or act of hostility against any Mehomitan nation, it is declared by the parties that no pretext arising from religious opinions shall ever produce an interruption of the harmony existing between the two countries.[91]

As in Tyler's dramatic encounter with the Mollah's disarming rationality, the rhetoric of this treaty demonstrates another critical valence of islamicist discourse in the early United States. Unwilling to relegate reason to a cultural resource associated with Islam, nor to allow Christian belief to display itself as a form of superstitious emotional dependence, some philosophical Americans sought to redeploy rational logic itself as a means of strengthening the foundations of American democracy. This approach is most compellingly expressed through another fascinating and unexamined example of the Muslim spy genre in the early republic, one that satirizes the religious wrangling and evangelical sectarianism during the time of the disestablishment of religion in New England through the rational contemplation of a Muslim philosopher seeking to undermine Christian belief in the "city upon a hill" of Boston society.

Extracts from a Journal of Travels in North America was written under the pseudonym Ali Bey and published in Boston in 1818 after the Barbary States had been subdued by American and then British naval power.[92] This later historical context helps explain why the domestic weaknesses uncovered by Ali Bey are religious and social rather than political, and the threat of Islam represents the detachment of philosophical rationalism rather than attachment to sensual excess or submission to despotic authority. The book's real author was Samuel Lorenzo Knapp, a Boston editor who was called in the *Cyclopedia of American Literature* a "voluminous and useful miscellaneous writer" and was known for authoring biographies of Aaron Burr, Andrew Jackson, and Daniel Webster, as well as the 1829 "Lectures on American Literature," one of the earliest attempts to distinguish a national literary

---

(Bloomington and Indianapolis: Indiana University Press, 1996), 39–51; Herbert M. Morais, *Deism in Eighteenth-Century America* (New York: Russell & Russell, 1960), 144.

[91] "Treaty of Peace and Friendship, Signed at Tripoli November 4, 1796," in *Treaties and Other International Acts of the United States of America*, ed. Hunter Miller, 8 vol. (Washington, DC: GPO, 1931) 2: 365.

[92] Samuel L. Knapp, *Extracts from a Journal of Travels in North America, Consisting of an Account of Boston and Its Vicinity* (Boston: Thomas Badger, 1818).

tradition.[93] The innovation of Ali Bey's journal was to domesticate the popularity of an actual travel narrative, *The Travels of Ali Bey* – a book published in London in 1816 and in two American editions that same year – by applying its transnational intelligence to American subjects. Ali Bey was a pseudonym of a Spanish traveler named Domingo Badía y Leblich, whose knowledge of Arabic, geology, and botany earned for him financial backing for an opulent voyage through the lands of the Muslim Mediterranean between the years 1803 to 1807. Badía's account of his actual pilgrimage to Mecca was the first presented to Western readers in over a century, and this status as a Hajji opened the doors to the Mosque of Omar in Jerusalem that had been closed to Christians since the times of the Crusades.[94]

Knapp draws upon this vogue by assuming the narrative voice of the same Ali Bey, who takes on the disguise of a Frenchman named Monsieur Desaleurs but is really a spy for the Ottoman Empire, sent to the States on a "great project" to determine how the New World might be converted to Islam. Ali Bey's journal registers his attempt to "unravel the secret folds and reduplications" of Boston society, most of whose citizens he views as "slaves of fashion and opinion." Knapp uses multiple masks in Ali Bey's journal to protect himself from his withering indictment of the Bostonians' "mental vassalage" to superficial emulation, a situation stemming from a frivolous system of education and an inordinate respect for the privileges of wealth. Ali Bey's own narrative voice is frequently blended with the Americans he discourses with, especially the American Southerner he befriends at the Exchange Coffee House where he resides, indicating that there are resources of domestic subversion he can count upon for assistance and intelligence.[95]

Of greatest interest in the work is the appendix that consists of Ali Bey's report to the Turkish Sultan about why Boston is an appropriate place to introduce Islam into North America and how such a project might be successfully accomplished. He believes that the denominational disunity resulting from the "religious interregnum" between Calvinism and Unitarianism offers an opportunity for Islam to breach the bulwarks of Boston society. "To those who are offended with the fanaticism of one party or the levity and affectation of the other," Ali Bey asserts, "we should offer simplicity, sincerity, solemnity, truth!" Part of Ali Bey's satire involves inhabiting the viewpoint of a missionary-in-reverse and arrogating such a presumptive privilege as the barb of his critique. To succeed in North America, Ali Bey suggests, Islam would merely have to display itself with enough wealth and

---

[93] Evert A. and George L. Duyckinck, eds., *Cyclopaedia of American Literature*, 2 vols. (New York: Charles Scribner, 1856), 2: 61–2.

[94] *The Travels of Ali Bey in Morocco, Tripoli, Cyprus, Egypt, Arabia, Syria, and Turkey, between the Years 1803 and 1807* (Philadelphia: M. Carey, 1816). The author seems to have devised his pseudonym from a rebellious Egyptian named Ali Bey whose exploits were trumpeted in a 1783 book by Sauveur Lusignan called *A History of the Revolt of Ali Bey against the Ottoman Porte* (London, 1783).

[95] Knapp, *Extracts from a Journal*, 14n, 13, 96.

style that it would become the new fashion of the city to which the citizens, given their "mimetic dispositions," would flock for social recognition. Ali Bey's imperial desire to colonize Boston is displayed when he climbs to the cupola of the Boston State House and looks out over a countryside he finds unsurpassed in all his travels and imagines the twenty church spires that rise in front of him being replaced with the minarets of mosques.[96]

While Mehemet's naturalization in *The Algerine Spy* enables Markoe to fantasize the capacity of American virtue to convert the devious designs of the Muslim spy, Knapp's Ali Bey exposes the infidel barbarities of a civilization that is blinded by its "preposterous itching for style and parade" and its deluded devotion to what Alexis de Tocqueville would later call "the tyranny of the majority." The "translator" of Ali Bey's *Journal* overcomes his scruples about publishing writing "not intended for a Christian audience" by the rationalization that such a "covert project" has been "happily detected." The publication of these intercepted missives to an American audience effectively coopts the potential subversion of the spy through the social circulation of their "intelligence." The antidemocratic conspiracy that emerges from the conjunction of espionage with the epistolary mode is thus defused through publication. Texts such as Knapp's and Markoe's, offered to the readers by so-called "translators," thus serve as a compelling means of rational counterintelligence through which the American press, itself one of the stays against domestic despotism, exposed the dangers of an uncritical or hypocritical citizenry, thereby reminding readers of the vigilance necessary to maintain liberty and the precarious paradox of democratic independence. The fact that these letters are read by Americans in English and not by Muslims in Arabic also dramatizes the capacity of American literature to globalize its national mission. By registering the Muslim desire for America, these spy narratives also universalize democracy and thereby fantasize a global prominence for the new nation that was distinctly at odds with its political status in the Muslim world.[97]

Captivity narratives celebrated the survival and persistence of the American desire to experience liberty; in contrast, the islamicist tropes of the Algerine captive and the Muslim spy naturalized the discriminating intellect as an effective resource of cultural analysis. Positing an islamicist observer emancipated the author to provide rational latitude on how provincial perspectives and a parochial education held Americans captive to a type of cultural insularity. The invention of an alien and naïve interlocuter empowered Tyler, Knapp, and Markoe to levy a direct criticism of common practices without the charge of being labeled uncharitable, displacing this ingratitude through the transgressive form of islamicism itself. Although derived from European literary practices, the ways that these narratives transposed comparative commentary onto American subjects enabled critical imagination to serve as literary diplomacy in the cause of republican reform, and thereby

---

[96] Knapp, *Extracts from a Journal*, 119, 100, 58–9.   [97] Knapp, *Extracts from a Journal*, 91, 5.

to recycle the energies of revolutionary liberty as a reinvigorating national resource.

Part of the difficulty that diplomats experienced in stabilizing foreign policy in North Africa was that once promises or gifts had been granted to one regency, the others often felt entitled to demand similar treatment. In response to these unreasonable demands, American men performed their own republican resistance by refusing to submit. Such resolve also manifested itself in the corresponding gesture of discounting the historical threat posed by despotism and emasculating the authority of its male leaders. The treaty mentioned earlier that the United States signed in 1796 with the Pasha of Tripoli did not require the payment of tribute, and when the American government later refused to renegotiate this treaty and offer the Pasha similar terms as it had offered to Algiers, Tripoli declared war. It was during this Tripolitan War of 1801–5 that the American navy first displayed some measure of active valor in the suppression of North African tyranny. The building of the naval ship the *U.S.S. Constitution*, for example, was authorized by Congress to defend American shipping from North African harassment (a military counterpart to the manner in which the written Constitution protected Americans from the threat of domestic despotism). An engraving depicting the Navy's first bombardment of a Barbary ship in 1801 contains the caption "Capt STERRETT in the Schr. ENTERPRISE paying tribute to TRIPOLI" (Fig. 1.3).[98]

Ironically, however, the most celebrated naval events of the Tripolitan War were the results of American failures. Stephen Decatur gained enormous fame by sneaking a force of seventy into the harbor of Tripoli and burning the *U.S.S. Philadelphia* on 16 February 1804 after it had run aground there the previous year and its crew of 307 had been coerced into captivity. When the American ship *Intrepid* – after it had been loaded with ten thousand pounds of gunpowder as a floating bombship in Tripoli's harbor and renamed the *Infernal* – exploded in September of 1804, its martyred sailors gained legendary acclaim by supposedly choosing death, Cato-like, rather than surrender their ammunition to the Tripolitans. A naval ode celebrated this "band ... Who well aveng'd our injured land; / And drove the crescent, bath'd in blood, / To hide its blushes in the flood./ But when no effort could withstand / The willy [sic] Turk's ensnaring hand, / Snatch'd for themselves the lighted brand, / And mounting in a shroud of flame, / Died to the world – to live in fame!"[99] By celebrating national martyrdom,

---

[98] Engraving by M. F. Crone, in *Naval Documents Relating to the U.S. Wars with the Barbary Powers,* 6 vols. (Washington, DC: GPO, 1939–45), 1: frontispiece.

[99] "Ocean – A Naval Ode," in *American Naval Battles* (Boston: J. J. Smith, Jr., 1831), 265, see also p. 40. A captive in Tripoli at the time, Dr. Jonathan Cowdery, grounds such lofty rhetoric in his journal

FIGURE 1.3. This image of thirteen ships before the rock of Gibraltar dramatizes the might of American naval power at the conclusion of the conflicts with the Barbary Regencies. M. Corne, "Triumphant Return of the American Squadron under Com. Bainbridge from the Mediterranean 1815." *The Naval Temple* (Boston: Barber Badger, 1816), frontispiece.

Americans were able to mythologize both cultural strength and male vigor out of the very midst of failure, broadening the cultural strategy employed by individual captives when narrating their exploits of endurance and survival under Muslim bondage.

As American military power grew in strength, narrative performances of nationality found fuller embodiment in masculine myths of naval honor. Triumphant cultural expression about the Tripolitan phase of the Barbary wars vitalized national fortunes by celebrating a second generation of American military heroes, men who refused to cower before the "pirates" of Barbary and embodied instead the triumph of republican resolve over the "savage Mussulman."[100] Commodore Edward Preble's aggressive resistance to Tripoli's demands culminated in four separate shellings of the city in August and September of 1804. Stephen Decatur, whose exploits included revenge on the treacherous Tripolitans who had killed his brother James, was celebrated as both a contemporary crusader and a latter day Homeric hero – such as in a poem called "The Mussulmen Humbled,"

by describing how he saw "the mangled bodies of his countrymen precipitated into the air" and how their corpses lay in putrefaction on the beach weeks after the incident because the Algerines refused to handle the bodies of Christians. *American Captives in Tripoli; or, Dr. Cowdery's Journal*, 2nd ed. (Boston: Belcher and Armstrong, 1806), in Baepler, *White Slaves*, 171, 175.

[100] For a useful presentation of the flurry of cultural production see "Remembering the Tripolitan War" in Allison, *Crescent Obscured*, 187–206.

which portrayed him as a triumphant Achilles braving the new Muslim Trojans. Americans promoted Decatur into a popular hero as registered by the dozen cities and towns throughout the country that were named after him.[101] Indeed, the retaliatory destruction of the *Philadelphia* took its place among the select accomplishments around Americans' invented traditions of national honor. For example, in 1807 a national panorama joined the burning of the *Philadelphia* and the bombing of Tripoli with one depicting the Battle of Bunker Hill.[102]

If Jeffersonians celebrated Decatur for his deeds in avenging national failures at sea, Federalists fostered another hero in the figure of William Eaton, the general who gained fame for a land-based operation that ultimately proved abortive because of the signing of the peace treaty. As the war with Tripoli was launched, Eaton discovered (from his official position as consul to Tunis) that Jusef Caramalli (Yusef Qaramanli), the bashaw of Tripoli, had unjustly usurped leadership by killing his father, murdering his eldest brother, and forcing into exile his other older brother, Hamet Caramalli (Ahmed). Eaton reasoned that if the United States supported the ex-bashaw Hamet in retaking his rightful authority, the Americans could simultaneously liberate their captives and depose a despot, as well as gain an ally by standing on the side of justice. Eaton devised an "experiment" whereby he would travel with a guard of eight Marines to Cairo and Alexandria, where Hamet was living, and support him in raising a force to retake the eastern city of Derne. After many preparations and deliberations, a camel caravan set off from Egypt in March of 1804 across over five hundred miles of formidable Libyan desert, during which his mixed army of Arabs, Greeks, Egyptians, and Americans experienced trials of dissent, deprivation, and desertion. Finally at the end of April, supported by the naval ships the *Hornet*, *Nautilus*, and *Argus*, the force victoriously attacked Derne resulting in the raising of the American flag above the city's ramparts, the first time that the United States had so established its power outside of the Americas. The victory at Derne was trumpeted throughout the States as an example of American courage in the world, and Eaton, who was injured in the attack, was celebrated by schoolchildren as a legendary American Alexander or Scipio.[103]

These events came as a threat to the bashaw Jusef Caramalli in Tripoli, who feared the combined assault of the American naval squadron and

---

[101] Joseph Hanson, *The Mussulmen Humbled; or, A Heroic Poem in Celebration of the Bravery Displayed by the American Tars, in the Contest with Tripoli* (New York: Southwick and Hardcastle, 1806).

[102] *Companion to the Historical Paintings of the Ever Memorable Battle of Bunker's Hill and Grand View of the Destruction of the Frigate Philadelphia and the Bombardment of Tripoli* ... (Boston: B. True, 1807).

[103] Charles Prentiss, *The Life of the Late Gen. William Eaton* (Brookfield: E. Merriam & Co., 1813); Kitzen, *Tripoli and the United States at War*, who borrows heavily from Wright and Macleod, *The First Americans in North Africa*. a book whose research was stimulated by the African landings of American troops to fight German General Rommel in World War II.

the rebellion of his brother's advancing troops. When three navy frigates appeared on the coast of Tripoli at the end of May, he was eager to sue for peace, and on June 4, Tobias Lear arranged a treaty through which the almost three hundred prisoners from the *Philadelphia* were finally ransomed for $60,000 and released. Eaton, however, remained bitter about the dishonorable betrayal of Hamet and the failure of the United States to establish its prestige by carrying through on the campaign to remove both the payment of tribute and the bashaw's despotic authority once and for all.

Narratives written about prisoners in Tripoli dramatize their attempts to maintain their masculine pride among their Muslim captors. Several sailors even converted to Islam or "turned Turk," including one Lewis Heximer who assumed the name Hamet Amerikan.[104] In contrast, a few days after being taken from the *Philadelphia*, Elijah Shaw recounts how he retaliated against the cruelty of one of his drivers by knocking the man down. The price of his pride was 182 strokes of the bastinado on the bottoms of his feet. Masculine rehabilitation was more fully dramatized in a play called *The Young Carolinians* in which a drunk gambler is redeemed by following the noble example of the American tars and setting off to help rescue the captives. He announces that "treaties with pirates are as pearls cast before swine" and foresees the day, accomplished by the date of the play's publication, when "our sailors shall make the crescent bend to our fixed stars."[105] When the captive sailors from the *Philadelphia* were finally restored to Washington, D.C., they were welcomed by thousands of spectators who were fascinated by the Turkish dress and long beards that they patriotically wore as badges of their exotic experience.[106]

DEFLATING THE DESPOT: NORTH AFRICAN MUSLIMS IN THE UNITED STATES, 1804–1807

If exalting the exploits of American military men served as one means of disposing of the challenge of despotism, a correspondingly important cultural strategy was deflating the legendary male power of Muslim authority. The caving in of the Tripolitan bashaw in the face of force demonstrated that Barbary power had proven to be an exaggerated threat, and this was a lesson later taken to heart by political leaders in France and Britain. These images promoted a burlesquing of despotic power that portrayed it as an opposing model of ineffectual and hypocritical manhood against which the honor of republican masculinity could be revived. At the end of the Tripolitan War, East coast Americans had opportunities to view North Africans at first hand

---

[104] Cowlery, *American Captives in Tripoli* in Baepler, *White Slaves*, 171–2 (renegades Prince, Wilson, and West are mentioned on pages 165, 178, and 180). See also *Naval Documents*, 3: 347.

[105] *The Young Carolinians*, 100; see note 77.

[106] *A Short Sketch of the Life of Elijah Shaw* (Rochester, NY: Strong & Dawson, 1843), 53.

through the visit of a Tunisian ambassador to the United States and the presence of Tripolitan prisoners in New York City. These exotic representatives failed to uphold the fearsome heritage of Muslim male power and ruthlessness but rather served as ludicrous examples that helped to undercut the cultural fear of an idealized Islamic despotism.

After the American navy had displayed its power in June 1804 by pressuring Tripoli to end its actions against the United States, a military squadron sailed west to the regency of Tunis to force the Bey to abide by the existing treaty of 1797 and abandon his requests for a cruiser and more tribute. Hamuda Pasha accepted this ultimatum provided that the United States agree to negotiate with his representative in Washington about indemnification for Tunisian vessels that the Navy had captured during the Tripolitan War. He appointed as ambassador Sidi Soliman Mellimelni (or Mellimelli) who, with a suite of attendants, arrived in Virginia on board the *Congress* on 4 November 1805, reaching Washington three and a half weeks later during the fast of Ramadan. For the next six months, Mellimelli and his colorful retinue were the talk of the capital. During the first month, Mellimelli dined (precisely at sunset) with President Thomas Jefferson and a party that included John Quincy Adams. The federal government had to post a guard of marines outside of Stelle's Hotel keep at bay the swelling spectators eager to catch a glimpse of the tall-turbaned and yellow-slippered "Turk." Part of his hotel expenses included prostitutes provided by the government to replace the harem that he had left at home.

But the Tunisian Ambassador's exotic splash – which included debates with a delegation of Cherokees about the nature of religious worship – did not ripple for very long among government leaders. Mellimelli refused financial compensation for the ships and then rejected the brig that the government had acquired as a replacement after it was already loaded for the return trip. Between May and September, his journey up the eastern seaboard to Baltimore, Philadelphia, New York, and Boston caused many annoyances for the officials in charge of his visit. His demands for gifts and supplies for the Bey, his avaricious speculation and refusal to pay duties, his inability to keep his barber and cook sober and in line (they eventually refused to join him for the return home), and even the disposal of the four unremarkable horses he had presented to President Jefferson as gifts were among the problems arising from his irregular conduct. His guide James Leander Cathcart, himself a former captive who had risen to become secretary to the Dey of Algiers and later appointed consul to Tripoli, was outraged by the ambassador's selfish insolence and threw up his hands in a letter to James Madison, labeling Mellimelli a "political pest of society."[107] After the government had gone the extra mile to facilitate his journey and to send him back home content, Mellimelli left Boston on 17 September 1805 and arrived home in December, where he was eventually rewarded for

---

[107] James Leander Cathcart to the Secretary of the Navy, 20 August 1806, in *Naval Documents*, 6: 475.

this services with an ambassadorship in Spain. Tobias Lear, the American diplomat, still had to pay the Bey a $10,000 indemnity for the ships that Mellimelli had agreed were worth less than half that amount.[108]

Mellimelli and his suite were not the only North Africans in the eastern United States during the 1805–6 season. A group of Tripolitan prisoners who had been captured in August of 1804 had been sent back to the States in the frigate *John Adams* where they too became a social spectacle. On 6 March 1805, they attended a New York performance of the play *Bluebeard* where their appearance in the stage box attracted as much attention as the actors on stage. A historian of the New York theater noted: "The atrocious taste of these proceedings [was] only equalled by the vulgarity of the audience that flocked to the show." By popular acclaim, they returned a week later to see another play that featured fictional Moors as characters. Later that month, a theater held a benefit drama to raise money to buy new clothes for these Tripolitan captives who apparently had not changed their apparel since their capture. On April 5th, they gave an encore appearance at another performance of *Bluebeard*, presumably wearing their new Yankee duds.[109]

For the first time, domestic Americans were able to witness live Muslims in their midst rather than read about fictional creations, and the result both confirmed their exotic interest and deflated the menace of Muslim despotism. Juxtaposing ragged captives with the often orientalized theatrical figure of Bluebeard, whose punitive violence against women resembled Shahriyar in the *Arabian Nights*, made a charade out of the fear of despotism and dramatized how domestic cultural repertoires helped to defuse the legendary threat of oriental power.

The presence of Tripolitan prisoners in New York, specifically one "Mustaffa, Captain of the Ketch," provided the model for the most well-known epistolary commentary by a fictional islamicist observer in the early republic. The nine letters of one Mustapha Rub-a-Dub Keli Khan to his acquaintances in Tripoli were translated from the "Arabic-Greek" and published as part of the 1807 volume *Salmagundi* written by Washington Irving, his brother William, and James Kirke Paulding.[110] The Mustapha letters dramatized the utility of the Muslim interlocutor as a means of commenting

---

108 *Naval Documents*, 6: 334, 336, 343–4, 349; Ray Watkins Irwin, "The Mission of Soliman Mellimelni, Tunisian Ambassador to the United States, 1805–7," *Americana* (October 1932): 465–71; Louis B. Wright and Julia H. Macleod, "Mellimelli: A Problem for President Jefferson in North African Diplomacy," *The Virginia Quarterly Review* (1944): 555–65. Senator William Plumer of New Hampshire viewed him in his diary as a "half savage, half Brute – whom we have deigned to receive in the dignified character of an ambassador from Tunis" (469). *Plumer's Memorandum of Proceedings in the United States Senate, 1803–1807* (New York: Macmillan, 1923), 358–9.

109 "The Turks to the Rescue," Odell, *Annals of the New York Stage*, 2: 228–9.

110 The Mustapha Rub-a-Dub Keli Khan letters are included in Washington Irving et al., *Salmagundi or the Whim-Whams and Opinions of Lancelot Langstaff, Esq. and Others* (1808; London: J. M. Richardson, 1810).

on local politics as did the letters of Mehemet and Ali Bey; at the same time, they also satirically displayed caricatures of oriental male excess.[111] The three recipients of the letters are given full Arabic names and titles, as is Mustapha himself, but such exaltation is satirically undercut by the positions each holds in Tripolitan society. Seven of the letters are sent to Asem Hacchem, the "Principal Slave-Driver to His Highness the Bashaw of Tripoli," and the other two recipients hold the offices of "the Chief Mountebank and Buffa-Dancer to his Highness" and military sentinel at gate of the Bashaw's palace – called "the snorer" as a sneer at the weakness of North African military power. The device of a lowly infidel narrator beyond the pale of class and religious orthodoxy licensed the authors to invent absurd titles and to publish profane oaths. Mustapha swears twice each on the "beard" and the "head of Mahomet," "by the hump of Mahomet's camel," "by the whiskers of our sublime bashaw," and, most ludicrously, "by the nine thousand capers of the great mountebank of Damascus."[112] Such satire capitalized on the fantastic conventions of literary orientalism, and Mustapha's allusions refer more to such works as William Beckford's *Vathek* and Robert Southey's poetry than to actual Islamic beliefs.[113]

While such transactions accomplished important ends in liberating American satire from conventional restraints, they also opened the space for Mustapha's critical observations about democratic society. Mustapha calls the United States a "logocracy" because he saw its citizens constantly engaged in "somnifereous debates about the most trivial affairs." The frequent refrain of his letters is that the "gigantic genius" of Americans is their "faculty of swelling everything up into importance." Mustapha encourages his friend Asem in Tripoli to "rejoice that . . . thou livest in a country where the people instead of being at the mercy of a tyrant with a million of heads, having nothing to do but submit to the will of a bashaw of only three tails."[114] By rendering republican conventions the satirical focus of an upstart despot (who was himself a lowly prisoner), *Salmagundi* identified the petty debates of American politics as themselves a source of oriental excess. Moreover, Mustapha's satirical comments also ironically embodied the capacity of American expression to generate and incorporate islamicized difference as a critical, inclusive, and even humorous resource for establishing the authority of democratic culture.

[111] See Mary Wetherspoon Bowden, "Cocklofts and Slang-Whangers: The Historical Sources of Washington Irving's *Salmagundi*," *New York History* 59 (April 1980): 133–60, esp. 138.

[112] Irving et al., *Salmagundi*, 204, 243, 377, 414. Other subjects of oaths in the letters are the "head of the immortal" or "mighty Amrou" [424]; the "sword of the immortal" or "puissant Khaled" [149, 376].

[113] As early as 1770, American fiction was featuring the trappings of Islamic orientalism, see *Father Bombo's Pilgrimage to Mecca*. ed. Michael Davitt Bell (Princeton, NJ: Princeton University Library, 1975).

[114] Irving et al., *Salmagundi*, 111, 321.

GREEK INDEPENDENCE AND THE METONYMY
OF MUSLIM MANHOOD

The American armed forces, especially the U.S. Marine Corps, gained fame through its support of Eaton's march under Lieutenant Presley O'Bannon, which led to the adoption of a curved scimeter given by Hamet Caramalli as the symbol of the Corps, as well as the phrase "To the Shores to Tripoli" in its official hymn. The prestige and experience of the American Navy, symbolized by the presence of Tripolitan captives in New York, grew so much that in 1812 a new war with Britain was being entertained, in part to end the impressment of U.S. sailors. John C. Calhoun called the Mediterranean Sea "the school of our naval virtue" and had elevated expectations that the United States would never again accept insult with impunity.[115] With its confidence strengthened by another victory over Britain, the Navy was then able to sail in full force under Stephen Decatur, now commander of the Fleet, to dictate new treaties to the Barbary Regencies that dispensed forever with the paying of tribute, actions that paved the way for the subjugation of Algiers by the British in 1816. Through these exploits of Decatur and others, the Navy was no longer a threat to Americans but had itself been transformed into an emblematic instrument of national honor.

After North Africa was subdued by Euroamerican naval powers, American attention migrated further east into the Muslim lands that began to be called the Near East. When Greek nationalists rose in rebellion to demand their independence from Turkey in 1821, a new phase of Mediterranean orientalism emerged in popular expression in the United States. Philhellenism was stimulated by a Byronic desire to revive the noble qualities of Greek democracy and heroism that so permeated the classical texts of the American educational curriculum. The successful revolt of the Greeks against their Ottoman masters legitimated the national project by encouraging Americans that their example was revitalizing the tradition of democracy in the land of its origin. The Greeks, like the Americans struggling against the British, were vastly outnumbered. However, their desire for liberty and democratic self-rule demonstrated the hope of exporting democracy back to Greece, even as it had just began to spread through the hemisphere of the Americas. President James Monroe announced to Congress that it had been "a cause of unceasing and deep regret... that such a country should have been overwhelmed, and so long hidden, as it were, from the world, under a gloomy despotism."[116] The cause of Greek independence stoked the sympathies of American citizens who formed dozens of local Greek

---

[115] J. C. Calhoun, Speech on the Merchants Bonds, 8 December 1812, *The Papers of John C. Calhoun*, ed. Robert L. Meriwether 28 vols. (Columbia: University of South Carolina Press, 1959), 1: 144.

[116] Monroe's Message to Congress, 3 December 1822, *The Debates and Proceedings of the Congress of the United States*, 17th Congress, 2nd Session (Washington, DC: Gales and Seaton, 1855), 19.

committees to raise funds to send out supplies to the Greek nationalists. Manuel Mordecai Noah, a former U.S. diplomat to Algiers, wrote a play in 1822 called *The Grecian Captive* in which the victory of Alexander Ypsilanti was guaranteed by artillery from a frigate called the *United States*, even though the U.S. Navy actually remained neutral in the contest. (The play ended with Turkish captives being led in chains under the Acropolis – including one whose name is the pun Nadir – under banners bearing the names of the heroes of ancient Greece, as well as Ypsilanti, Washington, Bolivar, and Lafayette.)[117]

The Greek conflict was also interpreted as a struggle between the Cross and the Crescent in which the empire of Turkey was again denigrated into a caricature of monstrous despotism. The belief that Muslims were bewitched by a religion that prevented any prosperity is revealed by the frequent use of dehumanizing metonymies to explain their backwardness. "The foot of the Turk, wherever placed, leaves sterility and wretchedness," averred the Philhellene Samuel Woodruff; Fisher Howe emphasized "the blighting hand of the Turk," a hand which John L. Stephens felt "withers all that it touches."[118] Images of Ottoman leaders (such as the terrible Ali Pasha) as heartless brutes (along with the contrasting image of the enslaved Greek maiden) were frequently enlisted in Philhellenic propaganda and poetry. One ode to Greece, sung on George Washington's birthday, celebrated the Greek resolve to "Spurn the turban'ed Tyrant's power" and "Lay the ruthless Moslem low."[119]

Many Americans were so enamored with the Greek cause that they explained away any defects or dishonor in their behavior as the result of Turkish oppression.[120] One historian explained that "the press and other organs of American public opinion . . . although eloquent and verbose on the subject of Turkish atrocities, were silent concerning the brutalities of the Greek armed forces."[121] Henry A. V. Post, an agent sent to the Aegean by

---

[117] Mordecai Manuel Noah, *The Grecian Captive; or, The Fall of Athens* (New York: E. M. Murden, 1822), 48. The pageantry of this scene was destroyed during its performance when the elephant shook his skin, nearly tumbling the victorious Ypsilanti from his howdah and then relieved itself with a steady stream of urine that threatened to deluge the pit. Joe Cowell, *Thirty Years Passed Among the Players in England and America* (New York: Harper and Brothers, 1844), 63–5. Noah wrote another play about Eaton's march that is no longer extant called *Yusef Caramalli, or the Siege of Tripoli.*

[118] Samuel Woodruff, *Journal of a Tour to Malta, Greece, Asia Minor, Carthage, Algiers, Port Mahon, and Spain in 1828* (Hartford, CT: Cooke & Co., 1831), 140; Fisher Howe, *Oriental and Sacred Scenes* (New York: M. W. Dodd, 1854), 109; John L. Stephens, *Incidents of Travel in Egypt, Arabia Petraea, and the Holy Land* (1837; Norman: University of Oklahoma Press, 1970), 152.

[119] Quoted in Harris John Booras, *Hellenic Independence and America's Contribution to the Cause* (Rutland, VT: The Tuttle Co., 1934), 190–1.

[120] *A General View of the Rise, Progress, and Brilliant Achievements of the American Navy* (Brooklyn, NY, 1828), 426.

[121] E. M. Earle, "American Interest in the Greek Cause, 1821–27," *American Historical Review* 33 (October 1927): 62.

the New York Greek Committee, revealed this anti-Turkish prejudice even in his attempt to qualify it. Admitting that the Turk's "ferocity and cruelty are vastly magnified in the minds of the ignorant and vulgar," Post goes on to explain that in peace he is a "good natured animal," but "once excite him – once rouse him to wrath, and he is a wild beast . . . tearing and rending without mercy, wherever he can find a prey." "Even his hospitality and bravery are but the virtues of barbarism," Post avers, alluding to the heritage of the biblical Ishmael, "and wild, fierce, and bloody he will remain, until the purpose of desolation, for which he was brought from his desert shall be done."[122]

Despite feverish pro-Greek sentiment condemning the turbaned Turkish "beast," the U.S. government, following the Monroe Doctrine, remained officially neutral in the war for their independence. Ironically, the Turks interpreted this neutrality as a sign of "friendly disposition" and assumed that Americans "if not exactly Mahometans, were something much better than Christians."[123] This viewpoint assisted the United States eventually to sign a Treaty of Commerce with Sultan Mahmud II in 1830, the same year that Algeria became a colony of the French. As a result of Greek independence and Russian encroachment, the Ottoman Empire shrank so much in stature that in 1833 Czar Nicholas I famously diagnosed it as "the sick man of Europe."

It was in the cultural context of the Greek War of Independence with symbolic attempts to emasculate the Turkish despot as a sick and dehumanized metonymy of a man that the most famous Muslim yet to visit the shores of the United States traveled to the eastern seaboard. On 16 April 1826, a crowd of New Yorkers gathered at the National Hotel to witness the debut of this improbable American appearance of a Turk who was, according to James Cook, "the preeminent entertainer of the late eighteenth and early nineteenth centuries."[124] This international celebrity was the Great Chess Automaton – dressed in the robes and turban of a Turk – who the Bavarian

---

[122] Henry A. V. Post, *A Visit to Greece and Constantinople in the Year 1827–8* (New York: Sleight & Robinson, 1830), 310–11, 411–12.

[123] Howe, *Oriental and Sacred Scenes*, 210–1.

[124] James W. Cook, *The Arts of Deception: Playing with Fraud in the Age of Barnum* (Cambridge, MA: Harvard University Press, 2001), 232. The most thorough treatment of the American career of the Turkish automaton was written by its first "American historian," George Allen, "The History of the Automaton Chess-Player in America," in Daniel Willard Fiske, *The Book of the First American Chess Congress* (New York: Rudd & Carleton, 1859), 420–85. Recent book-length treatments are Gerald M. Leavitt, *The Turk, Chess Automaton* (Jefferson, NC: McFarland & Co., 2000) (which includes several important sources and documents) and Tom Standage, *The Turk: The Life and Times of the Famous Eighteenth-Century Chess-Playing Machine* (New York: Walker & Co., 2002). Scholarly articles and chapters devoted to the Turk include James W. Cook, Jr., "From the Age of Reason to the Age of Barnum: The Great Automaton Chess-Player and the Emergence of Victorian Cultural Illusionism," *Winterthur Portfolio* 30:4 (Winter 1995): 231–57, (revised for *The Arts of Deception*, 30–72); Stephen P. Rice, "Making Way for the Machine: Maelzel's Automaton Chess-Player and Antebellum American Culture," *Massachusetts Historical Society* 106 (1994): 1–16; Ernest Wittenberg,

entertainment-entrepreneur Johann Maelzel (also known as the fabricator of the metronome) had imported into the United States two months earlier. With this performance, Maelzel inaugurated a tour that continued for over a decade during which he displayed the Turk as one of the central acts of a successful exhibition that toured New York, Boston, Philadelphia, Washington, Richmond, Pittsburgh, Cincinnati, and New Orleans before Maelzel met his end in 1838 on a ship returning from a venue in Havana, Cuba.

The core attraction of Chess Automaton was its curious combination of human intelligence and mechanical operation, producing what Cook calls "one of the greatest cultural conundrums of the modern era."[125] At the beginning of a performance, Maelzel rolled in a large cabinet on casters with a chessboard on its top and three doors above a long drawer on its front. Sitting on a bench behind the cabinet was the larger-than-life figure of an expressionless and turbaned wooden Turk with a black beard and gray eyes whose legs were crossed with his slippered feet turned to the side and whose left hand held a long Turkish pipe known as a chibouque. Maelzel successively opened or removed the cabinet doors and invited the audience to inspect its cavities, which were filled either with empty space or a perplexing assortment of wheels, cogs, and levers through which he displayed the light of a candle. The cabinet was also turned around and the Turk's robes were lifted, revealing two ten-inch doors in its thigh and lower back, which when opened, likewise revealed no space for any human inhabitant. The cabinets and drawers were opened from which the chess pieces were taken along with a pillow that was placed under the Turk's elbow after his pipe was removed.

While playing the game, the exhibitor would place a key into the cabinet and crank it up creating a whirring sound that might last for ten to twelve of the Turk's moves before requiring rewinding. The Turk had the privilege of the first move (although at times it would defer to a novice, female, or famous opponent). Once the challenger made a move on a board on a separate table twelve feet away, Maelzel would replicate the move on the Turk's chessboard. Depending on the nature of that move, the Turk with "all the dignity of a sultan" would shake his head and survey the board, nod his head and roll his eyes, or even return the piece to its prior position or remove it if tested with an illegal move.[126] During his own turn, the Turk would lift his left hand, place his fingers over a piece, grasp it, and mechanically move it to a new space of attack until he earned the right to say out loud "Échec!" and eventually "Échec et Mat" (the French words for "check"

"Echec!: The Bizarre Career of the Turk," *American Heritage* 11:2 (February 1960): 34–7, 82–5. See also Charles Michael Carroll, *The Great Chess Automaton* (New York: Dover, 1975).

[125] Cook, *Arts of Deception*, 33.

[126] John Timbs, *Stories of Inventors and Discoverers in Science and the Useful Arts* (New York: Harper & Brothers, 1860), 91.

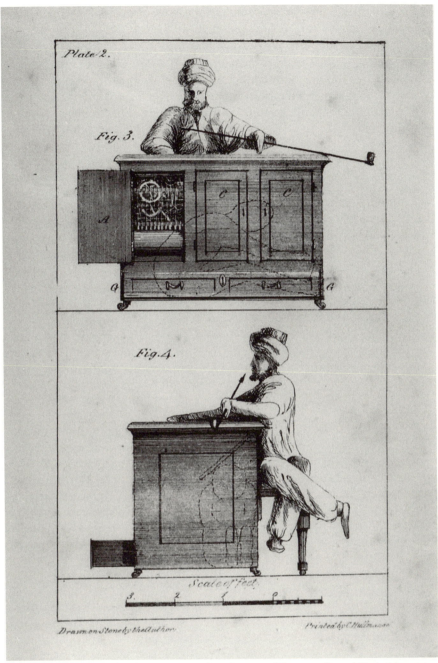

FIGURE 1.4. Robert Willis drew on stone these images of the cross-legged Turk Automaton with his long chibouque pipe in his attempts to surmise the manner by which its operator hid inside. *An Attempt to Analyse the Automaton Chess Player of Mr. De Kempelin* (London: Booth, 1821)

73

and "checkmate"). Edgar Allan Poe in his famous 1836 essay on the automaton emphasized how the mechanistic illusion of the chess player was aided by the "artificial and unnatural . . . deportment of the Turk," his "indifferent" countenance, and the "exceedingly stiff, awkward, jerking, and rectangular manner" with which he moved his pieces.[127]

The complexity and ingenuity of this curious object invited consistent scrutiny and analysis. The primary focus of this inquiry emphasized what Poe called "the mysteries of its evolutions" – the task of fathoming the governing principle of its supposedly intelligent mechanical operation.[128] The secret of the Turk's operation was actually discovered by two teenagers spying from a nearby roof and reported by the *Baltimore Gazette* in June of 1827, but their revelations were treated by the *National Intelligencer* as a rumor emanating from Maelzel himself to enhance interest in his performance.[129] The full workings of the Turk's operation were not publically revealed until 1840 after a club led by the famous physician John Kearsley Mitchell, raised money to resurrect the Turk, dissect its anatomy, and verify its secret. The wooden warrior was in fact operated by a hidden human director – for most of Maelzel's American career it was a chessmaster named William Schlumberger – who sequestered himself inside the cabinet (deftly moving on a sliding chair as Maelzel opened its doors and drawers), employed a device called a pantagraph to operate the Turk's arm, and examined magnetic disks under the board that registered his opponent's moves with the help of a candle whose heat was channeled by tubes through the top of the Turk's head and whose smell was disguised by the presence of a candelabra placed on the cabinet.

Recent books by Gerald M. Leavitt and Tom Standage have charted the history and mystery of the automaton's eighty-five-year career from its invention near Vienna in 1769 to its destruction in 1854 in a New York fire in the Chinese Museum (formerly Peale's Museum). The Chess Automaton registered triumphs over such noble adversaries as Napoleon, Frederick the Great, Benjamin Franklin, Andrew Jackson, and the Sultan himself in Constantinople. The popularity of Maelzel's Chess-Player has also attracted the attention of antebellum cultural historians seeking to interpret the significance of the Turk's career. Stephen P. Rice reads the automaton as a site that "modeled the social ills of mechanical production" affecting middle-class reorganization of work during the market revolution. James Cook's insightful *The Arts of Deception: Playing with Fraud in the Age of Barnum* celebrates the automaton as "the very first exhibition in the history of American show business to make dubious authenticity a perpetual – and

---

[127] Edgar Allan Poe, "Maelzel's Chess-Player," *Southern Literary Messenger* 2 (April 1836): 318–26; reprinted in Leavitt, *The Turk, Chess Automaton*, 232–3.

[128] Poe, "Maelzel's Chess Player," in Leavitt, *The Turk, Chess Automaton*, 228.

[129] Allen, "History of the Automaton Chess-Player," 452.

profitable – source of popular entertainment."[130] The automaton's Turkish "ethnicity" also renders it a fascinating artifact of antebellum islamicism, and examining this dimension reveals new insights into both the cultural significance of Maelzel's performances as well as American attitudes toward Muslim power and masculinity during the 1820s and 1830s.

The mysterious problem of the chess player replicated the challenge that faced Westerners in understanding the significance of the worldly ascendancy of Islam and its contest to the Christian cultures of Eastern Europe. The cultural genesis of the automaton and its Austro-Hungarian matrix helps to explains some of the strategic symbolism of its Muslim identity. In 1789, Freyherr Racknitz intepreted the "advantage" of the automaton's Turkish clothes and "stylish" pipe merely in terms of their effect in enlarging the figure so that the cabinet would appear smaller than it was and thus maintain the illusion that it was incapable of holding a human.[131] (Poe noted in his essay that the Turk was at least eighteen inches taller than Maelzel when he stood next to it, even though the former was sitting down.[132]) The game of chess itself had an oriental genealogy and was known to be an "Eastern Game" that originated in India around the time of the appearance of the Prophet Muhammad.[133] More importantly, Baron Wolfgang von Kempelen's original performance of his invention before Queen in the Viennese court in 1770 took place only eighty-seven years after the Ottoman armies had been turned back from the gates of that city. Dressing the automaton in the guise of the Turk clearly associated his victorious intelligence with the worldly might of the Ottomans and their long history of overtaking the kings of Byzantium and the Balkans.[134]

By the time of the automaton's American campaigns under Maelzel, the Russian army was pressing the Ottomans further back toward Asia and the Greeks were in the midst of their bloody attempt to gain their independence

---

[130] Cook, *Arts of Deception*, 34.

[131] Freyherr zu Rachnitz, *Ueber den Schachspieler* (Leipzig and Dresden, 1789) translated in Leavitt, *The Turk, Chess Automaton*, 214.

[132] Poe, "Maelzel's Chess Player," in Leavitt, *The Turk, Chess Automaton*, 233.

[133] The illustration of a sphinx on the cover of the antebellum journal *Chess Monthly* has the caption "Ex Oriente est Ludus Scaccorum" (Out of the Orient is the game of chess).

[134] James Cook examines the ways that the exhibition of the automaton shifted in significance and presentation as its career transformed from a curiosity of the European enlightenment to a commodity of American entertainment. Yet, despite his acknowledgment that the automaton's puzzle enabled the negotiation of cultural issues such as "a wide variety of geo-cultural rivalries symbolized and contested through a caricatured non-Western other," his attention to the automaton's contingent significances resists a full tracing of the changing meanings of the chess-player's "Turkishness" as it toured the United States. Cook, *Arts of Deception*, 71. In the article that was revised for the chapter in *The Arts of Deception*, Cook had suggested that in the United States "the automaton's 'Turkishness' ceased to function as a signifier for a specific cultural Other" and had "no local symbolic resonance." Cook, "From the Age of Reason," 249–50.

from the Empire. Overshadowing the Turk's playful victories within the arena of American entertainment was the contemporary historical match being played out on real battlefields between the Greeks and Ottomans. The gain and loss of fortresses, towns, and islands were reported daily in the press. The very week that the Turk began his first public engagement in New York, the Greeks had lost their heroic struggle to save their stronghold at Missolonghi. As Maelzel's exhibition gained popularity in the United States, the Ottomans marched on Athens and besieged the fortress of the Acropole, which eventually fell to the Turks on 24 May 1827. In its first year in the United States, the Turk's prowess on the chessboard matched the progress of the Ottomans (with the help of the forces of Ibrahim Pasha of Egypt) in regaining the territory they had lost in the Aegean. That American philhellenism served as a cultural context for interpreting the chess-playing Turk is evident in the report of a Baltimore newspaper on May 8 that "Mr. Maelzel's Grand Turk holds two divans every day, and as the ladies are at present much interested in his movements, probably with a view of giving intelligence to the Greeks, they attend among the rest with great punctuality."[135] Under domestic pressure in support of the Greeks, the governments of Britain, France and Russia intervened, demanded a cease-fire, and eventually decimated the Turkish-Egyptian armada (which included many ships from the Barbary Regencies) at the Battle of Navarino on 27 October 1827. The Turk's chess campaign thus was launched within the context of the unfolding geopolitics of the "Eastern Question," which involved the ebbing hegemony of the Ottomans and the political question of which Western power would replace their authority in the East. Understanding this cultural context provides new insights into the islamicist significances of the Turk to American audiences.

The popular tour of the automaton Turk embodied many changing and ambiguous cultural attitudes toward Islamic despotism as the new nation expanded its democracy under the administrations of Andrew Jackson. The personalization of the Turk no doubt provided an exotic mystery to the machine that helped to lure American audiences to its tournaments. One article reported that "we confess we are inclined to attribute something also to a kind of superstitious fear in the players, who found themselves vis-à-vis with a black-bearded wooden Turk."[136] The same aura of "certain mysterious awe" was felt by Weir Mitchell who confessed that the Turk "with his oriental silence and rolling eyes, would haunt your nightly visions for many an evening after."[137] On the surface, the invincible Turk represented a

---

[135] *Baltimore American and Commercial Daily Advertiser* (8 May 1827), 2. Thanks to Tom Knoles at the American Antiquarian Society for this source.

[136] *Living Age* 22 (18 August 1849): 293.

[137] Weir Mitchell wrote: "we confess, to this day, a certain mysterious awe of his eternal cross-leggedness, his turbaned front, and left handed activity," in Leavitt, *The Turk, Chess Automaton*, 237.

combination of the strategic force and technical skill that had enabled Islam to gain ascendancy throughout Asia and Africa. But such power, although premised on the refinement of intellectual reason, seemed devoid of the human qualities of expressive choice. On the one hand, the solemn and imperturbable play of the Turk routinized his functions as feats of machine-like efficiency that were ruled by chance and fatalism rather than by human intelligence. "The Turks believe in the doctrine of predestination so implicitly, as to prevent their taking precaution against the plague and other evils," wrote a Greek who had been held captive by the Ottomans, "and they endure pain and afflictions with wonderful patience and fortitude."[138] On the other hand, the failure of Western audiences to penetrate the principles of his operation also communicated the almost magical powers of oriental necromancy, one whose claim to mastery was compromised by ungraspable ulterior motives. The Turk's uncanny ability to defeat his opponents as well as to delude all who came to see him play mirrored the mystery of Muhammad's capacity to enlist his votaries in what Westerners viewed as the corrupt heresy of Islam.

Even though the Turk seemed able to win the battle on the sixty-four squares of the gameboard, he ultimately was a loser in the global war of cultural politics. The very intelligence that the Turk appeared to embody was deeply compromised by the truth that the automaton was the creation of a European Christian who contained his force within a material machine employed for entertainment and profit. Separating the Turk's intellectual acumen from his humanity effectively contained and immobilized his conniving skill and revealed the automaton as a metonymy of the essential soullessness of Islamic manhood. This reduction of Ottoman sultanship (who was also the spiritual leader of Sunni Islam) into a mere mechanical sign provides a material manifestation of Edward Said's thesis about the discursive power of orientalism to evade the substance of Islam and construct the Orient instead as an expression of Western desire and control. The automaton literally allowed Euroamericans to hollow out the form of Turkish power and create in its place an ironic resource for performing the ultimate mastery of Western science. The Turkish automaton caricatured the islamicist resource of philosophical reason while at the same time erasing the sensual excess of the Muslim male. The despotic will of the Turk, far from being the threat it was rumored to be, became ultimately a spectacular creation of Western intelligence, which was capable of inhabiting, animating, and possessing the emptiness of Islam for the purpose of generating new imperial energies for its own cultural advancement. Just as the Turk vanquished monarchy by sweeping away a series of kings on the chessboard, his own despotic "intelligence" and power was enlisted in support of the vitality of republican ingenuity. One of the rare losses of the Turk occurred

---

[138] *The Personal Narrative of the Sufferings of J. Stephanini* (New York: Vanderpool & Cole, 1829), 71.

on 23 May 1827 when it conceded a game to Charles Carroll, the last living signer of the Declaration of Independence.

THE ASCENDENCY OF AMERICA NAVAL POWER, 1831

Faced with their defeat in the Greek War of Independence, the Turks turned to American technical ingenuity to rebuild and modernize their navy and to reinvigorate their trade. The U.S. Senate rejected a secret article in their Treaty with the Ottomans that would have directly provided them with timber and talent for shipbuilding. Commodore David Porter – the newly appointed diplomat in Turkey and naval veteran of the Tripolitan War – offered surrogate naval support by welcoming in Constantinople the expert naval architect Henry Eckford, who had skillfully designed state-of-the-art American ships of war during the War of 1812. Eckford arrived in Turkey in 1831 with a sloop of war that so pleased the Sultan that he was hired as the chief naval constructor for the Ottoman Empire and given charge of a ship-yard with five hundred laborers (which included a group of firefighters from New York City).[139] After Eckford's death in 1832, the shipbuilding program continued under his foreman Foster Rhodes, and the navy that Turkey had lost at Navarino was soon restored to parity with Russia's Black Sea Fleet. The favor with which American naval power found itself in the Turkish capital city contrasted dramatically with the fate of one of its first ships – the *George Washington* – when it arrived in indignity as a commandeered ship thirty years before.

The global ascendancy of naval power as an expression of the nation's power to defeat despotism during Andrew Jackson's administration can be measured by another event of 1831. Although this chapter has focused on responses to violence in the Muslim Mediterranean, the global expanse of both American trade and islamicist counterdespotism is intimated by the first massive use of United States' military force against Malays in Southeast Asia. In 1787, the 300-ton ship called *The Grand Turk*, which had served as a privateer during the Revolution, became the first trading vessel from Salem to sail through the Malaccan Straits and return from East Asian ports laden with richly exotic goods, giving rise to the motto of the City of Salem: "To the Farthest Port of the Rich East."[140] In the 1790s, the Muslim islands of Java and Sumatra were established as valuable entrepôts for the purchase of

---

[139] David Porter, *Constantinople and Its Environs*, 2 vols. (New York: Harper & Brothers, 1835), 1: 13, 158; 2: 7–8. Eckford brought a group of New York firefighters as shipbuilders with him to Constantinople; upon their return, the company was known as the Old Turks and had Turks with scimitars depicted on their engines. Augustine Costello, *Our Firemen, The History of the New York Fire Departments* (New York: A. E. Costello, 1887), Chapter 35, Part IV, no. 44 .

[140] American trade routes to India began even earlier. In December of 1784, the ship *United States* docked in the east coast port of Pondicherry (near where Elihu Yale a century before made the

coffee and pepper, but, by the 1820s, disputes over weighing practices led to the detainment of American ships in East Indian ports. In February of 1831 Malays from Kuala Batu (Quallah Battoo) captured the trading vessel *Friendship*, killed five crew members, and confiscated its load of specie and opium.[141]

Such an affront to national honor did not go unheeded by President Andrew Jackson who quickly gave new instructions to the *U.S.S. Potomac*, the finest warship in the U.S. Navy, to sail to Sumatra and demand injury and indemnity for the murder of American citizens. Instead of following instructions to investigate the incident and negotiate for restitution, Commodore John Downes disguised the *Potomac* as a Danish merchant ship and attacked the town at dawn the day after its arrival. The ensuing raid claimed the lives of a hundred Malays. According to one eyewitness:

> The greater part of the town was reduced to ashes. The bazaar, the principal place of merchandise, and most of the private dwellings, were consumed by fire. The triumph had now been completed over the Malays; ample satisfaction had been taken for their outrages committed upon our countrymen.[142]

R. N. Reynolds's account of the *Potomac*'s voyage (which features as its frontispiece the motto "Naval Power Is National Glory") romanticizes the band of armed American sailors on the Sumatran beach at dawn prior to their attack: "what an interesting spectacle must they have presented to an American eye! . . . they presented a picture that was by no means deficient in those exquisite touches which constitute the 'moral sublime.' "[143] A broadside that was sold in Boston, called "Battle of the Potomac with the Malays," told the same sublime story from the perspective of a crew member: how the Americans courageously advanced on the "piratical host" by night "To revenge the sad wrongs that our friends and our nation, / so oft have sustain'd from those demons of hell." In his Fourth Annual Message to Congress, President Jackson applauded these attacks against a "band of lawless pirates," claiming that they would deter further aggressions and lead to increased respect for

---

wealth that led Yale University to be named after him). G. Bhagat, "America's First Contacts with India, 1784–5," *American Neptune* 31 (1971): 38–48.

[141] James Duncan Phillips, "Sumatra and the Pepper Trade," in *Salem and the Indies* (Boston: Houghton Mifflin, 1947), 92–100. In 1795, trade in coffee began with the port of Muscat on the Arabian Peninsula (186).

[142] Francis Warriner, *Cruise of the United States Frigate* Potomac *Round the World, during the Years 1831–34* (New York: Leavitt, Lord & Co. 1835), 91.

[143] J. N. Reynolds, *Voyage of the United States Frigate* Potomac (New York: Harper & Brothers, 1835), 97, 109. In addition to Warriner and Reynolds, see the secondary accounts of Kuala Batu by David F. Long, "'Martial Thunder': The First Official American Armed Intervention in Asia," *Pacific Historical Review* 42 (1973): 143–62; and John M. Belohlavek, "Andrew Jackson and the Malaysian Pirates: A Question of Diplomacy and Politics," *Tennessee Historical Quarterly* 36 (1977): 19–29. See also James W. Gould, "Sumatra – America's Pepperpot, 1784–1873," *Essex Institute Historical Collections* 152 (1956): 83–152, 203–51, 295–348, especially 229–41.

FIGURE 1.5. Moorish faces on the Naval (or Tripoli) Monument, the oldest national military monument. It was imported in 1808 and is now in the U.S. Naval Academy in Annapolis, Maryland. Moved to its present site in 1860, it was the earliest monument on the grounds of the U.S. Capitol. Photograph taken by author.

the flag of the United States. Overcoming the "savages" ("the God of the Christians they never had known" read the broadside), the sailors hoisted the American flag on the ramparts of Kuala Batu (as they had done earlier in Derne) as an emblem of the will to establish the glory and honor of the nation in the eyes of the world.[144]

The illustrative power of the Navy in the symbolic constitution of national power was dramatized in the same year as the attack on Kuala Batu by the conspicuous relocation of the most elaborate national monument then in existence. The Naval Monument that honored the lives of the six officers who lost their lives in the explosion of the *Intrepid* during the Tripolitan War was moved from Washington's Ship Yard to a prominent place on the western terrace of the Capitol (Fig. 1.5). Built by Italian sculptor Charles Micali in 1806–7 from subscriptions elicited by David Porter (who had been captured when the *Philadelphia* ran aground), the marble monument features a fifteen-foot column decorated with the bows of warships surrounded by allegorical representations of Fame, History, Commerce, and America – the latter represented as an Indian princess. The top of the monument's base is ringed with the faces of Muslim masks and trophies from the war. These Moorish faces in stone peered forward onto the grounds of the capitol standing as visible demonstrations of the many ways that islamicist representations were integral to the symbolic construction of early American nationalism.[145] In a comment that could apply to both Moors and Malays, an early history of *American Naval Battles* published that same year in 1831 affirmed the usefulness of oppositional islamicism when it concluded that "the nation acquired singular honour, in humbling and chastising a race of lawless pirates, who have long been the inveterate scourges of the christian world."[146]

---

[144] "Battle of the *Potomac*, with the Malays. Written by one of the Crew" (1832), original in Boston Public Library. Andrew Jackson, Fourth Annual Message to Congress, 4 December 1832, in *Register of Debates in Congress*, vol. 9, part 2 (Washington: Gales and Seaton, 1833), Appendix, p. 3. In his message the year before, Jackson spoke of sending out the *Potomac* in response to the "daring outrage" committed by "piratical perpetrators belonging to tribes in such a state of society that the usual course of proceeding between civilized nations could not be pursued." *Register of Debates*, vol. 8, part 3 (1832), Appendix, p. 4. There were those that found Downes's actions neither sublime nor moral, partly because Malay women and children who had not taken to arms against the attack were killed in the Kuala Batu raid. Anti-Jackson forces in the United States denounced him as a despot for sending the Navy into combat without the permission of Congress.

[145] The best analysis of the monument is Janet A. Headley, "The Monument without a Public: The Case of the Tripoli Monument," *Winterthur Portfolio* 29 (1994): 247–64. See also C. A. Wright, "The Tripoli Monument," *United States Naval Institute Proceedings* 58 (1932): 1930–41. See *Naval Documents*, 6: 362, 365–6, 384–6, 497, 519, 572, 580. The monument came to be known as the Tripoli Monument and was transported again to its present location on the grounds of the Naval Academy at Annapolis in 1860.

[146] *American Naval Battles*, 262.

Chapter 2

"Drying Up the Euphrates": Muslims, Millennialism, and Early American Missionary Enterprise

STORMING SATAN'S STRONGHOLD

"What would you think of a man approaching you of gigantic stature, long beard, fierce eyes, a turban on his head, which if stretched out would make a blanket, long flowing robes, a large belt, in which were four or five pistols and a sword?" Levi Parsons – one of the first American missionaries sent to the eastern Mediterranean – posed this question to his sister in a letter from Turkey in 1820.[1] The fearsome stature of the Turk was augmented by the status given to him by a powerful heritage of biblical commentary that portrayed the Ottoman Empire as "the strong holds of Satan's kingdom." Although Parsons thought himself a mere "grasshopper" in the sight of the Turks, he felt called to the prodigious duty of confronting this contemporary Goliath because he believed it was an essential part of the Christian plan for global redemption. "What are *we* in such an empire?" he humbly asked, "what is our strength before Leviathan?"[2] While standing in a mosque in Turkey where the first Christian churches had been established in the time of the apostle Paul, Parsons felt the atmosphere to be "more like a prison than a place of worship," and reflected that "[i]t was impossible to forget that this people have power to make war with the saints, and to overcome them."[3]

The situation that the early American missionaries found in the Holy Land was even more appalling. After Jonas King arrived in the Near East in 1822, he was horrified by the Arabs he encountered during a land journey to Jerusalem from Egypt through the desert of Sinai. Sinai had once been the passage of the Hebrews toward the Promised Land, but it seemed to King

---

[1] Daniel O. Morton, ed., *Memoir of Reverend Levi Parsons*, 2nd ed. (Burlington, VT: Chauncey Goodrich, 1830), 248.

[2] Morton, *Memoir*, 286, 255. These sentiments are echoed by William Goodell, who arrived in Turkey in 1823 to spend over thirty years in the eastern Mediterranean. "When we first went into those countries, the Turks walked proudly about with their bosoms stuffed with pistols and yataghans; and certainly they were very terrible in their appearance." *The Old and the New; or, The Changes of Thirty Years in the East* (New York: M. W. Dodd, 1853), 43. Another early missionary, Eli Smith "distinctly recall[ed] the involuntary dread . . . with which I shrunk from the haughtiness of the turbaned Turk, as I landed in Egypt, a single-handed missionary, aiming to undermine the faith he adores." *The Trials of Missionaries* (Boston: Crocker and Brewster, 1832), 4.

[3] Morton, *Memoir*, 244.

a Sodom, and he viewed the Bedouins as "fiends from the world below." When the party arrived in Jerusalem in the spring of 1823, King found it "a place, cursed of God and given over to iniquity." He judged Palestine's Muslim residents to be "full of hypocrisy and lying" for "exalt[ing] the name of their false Prophet above [Christ's] most glorious name."[4] Requesting prayers from his fellow Protestants back in New York, King wrote, "Oh, that you could be with me in Calvary, where I am writing, and hear the roaring of the Turks from the minarets, and see the deep iniquity with which this Holy Land is polluted!...Everything around me seems blasted and withered by the Curse of the Almighty."[5]

If these missionaries viewed the Islamic world as a realm of dark destruction, why did they dare venture as mere individuals onto its dangerous ground? To them the curse of Islam had been divinely sanctioned to punish Christians for corrupting worship with rites and rituals alien to the spirit of the Bible. Exporting Christian purity back to the Holy Land was a crucial divine duty they believed would culminate in the establishment of the Kingdom of God on earth. Indeed, the central reason for the interest of many early Americans in the fate of the Ottoman Empire was that its removal or destruction stood as an essential prerequisite to the restoration of the Jews to Jerusalem, signalizing that the second advent of Christ was imminent. Just before Levi Parsons sailed in 1819 to inaugurate the mission of the United States to the Holy Land, he professed this clear path: "Destroy the Ottoman empire and nothing but a miracle will prevent the Jews' immediate return from the four winds of heaven."[6] Parsons followed the pattern of many educated Christians of his age and tried to resolve the confusing conundrum of Islam's dominion by consulting the prophetic verses of the Bible. "I desire to know, if it be revealed, the divine purpose in regard to this great empire of sin," he wondered, "How long will it remain? By what means will it be subdued?"[7] The faith in biblical prophecy assured the missionaries of Christ's ultimate victory over the worldly reign of Islam despite the possibility of their own martyrdom and the pragmatic challenges of converting the Muslims.[8] Indeed it was in large part the power of millennial promise that encouraged the missionaries to undertake their mission to Western Asia and ally themselves and their nation with this divine plan.

---

[4] Jonas King, *Diary, 1823* (unpublished manuscript, American Antiquarian Society, Worcester, MA). Henry Harris Jessup called King "the third of the remarkable trio who began the work of giving the Bible to Bible lands." *Fifty-Three Years in Syria*, 2 vols. (New York: Fleming H. Revell Company, 1910), 1: 38.

[5] F. E. Haines, *Jonas King, Missionary to Syria and Greece* (New York: American Tract Society, 1879), 123.

[6] Quoted in James L. Barton, *Daybreak in Turkey* (Boston: Pilgrim Press, 1908), 86.

[7] Parsons had earlier read eschatological projections in the popular commentaries of Bishop Thomas Newton, George Stanley Faber, and Thomas Scott and wrote a letter from the Near East to the noted eschatologist Ethan Smith. Morton, *Memoir*, 301, 304–8, 357.

[8] Morton, *Memoir*, 350, 357.

During the half century following the American and French Revolutions, several boards and societies were convened in the United States to raise funds to publish tracts and Bibles and to coordinate missionary efforts. This proliferation of efforts aimed at the evangelization of the world reveals "the tremendous force of the eschatological motive in the rise of the American foreign and domestic missionary agencies."[9] The most prominent of these societies and the first devoted to the international field was the American Board of Commission for Foreign Missions (hereafter ABCFM or American Board) founded in 1810 by eager students and evangelical leaders in Massachusetts. Propelled in part by prophetic promises, the ABCFM, in 1812, expanded beyond its domestic missions to native Americans by sending out its first international missionaries to Bombay in India and Jaffna on the island now known as Sri Lanka, and in 1818 to the Sandwich Islands (Hawai'i) in the Pacific.[10] The following year, the American Board organized the mission to Palestine or "Western Asia" and selected Parsons and Pliny Fisk – both graduates of Middlebury College and Andover Theological Seminary – to serve in the sacred field they called "the Land of ancient Promise, and of present Hope."[11] Armed with Bibles and tracts, Parsons and Fisk prayed that their active presence in the field might help to instigate the events of the last days culminating in the Second Coming of the Savior. Fisk believed himself to be linguistically, culturally, and spiritually unequipped to proselytize the learned Muslims whom he found "so wise in their conceits." Nevertheless, he remained convinced that "it is not more certain, that the walls of Jericho fell before the ancient people of God, than it is, that the whole Mahommedan world will be subdued by the Gospel."[12]

Many educated American Protestants, including Fisk, King, and Parsons, believed that the new American nation had a providential mission to help redeem the world and bring about the millennium, the thousand-year reign

---

[9] R. Pierce Beaver, "Eschatology in American Missions," in eds. Jan Hermelink and Hans J. Margill, *Basileia: Festschrift für Walter Freytag* (Stuttgart: Evang. Missionsverlag, 1959), 67.

[10] Although American missionaries in India and Sri Lanka encountered Muslims, there were also "large groups of depressed classes, Hindus, and others to which the missionary could turn when frustrated by the exhausting nature of Muslim evangelization." Lyle L. Vander Werff, *Christian Mission to Muslims: The Record* (South Pasadena, CA: William Carey Library, 1977), 101. Although this area should be opened to renewed inquiry, a scholar of the American presence in India, Bernard Saul Stern, notes in relation to that contact "a singular lack of comment on Islam in India" and claims that "one is struck by the absence of discussion on Islam and the way of life of its followers." "American Views of India and Indians, 1817–1900" (Ph.D. diss., University of Pennsylvania, 1956), 245.

[11] *The Missionary Herald* 15 (1819): 546.

[12] Alvan Bond, *Memoir of the Rev. Pliny Fisk, A.M.: Late Missionary to Palestine* (Boston: Crocker and Brewster, 1828), 114. William Goodell viewed his mission in these terms: "We have had to go into the very heart of the kingdom of darkness, 'where Satan's seat is,' and there, amidst conflict, noise, and strife, and deadly hate, to break open the prison doors, and proclaim liberty to the miserable captives." *The Old and the New*, 64.

of Christian peace. By figuring the Arab residents of the Ottoman Empire as living embodiments of the ancient peoples of Judea who had been forced to succumb to the advances of the chosen Hebrews, American missionaries framed a righteous enterprise of following in their footsteps as representatives of the New Israel. Levi Parsons viewed the Muslims of Smyrna ("most ... dreaming of the sensual paradise of Mahomet!") as emblems of the tragedy of false belief, and exclaimed: "How fatal the dream! How certain their destruction!"[13] Parson's assurance about the emptiness of Islam was most evident when he mused over the cypress-shaded cemeteries of the Turks and bemoaned the despair that would descend upon followers of the false prophet on the Day of Judgment. To these missionaries, the strong faith of millions of Muslims appeared a delusive fiction grasped by blind fatalism, one that would be dissipated by the reintroduction of a purified practice of Christianity to the sites of its original emergence. "The land is an exceedingly good land, and the Lord our God will give it to us for a possession," Pliny Fisk assured his readers when requesting that more missionaries be sent, "There is no ground to fear unless our unbelief should prevent success."[14] Fisk's statement exemplifies how faith in biblical promise served as a strong foundation for a spiritually sanctioned form of religious mission that ultimately failed to explain the complexities of cultural difference in the Near East.

Both Pliny Fisk and Levi Parsons died from disease less than five years after they ventured into the field. Although unnoticed by those they had hoped to convert, the American Board back in Boston celebrated them as martyrs and heroic models of devoted sacrifice in the cause of Christ. (One requiem, for example, sang of "Thy spirit, Parsons, lur'd by seraph's song / ... who like him [shall] destroy Mohammed's sway?"[15]) The passing of Parsons and Fisk, combined with political instability in the Mediterranean in the 1820s, barred immediate avenues to the direct evangelization of the Muslim populations of the Near East. Their prospects for success were further weakened by the facts that Qur'anic theology already accepted the dispensation of Christ, and Ottoman law punished apostasy from Islam. In 1824, the Ottoman government forbade the circulation of Bibles printed in Europe because they feared "disputation and disturbance" among their Christian subjects, a decree that was indifferently enforced.[16] William Schauffler canceled his proposed mission to the Muslims in 1826 partly because of the hostilities surrounding the Greek rebellion against the Turks. Henry Augustus Homes, a missionary sent by the ABCFM to Constantinople to proselytize the Muslim

---

[13] Morton, *Memoir*, 295.   [14] Bond, *Memoir*, 215.

[15] *Missionary Register of 1823* (London, 1823), 122–4, quoted in David H. Finnie, *Pioneers East: The Early American Experience in the Middle East* (Cambridge, MA: Harvard University Press, 1967), 152.

[16] A. L. Tibawi, *American Interests in Syria, 1800–1901* (Oxford: Clarendon Press, 1966), 28–9.

population, soon returned to New York because he found "no access to the mind of Islam."[17] Despite these formidable setbacks, American Protestants in the Near East remained committed to and assured of the ultimate conversion of Muslims, the group whom Isaac Bird – who entered the Near Eastern missionary field in 1823 – called their "long-avowed and oppressive enemies."[18]

ISLAMICISM IN THE ESCHATOLOGICAL IMAGINATION

Early Protestant Americans of various political and religious stripes found the Islamic world to be a distant site of oriental opposition. Against this difference, they affirmed a united destiny for the new nation that joined religious and republican worldviews in a broad vision of Christian patriotism. The first chapter examined how American republicans, by figuring the Islamic world as a domain of despotism, were able to articulate and express gendered versions of their national vitality even in moments of cultural and political weakness. This emphasis on the political dimension of tyranny in Islamic lands accorded with the deist critique of the excess power and passions of clerical religion. While secular expression in the new republic projected creative options for how Americans could exercise virtuous behavior in the face of the temptations of independence, an established religious discourse remained an integral part of the founding vision of national liberty. Many Protestant thinkers believed that the foul fruits of political despotism stemmed from the deeper and darker roots of religious infidelity that poisoned the cultivation of virtue. In their sermons and commentaries, religious-minded Americans drew less on literary genres, classical models, and political philosophy to stimulate the global relevance of American public culture and focused instead on the Bible itself and its system of typology to explain the significance of secular events. The Bible's assurance that "this gospel of the kingdom shall be preached in all the world for a witness unto all nations; and then shall the end come" (Matthew 24:14), encouraged Americans to expand both the geographical and millennial scope of their missionary enterprise in ways that dramatized a broad international interest in its outcomes, especially an intense apocalyptic focus

---

[17] Cyrus Hamlin, *My Life and Times*, 2nd ed. (Boston and Chicago: Congregational Sunday School and Publication Society, 1893), 203–4. Henry Augustus Homes returned to New York to long service as a historian and as librarian of the State Library in Albany. In 1873, he published his English translation of Al-Ghazzali's *The Alchemy of Happiness* (Albany: Munsell). Cyrus Hamlin, a long-time missionary in Constantinople saw the conversion of fifty Muslims in twenty years as "not to be despised" given the lesser number converted in the Muslim colonies of Russia, England, and The Netherlands. *Among the Turks* (New York: R. Carter, 1878), 91.

[18] Isaac Bird, *Bible Work in Bible Lands; or, Events in the History of the Syria Mission* (Philadelphia: Presbyterian Board for Publication, 1872), 16.

on the politics of the Holy Land, then under the hegemony of the Ottoman Empire.

As shown in Chapter 1, many Americans first encountered Muslims on the historical and rhetorical shores of North Africa, but the attentions of millennium-minded Protestants were drawn to the Asian continent further east – the heartlands of the Holy Land where Christ had once appeared and had promised to come again. Diligent study of the prophetic verses of the Bible was a major means that Christian thinkers employed to illuminate what they saw as the divine plan of world redemption. These prophetic projections about the apocalyptic events leading up to the return of Christ – the cultural logic known as eschatology – became so closely aligned with the fibers of religious faith that a belief in the imminent fall of Islam formed one of the dogmas of Protestant evangelical belief in early U.S. history. Although many scholars of Protestant eschatology have pointed out the frequent and persistent reference to Islam (under the names Saracens and Turks) in biblical commentary, none have focused their analysis on the powerful implications of this genre of orientalist narration.[19] Many Protestant intellectual leaders in early America not only regarded prophetic speculation as a respectable form of religious understanding but also viewed it as a means of using their education to discover a role for the new nation in the salvation of the world. Islam embodied for them the powerful forces of antichristianity that continued to impede the future of Christian salvation. Since early American political visions were often imbricated with this religious desire, anticipating the removal of Islam comprised a crucial element of the nation's unmanifest destiny.

This chapter unfolds a contrapuntal drama between the discursive power of eschatological expectation and the commitment of early missionaries to evangelize the Muslim peoples of the eastern Mediterranean. It charts the contours of Protestant eschatology and its evolutions as a centuries-old foundation of islamicist cultural imagination from the days of the Reformation

---

[19] Paul Boyer, in his 1992 study of prophecy belief in American culture, argued that there has existed a "constant" interest in Islamic leaders and their prophetic significance since the time of the Crusades. *When Time Shall Be No More: Prophecy Belief in Modern American Culture* (Cambridge, MA: Harvard University Press, 1992), 78. According to Peter Toon, a historian of the biblical commentary of the British Reformation, "references to the Turkish empire appear in virtually every commentary on the Apocalypse of John which was produced by English Puritans, Independents, Presbyterians and Baptists." *Puritans, the Millennium and the Future of Israel* (Cambridge: James Clarke, 1970), 19–20. The Adventist Le Roy Edwin Froom, in his massive four-volume study of the historical development of prophetic interpretation, argues that the application of verses from the Book of Revelation to account for the rise and fall of the Saracens and Turks was "almost axiomatic" and that "the final drying up of the Turk and his crucial place in the closing events of earth were of deepest and immediate interest, and frequent exposition." *The Prophetic Faith of Our Fathers: The Historical Development of the Prophetic Interpretation* (Washington, DC: Review and Herald, 1946–54), 2: 786; 4: 399–400. See also Thomas S. Kidd, "Is it Worse to Follow Mahomet Than the Devil?: Early American Uses of Islam," *Church History* 72 (2003): 766–90.

and Puritan settlement through the early national and antebellum periods of U.S. history. Examining the sophisticated projections of how prophecy formulated the fate of Islam in the world reveals valuable insights into the motives propelling the missionary enterprise, which generated the most sustained early encounters between American Christians and Near Eastern Muslims. Understanding the influence of religious interpretations of the meaning of Islam in the prophetic mode, moreover, reveals islamicism to be a sacralized vehicle of imagination employed to dramatize the salience of American behaviors on a global and even a cosmic stage.

The great lengths to which commentarists applied rational means to justify findings that were ahistorical and teleological is part of what makes eschatological discourse so compelling as a field of cultural imagination. Eschatology was above all an ingenious artistic act that enabled religious thinkers to deal with intractable problems – such as the existence of Islam – by resolving them through the interpretation of scriptural promises. The practice of eschatology involved an arcane process of harmonizing the symbols and sequences describing the "time of the end" and then aligning these scriptural types with the chronology of secular events. The labor of exegesis empowered the believer to be an active collaborator in uncovering the historical relevance of biblical revelation. Eschatology enabled thinkers to reinvigorate the relevance of the Bible and preserve it from radical threats of infidelity that challenged its authority, challenges that ranged from the millions of unredeemed populations on the global front to the popular trends of secularization in their midst. Armed with eschatological imagination and conviction, Christian thinkers could simultaneously parade the worldliness of their wisdom and demonstrate the firmness of their faith. The secular tools of Enlightenment science and classical learning – such as rhetoric, etymology, numerology, and historiography – did not have to subvert faith because their techniques of reason could be harnessed to promote the validity of religion. Realizing the secular references indicated by scriptural signs fortified the interpreter's religious faith by situating personal intelligence, itself a divinely endowed faculty, in sanctified alignment with both the divine will and the events of history.

Eschatology had a special mission for Anglo American Protestants of the colonial era and early republic for it empowered them to identify with a global drama that addressed anxieties about their worldly isolation in the western hemisphere. Engaging with this tradition of imagination connected them with a transatlantic enterprise that supported a common explanation of the world but also saw such a field as a redemptive opportunity in which the vitalities of American intelligence and commitment could compete with Protestant Europe. Eschatology could transform American expression from a voice in the wilderness into a force enunciating the moral direction of human evolution and instigating the Kingdom of God on earth. Anxious about the peripherality of their region and the tenuousness of their republic, some Protestants imagined an American religious mission that promoted their community as a new type of Israel committed (if not cho-sen) to help raise up a promised new Jerusalem. Before a liberty consonant with Christian belief could ever become established as a global phenomenon, however, the powerful Ottoman Empire and its Sultans (the contemporary types of Egypt and the Pharoahs) would have to be converted or subdued.

Biblical exegesis authorized American missionaries and commentators – including such prominent religious thinkers as John Cotton, Increase and Cotton Mather, Jonathan Edwards, and William Miller – to imagine the removal of the Ottoman Empire as a necessary stage signalizing the onset of the millennium of peace. Biblical commentaries established strong and persistent interpretive communities around consensual readings of scriptural verses, and their conclusions – sanctioned as they were with some of the power of the sacred – comprised an important part of the apparatus of Christian belief. In the era before the formal development of the study of comparative religion, eschatological imagery and typology functioned as an important religious buttress supporting other constructions of Euroamerican islamicism. This process of millennial projection established a discursive formation that contained the transgressive threat of Islam within the Bible itself and subordinated it into a confirmation of Christian victory. The powerful tradition of eschatology in this way helped to form fundamental dispositions about Islam and Muslims in transatlantic Protestant imagination.

The details of eschatological reasoning reveal significant insights into how dismissive and even dehumanizing notions about Islam were implanted within the cultural perspective, and even the religious faith, of many edu-cated early Americans. Applying biblical verses to understand the reality of Islam was ultimately a process of *eisegesis* in which Americans read their own fears and desires into religious revelation as a fantasy of their own cul-tural superiority. Unwilling to view Islam as a religious system with its own internal logic and practices, and unable to convert Muslims to Christian belief, many American Protestants contained its challenge by interpreting the Islamic world as a theater for imagining and projecting cultural dramas of their own global dominance.

ESCHATOLOGY AND THE PROTESTANT INVENTION OF THE EASTERN ANTICHRIST

The rise of Islam in the seventh century after Christ and its successful spread from Spain to Southeast Asia created a military problem for Europeans, but it also posed a religious enigma for all Christian thinkers, creating what one scholar has called a permanent "divine scandal."[20] Unlike the Jews, whose biblical lineage Christians believed they had fulfilled and superseded and

---

[20] Hichem Djait, *Europe and Islam*, trans. Peter Heinegg (Berkeley: University of California Press, 1985), 13.

who were minorities within Christian territories, the spiritual status of the distant and powerful Muslims was difficult to fathom.[21] There was little doubt about the history of Islamic military prowess. For centuries, the Ottomans had possessed Jerusalem and the Holy Land, and they had also conquered Byzantium and made mosques out of the churches of Constantinople. Muslim military forces had twice threatened to overrun Europe first with Saracen sallies into France in the eighth century, and again when Turkish forces advanced on Eastern Europe before being resisted at the gates of Vienna in 1683. When the United States became an independent nation, the Balkans and the Caucasus, as well as Greece and parts of North Africa (comprising over half the Mediterranean littoral), were still under Ottoman hegemony. Because Christians resisted viewing Islam as a legitimate religious dispensation, they were forced to invent explanations of why divine wisdom had permitted so much worldly power to such a false religion.

The earliest Western images of Muslims had been fabricated out of fear and ignorance and had demonized Muslims as fabulous monsters with the heads of dogs.[22] Medieval polemicists employed what R.W. Southern has called "the ignorance of triumphant imagination" to argue that Islam was either a heresy or an imposture that gained its adherents by a combination of appealing to carnal desires and coercing belief at the point of a sword.[23] The crucible of the Crusades with its ideological rivalry developed derogatory images of Islam that were little more than "tenacious fictions and mythical legends which took on literary lives of their own."[24] Islamicist legends took the place of comparative investigation. "The soothsayers could be convinced by the products of their own imaginations," wrote Kenneth M. Setton, "and thus be duped by their own ingenuity."[25] The fact that Islam claimed a direct revelation from God after Christ and therefore could not easily be placed within a Christian worldview spawned the need to explain its

---

[21] The historian of the American missionary movement William S. Hutchinson has noted that missionaries believed that faiths other than their own were inadequate in responding to the human condition, arguing that "[v]irtually all other faiths – with Islam the important exception – were seen as introverted rather than expansive" and "[t]heir alleged lack of concern for the salvation of humankind was taken as a tacit acknowledgement of Christianity's right of conquest." "New England's Further Errand: Millennial Belief and the Beginnings of Foreign Missions," *Proceedings of the Massachusetts Historical Society* 94 (1982): 54.

[22] John Block Friedman, *The Monstrous Races in Medieval Art and Thought* (Cambridge, MA: Harvard University Press, 1981), 62–9.

[23] R. W. Southern, *The Western View of Islam in the Middle Ages* (Cambridge, MA: Harvard University Press, 1962), 28.

[24] Southern, *Western View of Islam*, 28–9. "By misapprehension and misrepresentation an idea of the beliefs and practices of one society can pass into the accepted myths of anther society in a form so distorted that relation to the original facts in sometimes barely discernible." Norman Daniel, *Islam and the West: The Making of an Image*, revised ed. (Oxford: Oneworld, 1993), 2.

[25] Kenneth M. Setton, *Western Hostility to Islam and Prophecies of Turkish Doom*, vol. 201 (Philadelphia: American Philosophical Society, 1992), 17.

presence. Islam's very existence shook the foundations of Christian belief, spelling spiritual ruin and a return to moral chaos, and therefore requiring a religious response.

Islam was rarely considered the embodiment of the final Antichrist, a station usually reserved in Protestant eschatology for the Pope, but it was specifically prophesied as an antichristian force in league with Satan.[26] The notion that the Antichrist and his empire was split into an Eastern and Western manifestation, with Islam and Catholicism as the two legs of a satanic colossus, was a common belief of Protestant biblical exegetes from the time of the earliest years of the Reformation, when the Turkish threat to Europe was a topic of intense public discussion. Prophecies about the reign of antichristian forces enabled Protestants to link Islam and Catholicism as a connected system of corruption and subversion. The invention of an Eastern Antichrist also enabled early Protestant interpreters to extend the jurisdiction of Satan beyond Europe, and, by linking the unknown horizon with the forces of evil, to promote a more vigorous call for reform and regeneration.[27] The Turks, a label frequently and indiscriminately applied to all contemporary Muslims, were frequently viewed as the newest type of Eastern horde and assumed the status previously held by the Babylonians, Scythians, Assyrians, and Persians; they were also sometimes linked with the mysterious tribes of Gog and Magog.[28] The conversion of Tartars and some Mongols to Islam and the fact that their societies impeded land routes to Eastern Asia both challenged and preserved the hopes of Christians that they might find allies in the peoples of the further east. In fact, the technology of navigation was partly stimulated by the necessity for Europeans to take to the seas to bypass the lands of Islam on the way to east Asia. Columbus himself maintained millennial aspirations that he might find Eastern potentates who might join with Christian Europe to push Islam from its strongholds in the Holy Land where it had waxed powerful since the Crusades.[29]

---

[26] Richard Bauckham, *Tudor Apocalypse* (Oxford: Sutton Courtenay, 1978), 99. Samuel Chew mentions that while Protestants "associate[d] Rome and Islam together as partners in iniquity," Roman Catholics "asserted that Satan worked for the Turks by stirring up hatred of heretics against the true church." For example, opponents of Wyclif called him "mahomet." *The Crescent and the Rose: Islam and England during the Renaissance* (1937; New York: Octagon, 1965), 101. John Calvin saw Muhammad and the Pope as "two horns of the Antichrist." Wilhelm Baum et al., eds., *Ioannis Calvini, Opera Quae Supersunt Omnia*, 59 vols. (Neukirken, Germany: Neukirchener Verlag der Buchhandlung des Erziehungsverein, 1863–1900), 27: 502.

[27] Paul Christianson, *Reformers and Babylon: English Apocalyptical Visions from the Reformation to the Eve of the Civil War* (Toronto: University of Toronto Press, 1978), 17.

[28] "[M]ost millennialists of the day identified [Gog] with the powerful Ottoman Empire, which played a significant role in Anglo-American eschatology." Reiner Smolinski, ed., *The Threefold Paradise of Cotton Mather: An Edition of "Triparadisus"* (Athens: The University of Georgia Press, 1995), 360 n 23. The account of Gog and Magog can be found in Ezekiel 38.

[29] Djelal Kadir, *Columbus and the Ends of the Earth: Europe's Prophetic Rhetoric as Conquering Ideology* (Berkeley: University of California Press, 1992).

Although Protestants were also interested in the destruction and removal of Islam, they focused more on the spiritual elements of the war against Islam than the physical crusade. This was evident in the writings of Protestantism's founder, Martin Luther. Luther claimed that "the person of the Antichrist is at the same time the pope and the Turk." He went on to clarify: "Every person consists of a body and a soul. So the spirit of the Antichrist is the pope, his flesh is the Turk. The one has infested the Church spiritually, the other bodily. However, both come from the same Lord, even the devil."[30] Luther's notion of the Turk as the fleshly embodiment of the Antichrist was in part based upon his notions of the fate of Ishmael and his seed from the Book of Genesis. Born from the union of Abraham and his slave Hagar, Ishmael, according to Luther, took glory in his physical birth and the material provenance of Abraham at the expense of his spiritual blessing.[31] The Turks, as inheritors of the mantle of Islam, likewise gloried in their temporal power and potency, confusing these works and effects as signs of divine election. For Luther, the apparent worldly success of Islam deceived its adherents into believing they had the scriptures on their side, when in fact they were "set on a slippery place to be hurled headlong to their destruction."[32] Even if the allegorical Turk had no spiritual leg to stand upon, Luther still found a religious function in his physical presence. Islam and the Turks were seen as a worldly manifestation of the corruption within Christianity. Luther interpreted the Turkish invasions of Europe as "the rod of punishment of the wrath of God" that had been raised up to chastise Christians for their infidelity to the spirit of the Bible.[33] Because the ultimate defeat of the Turkish military challenge corresponded with the spiritual reform of the Church, Luther viewed any weakening of the Turkish position as a clear sign of the imminence of the "Judgment Day."[34]

---

[30] *Luther's Works*, 55 vols. (Philadelphia: Fortress Press, 1965), 2: 181. "We regard and condemn both the Pope and the Turk as the very antichrist" (2: 189). Since the Antichrist had to undermine the Church from within, Luther was in a quandary when determining the precise diabolical status of the Turk. "It is more in accordance with the truth to say that the Turk is the beast," argued Luther, "because he is outside the church and openly persecutes Christianity . . . ; The Antichrist, however, sits in the temple of God" (3: 122). If the Pope was that Antichrist, therefore the Turk was "the very devil" or the "incarnate devil" (5: 98). The key point for Luther, in any case, was that that both were conceived as "most powerful monsters" (3: 37). See Harvey Buchanan, "Luther and the Turks 1519–1529," *Archiv Für Reformationsgeschichte* 47 (1956): 155; and George W. Forell, "Luther and the War against the Turks," *Church History* 14 (1945): 264.

[31] The name ascribed to Ishmael's progeny, the Saracens, is taken by Luther to be in imitation of Sarah, the lawful wife of Abraham, and therefore a perversion of respectability in maintaining the pretense that physical birth determined God's favor. *Works*, 4: 70, 292, 346.

[32] *Luther's Works*, 2: 196; Buchanan, "Luther and the Turks," 149.

[33] *Luther's Works*, 5: 88. Luther contemptuously called the Turkish Empire "nothing but a morsel of bread which a rich head of a household throws to his dogs" claiming that they "have no promise of God only their stinking Koran, their victories, and the temporal power on which they rely" (4: 29).

[34] "When the Turk shall have reached his end, we can surely predict that the Judgment Day must be before the gate," quoted in Buchanan, "Luther and the Turks," 158. "After the Turks, the Last

Protestant thinkers after the early days of the Reformation perpetuated these islamicist legends by rooting them more firmly within interpretation of the Bible's prophetic verses – especially those from the Books of Daniel and Revelation. During the medieval period, leaders of the church had feared the eschatological imagination as an engine of social revolution and branded it as heretical. They saw the events alluded to in the prophetic visions of the Bible as having already occurred in the past. But during the sixteenth and seventeenth centuries, the belief in a future millennium became a respectable tenet of Christian faith.[35] Protestants became attuned to the high stakes of the divine drama between the Church and Antichrist and sought out scriptural indications of the nature of the coming apocalypse. Because the Holy Land remained in the hands of the Turkish "empire of sin," the status and condition of Islam played a central role in this eschatological drama.

Early American understandings of Islam emerged therefore neither from substantial comparative dialogue with Muslims nor from engaged scholarly study of Islamic texts, but largely from investigation into what the Bible seemed to reveal prophetically about its existence and duration as a worldly challenge to the Christian church. The threatening fact that Islam had arisen centuries after the Bible itself was defused by the staunch belief that the Old and New Testaments, the most accessible textual sources, had been sanctioned with the authority to explain the direction of human history. Christian exegetes believed it was the duty of true believers to interpret the oracular signs scripted in the Bible as a means of making steadfast their faith. They believed that the hand of providence had placed verses within the Bible that prophesied the glorious future of Christian victory and intimated the prior stages through which history had to pass on the way to the promised millennium. One of the most important of these was the expiration of Islam. It was this faith that encouraged the missionary desire to evangelize in Muslim lands.

Biblical verses have of course regularly been used to comprehend the place of non-Protestants in divine creation and therefore justify their fates as peoples of history. Not only has the Bible been consulted to make sense of American religious minorities such as Jews and Catholics, but it has also been applied to ethnic others, such as the way that Africans were branded with the "curse of Ham" to justify their enslavement as "hewers of wood," and how Native Americans were linked with specific biblical designations, such as

Judgment flows quickly." "Preface to the Revelation of St John" (1545) in *Works of Martin Luther,* 6 vols. (Philadelphia: Muhlenberg Press, 1930), 4: 486. The fate of the Turks, according to Luther, was to ultimately end up as the "stubble" of Isaiah 47:14: "Behold, they shall be as stubble, the fire shall burn them; they shall not deliver themselves from the power of the flame." *Luther's Works,* 17: 153.

35 Toon, *Puritans, the Millennium and the Future of Israel,* 19; Christopher Hill, *Antichrist in Seventeenth-Century England,* revised ed. (London: Verso, 1990), 9, 13.

one of the lost tribes of Israel or remnants of sinful Babylonians.[36] However, commentators of biblical prophecies read a fuller and more dramatic story of the place of Islam in divine history because the religion established by Muhammad included a powerful political system that arose after Christianity and stood outside America, one whose presence still impeded the recovery of the Holy Land and the fulfillment of the events of the end times.

The Ottoman Empire and its fate became a topic of great political and religious consideration during the years of the early republic because its expansive power had been checked and its dominions eroded away by European encroachment, especially by Russia. In European politics, the Eastern Question raised concerns about how the instability of the Ottoman Empire promoted imperial competition that endangered the balance of power of European nations. After the Barbary Wars and the Greek War of Independence, the Eastern Question in the United States became for many Protestants primarily a religious question. Because American political ideology was opposed to extracontinental colonization, the religious vision through which the divine will orchestrated the universal success of Protestant aspirations became a strong cultural means of consolidating national power and pride. Islamicism broadened the ideology of removal that characterized the continental colonization of Native Americans into a transnational cultural imagination that allowed Americans to project their own aspirations to global power by fantasizing the symbolic termination of the Turkish Empire.

LOCUSTS FROM THE BOTTOMLESS PIT: ISLAM IN
PROTESTANT PROPHECY

To more fully understand the power of eschatology as a discursive shaper of early American cultural understandings of Islam, it is insightful to excavate the layers of its exegetical imagination. Examining the prophetic genealogy of the Eastern Antichrist reveals an influential transatlantic interpretive tradition that coalesced around a consensus of varied Protestant commentators from the sixteenth through the nineteenth centuries. During the colonial and early national years, the eschatological imagination was a mainstream Protestant enterprise and served as a nexus for understanding world events and for projecting the meaning of American actions on the global stage. Reinhabiting this tradition of transatlantic prophetic imagination restores a

---

[36] See, for example, Sylvester A. Johnson, *The Myth of Ham in Nineteenth-Century American Christianity: Race, Heathens, and the People of God* (New York: Palgrave McMillan, 2004); Stephen R. Haynes, *Noah's Curse: The Biblical Justification of American Slavery* (Oxford: Oxford University Press, 2002); Thomas Virgil Peterson, *Ham and Japheth: The Mythic World of Whites in the Antebellum South* (Metuchen, NJ: Scarecrow Press, 1978). For one account of Native Americans as descendants of the lost tribes of Israel, see Israel Worsley, *A View of the American Indians* (London: Printed for the Author, 1828).

crucial dimension of early American religious discourse that provided abiding interpretations of Islam that captivated many educated Protestant leaders and shaped American dispositions about Muslim belief and culture.

The commentaries published by major European millennial thinkers such as Joseph Mede, Thomas Brightman, Pierre Jurieu, Charles Daubuz, Bishop Thomas Newton, John Gill, and George Stanley Faber progressively established a foundation upon which an American tradition of exegesis was built and elaborated.[37] According to these interpreters, the fifth and sixth trumpets of the Book of Revelation, whose blasts were called the first two trumpets of woe, described the history of Islam. The great importance of these trumpets lay in the fact that, according to Revelation's angel, when the second woe corresponding to the Turks was passed, the third and final woe would "come quickly" – an advent heralding the Day of Judgment that would destroy all manner of infidelity and cleanse the earth for the kingdom of Christ. It was primarily through the agency of this "Turkish theory" that, as early as the first generation of Puritan settlers, the fate of Islam came to be intimately connected with apocalyptical expectation. It was the "intelligence" that American Christians garnered from this arcane prophetic landscape that informed the missionary efforts like those of Parsons, King, Fisk, and Bird who aimed to bring the Gospel to the Islamic orient.

As early as the late sixteenth century, Protestant commentators of the Bible began to develop a powerful discursive tradition that centered on the figure of fifth trumpet to explain the rise of Muhammad and Islam.[38] The first twelve verses of the ninth chapter of Revelation tell of the "angel of the bottomless pit" who was commissioned to take vengeance on a corrupt Christianity. The smoke that this angel summoned out of the abyss seemed to these commentators to be an appropriate symbol of the false religion of Islam that had occluded the teachings of Christianity. The locusts with tails like scorpions that emerged from that smoke suggested the early Muslims (or Saracens) who, while spreading their religion from France to the Far East, tormented Christian lands with both the force of their arms and the poison of their doctrines (Fig. 2.1). The verses of the fifth trumpet confirmed orientalist stereotypes of Muhammad as an apostate from Christianity who perverted its teachings to his own ends through deception

---

[37] Joseph Mede, *The Key of the Revelation* (London, 1650); Thomas Brightman, *The Revelation of St. John* (Amsterdam: Thos. Stafford, 1644); Pierre Jurieu, *The Accomplishment of the Scripture Prophecies* (London, 1687); Charles Daubuz, *A Perpetual Commentary on the Revelation of St. John* (London: Benjamin Tooke, 1720); Bishop Thomas Newton, *Dissertations on the Prophecies* (1754; London: B. Blake, 1840); John Gill, *An Exposition of the Revelation of St. John the Divine* (London: George Keith, 1776); George Stanley Faber, *The Sacred Calendar of Prophecy* (London: Rivington, 1828).

[38] In 1593, John Napier dissented from the early Reformation views that had applied this verse to Christian heretics, arguing that they must apply to "some other godlesse tyrant ... whome wee shall proove to be the Apostate Mahomet." John Napeir [sic], *A Plain Discovery of the Whole Revelation of St. John* (Edinburgh: R. Walde-Grave, 1593), 4.

A Sketch from imagination, illustrative of the possible combination of the details of the Apocalyptic symbol.

FIGURE 2.1. "And there came out of the smoke Locusts upon the earth: and unto them was given power, as the scorpions of the earth have power. . . . And the shapes of the locusts were like unto horses prepared unto battle; and on their heads were as it were crowns like gold, and their faces were as the faces of men. . . . And they had breastplates, as it were breastplates of iron; and the sound of their wings was as the sound of chariots of many horses running to battle. And they had tails like unto scorpions, and there were stings in their tails: and their power was to hurt men five months." Revelation 9:3, 7, 9–10. "The Apocalyptic Scorpion-Locust," E. B. Elliott, *Horae Apocalyticae; or, A Commentary on the Apocalypse.* 3 vols. (London: Seeley, Burnside & Seeley, 1844), 1: 411; Plate 12.

and coercion. Early Protestant commentators linked Muhammad with the "angel of the bottomless pit" and viewed the epithets Abaddon and Apollyon (which mean destroyer) as an apt title for Muhammad and the Caliphs. Commentators also found it fitting that Islam, conceived of as a delusion introduced by the Arabian destroyer, emerged from some subterranean hell and not from any heavenly inspiration. The fact that Islam was prophetically figured as a smoke at once emphasized both its capacity to block out the sun of Christian truth and its status as an empty and superstitious form of worship that was doomed to vanish. That such a smoke was also associated with pestilence and plague is made clear by the fact that Cotton Mather justified his practice of adopting the Eastern practice of inoculating individuals against smallpox to his critics by claiming that the disease itself had "been brought into *Europe* throe' *Africa*; on the Wings of those *Arabian* Locusts, that in the *Saracen Conquests* did *spread over the Face of the Earth.*"[39]

As did Mather, most Protestant expositors of the Book of Revelation were convinced that the locusts that emerged from the smoke symbolized the invasions of the Saracen armies that rapidly spread the Islamic religious community through Asia and Africa and into Europe.[40] In arguing for the correctness of this typology, interpreters put forth several forms of logical evidence including intertextual analysis of other references to locusts in the Old Testament, comparison of the Saracen diaspora with the migratory patterns of natural locusts, and the correspondence of these biblical references with events related in works of Islamic history. The influential British commentator Joseph Mede even envisioned the swarm of locusts transformed into a transcontinental "Saracenicall body" whose foreparts faced east into Damascus and Baghdad, but whose tail inflicted and infected Europe with its horrible poison.[41]

It was of great significance to Protestants that the vengeful decrees of divine Providence had authorized the rise of Islam. It certified that the power of Islam was temporary and that its woes were part of God's plan to

---

[39] Cotton Mather, *The Angel of Bethesda* (New London, CT, 1722), 112, quoted in Mukhtar Ali Isani, "Cotton Mather and the Orient," *The New England Quarterly* 43 (1970): 49–50. Mather calls Muhammad "the smoke of Ignorance and Blasphemy" and "a Blade Actually possessed by the Divil [sic]" and his religion a "new Antichristianism, in the east, intended for the Derision and Vexation" of the Papal Antichrist. Cotton Mather, *Things to be Look'd For* (Cambridge, 1691), 39–41.

[40] The concordance on this interpretation of the fifth trumpet is prodigious. When William Whiston wrote in 1706 of this verse prefiguring the rise of Muhammad, he claimed that it was a "Judgement" that was "very obvious, and cannot easily be mistaken," one that was "allow'd by almost all the Protestant Expositors." William Whiston, *An Essay on the Revelation of St. John. So Far as Concerns the Past and Present Times* (Cambridge: University Press, 1706), 168. One American missionary journal announced about Revelation 9 that "the Turks are so clearly pictured in the remaining verses, that all Protestant interpreters, of any eminence, from the time of Mr. Brightman to that of Bishop Newton, consider the meaning almost as self-evident." "Juvenis," *The Christian Observer* 1 (1802): 763.

[41] Mede, *Key of the Revelation*, 101, 104. The etymology of these locusts – *arbim* or *arpim* in Hebrew – were variously linked with the savage female "Harpies" from Virgil's *Aeneid*, "hargol" – the Arabic word for army, and even the word Arab itself.

punish the impieties of the church with the ultimate purpose of strengthening Christianity. For example, the first full-length American biography of the prophet Muhammad, written by a clergyman named George Bush, was published as a volume in the Harper's Family Library series in 1830 primarily to "show the intended providential bearings of the entire fabric of Mohammedan delusion upon the church of Christ." The author's ultimate goal was to strengthen his readers' own faith in Christianity by affirming the oracular miracle of the Bible and how it made spiritual sense of the otherwise perplexing ascendancy of Muhammad and Islam.[42] Nevertheless, until a new Adventist interpretation was established in the 1830s, the sting of the fifth trumpet remained a torment of the past. The most common interpretation of its duration was to view its prophetic five months as symbolizing 150 years, which, commencing in 612 when Muhammad reputedly began to teach his religion publicly, had elapsed in 762 when Al-Mansur founded the Abbasid caliphate and established Baghdad as the "abode of peace," signifying the settlement of nomadic Saracens into a stable nation no longer gaining in power and no longer led by one king.[43]

THE TURKISH WOE AND THE LOOSING OF THE EUPHRATEAN HORSEMEN

While the fifth trumpet had sounded well before the Reformation and the torment of the Saracens was apparently a matter for the historical record, there was less agreement about when the sixth trumpet, or second woe – the last plague prior to the great day of judgment – had elapsed or indeed whether it was still active. Commentators viewed this woe as prefiguring the rise of the Ottoman Turks and their Empire, a political force still to be reckoned with, and one that had retained sovereignty over Jerusalem and the Holy Land since the time of the Crusades. The fact that Islam was perceived as divinely ordained was never so clear to commentators as it was in verses 13 and 14 of Chapter 9 describing "a voice from the four horns of the golden altar which is before God" commanding the sixth angel to sound a trumpet that proclaims: "Loose the four angels which are bound in the great river Euphrates." Early Protestant commentators such as Thomas Brightman and Joseph Mede were convinced that these four angels referred

---

[42] "[I]t would not be easy to specify any admitted subject of prophecy, upon which history and Providence have thrown a stronger or clearer light." George Bush, *The Life of Mohammed* (New York: J. & J. Harper, 1830), 208, "Appendix A." See also *Helps to the Study of the Prophecies* (Baltimore: Young, 1832) for a discussion of the way that Islamic history proves biblical prophecy.

[43] Newton, *Dissertation on the Prophecies*, 548–9; Gill, *Exposition of the Revelation*, 764; Faber, *Sacred Calendar*, 3: 285; Aaron Kinne, *A Display of Scriptural Prophecies with Their Events, and the Period of Their Accomplishments* (Boston: Samuel Armstrong, 1813), 13; Isaac Taylor Hinton, *The Prophecies of Daniel and John. Illustrated by the Events of History* (St. Louis: Turnbull & Bray; Woodward & Mathews; David Keith, 1843), 111.

to different groups who had joined to inaugurate the Ottoman Empire, which the divine will had raised up to challenge the Roman Antichrist and limit his effectiveness in destroying the truth of the church.[44] Fear of the Crusades, intestine quarrels, and Mongol invasions from the East – all seen as the hand of providence – restrained these principalities from attacking the Christian Mediterranean and fettered them to the lands where they "hovered" around the Euphrates awaiting divine permission to punish an idolatrous Christianity.[45] The sounding of the sixth trumpet licensed the Turks to "creepe forth of those straits" and invade the West "like an inundation of waters" or "like so many furies."[46] These Ottoman conquests founded what Bishop Newton called a "new empire" inheriting the mantle of the Eastern Antichrist from the Saracens, and redoubling the vigor of their woeful incursions.[47]

Whereas the Saracenic woe was destined only to torment the Papal domains, the Turkish woe involved the "slay[ing] of the third part of men." Protestant commentators interpreted this verse as referring to the Eastern, or Byzantine, portion of the old Holy Roman Empire, whose idolatries had drawn down divine displeasure in the form of the Turkish armies that had captured Constantinople. Such surmisings enabled Protestants to rest assured, especially after the Turkish siege of the city of Vienna was rebuffed in 1683, that their territories would be preserved from the "rage of this savage enemy" even as "the waves of the raging seas, is stayed with the slender Sands."[48] Indeed, the vengeance meted out to the Eastern churches by the prodigious size and strength of the swift Turkish cavalry was brutal and unforgiving as figured by the fearsome depictions that John of Patmos described in Revelation 9:16–19:

> And the number of the army of the horsemen were two hundred thousand thousand: and I heard the number of them. And thus I saw the horses in the vision, and them that sat on them, having breastplates of fire, and of jacinth, and brimstone: and the heads of the horses were as the heads of lions, and out of their mouths issued fire and smoke and brimstone. By these three was the

[44] There was considerable disagreement in the prophetic commentaries concerning the identity of these four angels of retribution, and these attempts at associating them with the rise of the Ottomans required the consultation of all available secular sources about Islamic and Turkish history. Such feats of analogizing, whose inconsistencies led one critic to call it "a millstone about the neck of the whole Turkish theory of interpretation," were avoided by some critics who simply viewed four as a universal number, such as when it is applied to the four winds, or the four horns of the altar at the beginning of this particular prophecy. E. B. Elliott, *Horae Apocalypticae; or, A Commentary on the Apocalypse*, 4th ed., 4 vols. (1843; London: Seeley, Jackson and Halliday, 1851), 1: 490.

[45] "An Exposition of the Book of Revelation," *The Works of Thomas Goodwin*, ed. John C. Miller, 12 vols. (Edinburgh: James Nichol, 1865), 3: 57; "hovering" also used by Gill, *Exposition of the Revelation*, 767.

[46] Brightman, *Revelation of St. John*, 103; Gill, *Exposition of the Revelation*, 767.

[47] Newton, *Dissertation on the Prophesies*, 551.   [48] Brightman, *Revelation of St. John*, 104.

third part of men killed, by the fire, and by the smoke, and by the brimstone, which issued out of their mouths. For their power is in their mouth, and in their tails: for their tails were like unto serpents, and had heads, and with them do they hurt.

The open cruelty of these Turkish horsemen contrasted with the stealth of the Saracenic locusts, symbolized by the fact that the former had the heads as well as the teeth of lions, making them, according to the American critic John Haywood, "undaunted, mettlesome, and bold."[49] The fire, smoke, and sulfur emerging from the mouths of the horses seemed to a large number of interpreters to be a "most manifest allusion" to the ordinance and gunpowder believed to be invented by the Turks.[50] Many commentators could understand why those witnessing this firepower, who like the Apostle John were unfamiliar with its source, might assume that the fire and smoke were actually vomited from the horses' mouths and not from the guns of the horsemen.[51]

Once convinced that this sixth trumpet heralded and explained the rise of the Ottoman Turks, interpreters wanted to know how long this scourge of divine vengeance would endure. Verse fifteen of John's vision explained that the four angels "were prepared for an hour, and a day, and a month, and a year" during which they were to slay the third part of men. Depending on the calendar used to make these prophetic calculations, the woe of the Turks were slated to last either 391 years and 15 days or 396 years and 106 days. Yet even with this degree of concordance about its length, determining the date on which it had commenced involved intricate reasoning based upon the consultation of available historical sources. Some saw the Turkish woe as ending with the fall of Constantinople in 1453;[52] others thought that the defeat of the advancing Ottoman armies signified that it had fallen in the

---

[49] John Haywood, *The Christian Advocate* (Nashville, TN: Thomas G. Bradford, 1819), 85.

[50] Newton, *Dissertation on the Prophecies*, 554, also by Hinton, *Prophecies of Daniel and John*, 151; Faber, *Sacred Calendar*, 3: 289 (who quotes Gibbon on the use of artillery in the siege of Constantinople); Mede, *Key of the Revelation*, 116; Whiston, *An Essay on the Revelation of St. John*, 186; Elliott, *Horae Apocalypticae*, 1: 511; Gill, *Exposition of the Revelation*, 107–8 (Fig. 2.2).

[51] Mede, *Key of the Revelation*, 117; Isaac Hinton uses the Aztec and Inca response to Spanish arms as a parallel measure (*Prophecies of Daniel and John*, 151). John Haywood likewise takes the perspective of "simple Americans" (*Christian Advocate*, 86). Both Brightman and Mede cite as proof a reference from Laonicus Chalcondyl's *Turcicam Historia* about a great gun used in the siege of Constantinople, which was drawn by seventy yokes of oxen, claiming that the "Holy Ghost describes this enemy unto us by those war-like instruments, which should take their beginning almost with this tyranny." Brightman, *Revelation of St. John*, 104; Mede, *Key of the Revelation*, 117–18; Gill, *Exposition of the Revelation*, 108. The Enlightenment thinker Thomas Paine, found Thomas Newton's account of this enormous gun to be absurd, claiming "the bishop beats Gulliver." "Examination of the Prophecies," Philip S. Foner, ed., *The Complete Writings of Thomas Paine*, 2 vols. (New York: Citadel Press, 1969), 2: 877–8 n 37.

[52] For example, see Sir Isaac Newton, *Observations upon the Prophecies of Daniel, and the Apocalypse of St. John* (London: J. Darby and T. Browne, 1733), 307.

FIGURE 2.2. Eschatological depiction of "Mahometans" as the Fifth and Sixth Trumpets from the Book of Revelation. The Muslims on horseback represent the Saracens (with spear) and the Turks (with firearm). The commentary on the Turkish Woe, which that author dates as beginning to sound in 1449, is represented by "Fire arms first used on horseback by the Turks (fact in history)." The comment alludes to Revelation 9:17: "And thus I saw the horses in the vision, and them that sat on them, having breastplates of fire, and of jacinth, and brimstone: and the heads of the horses were as the heads of lions; and out of their mouths issued fire and smoke and brimstone." Lower right section of *A Chronological Chart of the Visions of Daniel and John* (Boston: J. V. Himes, c. 1843). Courtesy, American Antiquarian Society.

seventeenth century. In 1754, Thomas Newton popularized an interpretation that would become the standard interpretation of several of the most consulted Bible commentaries of the late eighteenth and early nineteenth centuries, ending the era with the capture of Kamieniec Podolski from the

Poles in 1672, which was seen as the last territorial aggrandizement of the Ottoman Empire.

The power of these dating schemes can be seen by examining how a third scenario of the waning of Turkish woe in the late seventeenth century influenced the millennial aspirations of the famous Puritan divines, Increase and Cotton Mather. Robert Middlekauff has claimed in his family biography that "Cotton Mather and his peers inaugurated an era of apocalyptical expectation in America" and noted the fervency of their chiliastic hopes based upon their reading of such noted eschatologists as Joseph Mede, Pierre Jurieu, and Thomas Brightman.[53] Brightman, citing the "one consent of all the Historians," claimed that the date of Turkish dominion had commenced in the year 1300, which, when added to the 396-year prophetic period of the second woe would expire 396 years later in 1696.[54] After reading this prophecy in 1682, Increase Mather expressed his hopes that the Turks would be permitted to expire on the prophetic schedule.[55] Increase Mather subscribed to the eschatological theory that "the Turk must be destroyed before all Israel be saved" because the Jews "shall never peaceably enjoy the Land of their Fathers again as long as he ['that Eastern Antichrist'] hath any power to hinder it."[56] His son Cotton shared this belief in the imminent end of the Turks. For example, both men interpreted the account of the Second Coming in the Gospel of Matthew, which refers to the moon failing to give her light, as symbolizing the waning of the Turkish crescent.[57] Cotton Mather, while preaching to the Artillery Company of Massachusetts in 1691 about the nearness of the time when the swords the soldiers were holding would be turned into plowshares, argued that a "dying *Mahometanism*" was a clear "symptom" of approach of the second advent of Christ and comprised one of the "Things to be Look'd For" of the title of his sermon. Mather prophesied "within less than *Seven Years* from this Time, the *Turk* should be under such Humiliations, as might Obstruct his ever giving *Europe* Trouble any more."[58] The Mathers viewed the termination of this "Plague" as a crucial precursor to the downfall of the Papacy and the restoration of the Jews. Cotton viewed the destruction of the Turkish power as a great sign of God's

---

[53] Robert Middlekauff, *The Mathers: Three Generations of Puritan Intellectuals, 1596–1728* (New York: Oxford University Press, 1971), 323.

[54] Brightman, *Revelation of St. John*, 103–4.   [55] Increase Mather, *Kometographia* (Boston, 1683), 137–8.

[56] Increase Mather, *The Mystery of Israel's Salvation* (London, 1669), 25–6. See also Increase Mather, *A Dissertation wherein the Strange Doctrine . . .* (Boston, 1683), 93–4, 110.

[57] Matthew 24:29–30. Increase Mather found the destruction of the Turkish monarchy to be "principally intended" by this verse (*Mystery of Israel's Salvation*, 30). "The Turkish moon must go down, ere the church come out of its night, or hear it said Thy Light is Come." Cotton Mather, *Problema Theologicum* (1703; unpublished manuscript, American Antiquarian Society), 55.

[58] Cotton Mather, *Things to Be Look'd For*, 31–4. Already by 1690, Cotton Mather was eagerly awaiting "the Happy *Chiliad*" because "'tis now past Question with me, *That the Second Wo is past*, and the *Third* you know then *cometh quickly.*" *The Present State of New England* (Boston: Samuel Green, 1690), 35.

mercy because he believed that no other conquerors since the beginning of the world "have hardly shed such Rivers of Blood as these *woful* Turks have done." Cotton Mather interpreted news of any reversal in the fortunes of the Turkish Empire as confirmatory "Declarations" of "the *Second Wo Passing Away*."[59]

As the date for the final termination of the Turks approached, Mather's prayers that Christ would deliver on his promise became passionate. On a Sunday in June of 1696, Cotton Mather preached to a large congregation about the dire fate of several New England sailors who had been taken into captivity in North Africa. Mather wrote in his diary:

> I received and uttered, my Assurance that the Lord Jesus Christ, had some wonderful Thing, to do for the deliverance of some of our Captives.
>
> Yea, several Times on the Lord's Dayes, before vast Assemblies, my public Prayers, have uttered this Assurance. O my sinful Soul, mark the Event!
>
> For I shall certainly see these poor Captives, wonderfully delivered, in Circumstances, that shall particularly furnish mee, with Opportunities, to glorify the Lord Jesus Christ exceedingly.[60]

This "Assurance" that moved Mather was nothing less than his belief that the Turks, among whom he included the Barbary states (known at that time as the "Turks of Zallee"), would cease to afflict the church close to the very time that he was preaching. In a fervent sermon that year, Cotton Mather proclaimed that he wished he could "speak with a voice as loud as the seventh trumpet" that the most wonderful revolution in history would be experienced within the lifetimes of most of his listeners: "*The Day is at Hand, when the Turkish Empire*, instead of being any longer a *Wo* to *Christendome*, shall it self become a *Part of Christendome*."[61] In "A Pastoral Letter to the English Captives in Africa" of 1698, he encouraged the Christians held in Barbary to resist conversion to Islam by fortifying them with faith that Christ had foretold both the rise of Islam and its destruction in the very near future.[62] When they were released in 1703, Mather's prayers seemed answered; he later penned in the margin: "In the Forty first year of my Life, this thing is wonderfully accomplished" and delivered a sermon called "The Glory of Goodness" in which he viewed the redemption of these individuals

---

[59] Cotton Mather, *The Wonders of the Invisible World* (Boston, 1693), 39–40.

[60] *The Diary of Cotton Mather*, 2 vols. (New York: Frederick Ungar, 1957), 1: 197.

[61] Cotton Mather, *Things for a Distress'd People to Think upon* (Boston: B. Green and J. Allen, 1696), 34–5.

[62] "He (Christ) foretold a thousand things, that we have seen exactly come to pass; but He particularly foretold, the Rising of the Mahometan Religion; its being propagated by the Arabian Arms; its obscuring the Christian Religion, with an horrid Smoke, and its Tormenting the Professors of the Christian Religion, after the Union of the Four Turkish Kingdoms in the One Ottoman Family, for Three hundred & Ninety seven years together." Cotton Mather, *A Pastoral Letter to the English Captives in Africa* (Boston, 1698), 7.

from the "filthy Disciples of Mahomet" as emblematic of the purification of the Church from the corruptions that had originally forced the hand of Turkish power.[63]

With the virtue of hindsight, both Mathers attempted to maintain their assurance that the downfall of the Turks had indeed commenced on schedule. The same year that the captives were redeemed, Cotton exulted in *Problema Theologicum* that believers should await the "Happy State" of the church's millennial reign and assured them that "the *Second Coming* of our Lord Jesus Christ, will be *Quickly after* the final loosing of the *Turkish Hostilityes* against Europe." Mather went on to assert:

> Pardon my freedome, if I venture to add; that in all probabilyty, not long after the year 1300 began the period for the Second Wo; and the Dispensations of Heaven towards the Turkish Empire, about the year 1697: are such as notably harmonize with our conjectures. But [then whom is] to come quickly? Tell me not that the Second Coming of our Lord is yett above a thousand years off! No, I have better News for you than so.[64]

In the case of the Mathers, the cultural work of islamicist eschatology empowered them with global proof of the imminence of the Second Coming without the need for an actual religious revival in America. The alien threat of Islam was contained within sacred biblical interpretation in a way that avoided the requirement to confront directly its religious challenge, a mission impossible to the Puritans whose hemispheric relocation had made them even more peripheral to the affairs of Muslim orient. Their faith was reassured by grappling with the unfoldment of secular events and viewing them with the interpretive lenses of eschatological imagination.

POURING OUT THE SIXTH VIAL: AWAITING THE END OF THE TURKISH WOE

Many exegetes through the early nineteenth century remained convinced that the second woe of Turkish ascendancy had terminated in the late seventeenth century – either in 1672 or 1697 – and the belief that Turkish spiritual hegemony was at its prophetic end continued to stimulate apocalyptic speculation. Protestant preachers used the examples of the first two woes as homiletic devices to intimate the imminent vengeance that would be

---

[63] Cotton Mather, "The Glory of Goodness," in *White Slaves, African Masters: An Anthology of American Barbary Captivity Narratives*, ed. Paul Baepler (Chicago and London: University of Chicago Press, 1999), 61–9. See Middlekauff, *The Mathers*, 339–44.

[64] Cotton Mather, *Problema Theologicum*, 53.

divinely dispensed to the unrepentant during the sounding of the seventh trumpet. However, the fact that Islam still held its ground after the sixth trumpet was widely believed to have sounded forced prophetic exegetes to seek out additional explanations for this perplexing paradox. Evidently the expiration of the 391 (or 396) years did not completely exhaust the worldly dominance of the Turks, even if further expansion of the Turkish state appeared to be contained. If the time allotted to the sixth trumpet to kill the one third of men had elapsed, then how much more time would the Ottoman Empire itself be permitted to exist?

Some interpreters accounted for this confounding lag by asserting that the sixth trumpet was still exerting its woeful reign. Two eighteenth-century presidents of American colleges subscribed to the Turkish theory of prophecy but dissented from the established belief that the Turkish woe had already expired. In 1757 Aaron Burr – president of the College of New Jersey (now Princeton) and the father of the notorious future Vice President of the United States – viewed Muhammad as the "great impostor" and saw Islam as a realm of darkness that he found to be "the greatest Obstacle in the way of spreading the Gospel." Burr saw the world as still groaning under the second woe, which would soon "end with the Total Destruction and Abolition of the Turkish Empire" – an event that would "open a Door for that Glorious Spread of the Gospel promised in the Latter Days."[65] Samuel Langdon, president of Harvard during the early years of the Revolutionary War and later head of the American Academy of Arts and Sciences, wrote his second book of prophetic interpretation in 1791 called *Observations on the Revelation of Jesus Christ to St. John*. Langdon subscribed to the eschatological theory that Muhammad was "an emissary of Satan," but he argued, however, that the hour, day, month and year should "not be summed up together" but suggested instead that they referred to a series of incursions of increasing duration with intervals between them and that the end of the Ottoman Empire was "not far off."[66] Burr's assertion that the second woe had not yet passed in 1757 and Langdon's later loosening of its strict dating schemes was necessary to explain the apparent failure of these first two woes, however punishing in their vengeance, to convince Christians of the necessity of reforming their churches and to put an end to Islam's worldly power.

Partly in response to this enigma, most prophetic-minded exegetes in the late eighteenth and early nineteenth centuries reevaluated another key prophetic sign of the end times from the Book of Revelation – the pouring out of the sixth vial – to explain the puzzling persistence of the Ottomans.

[65] Aaron Burr, *The Watchman's Answer* (Boston: S. Kneeland, 1757), 17–32.

[66] Samuel Langdon, *Observations on the Revelation of Jesus Christ to St. John* (Worcester, MA: Isaiah Thomas, 1791), 116–34.

While the trumpets of woe signalized a divine punishment of the church itself, the seven vials described in Revelation 16 poured out destruction upon its enemies. Verse 12 describes a scenario during which "the sixth angel poured out his vial upon the river Euphrates; and the water thereof was dried up, that the way of the kings might be prepared." If the sixth trumpet had loosed and then thrown back the tide of Turkish invasion from the Euphrates, exegetic logic reasoned that it was up to the pouring of the sixth vial to effect a complete evaporation of Islamic power. According to traditional interpretations, the first five vials had already been emptied, and the timing of the sixth vial's pouring was crucial because it immediately preceded the emptying of the seventh vial during which the wrath of God would destroy all antichristian forces in the battle of Armageddon, an event heralding the return of the Savior. Such a vision affirmed the orientalist belief that Islam was an insubstantial smoke or mist that would dissipate before the sun of Christ's promised millennium. The anticipated extermination of the Turk again served as a visible sign of the onset of the seventh trumpet, the Day of Judgment when "the mystery of God shall be finished" (Rev. 10: 7).

Prior to the end of the eighteenth century, the sixth vial had been interpreted as primarily signifying Rome and the Catholic Church as spiritual types of a New Babylon protected behind the symbolic bastions of the Euphrates. For example, John Cotton – a central intellectual presence in Puritan Massachusetts after he migrated there from Boston, England, in 1633 – claimed that "popish idolatry causes Turkish tyrannie" and continued to assert throughout his career that "it was for the sinne of Rome that the Turke was advanced, a barbarous and beastly enemy to punish a beastly religion."[67] In his exposition on *The Powring Out of the Seven Vials*, Cotton dwelt deeply on the meaning of the sixth vial of verse 12, presenting a vision of a fallen Garden of Eden, whose "streames of corruption" were not natural tributaries but the five evils of Revelation 9: 20–1: idolatries, murders, sorceries, fornications, and thefts. These were the sins of which Rome had failed to repent and which Cotton felt were "the Originall of the Turkish Dominion," the "walles" that protected them against the incursions of the crusades, and because of which Islam was permitted to persist.[68] "And how shall you overcome the Turkes?" he inquired, and then answered "dry up but the Fountaines of the Corruptions of religion, and you remove Antichrist, and make the Turkes easily Conquerable, he will not be defensible then, whereas now he standeth like a wall of brasse, and so will doe

---

[67] John Cotton, *The Powring of the Seven Vials* (London: R.S., 1642), 15; John Cotton, *An Exposition upon the Thirteenth Chapter of the Revelation* (London: Timothy Smart, 1656), 50, 54, 64. Cotton also wrote that "the staffe of the Turkish Monarchy, is the superstition of Antichristianisme." *Powring*, 30.

[68] Cotton, *Powring*, 19–23.

untill these streames of corruption be dryed up."[69] Through this process of "evaporation," the Catholic and Turkish monarchies would be simultaneously destroyed, opening the door first for the restoration of the Jews, and finally for the return of Christ.

To preacher and theologian Jonathan Edwards, the drying of the Euphrates' waters signified, as it had to Cotton, the "temporal supplies, wealth, revenues and incomes" that shored up Rome and would soon evaporate as had the pomp of the ancient Babylon after the Medes and Persians invaded from the east.[70] However, Edwards did surmise "that it may also have respect to another thing, somewhat nearer a literal accomplishment . . . that is the destruction of the Turkish Empire," which he believed, along with the subsequent conversion of those peoples under their domination, would surround the darkness of the Papacy and render it "compassed round with light." "For whenever the Mahometan Empire is destroyed," Edwards asserted, "it will doubtless be to make way for the kingdom of Christ's taking place in the room of it."[71]

This duality in Edward's thinking dramatizes the interpretive shift that progressively identified the drying of the Euphrates in Revelation 16:12 directly with the necessary removal of Turkey as a means of making way for the return of the Jews. The consolidation of this new consensus is evident in the energy of expectation exuded by a series of American commentaries between the French and Indian War and the War of 1812. Ethan Smith, an interpreter of the prophecies to whom Levi Parsons had written for guidance while in the Near East, exemplified the paradigm that viewed the Ottomans

---

[69] Cotton, *Powring*, 24. To Cotton, "the greate Turke" was also the "Leviathan" of Isaiah 27:1 who would be slayed by the Lord, not with the sword of a military crusade, but by the penetrating weapon of Christ's own Word, so that the Jews might be restored to the Holy Land and "blossom" again as Christians. *A Brief Exposition of the Whole Book of Canticles* (London: Philip Nevil, 1642), 255.

[70] After Jonathan Edwards had been converted (by his reading of the commentaries of Moses Lowman) to the belief that the church was presently in the time of the sixth vial, he wrote several descriptions of its meaning in his "Notes on the Apocalypse," in the *Humble Attempt*, and in a separate Tractate devoted to this issue, as well as in a notebook entitled "An Account of Events Probably Fulfilling the Sixth Vial on the River Euphrates" in which he collected items from the press that seemed to comment on its progressing fulfillment. *Apocalyptic Writings*. Volume 5 of *The Works of Jonathan Edwards*, ed. Stephen J. Stein, 14 vols. (New Haven, CT: Yale University Press, 1977), 5: 184–91, 416–27 passim, 298–305, 253–84. Jonathan Edwards, "Notes on the Apocalypse," 5: 186.

[71] Edwards, *Apocalyptic Writings*, 5: 188, 190. Increase Mather's account of Revelation 16:12 shows an early manifestation of this view. He interpreted this verse as either foreseeing another literal "exsiccation" of the waters as had occurred in Moses' time with the Red Sea, or signalizing the evaporation of the spiritual power of the Turkish Empire, "the Assyrian of the world at this day." Mather clearly stated that this verse denotes "that divine providence will by some means or other, bring fatal destruction upon the Turkish Empire, in order to make the way clear for Israel's salvation." Mather, *Mystery of Israel's Salvation*, 31–4.

as a spiritual type of the Euphrates. In 1811, he wrote that "the Ottoman Empire is to be overturned at a period not far from the present... and the judgment of the sixth vial appears strikingly to predict the accomplishment of this event." As an embodiment of the Euphrates, that "fatal obstacle" in the way of the resettlement of the Jews, Smith believed that Ottoman hegemony would evaporate in much the same way as the Red Sea was parted for the return of the Hebrews to Canaan in Moses's time.[72] Smith's prophetic writings echoed the voices of many others who viewed the drying up of the Euphrates as a typological reference to the extermination of the Ottoman Empire.[73]

Commentators gave the sixth vial such prominence during the early national period because it explained why the Turks had failed to fall despite the passing of their time of woe, but it also helped thinkers to resolve the Eastern Question – the troubling secular events occurring in Eastern Europe and Western Asia – within a religious worldview. Millennialist perspectives were bruited during the French and Indian War (and later in response to the Quebec Act) that had placed the contest for North America between France and England as an episode in the divine struggle between the true church and the legions of Antichrist.[74] But the alliance with France during the revolutionary years and the need to accommodate Catholic patriots had muted American attention to the antichristianity of Catholic France. With the coming of the French Revolution, however, with its radical challenge to both clerical power and revealed religion, biblical prophecies for many believers were confirmed, heightening the speculative fever that the time of the end was near. When Napoleon invaded the

---

[72] Ethan Smith, *A Dissertation on the Prophecies Relative to Antichrist and the Last Times* (Charlestown, MA: Samuel T. Armstrong, 1811), 326, 331–3.

[73] As early as 1757, William Torrey's *A Brief Discourse Concerning Futurities* stated that "God will some Way or other, first bring them [the Jews] into their own Land, and give them Advantage to return by drying up the River Euphrates, that is as I conceive by diminishing and abating the great Power of the Turk in and about that Part of the World; and that either by intestine Commotions, or Wars with other Nations, or both." (Boston: Edes & Gill, 1757), 58. In 1780, Thomas Wells Bray explained in his *A Dissertation upon the Sixth Vial* that the great Euphrates supported both Rome and Constantinople, and that the Antichrist had "set both his feet upon Christendome together." But to Bray the Euphrates primarily symbolized "that overgrown power of the Mahomitan destroyers... enslaved under the tyranny of Satan." The drying up of the Euphrates would signalize the defeat of the Ottoman Empire, one of the "great bulwarks of Satan's empire." (Hartford, CT: Hudson & Goodwin, 1780), 18n, 17. And ten years later, Asa McFarland – a Presbyterian from Concord, Massachusetts – preached in his *Signs of the Last Times* that "the decline of the Turkish empire will indicate that the end is near." "When that empire falls, which is already on the decline," assured McFarland, "the Jews will begin to be restored, together will the fullness of the Gentiles, and Christ will take to himself his power and reign." (Concord, MA: George Hough, 1808), 12. See also Joseph Galloway, *Brief Commentaries* (Trenton, NJ: James Oram, 1809), 312.

[74] John Berens, *Providence & Patriotism in Early America 1640–1815* (Charlottesville: University Press of Virginia, 1978), 32–50. James West Davidson, *The Logic of Millennial Thought: Eighteenth-Century New England* (New Haven, CT: Yale University Press, 1977).

eastern Mediterranean in 1798, the stage was set for imagining an apocalyptic showdown between the forces of light and darkness in the Holy Land.[75] David Austin from Elizabethtown, New Jersey, applied prophecies from the Book of Daniel to the Turks and argued that Napoleon's invasion of Egypt was "enter[ing] the wedge which eventually may produce a fracture upon the Mahometan empire," enabling the Jews an avenue back to Israel.[76]

It was the conjuncture of the apocalyptic desires raised by the American and French revolutions, the continuing conundrum of Turkish hegemony over Jerusalem, and the availability of this heritage of biblical commentary that led Islamic history to emerge in late eighteenth century as what Ruth Bloch, an historian of American eschatological thought, has called a "major theme in American millennial literature."[77] The prophetic linkage of the end of the Turkish hegemony over the Holy Land with a passionate faith in the promise of Christ's imminent return led prophecy-watching Americans of the early national period to follow historical events unfolding in the Ottoman Empire with surprising interest. "The destruction of the Mahometan power is the very epoch for the commencement of many other important matters," a 1798 commentary succinctly explained: "At that very time, the deliverance of thy people, or every one that is found written in the book, and the resurrection shall take place."[78] It is for the ironic reason of confirming that Christ's approach was impending that Protestant commentators paid such a fervent amount of attention to the vicissitudes of what was for them a distant and satanic empire. The conviction and logic with which these leaders viewed the imminent end of the Ottomans exemplifies the power of eschatology as a shaper of early American cultural imagination.

Apocalyptic thinkers sought additional elucidation for Turkey's fall by examining intertextual harmonies between the prophecies in the New Testament's Book of Revelation and the Old Testament's Book of Daniel. These readings of chapter 11 of Daniel explained the eventual downfall of Islam in a way that complemented the pouring out of the sixth vial of Revelation. Verses 40–3 of this chapter spoke of "the time of the end" during which the "king of the south" would push at Antichrist while the "king of the north" would "come like a whirlwind" and conquer many countries,

---

75 Joseph Lathrop envisioned Napoleon as "king of the Mahometans" and asserted that God had literally foretold this event by the fact that the appellation "Apollyon" was only one letter away from Napoleon's own. *A Sermon, on the Dangers of the Times* (Springfield, MA: Francis Stebbins, 1798), 44.

76 David Austin, *The Millennial Door Thrown Open* (E. Windsor, CT: Luther Pratt, 1799), 23.

77 Ruth H. Bloch, *Visionary Republic: Millennial Themes in American Thought, 1756–1800* (Cambridge and New York: Cambridge University Press, 1985), 145.

78 *Characteristics in the Prophecies Applicable to and Descriptive of, the Power and Duration of the French Republic* (New York: John Tiebout, 1798), 10.

including the "glorious land."[79] Chapter 11 ends with these two verses (44–5):

> But tidings out of the east and out of the north shall trouble him: therefore he shall go forth with great fury to destroy, and utterly to take away many. And he shall plant the tabernacles of his palace between the seas in the glorious holy mountain; yet he shall come to his end and none shall help him.

Biblical commentators viewed this scenario as an explanation of the ravages of the Turks who were divinely licensed to "overflow and pass over" the Near East and North Africa and to conquer its peoples with furious destruction before ultimately meeting their own demise. As early as the 1640s, Ephraim Huit and Thomas Parker, the first American expositors of the Book of Daniel, both agreed that the "king of the south" referred to Saracen incursions into the Holy Land; the Arabs were able to "push at" the Byzantine empire but never conquer it, a position maintained in the early national period. The "king of the north" seemed to many expositors clearly to describe the expansion of the Ottoman Turks over the Mediterranean littoral as far as Algiers ("Egyptians, Libyans, Ethiopians") and at the same time explain their incomplete subjugation of the Arab Bedouins (indicated by "Moab, Edom, and Ammon"). These verses also explained the Ottoman control over the Holy Land (the "glorious mountain" between the Mediterranean and Dead Seas) and prophesied that such a dominion was doomed to ultimate failure.[80] The application of Daniel 11:40–5 to Islam was heavily subscribed to by American writers on eschatological themes during the early national period. Benjamin Gale, a Yale graduate who studied surgery and settled as a lawyer in Killingworth, Connecticut, linked this "king of the north" to the Turks, Persians, and other Muslims who had "imbibed that imposture," seeing them as the "Mahometan part of the Spiritual Babylon."[81] A chorus of other Bible commentators was also

---

[79] "And at the time of the end shall the king of the south push at him [i.e., Antichrist]: and the king of the north shall come against him like a whirlwind, with chariots, and with horsemen, and with many ships; and he shall enter into the countries, and shall overflow and pass over. He shall enter also into the glorious land, and many countries shall be overthrown: but these shall escape out of his hand, even Edom, and Moab, and the chief of the children of Ammon. He shall stretch forth his hand also upon the countries: and the land of Egypt shall not escape. But he shall have power over the treasures of gold and of silver, and over all the precious things of Egypt: and the Libyans and the Ethiopians shall be at his steps." Daniel 11:40–3.

[80] Ephraim Huit, *The Whole Prophecie of Daniel Explained* (London: Henry Overton, 1643), 332–44; Thomas Parker, *The Visions and Prophecies of Daniel Expounded* (London: Edmund Paxton, 1646), 122–4; James Winthrop, *A Systematic Arrangement of Several Scriptures* (Boston: Thomas Hall, 1795), 141; Eliphaz Chapman, *Discourse on the Prophecies* (Portland, ME: John K. Baker, 1797), 13.

[81] Benjamin Gale, *A Brief Essay, or, An Attempt to Prove, from the Prophetick Writings of the Old and New Testament, What Period of Prophecy the Church of God Is Now Under* (New Haven, CT: Thomas & Samuel Green, 1788), 16, 53.

convinced that the Book of Daniel explained the expansion and doom of the Turks in the Holy Land. Former Postmaster General Samuel Osgood perhaps spoke for these commentators, if not most of Protestant America, when he argued in 1794 that the king of the north was "so naturally applicable to the Ottoman power, that little need be said to elucidate the same."[82]

This promise of Daniel, combined with the pouring out of the sixth vial linking the drying up of the Euphrates with the decline of Ottoman power, signaled that the need for Islam to punish an erring Christianity was over. Attempts to read "the signs of the times" as it related to the Turks centered on speculation about who was east and north of the Ottoman Empire and opened Western curiosity about the further east. The object of the drying up of the Euphrates was to "prepare the way for the kings of the east" (Revelation 16:12), and Daniel had spoken of "tidings out of the east and out of the north" (11:44) that would provoke antichrist to set in motion the train of events that would culminate in his destruction.

Efforts at identifying the secular referents of these "kings" and "tidings" opened up a wide variety of possible historical situations and demonstrated the creative reaches of eschatological reasoning vying to align scriptural verse with actual event. There was considerable latitude in defining the populations designated by these prophecies. Many were committed to viewing the "kings of the east" as the return of the Jews, no doubt believing that substantial numbers of Jews still remained in the East near their ancient site of Babylonian captivity. In 1759, for instance, Harne Kilco believed that weakening of Turkish power would rouse the Jews to "zealously make their Way through . . . the Mahometan and Turkish Countries, bearing loud testimony against the false prophet" as they atoned for their sins against Christ.[83] Ethan Smith argued that the eastern population of the Afghans might be the kings of the east because they "call themselves *Melchim*, the Hebrew word for *kings*."[84] In 1788, Benjamin Gale argued that the Turks would be defeated by invasions of the Russians and Persians, the "kings of the east."[85] Others viewed the "kings of the east" as the Ottoman Sultans themselves who would be divinely induced to invade Italy and eventually

---

[82] Samuel Osgood, *Remarks on the Book of Daniel* (New York: Greenleaf's Press, 1794), 248–50. Eliphaz Chapman argued that Daniel's vision had been fulfilled "even as to the letter of the prophecy" by the geographical extent of Ottoman control. *Discourse on the Prophecies*, 3–5. Jedidiah Morse likewise preached: "the victories of Mahomet, of the rise and establishment of his dominion, and also the destruction of his power, seem plainly foretold and described in the last five verses" [of Daniel 11]. *Signs of the Times* (Charlestown, MA: The Society for Propagating the Gospel among the Indians and Others in North America, 1810), 6.

[83] Harne Kilco, *From a Folio Manuscript, in the Archive of a Certain Aged Gorgomon* (Boston: Thomas and John Fleet, 1759), 7–8, 15.

[84] Ethan Smith, *Dissertation on the Prophecies*, 332.   [85] Gale, *A Brief Essay*, 13.

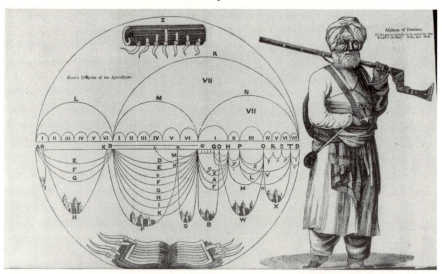

FIGURE 2.3. A prophetic chart featuring an image of an "Afghaun of Damaun" adapted from a watercolor by Robert Melville Grindlay originally included in the second edition of Mountstuart Elphinstone's 1815 narrative, *An Account of the Kingdom of Caubul* (London: Longman et al.). The Afghaun is described as a representative "Of the nations thought to be meant by 'the Kings of the East.' Note, Rev. 16:12."

France.[86] The great variety of these interpretations only served to accentuate the established view that the drying up of the Euphrates signified the promised removal of the Turkish Empire to make room for the restoration of the Jews to Israel and their subsequent conversion to Christianity, a harbinger of the end of the antichristian empire.

The fact that the Sultan's dominion had been shrinking in the face of European encroachment was frequently employed as secular proof of the desiccation of the eschatological Euphrates. In 1830, the terrible Algiers had become a colony of France. Russian aggression against the Sultan had resulted in a series of treaties, up until the Crimean War in the late 1850s, in which the Sublime Porte was forced to cede territories in the Balkans, on the Black Sea, and in the Caucasus to that power to their north. Other expositors charted the weakening of the Ottoman Empire by focusing on signs of decay in the internal politics of the Sublime Porte. Joseph Galloway theorized how the Sultan's control might self-destruct from within because of the indifference of Turkish subjects caused by the use of opium and

---

[86] Austin, *Millennial Door*, 23; William Cummins Davis, *The Millennium* (Salisbury, NC: Coupee and Crider, 1811), 39; Benjamin Farnham, *Dissertations on the Prophecies* (E. Windsor, CT: Luther Pratt, 1800), 8. William F. Miller, *Christ the Rod of Iron upon all Antichristian Kings and Nations* (Hartford, CT: Hudson & Goodwin, 1804), 63.

"licentious and satanic spirit of liberty," as well as the disaffection caused by resentment of despotism and French intrigue. Islamic sectarianism was also cited as a sign of the impending doom of the Ottoman Empire. The rebellions of Mehemet Ali and Ibrahim Pasha from the south in Egypt signified to prophecy-minded Christians that all was not well in the state of Satan.[87] The schism caused by Shi'ism was also seen by some as offering some hope that Islam would continue to disintegrate from within and that Persia might provide forces for the decimation of the Turks. Some Americans even interpreted the rise of the Wahabi movement in the Arabian peninsula far from a form of "fundamentalist" retrenchment, but rather as an Islamic equivalent of the Reformation that would lead to more receptivity to Christian ideas and hence contribute to the downfall of Islam.[88] The beginning of the Greek War of Independence in 1821, however, provided the most dramatic historical template upon which the decline of the Turks could be charted. Both George Stanley Faber and Ethan Smith popularized the view that the Turks' loss of Greece manifested the pouring out of the sixth vial.[89] To watchers of the signs, the sanctuary of Daniel 8:14 seemed to be becoming more cleansed by the year.

Signs of political weakness were not the only events that attracted the attention of Christians seeking confirmation for the divine punishment of the Turks by the pouring of the sixth vial. Ethan Smith saw such catastrophes as plagues, fires, earthquakes, and population decline as signs of the near collapse of the Ottomans pointing to the concomitant extinction of Islam.[90] Reverend George Bush reprinted an account in his *Treatise on the Millennium*

---

[87] Farnham, *Dissertations on the Prophecies*, 98; Galloway, *Brief Commentaries*, 313; Ethan Smith, *Dissertation on the Prophecies*, 294.

[88] Edward Dorr Griffin preached in 1813 (using imagery from Daniel 9) that the rise of the Wahabis would "cleanse" the Arabs and leave nothing else wanting "to banish the religion of Mahomet from the world" except the Turkish and Persian empire which, as Gog, was soon "to be broken by a hand which in the very act should seal before the eyes of all nations the truth of the Christian religion." Griffin, *A Sermon Preached October 20, 1813, at Sandwich, Massachusetts* (Boston: Willis, 1813), 28n and 29n. Ethan Smith saw Abdul Wahab's effect on the Turks as similar to that of Illuminism on the Papacy. *Dissertation on the Prophecies*, 293.

[89] Smith, *Dissertation on the Prophecies*, iv, 292n, and 293–5. The fact that Greek independence seemed to confirm one of Smith's earlier prophecies was one of the major inducements for him to publish his lectures in 1833. "When the insurrection of the Greeks appeared, I ventured to express my belief that this was the entering wedge of the great event, as it has proved to be indeed. The wars and successes of the Greeks; the subsequent war of the emperor of the north; and the still later successful attacks of the Pacha of Egypt; and the present state of the empire of the Porte, are now well known, as before the eye of the world. And we have here the manifest fulfilment of our text; – the drying of the river Euphrates!" Ethan Smith, *Key to the Revelation. In Thirty-Six Lectures* (New York: J. & J. Harper, 1833), 318. In keying in on 1821 as the year in which the sixth vial was poured out, George Stanley Faber labeled himself an "impatient speculatist." *The Sacred Calendar of Prophecy*, 2nd ed., 3 vols. (London: W. E. Painter, 1844), 3: 353, 287. See also John Thomas, *The Coming Struggle among the Nations of the East* (Toronto: Maclean & Co., 1854), 16–17.

[90] Smith, *Dissertation on the Prophecies*, 292–4.

from the *London Record* of 13 November 1831 that spoke not only of cholera and fires, but also of a storm that dumped "*lumps of ice*, as large as a man's foot."[91] Any mention of natural calamities in the press, travel narratives, or any other form of intelligence that made its way from the East was promoted as proof of the overdue evaporation of Islam. Evidence from the historical record was consulted by millennialist writers not to understand the ethos of Muslim religious experience but rather to consolidate their faith in the oracular power of the Bible by confirming prophecies of the tottering of the Ottoman Empire.

THE MILLERITES AND THE END OF THE OTTOMANS

Many years of watching the long trail of signs symbolizing the "drying up of the Euphrates" proved unsatisfactory to the influential leaders of the new American Adventist movement that gained increasing popularity through the 1830s. William Miller, the most celebrated American eschatologist of the nineteenth century, thought he had found firmer ground for believing in the proximity of Islam's demise by arguing that the second woe had never ended. This interpretation revised the timetable of the sixth trumpet so as to place the end of the Islamic woe in the future, thereby setting the speculation about Islam's end on an apparently more rational chronological schedule. Following the intricacies of his logic reveals the continuing vitality and creativity of eschatological reasoning as a powerful form of intercultural imposition. As early as an 1828 lecture, Miller applied both woe trumpets only to the rise of the Turkish Empire and not to the earlier Saracen incursions. Accordingly, he began the "five months" of the locusts in 1298, the time traditionally associated with the rise of the Ottomans, claiming that the angel of the bottomless pit was not Muhammad himself but rather Othman, the first Ottoman sultan. This period of 150 years led immediately into the 391 years of the sixth trumpet's "hour, day, month and year" to create a combined period of Turkish woe of 541 years. According to this logic, Islamic oppression of the Christian global community would evaporate when the sixth vial was poured out sometime during the year 1839 followed quickly by the sounding of the last trumpet. This argument would be elaborated further in the many editions of his *Evidences from Scripture* published in the decade after the local edition of 1833 and would be used to confirm his more renowned prophecy that Christ would return in 1844.[92]

---

[91] George Bush, *Treatise on the Millennium* (New York: J. & J. Harper, 1832), 244–5n. Bush also quoted the observations of the chaplain to the British ambassador in Constantinople reporting instances of "depopulation . . . conflagration, pestilence, and civil commotion," which seemed to confirm the decay of the Ottoman Empire (243–4). See also Elliott, *Horae Apocalyticae*, 3: 21–3.

[92] William Miller, *Evidences from Scripture* (Brandon, VT: Vermont Telegraph, 1833), 43.

Miller's associate Josiah Litch convinced Miller to recalibrate his scheme so that the second woe would pass on 11 August 1840. Litch's study of the fiftieth chapter of Edward Gibbon's *Rise and Fall of the Roman Empire* led him to view the first woe as beginning in 1299.[93] He confirmed this theory by learning from Vincent Mignot's *History of the Turkish, or Ottoman Empire* that 1449 was the year when the leader of the Eastern Church first required the consent of the Turkish Sultan, an event that symbolized to him the end of the Greek ascendancy and therefore of the 150-year duration of the fifth trumpet. Litch found this prophecy to be "the most remarkable and definite, (even descending to the days) of any in the Bible, relating to these great events."[94] When 11 August 1840 – the date set by Miller and his associates as the day that Turkey would fall – passed without apparent incident, Josiah Litch waited to hear the news arriving from the East. He learned that on that day, Mehemet Ali – the Pasha of Egypt who had been warring against the Sultan – had refused to accede to peace terms dictated by several European powers thus guaranteeing their support of the Ottoman Empire. Litch reasoned that this event, so similar to the circumstances he viewed as ending the fifth trumpet in 1449, signalized the moment when Ottoman sovereignty fell irretrievably into Christian hands and thus fulfilled the prophecy of the passing of the second woe. In *An Address to the Public* in 1841, Litch exhorted his listeners that the time of the end would arrive within the next three years. "But rest assured, dear reader, when you see the Turkish empire fall, that it [the third woe] is nigh, even at the door" to which he added a note in the published version: "It has now fallen."[95]

When Litch employed this apparent success at prophetic interpretation to alert a wider audience to the Second Coming scheduled to appear in 1844, some critics finally became vociferous in their opposition to his reasoning. One "Cosmopolite," who himself could see no definite reference to Islam in the verses describing the fifth trumpet, sardonically wrote that Litch's ingenuity in applying elements of the Turkish theory was "forced, strained and unnatural."[96] Others thought the notion that the Ottoman Empire had crumbled was preposterous because it in fact had been preserved by the combined actions of the European powers.[97] Litch tried to dispose of such

---

[93] Miller's waffling on this date was enough to convince one critic that Miller was a false prophet. See Otis Ainsworth Skinner, *The Theory of William Miller Concerning the End of the World in 1843 Utterly Exploded* (Boston: T. Whittemore, 1840), 185–6.

[94] Josiah Litch, *The Probability of the Second Coming of Christ* (Boston: David H. Ela, 1838), 154–8.

[95] Josiah Litch, *An Address to the Public and Especially the Clergy on the Near Approach of the Glorious, Everlasting Kingdom of God on Earth* (Boston: Joshua Himes, 1841), 117–25, 131. The same argument is put forward in a lecture that Litch delivered in Lowell in June 1841 that was published as *Dissertation on the Fall of the Ottoman Empire, the 11th of August, 1840* (1841).

[96] [By a Cosmopolite], *Miller Overthrown* (Boston: A. Thompkins), 92.

[97] Arguing in the interests of "an insulted and indignant community," James A. Hazen gave this retort: "With all their parade of history, are they so grossly ignorant as not to know that the interference

critics by asserting that the "re-organization" of the Ottoman Empire in 1840 had made it "to all intents and purposes, a Christian government, and is only ruled nominally by the sultan, as their vassal."[98] Imagining the fall of Ottoman power thus played an important part in Millerite thinking about the near approach of the Second Advent and the Adventist movement adopted it as an official dogma.[99] Historian Eric Anderson sees the strategy that the Millerites used to affirm the ending of the Turkish woe in 1840 as a model of how they would later deal with the "Great Disappointment" of Christ's apparent failure to return to earth four years later.[100]

The logic with which the Millerites framed the place of the Ottoman Turks in their millennial aspirations was remarkably similar to how the Mathers had imagined the same results almost a century and a half earlier, despite the historical changes in Ottoman power and the increased Western access to Turkey. Their common ingenuity in figuring the fate of Turkey by aligning the phantasms of Revelation with the political fortunes of the Sultan's realms dramatizes the durable power of the eschatological imagination in the formation of early American evangelical desire. This discursive tradition enabled Protestants to deal with the troubling intransigence of Islam by inventing a divinely ordained reason for its existence that served to confirm Christian power. The projective power of islamicist eschatology provided an effective biblical means of assuring Christian adherents of a teleological resolution to the problem of Islam. Eschatology, however, was a failure as a means of understanding the realities of Islamic religion and Muslim cultures. To grasp its limitations as a mode of intercultural interpretation, it is revealing to examine how this system of religious intelligence affected Protestant American evangelism in the eastern Mediterranean as missionaries were called back to the field following the Greek War of Independence.

of one kingdom . . . in the affairs of another, has been of frequent occurrence . . . do these men know these facts, or do they not? If they do not, what wonderful expositors of the prophecies must they be!" *The False Alarm* (Springfield, MA: Wood & Rupp, 1842), 9. Enoch Pond argued that "every child that looks into the newspapers" could see that the Ottoman Empire still stood, and, like Hazen, argued that the events of 1840 strengthened rather than subverted its existence, and went on to ask, "How is it that intelligent men and women can be led away by a theory, which is contradicted, as this is, by plain matters of fact?" *Millerism Destroyed* (Boston: S. N. Dickinson, 1842), 52–3.

[98] Josiah Litch, *Prophetic Expositions*, 2 vols. (Boston: Joshua V. Himes, 1842), 1: 190–1. Litch also cites a letter from William Goodell, missionary in Constantinople, which was published in the *Missionary Herald* and avers that "[t]he power of Islamism is broken forever" and that "they exist by mere sufferance" (189–90). See also Litch, *Dissertation on the Fall*, 9–10.

[99] Ellen G. White, in *The Great Controversy*, avers that Litch's Turkish calculation was "another remarkable fulfillment of prophecy," which "[w]hen it became known, multitudes were convinced of the correctness of the principles of prophetic interpretation adopted by Miller and his associates, and a wonderful impetus was given to the Advent Movement." (Nashville: Southern Publishing, 1911), 334–5.

[100] Eric Anderson, "The Millerite Use of Prophecy: A Case Study of a 'Striking Fulfilment,'" in *The Disappointed: Millerism and Millenarianism in the Nineteenth Century*, eds. Ronald L. Numbers and Jonathan M. Butler (Bloomington and Indianapolis: Indiana University Press, 1987), 78–91.

AMERICAN MISSIONS TO MUSLIMS IN THE 1830S AND 1840S

While William Miller was busy plotting the demise of the Ottoman Empire in prophecy, missionaries in the Near East redoubled their efforts with revived confidence that their efforts would bring on massive conversion and apocalyptical success. Missionaries who had taken refuge in Malta eagerly returned in the early 1830s to new missions in Syria and Constantinople under the protection of American government ministers and military officials posted in the eastern Mediterranean. Political changes in the Ottoman Empire had allowed more Western access to Turkey since Fisk and Parsons had first entered the field with what Eli Smith had acknowledged as "fear and trembling."[101] The French colonization of Algeria, the success of the Greeks in gaining their independence, and the institution of Ottoman political reforms (such as state support for transportation, communication, and education) opened doors for safer traffic to Levantine lands. The decimation in 1826 of the Sultan's janissaries, the destruction of the Turkish fleet in the Battle of Navarino, and the advance of the Egyptian army under Ibrahim Pasha into Palestine and Anatolia during the 1830s dramatized the weakness of the military resources of the Sublime Porte and its need to open avenues to the West for new sources of revenue. The eschatological belief in the evaporation of Islam combined with the emergence of a milder political climate in Turkey to generate a fervent resolve to reaniminate missions to Muslims. Historian Charles Foster gave the name "world-conquest fever" to this enthusiastic craze of domestic support for foreign missions during the years 1830–7.[102] In the eyes of Protestant missionaries, Islam was still the most prominent religious impediment in the way of this evangelical conquest of the world – but it was showing cracks in its armor and this apparent weakness emboldened a new surge of American missionary efforts to evangelize the followers of Islam.

Early American Protestants were embarrassed by the rituals of the Eastern churches and saw their Byzantine belief in saints and relics as a central obstacle that prevented Muslims – who they rightly believed viewed such practices as idolatry – from perceiving the merits of Protestant salvation. To them, the decrepitude of the Eastern denominations was demonstrable evidence of both the tyrannical oppression of Islam and the corruptions in Christianity that had fostered its rise. The ABCFM decided that the most pragmatic way to convince the Turk of the Gospel's continuing validity was to focus on the rehabilitation of these groups, especially the Armenians of Turkey and the Nestorians of Persia. Although millennial hopes of the conversion of Muslims (and eventually Jews) remained firm, the cultural,

101 Eli Smith, *Missionary Sermons and Addresses* (Boston: Perkins and Marvin, 1833), 211.
102 Charles Foster, *An Errand of Mercy: The Evangelical United Front, 1790–1837* (Chapel Hill: University of North Carolina Press, 1960), 210, 214–15.

political, and theological challenges of developing an effective dialogue with Muslims were pragmatically evaded by ministering to them indirectly by evangelizing the adherents of the Eastern churches. These denominations comprised minority communities in the Ottoman Empire who were more accepting of what the Protestants had to offer: if not their theology, then at least their publications, educational facilities, and medical knowledge.

Ten years after the passing of Parsons and Fisk, Eli Smith, translator of the Bible into Arabic and author of *Researches in Armenia* (a travel narrative used assiduously by the ABCFM in their strategic planning), declared: "The reformation of Christians seems an almost indispensable preliminary to the conversion of Moslems."[103] This approach was expressed in the American Board's 1839 "Instruction to Missionaries" which urged those in the field to regard missions to the Oriental Churches "as so many missions to the followers of the False Prophet."[104] Missionaries felt that if these nominal Christians could be liberated from their superstitions and express the true spirit of Christianity then "the Gospel might soon be proclaimed in its purity and power to the millions of Mohammedans who are pressing their way down to death."[105] Isaac Bird surmised that if the Muslim "adversary" could be convinced that Christianity and idolatry were incompatible, then "he might easily be persuaded to become a defender . . . of the Christian name," enabling "the gaining of a great nation" – a reference to the biblical promise granted the descendents of Ishmael.[106] "May not the day of its downfall [i.e. the 'monstrous heresy' of Islam]," wrote Episcopal missionary Horatio Southgate as he linked the removal of Islam with the glory of the apocalypse, "be that which shall see the Church in those lands restored to her pristine purity, and looking forth again, fair as the moon, clear as the sun, and terrible as an army with banners?"[107]

---

[103] Eli Smith, *Researches of the Rev. E. Smith and Rev. H. G. O. Dwight in Armenia*, 2 vols. (Boston: Crocker and Brewster, 1833), 2: 304. In a sermon called "Moral and Religious Conditions of Western Asia," Smith calls the reform of native Christians "a preparatory step by which to get access to the judgment and hearts of Moslems." Although he acknowledged this ultimate goal as "somewhat distant indeed," he views the presence of these Christians as a "door" to reaching the Muslims. "Reform the ungodly lives of the native Christians," exhorted Smith, "and the main support of Mohammedanism is gone; it must fall." *Missionary Sermons and Addresses*, 79.

[104] *Missionary Herald* (September 1839), quoted in James Thayer Addison, *The Christian Approach to the Moslem: A Historical Study* (New York: Columbia University Press, 1942), 94.

[105] David T. Stoddard, *Narrative of the Revival of Religion among the Nestorians*, 2nd ed. (Boston: ABCFM, 1848), 35–6.

[106] Bird, *Bible Work*, 16. "The Moslem will then have a true standard by which to test the Bible and the Koran; and it is not too much to hope that even he, surrounded by such influences, will be brought to lay down his native barbarity and put on the spirit of Christ." The Rev. S. W. Fisher, A. M., "The Turk and His Dominions," in *The Missionary Memorial: A Literary and Religious Souvenir* (New York: E. Walker, 1846), 247.

[107] Horatio Southgate, *Narrative of a Tour through Armenia, Kurdistan, Persia and Mesopotamia*, 2 vols. (New York: D. Appleton & Co., 1840), 2: 298. In imagining the triumph of Jerusalem's beauty, Southgate here quotes from the Song of Solomon 6:10.

These openings prompted the American Board to envision expanding its stations beyond the Mediterranean littoral, and as a result they initiated "Christian Researches," or exploratory journeys, deep into the Asian continent for the purpose of locating areas for future evangelical effort.[108] The first fruit of these ventures was the tour by Eli Smith and H. G. O. Dwight east out of Constantinople to Armenia and into Persia. The publication of Smith's *Researches in Armenia* in 1833 helped to heighten interest in the populations lying east of the Ottomans and encouraged the ABCFM to establish a mission to the Nestorian Christians living in northwest Persia. Smith delivered an address that same year at a meeting of the ABCFM in which he chose to focus on the topic "The Present Attitude of Mohammedanism, in Reference to the Spread of the Gospel." Smith viewed Islam as a "curse to man" whose oppression had blasted any chance of prosperity from visiting the rich lands of Asia Minor. Although Smith admitted that he did not want to raise expectations too high, he felt that "providential preparation" had set in motion changes that were "liberalizing" and "humbling the wall of arrogance" that had prevented earlier access to Turkish Muslims. "I have seen the wrath of the Turk restrained," he testified.[109] Smith ironically viewed the new interest of the Ottomans in Western military technology as having opened doors to renewed missionary efforts. Chastising his audience with the fact that those in the dark ages had been able to muster whole armies to challenge Muslim hegemony, Smith urged his listeners to enter these emerging fields so there might be "some one . . . ever at hand to throw the light of divine truth into the opening mind of every Mohammedan inquirer."[110]

Smith's researches and sermons reflected the optimism of the missionary movement in the 1830s and its conviction that it would soon be successful in evangelizing the world. The American Sunday School Union refocused attention on the exploits of British evangelist Henry Martyn, who had preceded Parsons and Fisk to Muslim lands dispensing his translations

---

[108] The model of this approach was the Christian Missionary Society's publication of William Jewett's *Christian Researches in the Mediterranean* in 1824 that reflects on the "deeply painful" fact of the continued prevalence of Islam in the region.

[109] Eli Smith noted these changes in a sermon Published as *Trials of Missionaries*, given in 1832 at the departure for the Holy Land of Elias Riggs, William Thomson, and Dr. Asa Dodge, that "[t]he Turks are so kept in check by fear of the power and vengeance of Christian nations, that, where you go, your life will rarely, if ever, be endangered by their wrath" (Boston: Crocker and Brewster, 1832), 8. The influence of Smith's points can be seen in a sermon called "The Aspect of the Age, with Respect to Foreign Missions": "Let the spirit of inquiry once be diffused and the refinements of European habits and character become popular, and the absurdity of the Moslem faith must and will be exchanged." *The Princeton Review* 5 (October 1833): 454.

[110] Eli Smith, *Missionary Sermons*, 29, 211, 228, 218. According to Smith, raising the standard of revolt where Satan "reigns lord paramount of all" required a courageous assurance to "exhort them [the Turks] to renounce their hereditary veneration for the Koran."

of the New Testament in Hindi and Persian. Martyn provided an inspirational model of a contemporary apostle who selflessly sacrificed his life to spreading the truths of the Bible in Asia. Martyn, who died on 16 October 1812 in the town of Tocat in eastern Turkey, was lionized in popular memoirs – much as the Quaker maiden Mary Fisher had been – for his devotion and courage in upholding Christian truths in dangerous situations. One biographical vignette presented Martyn responding to a Vizier's inquiry whether he believed that "God is God and Mahomet is the Prophet of God" with the unflinching retort "God is God and Jesus is the Son of God."[111] Another biographer noted that as a result of Martyn's audacity, "the imposture of the prophet of Mecca was boldly exposed, and the truths of Christianity openly vindicated, in the very heart and centre of a Mohammedan empire."[112]

Eli Smith's exhortations and Henry Martyn's efforts encouraged missionary boards to undertake new exploratory missions to determine the readiness of Muslims to receive the light of the Protestant Gospel. Examining the careers of two American missionaries who experienced strong callings to carry the Christian message deep into the interior of the Islamic orient reveals the powerful influence of the eschatological myth that Islam was nothing but an insubstantial error to be swept aside by Christian fact. The Presbyterian James Lyman Merrick and the Episcopalian Horatio Southgate were both inspired to evangelize the Muslims, and each journeyed into Persia under the aegis of their respective denominational boards for foreign missions. A comparison of their experiences dramatizes in different ways how actual encounters with Islam as a persistent religious tradition frustrated traditional hopes in its prophetic removal.

THE PROFESSIONAL DISAPPOINTMENT OF JAMES LYMAN MERRICK

James Lyman Merrick became enchanted by the sound of the word "Persia" while writing a poem as a sixteen-year-old "unknown ploughboy." By the time he was a senior at Amherst College, Merrick believed he had been "chosen by the great Captain of Salvation to plant the standard of the cross on the high lands and the lovely vales of Persia." The day he gained admission into Princeton Theological Seminary, Merrick charted a plan to "*preach*

---

[111] Miss Grierson, *Memoirs of the Rev. Henry Martyn* (Philadelphia: American Sunday School Union, 1825), 93. John Hall, *The Life of Rev. Henry Martyn* (Philadelphia: American Sunday School Union, 1832), 135.

[112] Rev. John Sargent, *A Memoir of the Rev. Henry Martyn . . .*, from the Tenth London edition (Boston: Perkins & Marvin, 1831), 385. Eli Smith wrote that "his artillery was that of heaven; and it shook the foundations of the ancient structure of Islam." "The Aspect of the Age," 453.

up . . . a holy crusade to Mahomedan Persia" that would "lay open for easy conquest the whole Mahomedan world."[113] Merrick devoted great efforts to this career and never abandoned his calling even after his plans were ultimately frustrated.

When illness forced him out of Princeton during in his first semester there, Merrick persevered in his seminary training by seeking out the more temperate climate of Union Presbytery Southern in Charleston, South Carolina. There Merrick's daily prayers remained focused on "my beloved Persians." His persistence at exhorting Christians to act on behalf of the "perishing Persians" eventually landed him a commission from the ABCFM as a Missionary to the Mohammedans of Western Asia.[114] Merrick was instructed to present "the truth, as it is in Jesus" directly to the Muslims "divested of superstitions and profane rites, and of all that paralizes [sic] its power upon the conscience and heart." To this ultimate end, Merrick was charged with the duty of *"collect[ing] information concerning the character and condition of the Mohammedans of Persia and Central Asia"* in order to *"ascertain where it is expedient for the Board to form missionary stations."* Merrick was expected to learn the Turkish, Persian, and Arabic languages; to acquire an intimate understanding of Islam in its doctrinal and mystical forms; and to travel extensively through the cities of Persia and, if possible, beyond to cities in Central Asia such as Kandahar, Kabul, and Peshawar, where the mysterious "kings of the east" may be awaiting the stimulus of the Gospel to play their prophetic parts.[115]

Merrick arrived in Turkey in November of 1834 and settled in Constantinople where for two years he studied languages while seeking an associate with whom he would travel to Persia. He wrote urgent letters to the American Board encouraging the seminaries to send out other missionaries to the Turks of both Constantinople and Broosa. Despite Merrick's insistence in letters to "no longer neglect the Mohammedans" and the American Board's call that it was of the "utmost importance" that someone arise to help in what they called "a difficult and somewhat hazardous, but momentous enterprize," no companion was sent to assist him.[116]

---

[113] The influence of prophecy can be seen in Merrick's statement that "truly I expect that many will be convinced that a glorious day is coming in Persia, before the year 1840 closes on the world . . . yet I hope, I trust, that *christian hearts* will beat [and burn] in *Persian bosoms* ere many years have sped their flight." Merrick's focus on the year 1840 seems to demonstrate his familiarity with the theories of William Miller. Merrick, James Lyman, Diaries, Alumni Class Shelves, Class of 1830, Archives & Special Collections, Amherst College Library, Amherst, MA.

[114] *The Missionary Herald* 30 (1834): 237, 351.

[115] "Instructions of the Prudential Committee, to the Rev. James Lyman Merrick," *The Missionary Herald* 30 (1834): 402–5. The American Board may have expected a document similar in scope and insight to Eli Smith's and H. G. O. Dwight's *Researches in Armenia* that was responsible for the American Board's decision to set up a mission to the Nestorians in Persia.

[116] *The Missionary Herald* 31 (1835): 366–8; 32 (1836): 9–10, 165–6.

Merrick did receive assistance, however, in the form of a series of twenty letters written by a German-born missionary William S. Schauffler, who had been educated at Andover and had himself planned a mission to Muslims in 1826 that included preparations for the journey to Persia that Merrick was to take ten years later.[117] Schauffler's advice to the idealistic young missionary apparently played a significant role in maturing Merrick's views of the preparation and resolve required by a mission to "the followers of the false prophet." Schauffler provided Merrick with a course of study designed to prepare him to teach Muslims effectively, including Qur'anic verses that he could employ in his "conversations" to refute Islam.[118] Perhaps sensing that Merrick's devotion to his vocation exceeded his understanding of its difficulties, Schauffler instructed his charge to be more calm and deliberate in his preparations and to expect results only from "a slow and sober process of experience." Schauffler expressed his scorn for the "beau ideal" that many Americans had of the missionary that placed him "upon the highest gravestone . . . to proclaim with a loud voice the terms of salvation." Such fanaticism lacked Paul's "delicate regard" for the social institutions he came across, Schauffler believed, and would only result in a martyrdom that would "shut up a thousand doors of usefulness." Schauffler specifically counseled Merrick to bear his responsibility to God alone and not be tempted to write "fair representations" back to the American Board to justify his mission, but rather "to write home plain truth, whether it be sweet or bitter."[119]

Schauffler himself viewed evangelizing the Jews and Muslims as fields that were "parched and forbidding above most others, if not above all." He was especially repulsed by Islamic scripture and claimed: "the dry dead Koran is perhaps the most powerful positive obstacle to the promotion of religion among the Muslims."[120] Despite the difficulties of Merrick's mission, Schauffler was ultimately cheered by the eschatological decomposition of Islam that promised to open timely new doors for the doing of wonders. In expressing this hope, he expanded the figures of the fifth trumpet to

---

[117] William Schauffler, *Autobiography* (New York: Anson D. F. Randolph & Co., 1887), 25.

[118] William S. Schauffler, "Thoughts on the Hints and Cautions of Goodell, Dwight, and Temple to Merrick, 25 August 1836," ABCFM Papers, Houghton Library of Harvard University, Unit 5 (16.5), especially letters 3, 13 and 14.

[119] Schauffler, "Thoughts," 257, 211, 256.

[120] Schauffler, "Thoughts," 224, 354. Schauffler's "instinctive horror" in responding to the Qur'an's "mess of nonsense, of ambiguities, or indecencies, and . . . intolerable repetitions" was a common refrain in criticizing the Muslim holy text (256). Jonas King, who left his professorship at Amherst to serve out his life as a missionary to the Greeks, claimed "the beauties of the Koran consist principally in the language, in the fine jingle of words which it is utterly impossible to convey through the medium of any European language. But I cannot conceive that any man of decent morals and of good understanding, who admires thoughts rather than words, should ever leave the Bible for the Koran. This would be leaving a pure crystal fountain, to drink out of a dirty slough; . . . The Bible is as much above the Koran . . . as the heavens are higher than the earth." Haines, *Jonas King*, 163–4.

describe Islam as the past eruption of a volcano that left deposits of lava that still could be remolded into a new foundation.

> The bottomless pit spits no more flames on this side, it does not even emit a vapour; or a smoke. If I mistake not, it was quite time for you to come, and I trust you will be followed by many more. Now dig the foundation of that building which will stand forever. The lava is warm yet.[121]

Merrick took all this advice to heart, even as it confirmed his deep personal resolve to carry the Gospel to the Persians. On 15 October 1836 he accompanied Asahel Grant and his wife – who were beginning their medical mission to the mountain Nestorian Christians – on their journey to Tabriz in Persia. Like Merrick, Grant was fully convinced that the long night of the "persecuting Mohammedan beast" was over. He chose to brave the "stiff hauteur of the Turk" and minister to the Nestorians because he believed that that nation embodied the "kings of the East" who, liberated from Turkish control, would lead the march to Zion that would inaugurate the events of the end. Grant believed that the Nestorians' belief in the Bible ("the seals of God on their foreheads") had protected them from incursions of the Islamic locusts and preserved them to play their present role: "For who of God's servants, under Mohammedan domination, can with so much propriety be called 'the kings of the East' as 'the remnant of his people which shall be left in Assyria?' "[122]

Merrick's heart, however, was focused directly on the Muslims themselves. After studying Persian through the winter in Tabriz, Merrick joined up with two German missionaries and visited Tehran and Isfahan before settling in Shiraz for the winter. In the course of this trip, Merrick lost any innocent idealism about the readiness of Muslims to accept Christian salvation. Merrick's communications to the American Board were candid. The lava did not appear to be very yielding. Public evangelism was a dangerous enterprise that increased Persian resistance to Christianity. More importantly, Merrick's obedience to his instructions "to become intimately conversant with Mohammedanism" had caused him to reassess the common attitude held by Schauffler and others that Islam and its teachings were nothing more than a "powerless hush."[123] In this sensitive statement Merrick grasped part of the reason for the endurance of Islam.

> Perhaps the general impression in Europe and America respecting Mohammedanism is, that it is such a flimsy, frostwork structure, that a few rays of science, a smattering of literature, or a modicum of the arts would annihilate it at once. Whatever may have been the origin of the materials of

---

[121] Schauffler, "Thoughts," 330–1.

[122] Asahel Grant, *The Nestorians; or, the Lost Tribes* (New York: Harper & Brothers, 1841), 322, 54, 353.

[123] Schauffler, "Thoughts," 224.

Mohammedanism, they have been so artfully built on truth, and cemented by excellent sentiments, that the fabric, the more I examine it, appears in every joint and angle a master-piece of skill and power. If I should take my own experience as a criterion, I should say that few have understood Mohammedanism, who have not bestowed laborious research on the subject. The small advantages I have hitherto enjoyed to arrive at the truth of the case, only convince me, that it is a "bottomless pit," not easily fathomed or filled up.[124]

By revising the traditional meaning of the "bottomless pit" and applying it to Christians' own inability to appreciate Islam adequately, Merrick challenged the eschatological status quo and displayed an appreciation of Islam as a religious system that other Americans of his era were incapable of perceiving.

Unfortunately, this sensitivity was not the intelligence that the ABCFM was looking for. The American Board learned from the "tenor" and "tone" of Merrick's letters that the prospect of a direct mission to the "Perso-Mohammedans" was "by no means favorable."[125] As early as 1836, the American Board believed that "the set time to favor Persia has [not] yet come" and began to consider other fields in which Merrick might serve.[126] Merrick continued his mission by focusing on three important areas: "translation, literary and scientific instruction, and general religious influence."[127] He carried on his discussion with Persians on sacred subjects and even negotiated with Persian government officials for the formation of schools. During his time in the field, Merrick translated into English a Persian biography of the prophet Muhammad, the "Hyât-ul-Kuloob" (The Life of Hearts), and into Persian an astronomy text and an edition of Alexander Keith's biblical commentary, *Evidences of Prophecy*, a work that espoused the eschatology of the Turkish theory.[128]

However, the American Board desired neither translations nor schools from Merrick's exploratory mission. It refused to support a school in Tabriz

---

[124] "Letter from Mr. Merrick, dated at Oroomiah, June 19, 1837" in *The Missionary Herald*, 34 (1838): 64.

[125] See the Annual Reports of the ABCFM for 1838 and 1839 in *The Missionary Herald* 34 (1838): 7; 35 (1839), 7–8.

[126] Rev. J. L. Merrick, *An Appeal to the American Board of Commissioners for Foreign Missions* (Springfield, MA: John Wood, 1847), 26.

[127] Merrick, *Appeal*, 9. Merrick came to be known of by the Shah of Iran who called him "a Man of God and a Man of Science."

[128] After the ABCFM refused to publish Merrick's translation of the "Hyât-ul-Kuloob," it was published by Phillips, Sampson of Boston in 1850. An article on Muhammad in *The North American Review* in October of 1850 reviews Merrick's book alongside Washington Irving's *Mahomet and His Successors*. For the references to Islam in the work he translated, see Alexander Keith, *Evidence of the Truth of the Christian Religion Derived from the Literal Fulfillment of Prophecy* (New York: Harper & Brothers, 1839), 247–7, 269–73.

to be administered by Merrick "where it would be regarded a violation of good faith to teach the Gospel of our Lord and Savior Jesus Christ directly to the pupils."[129] His marriage to an English missionary, Emma Taylor, in March of 1839 signaled to the American Board that his further travels in Persia and Central Asia would be curtailed. On 5 November 1839, Secretary Anderson wrote Merrick to notify him that the Prudential Committee had terminated his mission to the Muslims of Persia and requested that he and his wife join the mission to the Nestorian Christians in Urumiah. With great reluctance, they finally moved there in September 1842, where they served until February of 1845, when they were recalled, apparently in part for Merrick's unwillingness to abandon the Muslims as the primary focus of his mission.[130]

The American Board's decisions stunned Merrick and eventually led to a severance of their relationship. Believing that he had been unjustly treated, Merrick published a 125-page "Appeal to the American Board of Commissioners for Foreign Missions" two years after his return.[131] Merrick had followed Schauffler's advice to be forthright with the Committee with the result that he had been accused of "dwelling on the dark side," hamstringing any success in attracting an aspiring associate into the field. "My own acts are turned against my hopes," he voiced in despair.[132] Merrick was so deeply committed to ministering to the Muslims that, even after the American Board suggested a resignation and honorable discharge, he begged the Committee to "restore me to the people for whom my heart's desire and prayer to God is that they may be saved."[133] His services rejected, Merrick could only find solace once again in the divine promise that even if the ABCFM might "conclude to abandon a people as given up by God," the prophetic scheme had a different agenda. Merrick remained assured that the divine will was "carrying forward a providential work among the people of my choice and tender interest, which no resolution of missionary organs can repress." He testified: "The way of truth is preparing, and if neither you nor I lift a finger to remove obstructions, the great wheel of providential events will not be stopped, even should we be misguided enough to throw ourselves before its slow but irresistible progress."[134] While intending to belittle the Board that had meddled with his calling, this passionate metaphor – alluding to the relentless progress of the Hindu chariot known as the Juggernaut – also

---

[129] Annual Report for 1840 in *The Missionary Herald* 36 (1840): 8.

[130] For an account of a mission to evangelize directly the Muslims of India in the year of Merrick's recall, see Stanley E. Brush, "Presbyterianism and Islam in the Orient," *Journal of Presbyterian History* 62 (Fall 1984): 215–23; Elwood Wherry, *Our Missions in India, 1834–1924* (Boston: Stratford, 1926), 62.

[131] Merrick prefaced his appeal with Isaiah 59:4: "I have laboured in vain, I have spent my strength for nought, and in vain; yet surely my judgment is with the Lord, and my work with my God."

[132] Merrick, *Appeal,* 45.   [133] Merrick, *Appeal,* 111.

[134] "Letter to Rufus Anderson dated May 19, 1845," in Merrick, *Appeal,* 82.

dramatized the irresistible power of eschatological fatalism itself. Merrick ended his appeal by quoting the dream of Henry Martyn taken from Revelation 16:12 that he had hoped to help bring about: "The way of the kings of the East is preparing; thus much may be said with safety, but little more. The Persians will also probably take the lead in the march to Zion."[135]

THE FAILED CRUSADE OF HORATIO SOUTHGATE

The contrasting story of Horatio Southgate dramatizes both the exalted desires for Christian conquest and important transformations in missionary approaches to Muslims between the 1830s and the 1850s. Similar to Merrick (whom he met in Persia in July of 1837), Southgate in 1835 developed an ardent desire to evangelize the Muslims directly. But while Merrick never gave up his calling to preach to the Persians even after his career precluded it, Southgate's changing passions replicated important changes in the missionary enterprise during this period. By 1850, Southgate had come to reject the fundamental assumption that human effort in the field was necessary to bring on the hoped-for millennium.

A graduate of Bowdoin College, Southgate was raised as a Congregationalist, but he converted to Anglicanism while attending Andover Seminary and was ordained as a Deacon at Trinity Church in Boston in 1835. Southgate soon offered his services to the Foreign Missions Committee of the Protestant Episcopal Church because he was "thoroughly convinced that the time has come for a successful attack on the religion of the false prophet."[136] In 1836, Southgate traveled to Turkey and Persia to prepare the way for the establishment of missionary stations whose labors would lead to the "complete subversion of Islamism," an important step in the conversion of the world to Christianity.[137]

In a sermon called "Encouragement to Missionary Effort among Mohamedans," which he delivered just prior to his departure, Southgate exhorted his listeners: "The one hundred and fifty millions who are in bondage to the false and pernicious faith of the Koran look to you" and enumerated several reasons why he believed that the time was right for "a successful aggression" upon the Islamic world. Although Southgate paid little explicit attention to prophecy – which he felt was comprised of "appeals" that "might engender a groundless and ephemeral zeal" – the eschatological heritage nevertheless influenced what he called his "rational

---

[135] Merrick, *Appeal*, 125. Merrick's life-long devotion to his calling is manifested in his bequests to the educational institutions he attended in support of the study of the Persian language.

[136] Southgate to George Boyd, 9 November 1835. Horatio Southgate Papers, Manuscripts and Archives, Yale University Library, New Haven, CT. For an introduction to Southgate's writings, see Kenneth Walter Cameron, "The Manuscripts of Horatio Southgate – A Discovery," *American Church Monthly* 152 (October 1937): 155–73.

[137] "Letter to Rev. J. A. Clark, March 28, 1836," in *The Spirit of Missions* 1 (April 1836): 112.

and abiding conviction of duty."[138] Southgate asserted that, despite the centrality of the Islamic world as the "great thoroughfare" between Europe and Eastern Asia, Muslims had been "almost entirely neglected by the Christian church" and that it was time to send a new group of Protestant crusaders armed only with the sword of the Holy Word.[139] Southgate believed that Persian Muslims were intelligent and willing to engage in religious inquiry and saw signs of hope in Eli Smith's observations of the desires of Turks to imitate the arts and manners of Christian nations.[140] Southgate's understanding of Islamic belief and culture encouraged him also to believe that Qur'anic references to Christ would allow missionaries greater access to Muslims, who would reject Islam as a false system of external rites when shown its "scientific errors." "Let the Church send the unadulterated Gospel directly to the Mohamedans," preached Southgate, "and when they shall have bowed to its authority, how soon will the candlestick of the LORD be restored to its place in the fallen Churches of Asia!" Southgate figured the Islamic world as "a ruined fortress entrenched by a high mound and a deep mote. Throw a bridge over the moat, scale the mound, and the fortress is our own. If we can but gain a stand-point within the entrenchments of Mohamedan prejudice, we have little to fear from a religion which exerts so feeble a control over the mind, is so corrupted by superstition, and so weakened by defection."[141] Southgate imagined the missionary as a conquering crusader and his sermon demonstrates how the rhetoric of millennialism articulated a vision of Christian imperialism, one popular enough to elicit donations of two thousand dollars at a meeting at the Church of the Ascension in New York three weeks prior to his departure for Constantinople.

Exactly four years after he left for Turkey, Southgate had retreated to New York to finish the preface of his two-volume *Narrative of a Tour through Armenia, Kurdistan, Persia and Mesopotamia*. His intervening experience in the Near East had forced him to reevaluate his ardent beliefs about the readiness of Muslims to convert to Protestantism. Southgate had made the error

---

[138] *Encouragement to Missionary Effort among Mohamedans* (New York: Protestant Episcopal Press, 1836), 25, 30, 32, 26.

[139] Southgate's official instructions read: "Your mission will be directed immediately to the adherents of the false prophet in Persia . . . a very distant and almost untried field . . . Little direct effort, however, appears to have been since [the death of Henry Martyn] made for their conversion; and while this degrading system seems crumbling under the influence of the gradual spread of science and the arts, and the worldly policy of human rulers, the Church has been criminally tardy in putting forth her efforts for its demolition" included in *Encouragement to Missionary Effort*, 35–7. The Foreign Missions Committee testified: "We believe that no Mission to foreign lands has ever commenced with stronger encouragement or brighter prospects." "Mission to the Mohammedans," *The Spirit of Missions* 1 (February 1836): 52.

[140] "Perhaps no people excel the Persians in the higher qualities of intellectual character" Southgate asserted, "no unevangelized people are so intelligent and capable of receiving knowledge as the Mohamedans." *Encouragement to Missionary Effort*, 9, 10.

[141] Southgate, *Encouragement to Missionary Effort*, 8, 18–19.

of most of his generation of misinterpreting the apparent decrease of bigotry of Muslims in the Ottoman Empire as a sign of the waning of their faith in Islam. "At the end of my first month's residence in Constantinople, I might have promulgated my opinions on Turkish institutions and customs with the utmost confidence," confessed Southgate: "At the end of three months, I began to perceive the fallacy of most of my conclusions, and when six months had passed, I found that I knew next to nothing of the object of my study."[142] Part of Southgate's difficulty in fathoming Islam rested with his naive belief that he could easily equip himself with the linguistic capacities to carry out his explorations.[143] Like Merrick, he was surprised by "the comprehensive idea of religion" that he found in Islam (which he translated as "Devotedness to God"), a "genius" that accepted the divine origins of the Old and New Testaments and minutely explored its own traditions in an extensive heritage of religious commentary.[144] Such "factitious excellencies" ultimately convinced him of the degree of devotion with which Muslims held the forms of their religion. Despite Southgate's exalted intentions to engage in "Christian research" that would plot out a wholesale assault on Islam, his narrative ultimately expresses his perplexity about how to accomplish such an end.[145] In a letter from Constantinople written in 1843, Southgate's exasperation when debating Persians was evident in his own reference to the bottomless pit. He found the Persian to be a "wily antagonist" who "likes nothing better than to display his subtlety in disputing about essences, substances, and spirits...a metaphysical chaos, where there is neither shore nor bottom."[146] In short, Southgate desired a deeper understanding of Islam than he was capable or willing to gain. The shift in his metaphors from crumbling fortress to fathomless chaos reflected his own growing sense of Islam as a persistent religious mystery despite the decaying political system that surrounded it.

His desire to learn the truth encouraged him to assume Eastern clothing and mingle with the peoples of the lands he visited, voicing his willingness "to throw off those antipathies which the Christian world has too freely cherished against the followers of Mohammed, and to regard them as men and immortal."[147] This charity enabled him to glimpse some of the depths with which Muslims held their religious beliefs, owning that "I have

---

[142] Southgate, *Narrative of a Tour,* 1: 72.

[143] Southgate himself admitted: "Without a knowledge of his own, he [the missionary] cannot contemplate that perfect picture of the Eastern mind which appears in the language" (1: 185). Like Merrick, Southgate was frustrated in his expectation that a partner would arise to accompany him in his tour. He had wanted a partner well-versed in the Persian language and was forced to try to learn the language himself while in the field. The editors of *The Spirit of Missions* published extracts from Merrick's letters to apprise its readers of the difficulties that awaited Southgate. 2 (April 1837): 115–20.

[144] Southgate, *Narrative of a Tour,* 1: 9, 141, 17.   [145] Southgate, *Narrative of a Tour,* 1: 113.

[146] "On Missionary Efforts among the Mohammedans," *The Spirit of Missions* 9 (February 1844): 55.

[147] Southgate, *Narrative of a Tour,* 1: 73.

sometimes had my own mind quickened and benefitted by the reverence with which they spoke of the Deity."[148] After attending the Mosque of St. Sophia in Constantinople, he wrote "I had never witnessed greater solemnity in any Christian Church."[149] His most pronounced praise of Islam – one of its key contrasts with the Christian denominationalism that was spreading through the United States (which Southgate's Episcopal mission had itself fostered in the Eastern Mediterranean) – lauded the way that Muslims of all social classes forgot "all earthy distinctions" when they worshiped together. "The lowliest member of the community kneels side by side in the sanctuary, with the richest and the most powerful," observed Southgate; "There are no inferiors before God."[150] When he heard the verdict of a Muslim judge in favor of a wife who rejected her husband's polygamy – a practice he found rarely practiced in Turkey – Southgate praised Islam as a distinct improvement over paganism and chastised himself: "so gross did I find many of my former errors to be, that it seems to me now hardly less than a duty to acknowledge them."[151]

These surprising revelations about Islamic religious practice, while not able to dislodge Southgate's acquired belief that the spirit of Islam was "nearly extinct," did force him to shift the focus of his missionary endeavor. He no longer felt confident about his capacity to preach to the Muslims about Christian superiority and suffered from their "contempt and bigotry."[152] Early in his tour, Southgate had become "deeply excited" about the state of the Eastern churches (especially the Jacobite church of Mesopotamia), and by 1840 they had replaced Muslims as the goal of his evangelical effort.[153] In a letter published in 1844, Southgate explained that he had early been struck with the resemblance of the Oriental churches to Episcopalianism and that their oppression under the Muslims had fired his compassion and given him a new sense of duty.[154] Before his departure to the Near East, Southgate had firmly believed that "the great extension of Christianity among the Mohamedans would be the most powerful means to the enlightening and purifying of the corrupt Christian churches of the East." However, his

---

[148] Southgate, *Narrative of a Tour,* 1: 250–1. [149] *The Spirit of the Missions* 2 (May 1837): 146.

[150] Southgate, *Narrative of a Tour,* 1: 129–30. This attribute of Islam affected Southgate deeply. He also included mention of it in his 1879 novel, *The Cross above the Crescent,* claiming that "Christians might take a lesson, here, from the followers of Mohammed." (Philadelphia: J. P. Lippincott, 1878), 112–15.

[151] Southgate, *Narrative of a Tour,* 2: 202.

[152] Horatio Southgate, "Journal, August 5, 1840," *The Spirit of Missions* 6 (February 1841): 50.

[153] "While the author was pursuing his inquiries among the Mohammedans," Southgate wrote in the preface of his narrative, "he soon found his mind drawn, almost unconsciously, to the state of the Eastern Churches," *Narrative of a Tour,* 1: vi. For a discussion of the encounter between Southgate and a British traveler, see Charles MacFarlane, *Turkey and Its Destiny,* 2 vols. (Philadelphia: Lea and Blanchard, 1850), 1: 299.

[154] Southgate, *Vindication of the Rev. Horatio Southgate: A Letter to the Members of the Protestant Episcopal Church in the United States* (New York: Stafford and Swords, 1844), 16–17.

exposure to the intractability of Islam – as it had with many of the missionaries who preceded him – caused him to reverse his logic. He declared in his *Narrative of a Tour* that "it is impossible that [the Mohammedans] should in great numbers be converted to the faith of the Gospel, while Christianity appears before their eyes shorn of the beauty of holiness and stripped of her moral power."[155] As it had in the 1820s, the disunified state of Christianity again frustrated missions to the Muslims, a result that tended to confirm the belief that Islam existed as a result of corruption within the church.

When Southgate returned to Turkey in 1843, it was in the capacity of the "Missionary Bishop in the Dominions and Dependencies of the Sultan of Turkey" whose focus was the rejuvenation of "nominal Christians." His presence in Constantinople caused a great deal of denominational squabbling between the American Board and the Protestant Episcopal Church, especially over their respective claims and capacities to evangelize the Eastern churches with their respective brands of Christianity.[156] Nevertheless, by 1850, both Southgate and the Episcopal Church had abandoned their mission in Constantinople. One reason for this retraction can be clearly grasped by a sermon given by Southgate upon his return to Philadelphia in 1850. In "The Defects of the Present Foreign Mission Enterprise," Southgate assaulted its "false foundations," which, based on presumptive readings of prophecy, affirm that the "direct and immediate" instrumentality of missionaries is necessary to convert the world to Christian belief. Whether in part to justify his own abandonment of the missionary field or not, Southgate adopted a premillennialist stance that held that Christ's return would precede the conquest of the world. To expect such an end based on the accomplishments of missionaries seemed to Southgate nothing more than a "delusion by which their own minds are perverted." Southgate believed that such a fallacy would either exhaust their efforts or render "their hopes interpreters of their circumstances," resulting in exalted claims of success "that bear as romantic a character as the Arabian Nights' Entertainments."

---

[155] Southgate, *Narrative of a Tour*, 2: 297–8. Southgate nevertheless viewed this concern about the state of Eastern Christianity as "turning the current of my interest for the Mohammedans, not indeed away from them, but through a new channel and towards them still."

[156] Southgate believed strongly that the Episcopacy and the liturgy of his denomination offered a superior access to the Eastern churches, claiming "Congregationalism is a root which will not thrive in an Eastern soil" (Southgate, *Vindication*, 24). The American Board accused him of interfering with their efforts by using the trappings of Episcopalism to malign the efforts of the Congregationalists and to spread worry that they were attempting to cause an evangelical schism in the Armenian church. The American Board countered the publication of Southgate's *Vindication* with *Mr. Southgate and the Missionaries at Constantinople. A Letter from the Missionaries at Constantinople in Reply to the Charges by Rev. Horatio Southgate* (Boston: Crocker and Brewster, 1844); Southgate responded again with *A Letter to a Friend, in Reply to A Recent Pamphlet* (New York: D. Appleton; Philadelphia: George S. Appleton, 1845). There is no mention of any strategy of evangelizing the Muslims on any of the over 120 pages generated by this controversy.

Southgate argued that all the costly accoutrements of missions, including schools and printing presses, "will never succeed in subduing the world to Christ" because the millennium would be brought about only by Christ upon his return.[157]

THE CULTURAL TRAGEDY OF ESCHATOLOGICAL FATALISM

The termination of the missionary careers of Merrick and Southgate, callings that began with such ebullient hopes, reflect important changes in American evangelical approaches to the Muslim world. The rise in interdenominational competition in the missionary field and dissent about its direction and character shattered the unified evangelical front of the 1830s. The discredit into which the reading of the prophetic timetables fell after the Great Disillusionment of the Millerite movement qualified some of the vigor of expectation that had charged Americans before the 1840s. Decades of failures to rally large numbers of converts likewise challenged the commitment of missionaries to direct evangelical preaching and led to an increased reliance – for those permitted to remain in the field – on education, publication, and medicine as avenues to reach Eastern populations, cultural efforts that had lasting impact in the region and help to foster the rise of Arab nationalism.[158] The sense of eschatological expectation that was such a prominent motive in establishing the missionary movement became increasingly divorced from the apparatus of cultural uplift and more centered on a premillennial faith that Christ would return in his own time to bring on the millennium as a rapturous means of removing the corruption of religious belief.

Despite Southgate's retreat from the Orient, he never gave up his hopes that the religions of the East would be redeemed. However, his desires to purify the Eastern churches and subdue the Muslims took on the nostalgic form of romantic fiction. As a fifty-nine-year-old clergyman, Southgate serialized a "Tale of Oriental Life" called "Athanasius and Mirameh" in *The Christian Year* for 1871, which was published six years later as *The Cross above the Crescent: A Romance of Constantinople*.[159] Southgate's romance tells

---

[157] Horatio Southgate, "The Defects of the Present Foreign Mission Enterprise," (Philadelphia, January 1850) in The Horatio Southgate Papers (Group 17, Box 2, Folder 27). The seeds of such an approach were evident early in Southgate's career as a missionary. In 1836 he wrote: "If the hearts of the deluded disciples of Mohamed shall be turned to the knowledge and love of the divine Saviour, whom they despise, it must be by the power of the Spirit of God. Depend not on me to accomplish any thing of myself." "Letter to Rev. J. A. Clark," *Spirit of Missions*, 114.

[158] See George Antonius, *The Arab Awakening: The Story of the Arab National Movement* (London: H. Hamilton, 1938); and Samir Khalaf, *Cultural Resistance: Global and Local Encounters in the Middle East* (London: Saqi Books, 2001).

[159] *The Christian Year: A Monthly Magazine of Church Literature for the People* 1 (July 1871): 60–78; (August 1871): 171–87; (September 1871): 273–87; (October 1871): 403–14. See note 150.

the story of a rich and infertile Turkish couple who kidnap and adopt a young Greek boy named Athanasius (against his father's wishes) and rename him Mohammed Riza. But young Mohammed's belief in Islam proves to be a "mere holding of a form." Under the influence of an evangelical British missionary named Seymour, he is rescued from the harem and eventually becomes Gregory, a reformed Greek minister. "I call the work a Romance," wrote Southgate in its preface, but suggested that "it might, with equal truth, be called a Reality."

As this chapter has demonstrated, a similar effacement of the boundaries between romance and reality characterized early American religious responses to the Muslims of the Eastern Mediterranean. The predominant missionary response to Islam remained one that pitted it as a strong Satanic force that would ultimately bend to the power of the Holy Spirit, which the signs of the times seemed to be accomplishing regardless of their own direct efforts. Most antebellum American missionaries stationed in Ottoman lands redoubled their faith in the prophetic promises and increased the fervency of their declamations against Islam rather than launch new efforts at direct evangelism much less try to sympathize with its teachings. Islam, to these missionaries, was a dark and dreadful curse that rendered its followers into intolerant fatalists wallowing in superstition under Satan's despotic sway and blind to the clear light of Christianity. "Their religion is their destruction," Reverend Joel Hawes of Connecticut wrote after his 1844 visit to the eastern Mediterranean as a deputy of the ABCFM, "it represses all that is free, generous, noble . . . and subjects them to a miserable bigotry, ignorance, pride, and blood-thirsty cruelty."[160] William Goodell, writing in 1853 after spending thirty years as a missionary in the Eastern Mediterranean, was uncompromising in his contempt for Islam, claiming in tones of the fifth trumpet "there is not one right thought in their hearts about anything spiritual . . . I know of no words in the English language, by which I could fully express how thick, how gross is the darkness."[161] Sarah L. Huntington Smith, a missionary in Syria, rhetorically asked: "What else but evil can be told of the undisputed dominions of the enemy of God?"[162] Daniel Temple, the missionary in charge of printing tracts in the local languages during his twenty-three years in the Near East, never moved from the standard prophetic line during his more than two decades of service in the field. He called Islam "the most gross imposture that ever degraded fallen man," likening it to "the smoke ascending from the bottomless pit, [which] has filled all the eastern world with darkness," and was assured that the Turkish empire was "rapidly hastening to

[160] Joel Hawes, *Travels in the East, the Religion of the East, with Impressions of Foreign Travel* (Hartford, CT: Edwin Hunt, 1847), 114–15.

[161] Goodell, *The Old and the New*, 119.

[162] Edward W. Hooker, ed., *Memoir of Mrs. Sarah L. Huntington Smith, Late of the Mission in Syria*, 3rd ed. (New York: American Tract Society, 1845), 173.

its end" freeing the East "to become a part of the glorious inheritance of our Savior."[163]

By figuring Islam as a temporary scourge that God would soon remove, eschatology enabled American Christians to resolve the problem of Islam by explaining it within the terms of their own cultural desires and beliefs. Using scripture to authorize their utopian projections, they painted Islam as an enemy whose existence was a result of Christian error rather than an established religious tradition in its own right. Forcing diverse human communities into the procrustean bed of biblical metaphors – especially those describing them as locusts, scorpions, and other teratological beings – was a process of dehumanizing violence that sanctioned and even sanctified a religiously motivated prejudice. The eschatological faith held by many antebellum Protestants also absolved them of the need for meaningful dialogue with Muslims about the tenets of their religion, thereby limiting the ultimate effectiveness of any outreach. The hope of understanding Islam was therefore attributed to the culmination of a divine plan and not as result of the struggle of understanding intercultural difference. By their inabilities to engage the diverse Muslim cultures of the Ottoman Near East as peoples with highly developed systems and traditions of faith, these Christian thinkers demonstrated the degree to which the orientalism of eschatology prevented the appreciation of the diversity of the peoples and religions of the Eastern Mediterranean. The extensive efforts taken by students of the prophecies to globalize the relevance of their own religious beliefs ended up proving most profoundly the insularity of their own cultural imaginations. The deep fatalism that Christians saw as elemental to Muslim belief in the end ironically served more as an apt description of their own prophetic enterprise, as well as a sign of the strength of Islamic faith even at a time of political weakness and incipient colonization. The resurgence and persistence of Islam in the problematic postcolonial world of the twentieth century – even after the long-hoped-for end of the Ottomans and the return of the Jews to Israel – dramatizes the disappointment of this long heritage of apocalyptic expectation and the reason why some premillennialists continue to look to prophecy to explain enigmatic events of the East that ultimately refused to be contained within the ideologies of an American republic in the West.

---

[163] Daniel H. Temple, Jr. *Life and Letters of Reverend Daniel Temple, for Twenty-Three Years a Missionary of the American Board of Commissioners for Foreign Missions in Western Asia* (Boston: Congregational Board of Publications, 1855), 282, 251, 238, 244.

Chapter 3

Antebellum Islamicism and the Transnational Crusade of Antislavery and Temperance Reform

> Shall America be what the fathers and founders of her independence wished and hoped – a free democracy based on the foundation of human rights, or shall she degenerate into a miserable republic of Algerines, domineered over by a little self-constituted autocracy of slaveholding lynchers and blackguards, utterly disregardful of all law, except their own will and pleasure?
>
> R. Hildreth, *The White Slave; or, Memoirs of a Fugitive*[1]

In 1846, John Gorham Palfrey directly contrasted the "police laws" of Kuala Batu, the Malayan community that the U.S. Navy had decimated fifteen years earlier after its residents captured an American merchant ship, with those half way around the world in South Carolina, where any of African descent aboard an arriving ship were detained and subsequently enslaved if the ship owners were unwilling or unable to pay a fee. The principal difference between the two situations, asserted Palfrey – a Massachusetts abolitionist who had manumitted twenty-two of his own slaves (leading Senator Charles Sumner to claim that he had freed more slaves than had Stephen Decatur[2]) – was that "Qualla Battoo is in ruins, and Charleston stands to this day."[3] Palfrey's criticism of the abuse of habeus corpus by despotic regimes exemplifies a common rhetorical disposition of reformers in antebellum United States to equate American and Islamic situations as a means of expressing public opposition to immoral domestic practices. The Navy had used military reprisals against the Malays to chastise their piracy; reformers, however, deployed rhetorical exhortations to their audiences to arise and undertake a moral crusade that targeted injustices and excesses within the national body-politic. This comparative transposition of Sumatran practices with those of the U.S. South exemplifies the larger antebellum strategy of globalizing the relevance of American reform through a tactical deployment of islamicist expression.

This chapter examines the discourse of two major cultural movements – those centered on antislavery and on temperance – as case studies of the multivalent ways that reformers imported islamicist allusions and comparisons

---

[1] (Boston: Tappan & Whittemore, 1852), 467.

[2] Charles Sumner, *The Works of Charles Sumner*, 15 vols. (Boston: Lee and Shepard, 1870), 1: 457.

[3] John G. Palfrey, *Papers of the Slave Power* (Boston: Merrill, Cobb & Co, 1846), 45.

134

within the cultural enterprise of antebellum reform.[4] It examines a wide variety of rhetorical expression – including political speeches, polemical prose and pamphlets, fictional and autobiographical narrative, poetic verse, and travel writing – to analyze how references to distant Muslim cultures circulated in complex ways within the work of reform. Given the facts that the only Muslims inside the United States were subjugated African slaves and that many Americans were aware of the Muslim prohibition against alcohol consumption, the claim that islamicism played a significant and unexplored role in abolitionist and temperance discourse may seem surprising. This is partly because analyses of the contours of antebellum reform traditionally have been circumscribed within national situations, or at best set within transatlantic contexts. The chapter shows that reformers themselves required an even broader spatial and temporal compass to establish the global relevance of their projects. Islamicism's utility as a transhemispheric dimension within reform discourse resulted from the breadth of the comparative perspective it was able to encompass. The same process that maligned alien domestic practices that contradicted national visions of Christian democracy also provided some Americans with an imaginative means of addressing the obstinacy of Islam as an international contender. When Americans transposed observations about Islamic cultures onto American situations, they were simultaneously able to articulate the boundaries of acceptable domestic practices, to contain the cultural challenge of Islam, and to generate more hybrid and global national trajectories. An examination of the rhetorical play of abolitionists and temperance proponents reveals again the dialectical creativity that resulted from the tension between desires for national expansion and anxieties about geographical peripherality that characterized the antebellum cultural imagination.

As the prior two chapters have demonstrated, orientalist constructions of the despotism and antichristianity of Islam had become so ingrained in the consciousness of educated citizens in early America that the equation of Islam with cruelty, sensuality, and infidelity had become an almost proverbial disposition (Fig. 3.1). Indeed Islam, as it was orientally figured, served as a deep systematic symbol of slavery itself, supplanting or at least supplementing the biblical genealogy of Egyptian bondage. Early national foreign policy and missionary endeavors, especially in the lands surrounding the Mediterranean, involved attempts by Americans to extend or imagine their cultural influence within Muslim spaces, but the predominant direction of the exchange explored in this and following chapters focuses on how

---

4 Other reform movements that employed islamicist rhetoric as a transnational comparative resource include those associated with prisons and insane asylums, corporal punishment, rural cemeteries, and sabbatarianism. I do not discuss these in this book, but each merits further study within the transnational framework of islamicist comparison (Fig. 3.2).

islamicism was imported within domestic discourses as a constructed rhetoric of differentiation. Unwilling to colonize Muslim territories, some Americans transposed their desires for global influence into the registers of cultural imperialism. American Protestants likewise compensated for the inability of missionaries to convert Muslims to Christianity by transforming Islamic difference into symbolic capital for the cultural work of domestic reform. Analyzing alcoholism and slavery from the transnational perspective of islamicism reveals that both behaviors were figured as forms of infidel enthrallment that obliterated the virtuous self-control expected of Christian democrats. Despite the ethical differences between drinking and slaveholding, John W. Crowley has shown how temperance narratives resembled abolitionist genres in their portrayal of "slaves to the bottle whose bondage seemed comparable to that of plantation chattel."[5] An example of this linkage is an account of the debate between Senators John C. Calhoun and Thomas Hart Benton in 1849 over whether the transport of slaves should be allowed into Benton's state of Missouri. Frederick Douglass's newspaper *The North Star* took Benton to task for his inconsistency in supporting the prohibition against importing slaves while still preserving the institution itself. "If slavery be bad as an article of exportation, it cannot be better as an article of home consumption," the article commented before making an equivalence with the trade in alcohol, "If rum and brandy be ill-assorted with missionaries in a cargo to Heathen lands, they call loudly for extermination in our own."[6]

Some Protestant Americans desired to remove the challenge symbolized by Islam through the agency of their own cultural influence. It was therefore deeply disconcerting to recognize that some of the immoralities they associated with Turkish practices were thriving in the midst of their own democracy. The process of "domestic orientalism" transposed islamicist examples onto American situations as a means of maligning the practices of drunkenness and slave-holding. Aligning these repugnant domestic actions with those ascribed to alien infidels excommunicated them from the province of American acceptability. By branding such behaviors as beyond the pale of moral civilization, this defamiliarizing process of rhetorical exile enabled those employing such labels to reassure themselves of the righteousness of their own vision of America as a nation with a Christian mission. Such rhetoric was designed at times to motivate audiences to collaborate in rehabilitating these remaining pockets of domestic barbarism and backwardness. Protestant moralists thus confirmed their notions of progress and civilization though the process of constructing "domestic orients," cultural spaces

---

[5] John W. Crowley, "Slaves to the Bottle: Gough's Autobiography and Douglass's Narrative," in *The Serpent in the Cup: Temperance in American Literature*, eds. David S. Reynolds and Debra J. Rosenthal (Amherst: University of Massachusetts Press, 1997), 115–16.

[6] E.Q., "Mr. Calnoun," *The North Star* (17 August 1849).

TURKISH OR MAHOMETAN SCHOOL;

In which " the children learn to read the Koran and to receive the BASTINADO "
or BEATING on the soles of the feet; for, the Eastern nations have not yet learned
the *enlightened* and *Christian* method of FLOGGING, practised in the United States
and in Europe!

AN AMERICAN OR EUROPEAN SCHOOL;

In which the ROD is the ONLY means of discipline; " *kindness, mildness, persuasion*, and other *moral* and *religious* influences being INSUFFICIENT to preserve
ORDER!"

FIGURE 3.1. Comparative islamicism was deployed in many arenas of antebellum reform.
These satirical illustrations identify the beating of students in schools as an infidel and barbaric
Muslim practice. Frontispiece from Lyman Cobb, *The Evil Tendencies of Corporal Punishment
as a Means of Moral Discipline* (New York: Mark H. Newman, 1847). Thanks to Richard
Brodhead.

of American territory or expression stigmatized through their connection with Islamic (and other "Eastern") behaviors.[7]

While these reformers were infidelizing the behaviors they felt the nation had to forego, they were simultaneously engaging Islam through the vicarious complexities of orientalist imagination. Such rhetoric had the effect of domesticating Islam by linking it with the practices of American minorities, against whom reformers could struggle with more local fervency and with greater hope for ultimate success. This cultural conversion made it easier for reformers to imagine themselves as vanquishers of the inflexible evils of Islam and as exporters of the cultural principles they held to be universal. They thought that if only Americans could reform the behaviors in their own midst that tarnished their ideals of democracy and Christianity, then the nation would assume its exemplary power to influence the world, even before the act of venturing into foreign terrain. By compressing the millennium-old crusade between the Cross and the Crescent into the challenges of domestic reform, such rhetoric increased the religious validity, the global relevance, and the cosmic scope of American cultural activism.

However, as elucidated by the trajectory of eschatology examined in the previous chapter, this encounter with an Islam imagined as the idealized antithesis of notions of American destiny was frequently challenged by the increasing encounters with actual Muslims and their cultures. These encounters seemed to show that Muslims treated slaves more humanely and had a long tradition of temperance, leading many American reformers to experience a great deal of embarrassment. Americans had presumed that Islam was an embodiment of despotic backwardness and an incarnation of static evil that was destined to give way before the advances of republican democracy and Christian civilization. The fact that Muslims demonstrated more success in installing moral practices than did Americans themselves challenged their faith in both their national aspirations and their understanding of Muslims. These new understandings of Islamic cultural behaviors fostered the reemergence of a different valence of the domestication of Islamic orientalism. How could Christian Americans presume to be superior, much less convince Muslims to convert to their worldview, if some of their cultural customs were immoral and socially destructive? Emphasizing Turkish virtue thus became an effective method of highlighting the depths of American vice. Reformers used transnational examples of Turkish "wisdom" to lash Americans for the disappointments of their own purportedly moral civilization. Some reformers hoped that by evoking

---

[7] An example of how a "domestic orient" can be evolved with a single word can be seen in Louisa May Alcott's treatment of Amy March's "Last Will and Testament" in *Little Women*. Alcott signifies Amy's immoderate attraction to luxury when she talks of bequeathing a "turkquoise" ring she hopes to inherit. Even such a humorous marking of Amy's avarice with an islamicist misspelling announces it to be morally inappropriate (1868; New York: Bantam Books, 1983), 189.

a politics of embarrassment, one that John Greeleaf Whittier called the "crimson flush of shame," their audiences might be mortified into struggling harder to bring domestic practices more in line with their cultural ideals.[8]

Some of the contrasts that reformers drew between Islam and America contained valuable comparative insights that provided Americans with new models of cosmopolitan social behavior unavailable to them through transatlantic channels alone. Such a broadened perspective enabled a scathing critique of the hypocrisy of a country that aspired to a redeeming moral influence in the world at the same time that its own increasingly divided house was riddled with the barbaric practices it hoped to rid others of. Americans who expressed the positive difference of Islamic cultures through such comparisons often showed more openness to Islam than they had through earlier stereotypes. But the fact that they used such observations to define American situations precluded an evolving understanding of the full claims of Islam. The development of this comparative critique demonstrated afresh that islamicist discourse responded more to the cultural fears and fantasies of those who propounded it than to any abiding interest in the religion of Islam. In fact, such compensatory perceptions opened up the inverse danger of romanticizing Muslim cultures. The polemic of reform was designed to be excessive and hyperbolic in order to attract adherence to its program of active involvement. But the employment of Islamic orientalism in such a charged moral discourse had the effect of increasing the exoticism of Islamic behaviors, either by accentuating their repugnance (in the case of domestic orientalism) or their heuristic value (in the case of comparative orientalism). Such a process invested islamicism with a dual valence of sensationalism that expressed both its barbarity and its force as an exotic alternative. The fact that reformers applied both valences to domestic situations helped to solidify islamicism as a romantic resource with an emotional charge that less moralistic and more capitalistic Americans (like purveyors of popular fiction or entrepreneurial advertisers) would employ to manufacture audiences for the more secular productions and commodities that emerged as the nineteenth-century progressed.

THE BARBARY OF AMERICA: ISLAMICISM AND EARLY
ANTISLAVERY REFORM

In 1611, a Spanish caravel entered Chesapeake Bay and captured a young Englishman named John Clark, who would later become the first mate of the *Mayflower*, stranding three of its sailors on the Virginia shore in the

---

[8] John Greeleaf Whittier, "The World's Convention of The Friends Of Emancipation, Held in London in 1840," in *Anti-Slavery Poems*, Vol. 3 of *The Writings of John Greenleaf Whittier*, 7 vols. (London: Macmillan, 1889), 3: 79.

process. One of these castaways, a man named Don Diego de Molina, was incarcerated in Jamestown for four years, from where he smuggled letters back home to Spain in which he called the English colony "a new Algiers in America."[9] This anecdote demonstrates that even before the settlement of New England, situations of North American captivity had been compared with the older phenomenon of North African bondage.

Almost two hundred and fifty years later, in her blockbuster antislavery novel *Uncle Tom's Cabin,* Harriet Beecher Stowe narrates how Uncle Tom, after being sold down the river to New Orleans, is taken by his new owner to a plantation house that is constructed in a "moorish fashion" complete with courtyard, arched gateways, fountains, and "Arabian jessamines." Stowe describes its residents Marie and Augustine St. Clare as "a sultana" and "her slave" and portrays their other residence – a summer home on Lake Pontchartrain – as an orientalized East Indian villa with verandahs, bamboo furniture, and fragrant tropical plants. That Stowe confuses the two settings in various scenes of the novel suggests that she employs this islamicist architecture as a symbolic geography of the moral instability of slavery.[10]

These brief examples suggest how examining the changing field of domestic slavery affords insights into the process through which notions of Islam were applied to different American actualities. In similar and at times overlapping ways to how despotism served as a specter haunting the revived republican project, the infiltration and establishment of slavery as an American practice obstructed the national fantasy of liberty. The early national crisis of American captivity in Barbary was a founding moment establishing Muslim practices as a transnational mirror in which Americans perceived the dangers that the existence of slavery posed to democratic civilization. Fewer than five hundred Americans were ever held involuntarily in North Africa, and most of them were detained in captivity for no more than four years. In contrast, millions of Africans and their children, comprising up to twenty percent of the entire national population of the United States, were held in bondage in perpetuity, with no hope of ransom from afar. The persistence of slavery and its political support in the south led

---

[9] James R. Judge, "Between Columbus and Jamestown: Expressing our Forgotten Century," *National Geographic,* 173: 3 (March 1988). It was used as an example of "anecdote" in Thomas Clark et al., eds. *The Writer's Digest Guide to Good Writing* (Cincinnati, OH: Writer's Digest Books, 1994), 318. I am grateful to Woody Holton and Nessa Johnson for this reference.

[10] Harriet Beecher Stowe, *Uncle Tom's Cabin, or, Life among the Lowly* (New York: Penguin, 1986), 252–3, 243, 381. Lydia Maria Child also orientalized the sexual politics of a Southern plantation by linking the family with an Islamic seraglio in her short story "Slavery's Pleasant Homes," which features a morally quiescent wife who "had been nurtured in seclusion, almost as deep as that of the oriental harem." See Carolyn L. Karcher, "Rape, Murder and Revenge in 'Slavery's Pleasant Homes': Lydia Maria Child's Antislavery Fiction and the Limits of Genre," *Women's Studies International Forum* 9 (1986): 327.

Benjamin Franklin to fear "a new Barbary rising in America" and provoked Thomas Jefferson to worry that Virginia was "fast sinking" to the status of "the Barbary of the Union."[11] Enlightenment reformers domesticated Barbary as a mobile sign symbolizing the dangers faced by nascent liberty when suppressed by the iron hand of despotism.[12] Barbary captivity and "Algerine" bondage became transnational emblems of a contested domestic practice that would not be ruled as completely un-American until after the Civil War. By comparing Southern slaveholders with Barbary taskmasters, abolitionists challenged their claims both to American liberty and to civilized status. In so doing, they also brought to bear a scathing criticism of the moral defects of a nation whose mission was premised on liberty yet countenanced the enslavement of fellow humans. These faults could best be remedied through the application of abolitionism as a continuing American project of reforming antidemocratic political practices.

The captivity of American citizens in Algiers in the 1780s and 1790s reminded new nationals of how far the United States needed to progress if it was to escape the despotism it abhorred in the North Africans. Early abolitionists, stimulated by the emerging debate in the late eighteenth century over emancipation of slavery in the Northern states, accentuated this contradiction and tried to transform the national outrage over American captives in Algiers into a critique of the domestic institution of African slavery.[13] The rhetoric of early national abolitionist discourse focused some of its energies on a species-wide universalism that brought to bear transracial republican sympathies as a means of criticizing domestic failings. After American merchantmen had been captured in 1785, for example, John Jay saw little difference between the two cases of enslavement except that "the American slaves at Algiers were WHITE people, whereas the African slaves at New York were BLACK people."[14] A writer named "Humanus" wrote in 1786: "Negro masters doubtless shudder at the idea of slavery among the Algerines, and execrate them as barbarous tyrants, ... but are they less barbarous than the followers of Mahomet?"[15] This inversion of the problem

---

[11] Franklin to David Hartley, 8 May 1788, Jared Sparks, ed., *The Works of Benjamin Franklin*, 10 vols. (London: B. F. Stevens, 1882), 9: 521; Jefferson to Joseph C. Cabell, 28 November 1820, H. A. Washington, ed., *The Writings of Thomas Jefferson*, 9 vols. (Washington, DC: Taylor & Maury, 1854), 7: 187. Both are quoted in Charles Sumner's speech "The Barbarism of Slavery," *Works*, 4: 159–60.

[12] Lotfi Ben Rejeb, "'To the Shore of Tripoli': The Impact of Barbary on Early American Nationalism" (Ph.D. diss., Indiana University, 1981), 127–30.

[13] Both the Quakers of Germantown in 1688 and Reverend Samuel Hopkins in 1776 had attempted to arouse American commitment to antislavery by asking their audiences to empathize with the Africans by imagining the outrage they would feel if their friends and relations were carried into Turkish slavery. See Lotfi Ben Rejeb, "America's Captive Freemen in North Africa: The Comparative Method in Abolitionist Persuasion," *Slavery & Abolition* 9 (1988): 60–1.

[14] Jay is quoted in Charles Sumner, "White Slavery in the Barbary States," *Works*, 1: 449.

[15] *New Jersey Gazette* (18 September 1786), quoted in Arthur Zilversmit, *The First Emancipation: The Abolition of Slavery in the North* (Chicago: The University of Chicago Press, 1967), 117. Another

painted the United States as a racist and barbaric nation committed to the enforced large-scale captivity of Africans. American pretensions to democratic liberty, moral leadership, and enlightened religion rendered the slavery in its midst even more reprehensible than the cruel and infidel practices of the North African despots.

The crisis of North African captivity occurred at the same time as the debate over slavery during the creation of the Constitution, a crucial correspondence that made the symbol of Muslim bondage, especially in Barbary and Turkey, a highly charged resource for early American abolitionism. The Abolition Society of Pennsylvania implored the Constitutional Convention in 1787 to view the recent capture of Americans by Algerines as a providential warning designed to awaken its citizens "to a sentiment of the injustice and cruelty of which we are guilty towards the wretched Africans."[16] Their efforts failed when the drafted Constitution helped to ensure its own ratification by bartering away the rights of African slaves and allowing the slave trade to persist for twenty more years under the flag of the new republic. Benjamin Franklin, writing less than a month before his death under the pseudonym "Historicus" in the *Pennsylvania Gazette* of March of 1790, directly satirized an argument of a Congressman from Georgia about the need to protect the American slave trade. Franklin took the persona of a fictional Algerian courtier named Sidi Mehemet Ibrahim who pressed one century earlier for the preservation of enslavement in Algiers on the grounds that Christians were needed to cultivate its lands and represented an important source of wealth. By deftly transposing racial prejudice and religious allegiance, such as when he ironically argues that returning Christian slaves to their own countries would be to return to darkness from the "sun of Islamism," Franklin reveals the self-interest inherent in cultural constructions of liberty.[17] Franklin's parody is a prime early example of how islamicism enabled what Paul Giles calls "the critical process of virtualization." Giles explains how a comparative angle of vision that enables "seeing native landscapes refracted or inverted in a foreign mirror," like Franklin's transposition of Algiers onto Georgia, is "a process of aestheticization that highlights the manifestly fictional dimensions of their construction."[18]

---

correspondent pointed out with shame the awareness of the American captives in Algiers that the same country from which they desired ransom was engaged in depriving the Africans of their liberty, saying "Blush O ye Bostonians and Pennsylvanians for your degenerate sons, who have thus embarked in this monstrous and abominable trade and traffic!" *The New Haven Gazette and Literary Magazine* 11 (7 June 1786): 123–4.

[16] Quoted in Ben Rejeb, "America's Captive Freemen," 62.

[17] *Pennsylvania Gazette* (25 March 1790). This exchange was reprinted in the antebellum antislavery press; for example, see "Debates on the Slave Trade," *The African Observer* (November 1827): 235–8; "On the Slave Trade," *The Liberator* 1 (17 December 1831), 1; and *Republic of Letters* 10 (1834), 183.

[18] Paul Giles, *Virtual Americas: Transnational Fictions and the Transnational Imaginary* (Durham, NC: Duke, 2002), 1–2.

By inverting the argument about the value of human property, Franklin expressed the abolitionist strategy of confronting readers with the immorality of slavery and of forcing them to consider their fate as the chattel of Muslims, the people most fully associated in American imagination with systematic despotism. His satire was only one example of how imaginative works expanded the connection between Algerian and American bondage. Quaker abolitionist Warner Mifflin (who freed his own slaves in 1775) originally voiced this statement of universal sensibility in a letter that later circulated as a public statement. "I feel the call of humanity as strong towards an African in America, as an American in Algiers, both being my brethren; especially as I am informed that the Algerine treats his slave with more humanity," wrote Mifflin, "and I believe the sin of oppression on the part of the American, is greater in the sight of the Father of the family of mankind."[19] Such polemic dramatized the fear that continued domestic slavery rendered Americans worse than the most tyrannous of infidels. Islamicist perspectives were featured within several different genres of antislavery expression, including poetry and plays, didactic tales and moral exhortations, captivity narratives, confidence games, and geographical texts – works that circulated in dynamic ways to reach different audiences.

The return of the captives from North Africa in 1797 stimulated the publication of a variety of literature much of which aimed at raising national consciousness of the contradiction of permitting slavery to thrive in the land of liberty. Such a paradox is registered through the diptych structure of the 1797 poem, "The American in Algiers," whose two cantos juxtapose the tale of a Revolutionary War veteran captured by Algerian pirates with that of a "sable bard" ripped from his romantic life in Africa with his bride Zephra. To apprise his American audience of the continuing need to expand the republican revolution, the poet portrays slave-holders in the United States as "pious scourgers of the human race" and "feign'd friends to liberty" whose own possession of slaves "shall blast with shame Her boasted rights and prove them but a name." He argues that the "sacred instrument" of the Declaration of Independence should also apply to Africans and that the slave-holder George Washington should "convert" the sword he used to affirm American rights so that it might rend "slavery's galling chain."[20]

---

[19] Warner Mifflin, *The Colored American* (20 January 1838). The fact that Mifflin's private letter was published first in Gouveneur Morris's *Observations on the American Revolution* in 1779 and again in *The Colored American* in 1838 intimates the multivalent and persistent utility of these comparisons throughout the early years of the nation. See also Moses Fisk, *Tyrannical Libertymen: A Discourse upon Negro-Slavery in the United States* (Hanover, NH: The Eagle, 1795), reprinted in *The Life and Writings of Moses Fisk,* ed. Tim Barlow (Collegedale, TN: The College Press, 1980).

[20] *The American in Algiers or the Patriot of Seventy-Six in Captivity: a Poem, in Two Cantos* (New York: J. Buel, 1797), 21–5.

David Everett's play of the same year called "Slaves in Barbary," anthologized throughout the antebellum period in the popular *Columbian Orator*, dramatizes a turning of the tables in which an American slave-dealer named Kidnap and his slave Sharp undergo a partial role reversal during an episode of Algerian captivity. Sharp's capture actually elevates his social status by enabling him to testify against the vileness of his former master (even though he nevertheless remains caricatured as a degraded buffoon). Everett's attack on slavery as a system of enforced education strikes even more mordant tones of irony. The purchasers of Kidnap and Sharp joke that in the United States Sharp had been "under the benevolent instruction of a task-master, and converted to Christianity by lectures applied to the naked back with a rope's end"; they then sardonically devise a plan in which Kidnap will be placed under Sharp's instruction where he might "have the advantage of a whip-lecture from his former slave, whom he has treated so kindly." However, it is Hamet, the noble and humane Bashaw of Tunis, who ironically delivers the deepest philosophical lesson of the play when he suggests: "Let misery teach him, what he could never learn in affluence, the lesson of humanity."[21]

These literary productions demonstrate early American examples of how North African practices were emphasized both to highlight the cruelty of American slavery and to provide the space for cosmopolitan critique. To accomplish these ends, some drew upon the popular genre of the oriental tale that depicted Eastern lands as a sentimental space of benevolent humanity whose residents were content to rely upon the wisdom of Providence. At least one enterprising writer capitalized upon this moral inversion to attract audiences to his productions. *Humanity in Algiers; or, the Story of Azem*, is a tall tale that features an oriental story within the frame of a Barbary captivity narrative to authenticate its antislavery message. The author claims to have been a sailor on board the *Dauphin* when it was captured by corsairs from Algiers, where he faithfully served a wealthy planter for nine years before gaining his freedom from a legacy funded in honor of a former Senegalese slave named Azem.[22] However, it is evident that the writer has never spent any time in the actual Islamic orient, and his "best authority" is actually his reading of classical literature and the oriental tales

---

[21] David Everett, "Slaves in Barbary," in *The Columbian Orator* (Boston: Manning and Loring, 1797), 102–18. This anthology, which went through over twenty editions throughout the antebellum period, was the same book from which the twelve-year-old Frederick Douglass fed his unerring love for freedom. The documents in the *Orator*, he said, "gave tongue to interesting thoughts of my own soul, which had frequently flashed through my mind, and died away for want of utterance." *Narrative of the Life of Frederick Douglass, An American Slave, Written by Himself*, ed. David W. Blight (1845; Boston: Bedford, 1993), 61–2.

[22] *Humanity in Algiers, or the Story of Azem* [by an American, late a Slave in Algiers] (Troy, NY: R. Moffatt and Co. 1801; Utica, NY: Asahel Seward, 1806).

that were featured regularly in American periodicals of the early national period.[23]

The clearest borrowing of *Humanity in Algiers* from the tradition of the oriental tale, however, was its view of Islam as a potentially benevolent system of morality. "Taught and accustomed from infancy to think our own religious creed the only mark of a civilization," the author explains in the preface, "we can scarcely think it possible that a Mahometan should possess a feeling heart, or perform a virtuous deed." This beneficent face of Islam is dramatized most efficiently through the virtuous and noble Muslims Azem and Omri, one the former Senegalese slave and the other an Algerian physician, both of whom demonstrate the principles of the equality of all nations, the golden rule, and the Qur'anic precept (whose wording was taken directly from Franklin's parody) to "treat your slaves with kindness." The author consciously grants virtue to the Muslim in order to transpose the charge of immorality back onto the field of American slavery. If the charity of Azem certifies that there is humanity even in Algiers, the stereotypical abode of infidel bondage, then Americans must feel heavy reproach for not acting as virtuously in ending the inhumane slavery of the Africans in their midst. "'A vile, piratical set of unprincipled robbers,' is the softest name we can give them [the Algerians]," the narrator chastises, "forgetful of our former depredations on the coasts of Africa, and the cruel manner in which we at present treat the offspring of those whom we brought from thence."

Humanity in Algiers was published in New York in 1801 and 1806, with its first edition containing a list of more than two hundred subscribers from almost thirty towns in Vermont and New York. It would be charitable to assume that the author was raising a trust fund, similar to Azem's, for the manumission of American slaves. But the author's disingenuous tale seems to suggest another conclusion: that he was employing the currency of islamicism to capitalize on the guilt of his readers and their hope that Muslims could be redeemed and express virtuous behavior. The author may be employing the example of Azem's philanthropy and "enterprising genius" to model the benevolence he wishes from his own readers toward his own book as well as for slaves in the United States. By attracting his subscribers

---

[23] *Humanity in Algiers*, 10. His classical education is evident by the names he gives his Muslim characters (Selictor, Testador, Valaclus) which sound more Latin than Arabic, and he is appallingly unfamiliar with African geography such as when he places Elysium ("a landscape suited to captivate the imagination of every beholder" [56]) between Algiers and the desert. There is clear evidence that elements of the Story of Azem were lifted directly from oriental tales. The name of Azem's wife Shelimah is taken from the frequently reprinted tale "Almerine and Shelima" (sometimes called Almoran and Selima). Themes such as the near marriage of siblings, the appearance of Muhammad in a dream, and the lustful intoxication of Muslim males toward innocent virgins were also common motifs of the oriental tale.

to the virtues of Muslims to capitalize upon both their abolitionist and evangelical desires, he seems to be subjecting them to an American confidence game.[24]

The lash of such sentiments could also be registered through more sober genres such as a heavily subscribed volume designed to help Americans better understand the fate of their captive citizens in North Africa. *An Historical and Geographical Account of Algiers* eloquently probes the paradox of American slavery by erasing the distinction between Islamic and sub-Saharan Africa as well as any grounds for American criticism of North African piracy.

> With what countenance then can we reproach a set of barbarians, who have only retorted our own acts upon ourselves in making reprisals upon our citizens? For it is manifest to the world, that we are equally culpable, and whatever terms of opprobrium we may execrate the piratical disposition of the Africans, yet all our recrimination will recoil upon ourselves.[25]

For readers seeking information about Algiers, the encounter with this statement radically destabilizes any assumed American claim to moral authority. This approach persisted in abolitionist discourse throughout the antebellum period, although the tone became more insistently angry and fervid as the fires of sectionalism and ultraism heated up. In 1855, for example, Charles Sumner argued "every argument by which our own freedom is vindicated, – every applause awarded to the successful rebellion of our fathers, – every indignant word ever hurled against the enslavement of our white fellow-citizens by Algerine corsairs, must plead trumpet-tongued against the deep damnation of Slavery, whether white or black."[26] Laurilla Aleroyla Smith, one of five Connecticut sisters devoted to abolitionism and suffrage, exclaimed in exasperation about the treachery and murder that slavery allowed in the United States: "Oh, bring to me the flag of Europe's despot-kings; even the Sultan's crescent bring – Mahomet's standard bear – but take, oh take away the Bloody Banner of America!!"[27] Islamicism in this way instructively served as a potent means for weighing domestic practices in the balance of a more universal system of comparative morality. This comparative mirror defaced the legitimacy of American protest against North African depredations by dissolving it in the realization that the institution of slavery had made a Barbary out of America.

---

[24] *Humanity in Algiers*, 4, 98, 3, 105.

[25] James Wilson Stevens, *An Historical and Geographical Account of Algiers* (Philadelphia: Hogan & M'Elroy, 1797), 235. A second edition of the book was published in Brooklyn in 1800; it contained more eyewitness accounts of Americans in captivity. The quotation used here appears on page 243 in that edition.

[26] Charles Sumner, "The Anti-Slavery Enterprise," in *Recent Speeches and Addresses* (Boston: Higgins and Bradley, 1856), 486.

[27] Laurilla Aleroyla Smith, "The Bloody Banner," *Freedom's Gift: or Sentiments of the Free* (Hartford, CT: S. S. Cowles, 1840), 43–4.

ISLAMICISM AND THE RISE OF COMPARATIVE ANTISLAVERY

Even after the close of the official American slave trade and the subjugation of Barbary piracy, and especially as slavery emerged as a charged sectional issue, abolitionists such as Stowe continued to evoke the comparison as a means of constructing Southern territory as a domestic orient. During the Greek War of Independence, Americans contrasted the outrage over Turkish oppression with that inflicted by domestic slaveowners over Africans in America. "But say, do Turks alone enslave the free?" asked one poet in 1824, "Wrong'd Africa! the muse appeals to thee."[28] The African American *Freedom's Journal* wondered "how many of the most odious features of Turkish slavery may be fairly matched in this free and enlightened country" concluding that "in many parts of the slave territories, the despotism is exercised as absolutely as in Turkey."[29] When the African American community of New York City staged a ball to raise funds to support the independence of Greece, the *Freedom's Journal* denounced it by arguing that such efforts would be better spent helping to free blacks within the United States.[30]

Antislavery advocates frequently circulated islamicist examples throughout the antebellum period to sting the consciences of citizens who pretended to laud democracy while maintaining the slavery of millions in their midst. Such efforts not only framed slave-holding as an infidel practice but also constructed abolitionism as an attempt by a new generation of Americans to extend the righteous devotion to liberty manifested by their "fathers." Imagining abolition as an expression of the continuing American Revolution provided a symbolic act of ransom for slaves that also served as a prelusive form of political action. The islamicist charge of early abolitionists often measured American practices in the light of a universal morality; however, this strategy was progressively supplemented after 1830 by new insights into the nature of slavery and attempts at emancipation in Muslim lands. The symbolic status of the haughty Turk as the epitome of the despot was deflated not only by the persistence of American slavery and by Ottoman reforms but also by the way that Russian tyranny over the Poles after 1830 (and Austrian suppression of the Hungarian revolt in 1848) relocated despotism as a living practice within Christian Europe. The increasing weakness of the Ottoman Empire and the North African principalities was evident when both bowed to the pressure of encroaching European colonialism (masked partly by the civilizing mission of abolitionism) and took steps toward outlawing the slave trade and its manifestation in urban slave markets. Such actions altered American perceptions of Turkish slavery, enabling the emergence of a comparative orientalism that figured Muslim

[28] *The New York Mirror* 1 (3 January 1824): 182.
[29] "People of Colour," *Freedom's Journal* (6 April 1827).
[30] *Freedom's Journal* (30 March 1827): 3; (12 December 1828): 290–1.

slavery as a more benign alternative to the harsh racial bondage of the New World.

One of the first reforms of slavery in the Ottoman Empire reported in the American press was an 1831 edict of amnesty to those Greeks who had taken up arms against the sovereignty of the Sublime Porte.[31] The Sultan's proclamation included a prohibition of the practice of applying the epithet "dog" to Christians, prompting one writer to conclude: "Verily, the Turks are far superior in humanity and justice." He went on to ask "[w]hen will the Grand Sultan of this country – PUBLIC OPINION – pass an edict, forbidding persons of color to be classed with brutes and doomed to an interminable bondage?"[32] William Lloyd Garrison's new publication *The Liberator* compared this deep-rooted American prejudice against the African with "the narrow bigotry of the Mohammedan, who feels contaminated if a Christian shares his dinner," but nevertheless applauded the Sultan's edict by announcing: "Let us try to keep pace with the Turks in candor and benevolence." By positioning the Sultan as a leader of reform, American reformers gained an ironic moral ground for demanding a commensurate domestic response.[33]

When that same year Nat Turner and his accomplices staged a revolt against the white residents of Southampton, Virginia, antislavery advocates argued that both the complaints of the slaves and their eventual prospects of success were comparable to the revolts of the Greeks against the Turks, the Poles against the Russians, and the Americans against the British.[34] These other democratic uprisings highlighted what Garrison called the "odious inconsistency" of America's professed devotion to liberty and the persistence of its own domestic tyrannies.[35] He illustrated this dissonance in a speech before the American Anti-Slavery Society in 1835: "We boast that our country is the home of the oppressed, and yet there is not a nation on earth that holds so many slaves. We cheer on the Greeks to break the Turkish yoke, and we make contributions in aid of the Poles, and yet hold greater numbers in more cruel and crushing bondage."[36] An article on the "slave question" continued this comparison by emphasizing that the two million slaves in the United States equaled the colonial population of

[31] Bernard Lewis, *Race and Slavery in the Middle East* (New York: Oxford University Press, 1990), 79.

[32] [V.] "Walker's Appeal, No. 3," *The Liberator* 1 (14 May 1831): 78.

[33] *The Liberator* 1 (13 August 1831): 130.

[34] "The Insurrection," *The Liberator* 1 (3 September 1831); *Genius of Temperance, Philanthropist and People's Advocate* (26 October 1831): 1.

[35] "The Anti-Slavery Platform," in *Selections from the Writings and Speeches of William Lloyd Garrison* (Boston: R. F. Wallcut, 1852), 323. George Thompson wrote to Garrison on October 22, 1835: "Before you weep over the wrongs of Greece, go wash the gore out of your own national shambles" (393).

[36] Rev. A. Phelps, "Extracts from Speeches at the Anniversary of the American Anti-Slavery Society," *Anti-Slavery Reporter* 1 (June 1834): 83.

Americans when they revolted from Britain. It went on to suggest that Africans in the South merited the same support from American citizens as had the Greeks, by asking its readers to recall: "[W]hose arm was not instinctively raised to strike down the haughty Turk, as, in imagination, he beheld him brandishing his glittering scimetar over the head of his devoted victim?"[37]

By imaginatively mustering a physical response of indignation, such rhetoric aimed to enlist citizens in a renewed commitment to political revolution and religious mission. One of the most prominent Americans to apply islamicist perspectives to the antislavery effort was the poet John Greenleaf Whittier. His 1839 poem in honor of "The World's Convention of The Friends Of Emancipation, Held in London in 1840" exhorted the free world to enlist in this global crusade, not to recover the "long-deserted shrine" and "dull unconscious sod" of a distant Holy Land, but rather to free the earth from slavery. Smarting under the sting of American hypocrisy, Whittier suggests that "Moslem mercy yet may shame/All tyrants of a Christian name."[38] American tyranny seemed to these critics even more reprehensible than that perpetrated by the Turks, the Russians, and other powers of the Old World, who did not pretend to such an exalted devotion to constitutional liberty and Christian mission.

Abolitionists believed that enslaving people as property in one's own nation while loudly protesting the unjust treatments of minorities across the sea reeked of a double standard that augured the impending evaporation of America's moral authority in the world. One antislavery speaker asked: "Do, then, the essential principles of justice vary with geographical position; or do virtue and vice depend upon the color of a man's skin?" after stating that Americans held in Algiers had never allowed themselves to be considered the property in flesh of the "swarthy tyrants" of Barbary.[39] *The Anti-Slavery Catechism* of 1836 responded to the question of whether human slaves could ever be reduced to property by retorting, "If you were taken by an Algerine pirate, and an Arab bought you, and paid honestly for you, should you ever consider yourself the property of the Arab?"[40]

---

[37] "The Slave Question," *Worcester Spy* (8 July 1835) [reprinted from the *Lynn Chronicle*]. Thanks to James Moran for locating this source.

[38] Whittier, *Anti-Slavery Poems*, 72–80; see also [A Kentuckian], "American Slavery vs. Human Liberty," *Quarterly Anti-Slavery Magazine* 1 (October 1836). This mode of criticism was also heard in the African American press. "If it is a sin and a shame for a Turk to hold his fellow in bondage, it is a hundred fold more sinful for a Christian minister." "Why Always Harping at the Church?" *The Colored American* (8 September 1838).

[39] "Extracts from Godwin's Lectures of Colonial Slavery," *Anti-Slavery Reporter* 1 (October 1833): 80.

[40] Lydia Maria Child, *Anti-Slavery Catechism* (Newburyport, MA: Charles Whipple, 1836), 29. See also Samuel Brooke, *Slavery and the Slaveholder's Religion; As Opposed to Christianity* (Cincinnati, OH, 1846), 8; and Charles Elliot, *Sinfulness of American Slavery* (Cincinnati: L Swormstedt and J. H. Power, 1850), 95.

To abolitionists, any society that aimed to reduce humans into chattel was an infidel and soul-denying system. The heritage of islamicism led Americans to associate slavery with Muslim lands. Abolitionists armed themselves with this rhetoric to chastise Americans for imitating such a reprehensible practice.

Through this process of imaginative alchemy, islamicism generated a transnational sympathy with enslaved African Americans. Their plight was associated with the Americans sailors held in Algiers, and Southern slaveholders were identified as the imported embodiment of infidel Barbary taskmasters. This strategy of rhetorical inquiry worked for different speakers and a variety of audiences to increase awareness of the barbarism of slavery. In her autobiography of her experience as a slave, Martha Griffith Browne spoke before a group of white women (symbolic of her broader readership) and asked them to consider the wrong of slavery by imagining being gagged and forced to labor in Algiers and then being offered a path to freedom: "What would you think, if I were to decline, and to say I preferred to remain with the Algerines?" After they responded with silence, she pressed: "Oh, sisters, know ye not that this Algerine captivity that I have painted, is but a poor picture of the daily martyrdom which our slaves endure?"[41] Similarly, while speaking in Congress, Horace Mann challenged a "southern gentleman on this floor" by asking if he had "any doubt, for one moment, that if he were seized by a Barbary corsair and sold into Algerine bondage, and carried a hundred miles into the interior, that he would improve the first opportunity to escape, though at every step in his flight he should crush out a human life, and should leave an ever-widening expanse of conflagration behind him?" The horrors of slavery justified escape as well as retributive punishment of those responsible for its maintenance. Mann threatened, "Let them who live in a powder-mill beware how they madden pyrotechnists."[42] Domestic islamicism, in short, provided space for both a sentimental affiliation and a cutting critique whose contrasting perspectives combined to energize abolitionist polemic for women and men, whites and blacks.

A new comparative focus for antislavery islamicism developed when American newspapers reported that the Bey of Tunis, the leader of the smallest of the Barbary Regencies, had since 1841 actively opposed slavery

---

[41] Martha Griffith Browne, *Autobiography of a Female Slave* (New York: Redfield, 1857), 132. For another example, see *Narrative of the Sufferings of Lewis Clarke, during a Captivity of More than Twenty-Five Years, among the Algerines of Kentucky, One of the So Called States of North America*, Dictated by Himself (Boston: David H. Ela, 1845). The designation of "Algerines" as a symbol of despotism was also employed during the Dorr rebellion in Rhode Island in 1842 to identify those opposed to the People's Constitution.

[42] Horace Mann, *Slavery: Letters and Speeches* (Boston: B. B. Mussey & Co., 1853), 213; also, *Speech of Horace Mann . . . Delivered in the United States House of Representatives, February 15, 1850* (Boston: Redding and Co., 1850), 25.

in his dominions by preventing the slave trade, razing the slave market, emancipating all children born to slaves, and in January of 1846 finally decreeing that all slavery in his domains was prohibited.[43] One year later in 1847, the Sultan of Turkey also took the step of abolishing the slave market in Constantinople (which led to the abolition of the Ottoman slave trade ten years later), prompting the *New York Tribune* to ask: "What would these heathen Turks think of Slavery and the Slave-Trade, as it exists in this republican and civilized country, where Christian slave-breeders so often make merchandise of their own children?"[44] Although the complete removal of slavery in North Africa remained a long-term challenge, prominent Northern abolitionists such as Horace Mann, Theodore Parker, and Charles Sumner took advantage of the polemical charge that even Islamic nations seemed to be progressing in civility at a faster rate than the United States. Such a development was especially startling because of the heritage of orientalist notions about the fatalistic stasis of Islamic culture and the fact that Islam had itself long been figured as an emblem of enslavement.

Horace Mann responded to the abolition of slavery in Tunis by arguing in the House of Representatives that "Mahometanism precedes Christianity, and sets it an example of virtue," citing a tradition of Muhammad that "the worst of men is the seller of men."[45] Theodore Parker in his *Letter to the People of the United States Touching the Matter of Slavery,* was less willing to grant virtue to Tunis, but likewise tactically employed its abolitionist stance to attack the obduracy of the United States against ridding itself of the "Monster-Vice" of slavery. Parker communicated his outrage that the Bey of Tunis, "who knows nothing of unalienable rights and the inborn equality of man," was allowed to usurp the higher moral ground and that slavery could be considered a disgrace to Muslims while still being embraced by Christian nations. He was grieved that the United States, "the first of the foremost nations to proclaim Equality, and Human Rights inborn with all," persisted in protecting the right to own slaves, a practice

---

[43] On the background of the Bey's antislavery efforts, see Leon Carl Brown, *The Tunisia of Ahmad Bey, 1837–1855* (Princeton, NJ: Princeton University Press, 1974). See also See A. Adu Boahen, *Britain, the Sahara, and the Western Sudan, 1788–1861* (Oxford: Clarendon Press, 1964), 140; and John Greenleaf Whittier's article "Abolition in Tunis – Slavery in the United States," *The National Era* 1 (14 October 1847), 1. For an interesting 1863 letter from the mayor of Tunis in response to the American Consul's inquiries about the results of emancipation, see John Hunwick and Eve Troutt Powell, eds., *The African Diaspora in the Mediterranean Lands of Islam* (Princeton, NJ: Markus Wiener Publishers, 2002), 184–7.

[44] "Abolition of the Slave Market in Turkey [from the *New York Tribune*]," *The Liberator* 17 (2 April 1847): 57.

[45] Mann, *Slavery*, 202, 125. William Wells Brown used the decree of the Bey of Tunis as evidence of the infectious spirit of abolitionism to highlight the fact that "Christian, democratic, republican America is doing nothing at all" *A Lecture Delivered before the Female Anti-Slavery Society of Salem* (Boston: Massachusetts Anti-Slavery Society, 1847), 16.

that "restores Barbarism...[and] establishes Ferocity by federal law."[46] Parker even staged a divine judgment of American slavery that depicted the "Judge of all the Earth" reading the Golden Rule to Americans while delivering His verdict: "While the poor Mussulman, whom thou calls't Pagan and shuts't out from Heaven – sets free all men, how much more art thou thyself condemned; yea, by the Bible which thou sendest to the outcasts of the world?"[47]

The fullest response to the Bey's injunction abolishing slavery came from Charles Sumner who produced a prodigious history of Mediterranean slavery in 1847, which he called *White Slavery in the Barbary States*. Both a scholarly history and polemical tract, Sumner's essay draws a distinct parallel between North Africa and the American South. "There are no two spaces on the surface of the map of equal extent... which present so many distinctive features of resemblance," Sumner asserted, going so far to emphasize that the coast of Algiers and the line of the Missouri Compromise shared the common latitude of 36' 30". However, Sumner reserved his harshest judgments not for the slave-holders of Algiers, who he believed "had been reared in a religion of slavery," but rather for the Christian slave-owners of the United States. In fact, Sumner was aware of how Muslim slavery and Christian captivity in North Africa were both "mitigated by the genial influence of Mahometanism."[48] Sumner viewed Tunisian abolition as a sign of an immanent global conversion to antislavery beliefs that betokened the impending disappearance of the "barbarism of slavery" in the United States. He romanticized Algiers and Tunis as having undergone a conversion "like Saul of Tarsis" that placed them "in sacred fellowship with all those principles which promote the progress of man."[49]

Southern supporters of slavery recognized the rhetorical power of the ways in which the abolitionists linked them to Islam, and some Southern whites responded by invoking their own islamicism. In a variety of ways, they countered attempts by abolitionists to enlist Islam as part of their own arsenal of argument and deployed the currency of the Bey's edict to support their proslavery sentiments. To Southerners, Northerners who set up

---

[46] Theodore Parker, *Letter to the People of the United States Touching the Matter of Slavery* (Boston: James Munroe and Company, 1848), 117, 116.

[47] Parker, *Letter to the People*, 7, 108–10, 116–19.

[48] Charles Sumner, *White Slavery in the Barbary States* (Boston: W. Ticknor, 1847), 6, 53, 57. This was a theme that Sumner would return to many times in his oratorical career. Even in the heat of the Civil War, the year before the signing of the Emancipation Proclamation, Sumner spoke in the Senate of the effort to emancipate African American slaves in Washington with public money as a "complete parallel" to the raising of funds to free American captives in Algiers in 1796. Sumner, "Ransom of Slaves at the National Capital, Speech in the U.S. Senate, March 31, 1862," *Works*, 8:283–97.

[49] Sumner, "The Barbarism of Slavery, Speech in Senate, June 4, 1860," *Works*, 6: 161; Sumner, *White Slavery*, 60.

Mediterranean pirates as a "glorious example" of liberty demonstrated little more than their own despotic proclivities. They opposed this rhetoric of the "grand triumph" of freedom by reminding their readers that any proclamation of emancipation by a Muslim leader was a tautology because all the population of his realms remained his slaves.[50] Edward B. Bryan attacked this logic of abolitionist islamicism by claiming that the Qur'an, like the Bible, actually countenanced slavery and argued that Muhammad's support for emancipation was merely an effective means of swelling the number of converts. "The imposter in order to gain a follower, liberated a slave," wrote Bryan, "What a powerful argument for modern abolitionists!"[51] A critic of abolitionism writing in the *Southern Literary Messenger* scoffed at Charles Sumner's assertion that Christian America should learn from the examples of Muslim emancipation. "The Russian, the Turk, the Moor, the Algerine! Mild, estimable, tender-hearted people, how can we resist the contagion of their example!" This writer did not trust reports of the antislavery efforts of the Bey of Tunis, referring to classical history: "We are afraid the Bey lives too near the ruins of Carthage to escape the suspicion of Punic faith."[52] A report on the *Creole* case of 1841 during which African Americans mutinied to gain their freedom determined that the rebels should be punished because if a company of slaves held by a Barbary regent had murdered subjects of "any civilized nation" upon the high seas, they would be found guilty.[53] Another Southerner took the different strategy of islamicizing the abolitionists themselves when he claimed that their "rabid" doctrines were so "wildly insane" that they would "shock the moral sensibilities of a community of Barbary pirates."[54]

But these Southern counterattacks did not stop Northern abolitionists from regularly engaging the rhetoric of islamicism. In a series of articles in *The National Era* in 1847 and 1848 as well as in many poems, John Greenleaf Whittier testified how his republican and Christian sensibilities were mortified by the ways that Muslim actions shamed American failures. He engaged in the politics of critical displacement when he poetically imagined the retort of the "turbaned Turk and fiery Russ" to American criticisms of their despotism: "Go, loose your fettered slaves at home, Then turn, and ask the like of us!"[55] In response to Sumner's treatise on white slavery, Whittier

---

[50] Thomas P. Kettrell, "The Future of the South," *Debow's Review* 10 (10 February 1851): 135; and 21 (September 1856): 312.

[51] Edward B. Bryan, *The Rightful Remedy. Addressed to the Slaveholders of the South* (Charleston, SC: Walker & James, 1850), 115–16.

[52] "A Few Thoughts on Slavery," *Southern Literary Messenger* 20 (April 1854): 201.

[53] "The Creole Case," *Southern Quarterly Review* 2 (July 1842): 61.

[54] "The Present Aspect of Abolitionism," *Southern Literary Messenger* 13 (July 1847): 432.

[55] John Greenleaf Whittier, "Stanzas," in *The Anti-Slavery Picknick*, ed. John A. Collins (Boston: H. W. Williams, 1842), 68.

researched and reported on British attempts to encourage Muslim leaders to abolish slavery in their dominions. Whittier recounted the abolition of slavery from Ceylon (Sri Lanka) in 1816 during which "[t]he Mahomedan law offices admitted that 'all men are by nature free,' and that the Koran only allows of slavery as the punishment of the crime of the infidel who takes up arms against the faith of Islam." He compared Senator John Calhoun's defense of slavery and Secretary Daniel Webster's reticent position in the *Creole* case with a bold proclamation from the Muslim King of Oude that eloquently prohibited the selling of any slaves in one of the richest areas of British India.[56] In his famous poem "The Christian Slave," Whittier deployed the paradox of Muslim emancipation to emphasize the disgraceful ineffectiveness of the Church in resisting the South's deepening commitment to slavery:

> Oh, shame! the Moslem thrall,
> Who, with his master, to the Prophet kneels,
> While turning to the sacred Kebla* feels
> His fetter break and fall.
> Cheers for the turbaned Bey
> Of robber-peopled Tunis! he hath torn
> The dark slave-dungeons open, and hath born
> Their inmates into day.
> But our poor slave in vain
> Turns to the Christian shrine his aching eyes;
> Its rites will only swell his market price,
> And rivet on his chain.[57]

Whittier not only boldly challenged the religious legitimacy of Southern slavery, but he also championed the Christian patriotism of the abolitionists. In 1850, he wrote a poem called "Derne" that reenacted William Eaton's storming of that Tripolitan city forty-five years earlier. His purpose was to exhort his readers to transfer the sentimental heroism they celebrated in Eaton's past exploits into full support for the abolitionist activists of their own age who were striving to end the suffering of the "living dead" in their midst. William Eaton himself had paid heavy political costs for the equations

---

*Kebla = Qı̄blı̄h: the shrine in Mecca toward which all prayer in Islam is ordinated.

[56] John Greenleaf Whittier, "Abolition in Ceylon – Mohammedan and Hindoo Slaveholders," *The National Era* 1 (3 June 1847): 2. Whittier also wrote of a group of Persian mullahs who determined that slavery was an abomination against Islam, a ruling that was rejected by the representative of the Shah who felt it would be a sin to prevent thousands of Africans from embracing Islam. "The Shah of Persia and the Slave Trade," *The National Era* 2 (7 December 1848): 193.

[57] Whittier, "The Christian Slave," *Anti-Slavery Poems*, 3:86–9. Whittier's verses were widely distributed including a reprint in John Theophilus Kramer, *The Slave-Auction* (Boston: Robert F. Wallcut, 1859), 45–6.

he had made between North African and American slavery.[58] Whittier was dismayed by the fact that the American flag that Eaton had raised in Tripoli as a symbol of liberty now floated above a slave market in Washington, D.C., while the Bey of Tunis outlawed the sale of slaves in his domains.[59] Whittier contrasted the Bey's courageous stance with federal unwillingness to abolish the slave trade in the nation's capital by repeating the words of an exasperated Secretary of the Treasury who cried out in Congress: "Is the Crescent to be the symbol of freedom, and the Cross of slavery?"[60]

By suggesting that despotic lands were more successful in the antislavery campaign than the touted land of liberty itself, islamicist rhetoric transacted the very conversion of Islam to benevolence that missionaries were never able to accomplish in the field. In fact, long-term missionaries to Persia such as Justin Perkins viewed the persistence of slavery in the United States as "a most mortifying spectacle" to the world that had the effect of "confounding and astounding the gazing nations who would look to American for a hope of deliverance!"[61] Domestic abolitionism thus became another field for fighting the crusade against Islam.

As more travelers made their way to Islamic lands, Americans learned that Islamic slavery was a different beast than the race slavery of the U.S. South. The increased exposure of Westerners to Ottoman culture after the Greek War of Independence manifested itself in the publication of narratives and letters, many of which contained images of cultural life that contradicted stereotypes of Islam as a system of heartless bondage. An article in the *Pennsylvania Freeman* that was reprinted in *The Colored American* exemplifies the critical resources that comparative islamicism brought to African American abolitionism. The author learned the contrasts between Turkish and domestic slavery from reading a travel narrative by a British woman.

> The Turk never insults or injures the feelings of his slave – who is indeed nearly on terms of equality with him – he kneels side by side with his bondman in the mosque – he has no prejudice against color: – some of the highest offices of the State are in the hands of black men – and he who is a slave to-day may be raised to the dignity of a Pacha tomorrow. The hope of preferment, dignity, wealth and honor, reaches the humblest slave in the Ottoman Empire. But hope never visits the slave of our christian Republic.[62]

---

[58] Whittier, "Derne," *Anti-Slavery Poems*, 3: 155–9. Eaton quoted in Sumner, *White Slavery*, 53. William Goodell, *Slavery and Anti-slavery: A History of the Great Struggle in Both Hemispheres* (New York: W. Harned, 1853), 282–3.

[59] John Greenleaf Whittier, "The Spirit of the Age – Abolition of Turkish Slave Markets," *The National Era* 1 (1 April 1847): 3.

[60] *The National Era* 1 (14 October 1847): 1.

[61] Justin Perkins, *Our Country's Sin: A Sermon Preached to the Members and Families of the Nestorian Mission at Oroomiah, Persia, July 3, 1853* (Boston: John P. Jewett and Company; 1854), 10–11.

[62] "Turkish Slavery," *The Colored American* (9 June 1838).

If American abolitionist prose had infidelized the practices of American slaveholders by comparing them with the benighted terror of Turkish slavery, new images of the different system of slavery in Muslim lands shocked them with its comparative benignity. In this way, representations of the comparative practice of Turkish slavery offered ameliorative examples to those Americans wishing to reform their own peculiar institution and forced them to question whether "the Bible of the Christian [was] less merciful than the Koran."[63]

The fact that slaves could not serve as witnesses in either system of slavery did not mean that Islam did not provide more legal protections. Theodore Parker noted that in Turkey, unlike in the American South, "the marriage of a slave was sacred as that of a peer of the realm" as well as an inviolable contract protected by legal custom. Parker also argued that under Turkish law the slave received only half the sentence of free people for common offenses, whereas in Virginia there were six offenses that merited death for a slave but not for a white man. "In some States the law is milder," he attested, "but in none does the Christian Republican of Anglo-Saxon descent imitate the humanity of the Mussulman, and legally favor the weaker part – correcting slaves as the children of the State."[64] *A Buckeye Abroad* wrote in 1852 that "the slave of the Turk is not the slave of the planter, by a good deal" and reasoned that "it is the religion [Islam] which softens the harshness of the institution [slavery], and makes it a shadow."[65]

Examining the uses of comparative orientalism within the notices posted within one abolitionist's scrapbook from the early 1850s provides other examples of the ameliorative examples regularly relayed to American readers by travelers in the Near East. One account published in the *Salem Register* described the practice of slavery at the Arabian port of Mocha (the source of the coffee drink of the same name). Slaves were seldom worked severely, many learned to read and write, and they "frequently dress as expensively as their masters." Such refinement qualified them to undertake offices of trust for their masters that sometimes enabled them to earn their freedom

---

[63] This perspective had been voiced by earlier visitors to the Ottoman Empire such as a Russian ambassador who attested that "great misrepresentations hav[e] gone forth into all parts of Europe, respecting the state of slavery in the Ottoman empire, upon which subject no people on earth harbour such stupid prejudices as the freemen of the corporate cities of England." *The Philadelphia Magazine and Review* 6 (June 1799).

[64] Parker, "Letter of 22 December 1847," *Letter*, 89–90, 1. Comparative information also appeared in the Southern press. See, for example, William Boulware, "Extracts from Notes of a Voyage in the East in 1843," which discussed how Turkish slaves were trusted and "treated with great lenity and kindness," and that Muslims believed that "God will preserve from the torments of Hell as many parts of the body of an emancipator, as there are of the slaves set at liberty." *The Southern and Western Literary Messenger and Review* 12 (March 1846): 172–3.

[65] Samuel S. Cox, *A Buckeye Abroad* (New York: Putnam, 1852), 245–6.

and become wealthy merchants themselves.[66] "For even the Turk, bigoted as he is, does not refuse the liberty of his religion to his slave, for he and his bondsman kneel side by side in the same mosque," reported *The Colored American*, "but American Christians who would think themselves contaminated by sitting in the same pew with the descendents of those men from whom they have derived all their knowledge."[67] William Schauffler, the missionary who had advised James Merrick and who had been in the Near East for almost a quarter of a century, reported on aspects of Muslim manumission that he felt "put to shame our so-called Christian nation." These practices included not only the teaching that manumission was "a good and pious work" and that slaves were permitted to purchase their own freedom, but also protections for single slave women that gave them their liberty if they married a free man, and forced her master not to sell her or force her to marry another if she had borne his child – who, unlike in the United States, was free at birth. Any slave who acquired his or her freedom under his master's will or by an act of Providence was protected from the claims of heirs. Schauffler was so impressed by these regulations that he argued that should they "find a place on our statute books, they would be a deadly blow at some of the strongest roots of American slavery."[68] Another writer attacked Nathan Davis, an American Southerner who developed a plan to export slaves to work on the "model" cotton farm near Constantinople of his brother James B. Davis, by reminding him that under Turkish law such slaves would gain their freedom in seven years: "What turns would it make in American slavery, to have the Turkish trump of jubilee ring throughout all our slave borders every seventh year. Yet, *a la Turque*, to be as mean as a Turk, has passed into a proverb. Aye, go Christian slaveocrat, to the moslem Turk, learn of him, and be wise."[69]

In contrasting slavery among Muslims with the practice in the United States, the American abolitionists were right to point out the differences,

---

[66] "Slavery at Mocha [from the *Salem Register*, May 1851]," in *Antislavery Scrapbook* [unpublished manuscript at the American Antiquarian Society], 1: 19.

[67] *The Colored American* (3 March 1839), from an "Address to the Colored People of the United States" reported in the *Cleveland Observer*. A year earlier the same paper exclaimed "If it is a sin and a shame for a Turk to hold his fellow in bondage, it is a hundred fold more sinful for a Christian minister" (8 September 1838).

[68] William Schauffler, "Mohammedan Slavery, (1853–4)," *Antislavery Scrapbook*, 2: 101.

[69] P. S. B. "Slavery in Turkey," *Antislavery Scrapbook*, 1: 32. This man's name was referred to as Mr. Advise. Mary Boykin Chesnut's diary refers to a Nathan Davis, whom she called "Nathan the unlucky" after referring to "The Turkey fiasco, &c&c.>." *Mary Chesnut's Civil War*, ed. C. Vann Woodward (New Haven, CT: Yale University Press, 1981), 319, n4. For an account of the three-year fiasco of the Davis brothers (1846–9) that blames their failure partly on the laziness of his contracted Armenian laborers, see Charles MacFarlane, *Turkey and Its Destiny*, 2 vols. (Philadelphia: Lea and Blanchard, 1850), 1: 45–52; 2: 369–75. The only industrious laborers, according to MacFarlane, were four emancipated African Americans who "looked down with contempt on the lazy, loitering, *housemaid* blacks of this country" (2: 248).

but they did so in ways that at times overly romanticized Muslim slavery. Muslim jurisprudence, based on the fact that the Qur'an legitimated slavery, accorded the slave a clear legal status with protections never possessed by American slaves. The Prophet Muhammad himself had reformed ancient practices of slavery by outlawing abuses and appealing to the consciences of those who held slaves to respect their rights as humans. Islam taught that no born Muslim could ever be enslaved, a fact that rendered slavery a religious marker of unbelief rather than a racial badge of inferiority. With few exceptions, slavery in Muslim cultures was primarily domestic rather than economic and therefore symbolized consumption rather than production. The dynamic of this domestic slavery was quite different from slaves serving in the "big house" of American plantations in the U.S. South as Muslim slaves were often incorporated within the family structures of their owners, and fed and clothed accordingly.[70] Slavery in Islamic societies was also much less of a permanent condition because the Qur'an taught that manumission was a pious act of expiation and encouraged slave-owners to support the wish of slaves to buy their own freedom. The historian Bernard Lewis has likewise argued that at no time during the career of Middle Eastern slavery did a system of racial oppression arise with characteristics like that of slavery in the Americas.[71] As these elements of Muslim slavery were progressively revealed to American audiences, they not only contributed comparative ammunition to the arsenal of abolitionist argument but also effectively defused some of the harsh prejudices against the Turks.

Strategic uses such as these by the abolitionist press had the ironic effect of romanticizing Muslim slavery, contributing to an exoticization of oriental practices whose prominence reemerged as the nineteenth century progressed. Bernard Lewis wrote that the notion of Islamic racial innocence was a Western myth put in the service of arguments for abolition. "Not for the first time," he wrote, "a mythologized and idealized Islam provided a stick with which to chastise Western failings."[72] *The Anti-Slavery Record* published a traveler's letter that revealed the attitude of a Turkish government official about prejudice based on color: "It would be against the principles of the Mahomedan religion to treat any human being with disdain, or to suppose that God was a capricious or a partial parent in bestowing various

---

[70] Ronald Segal, *Islam's Black Slaves: The Other Black Diaspora* (New York: Farrar, Straus & Giroux, 2001), 107. One exception was the employment of slaves in the large-scale cotton cultivation that developed in Egypt as an alternative to American cotton that the Civil War had prevented from reaching traditional transatlantic markets. Slaves were also employed harvesting dates at desert oases and in the clove industry in Zanzibar. See Norman Robert Bennett, "Americans in Zanzibar, 1825–1845," *Essex Institute Historical Collections* 155 (July 1959): 239–62.

[71] Lewis, *Race and Slavery*, 99. Determining the nature of racism in Muslim societies, however, remains a complex endeavor. See John Hunwick, "The Same But Different: Africans in Slavery in the Mediterranean Muslim World," in *The African Diaspora*, xviii–xxi.

[72] Lewis, *Race and Slavery*, 101.

forms and tints on his children." To this the traveler responded: "Ought not Christians to blush at this contrast?"[73] While Islam did remedy some of the more abusive aspects of slavery more effectively than the Christianized cultures of the United States, slavery was in some ways legitimated by the Qur'an itself. Traditions of manumission in Islam also had the ironic effect of requiring new supplies of slaves.[74] The forced migration of African slaves through the Sahara and across the Red Sea into Islamic lands has been estimated to be larger in number and as grueling in duration as those forced to undergo the "middle passage" to the Americas, with such overland routes largely obscured from the eyes of Western abolitionists.[75] The fact that no popular abolitionist movement arose within the world of Islam, and the slow pace of Muslim leaders in completely ending slavery, can be explained partly by the fact that abolitionism itself could be construed as unislamic, much in the ways the proslavery advocates found biblical justification for their practices.

Nevertheless the practices of Turkish slavery mentioned in the writings of some of the most informed Americans did cast a more critical comparative glare on the inhumanities of the peculiar institution in the United States. These conjunctions between islamicism and antislavery reveal the deep extent to which the Islamic world figured in the cultural awareness of Americans before the Civil War. The contrasting logics of orientalist example within abolitionist polemic demonstrate the versatility of comparative history as a strategy for reproaching the immoralities of domestic slavery. Examining the transnational charge of such transactions reveals a process that broadened the cosmopolitan consciousness of early Americans at the same time that it confirmed, qualified, or sometimes romanticized orientalist constructions of Muslim practices.

CRUSADING AGAINST AL–COHOL: ISLAMICISM IN ANTEBELLUM TEMPERANCE REFORM

While reformers often employed the rhetoric of Islamic orientalism in their attempts to protest the injustices of slave-holding in the United States, many antebellum Americans viewed the thralldom of national citizens to alcohol as a more widespread, insidious, and longer lasting form of domestic bondage. It was the universality of alcoholism throughout American territories (especially in Northern cities), as well as the fact that alcohol itself could be

---

[73] "Mahometanism and Christianity. Extract of a letter from E. S. Abdy, Esq." *The Anti-Slavery Record* 2, Whole No. 24 (December 1836): 170.

[74] Segal, *Islam's Black Slaves*, 115.

[75] Ehud R. Toledano, *The Ottoman Slave Trade and Its Suppression, 1840–1890* (Princeton, NJ: Princeton University Press, 1982).

racialized as an alien other, that rendered temperance a more popular vehicle of antebellum reform than abolitionism. The prolific temperance author Lucius M. Sargent claimed in a Fourth of July address that Africans were not the only ones in bondage when he called the drunkard "a self-made slave, bowing before the unrelenting tyranny of his own unnatural appetites and passions."[76] The alcoholic binge that swept through the United States in the first third of the nineteenth century emerged as one of the most contentious issues in early antebellum cultural politics. The movement dedicated to temperance attracted a group of reformers as ethically engaged as the abolitionists, many of whom imagined both sobriety and emancipation as necessary prerequisites for the moral progress of the nation. The proliferation of temperance societies, especially after the founding of the American Temperance Society in 1826, and the publication of a steady barrage of temperance newspapers, tracts, sermons, and tales signaled that redeeming the nation from the ills of intemperance was a fervent aspiration of the culture of democratic reform beginning with the presidency of Andrew Jackson.[77]

Before the experiment with legal prohibition in the 1850s, temperance advocates focused their narrative attack most fully on trying to persuade fellow citizens that drunkenness prevented the United States from progressing toward the ideal of a prosperous democracy. Throughout this campaign, alcohol was essentialized as the vector propagating several national epidemics, including violence, crime, delinquency, insanity, idleness, and pauperism – all weaknesses leading to unproductive lives and untimely deaths that sapped the republic of its moral vigor. Aware that blaming the individual drinker might impede the recruitment of converts, some temperance advocates dramatized the social cost of inebriation through sociological,

---

[76] Lucius M. Sargent, *Address, Delivered at the Beneficent Congregational Meeting-house, July 4, 1838* (Providence, RI: B. Cranston & Co., 1838), 4.

[77] Jed Dannenbaum claims: "In popularity, longevity, and cumulative influence the 'temperance movement' . . . surpasses all other reform movements." "The Crusade against Drink," *Reviews in American History* 9 (December 1981): 497. Robert C. Fuller attests to the complexity of the temperance movement: "It would be wrong to interpret the growing prohibitionists sentiments as rooted solely in religious and ethnic prejudice. Prohibition was also very much an ideological agenda born of Christian commitment to moral sanctification, capitalistic concern with worker efficiency, moral outrage over the erosion of family stability, and patriotic defense of the need for an alert and sober citizenry. Yet without question, the call to prohibition had within it a certain resonance to the class and ethnic tensions of a rapidly industrializing society." *Wine and Religion, A Cultural History of Wine Drinking in the United States* (Knoxville: University of Tennessee Press, 1996), 86. The temperance movement also reflected the declining centrality of the rum-distilling industry to American manufacturing and the availability of a national grain market for farmers who had earlier preserved their crops as whiskey. See W. J. Rorabaugh, *The Alcoholic Republic: An American Tradition* (New York: Oxford University Press, 1979); and Ian R. Tyrrell, *Sobering Up: From Temperance to Prohibition in Antebellum America, 1800–1860* (Westport, CT: Greenwood Press, 1979).

statistical, and fictional vignettes of the destruction of family and community that drunkenness left in its wake. Other critics applied the findings of physiological science to the problem of alcoholism in order to expose its biological destructiveness. Both of these methods aimed to expose the evils of alcohol by displaying the damage it caused to both physical bodies and the national body-politic.

Temperance activists developed a more direct assault on the agency of alcohol when they constructed the substance itself as sinful and personified it as an emissary of satanic evil. The process of transforming alcoholic spirits into the "demon of the distillery" involved labeling liquor with a wide variety of aliases of the devil and cultural allusions to the sorcery it was imagined to perpetrate. Alcohol was often crowned with the title of King or Prince because of its capacity to tyrannize its votaries and dissolve their republican sensibilities. Polemicists expanded the identification of alcohol as fiend, beast, or villain by associating drunkenness with devotion to monstrous idols such as the biblical Belial, Moloch, or Leviathan or the mythological Hydra, Bacchus, or Juggernaut. The rhetorical excesses of these legendary allusions enlisted the energies of evil to convince citizens of the dangers of alcohol by allying it with traditional enemies of Christian patriotism.

Figuring alcohol as an offspring of Islam was a clear strategy in its construction as an inveterate enemy of American virtue. One example of the islamicization of alcohol was the tactic of comparing its destructive capacities with cholera and other desolating blights arising from the antichristian East, such as the Simoom wind of Arabia or the frequently figured poisonous Bohon Upas tree of Java, both of which were believed to destroy all life in its vicinity.[78] The portrayal of alcohol as an oriental agent of desolation is clear in the imagery of a temperance hymn from 1834: "A foe trod o'er the earth. This breath, / Like the sirocco's pois'ning blast / O'er verdant plains, left blight and death / And desolation where it pass'd."[79] But the most dramatic strategic use of islamicism in antebellum temperance literature was the

---

[78] One temperance lecturer asked his audience how they would explain to the next generation the harvest of iniquity associated with intemperance: can we persuade them that some baneful Simoom has sucked the virtue form the soil? that some nation stronger than we have scorched our fields with fire?" R. E. Selden, Jr. Esq., *An Address before the Middlesex Association, for the Promotion of Temperance* (Middletown, CT: Parmalee & Greenfield, 1829), 14. The frequently reprinted legend of the Upas described a tree whose roots poisoned the very soil in which it grew. One work, narrated in the form of a dialogue between a mother and her children, viewed cholera as an "Asiatic disease" that had been "prepared by the Almighty to show his abhorrence of the sin of intemperance." Harvey Newcomb, *History of Intemperance: With an Account of Temperance Reformation* (Boston: Massachusetts Sabbath School Union, 1833), 66–72. On cholera and intemperance, see also Harvey Newcomb, "On the Immorality of the Traffic in Ardent Spirit, Appendix to the Fifth Report of the American Temperance Society – 1832," in *Permanent Documents of the American Temperance Society*, Vol. I (Boston: Seth Bliss, 1835), 205–7.

[79] *American Temperance Intelligencer* 1 (March 1834): 2.

way that the orientalist charges of Islam as antichristian and despotic were transferred from an enemy alien to American shores onto alcohol itself, a domestically manufactured substance that infiltrated the homes, taverns, and workplaces of the United States.

Importing images of alcohol as a heathen evil poisoning the fabric of domestic morality rendered it into an emblematically un-American substance inimical to the progress of both democracy and enlightened religion. The portrayal of alcohol as an invader and ravager of the virtuous republic also summoned the traditional energies of the missionary crusade as a resource in the service of domestic reform. Moreover, this cultural conversion also attempted to compress the widespread hegemony of the Islamic world, against which missionaries had struggled with little avail, into a problem that could be controlled by Americans themselves. Without recourse to Muslims, Americans could register their triumph over the tyranny and infidelity associated with Islam simply by ridding themselves of their own drunken behaviors. At a time when American Protestantism was being "democratized," devotion to the cause of temperance reform allowed evangelicals a new cultural field upon which to carry out their millennial fantasies.[80] While the agents of such reform were local and domestic, the significance of their actions lay in the sacred and cosmic realms of Christian victory that had long motivated the millennial project of American nationalism.

Islamicism provided a versatile archive and cosmopolitan resource for the antebellum temperance movement and its contest of the cultural legitimacy of American drinking practices. Activists on all sides of the argument deployed islamicist rhetoric to register their varied commitments. Alcohol signified to some a material agent of the deception of Islam. To others the imperative of abstinence itself seemed a Muslim manifestation that contravened biblical teachings. The fact that Muslim lands had already established prohibition as a cultural norm led some activists to romanticize Turkish examples of temperance, as well as the surrogate practices of drinking water and coffee, as models for domestic consumption. Even while this complex rhetoric was imported into domestic discursive exchange, American rum itself circulated as a commodity of international trade in ways that challenged the Protestant commitment to temperance as a global practice of morality.

The identification of alcohol with Islam was possible because the process of distillation was known to have been invented by Arabian chemists, a fact that can be traced in the word "alcohol," which is derived from the Arabic

---

[80] Robert H. Abzug has suggested that "temperance provided an attractive version of ritual identity for Christians." *Cosmos Crumbling: American Reform and the Religious Imagination* (New York: Oxford University Press, 1994), 93. See Nathan Hatch, *The Democratization of American Christianity* (New Haven, CT: Yale University Press, 1989).

words *al-* (the) and *kohl* (fine, impalpable).[81] Secretary of War Lewis Cass, while addressing the newly formed Congressional Temperance Society in 1833, explained that "[t]he Arabian chemists were the first to introduce it, and not all the drugs of Arabia have been able to counteract its pernicious influence."[82] Allegories personified alcohol as a tempter and tyrant of Arabian birth, the offspring of the sorcery of the devil. "My great anxiety," wrote Alcohol himself in his *Memoir*, "has been to shun the imputation of a *low* extraction, which some have surmised belongs to me; for instance, that my birth-place was the '*Bottomless Pit*,' and my father, '*Beelzebub*' himself."[83] Similarly, Alcohol narrated his own oriental genealogy in a ballad published in the popular press:

> Away, away, in the Moslem land,
> They call me forth with a wizard wand;
> The burning sun of the Arab's sky
> Grew dim in the light of my flaming eye,
> And the serpent crown that bound my brow
> Betokened the power I'm wielding now.
> They call me a dark and poison thing,
> With a crazy brain, a serpent's sting,
> And they say my hot polluted breath
> Was the pestilential gale of death.[84]

The Arabian origin of alcohol led some temperance reformers to imagine an elaborate conspiracy theory about its malicious power to destroy religious principles. Expressing great indignation that Christians had so long been the "miserable dupes of *mahommedan* imposition," the Richmond Society for the Promotion of Temperance, in their First Annual Report in 1830, railed out against their fellow citizens who remained unaware of the "*diabolical*

---

[81] See, for example, "Alcohol," *The American Temperance Almanac, for the Year of our Lord 1835* (Albany, NY: Packard & Van Benthuysen, 1834), 30–1.

[82] Lewis Cass, "An Address Delivered in the Capitol...at the Formation of the Congressional Temperance Society, Feb 24, 1833," *Proceedings and Speeches at a Meeting for the Promotion of the Cause of Temperance, in the United States* (Washington, DC: Way and Gideon, 1833), 8–9, reprinted in Charles Yale, ed., *The Temperance Reader* (Boston: Hilliard, Gray, and Company, 1835), 12. Temperance advocates were unable to see the Arabian invention of distillation as an indication of Islamic advances in science that, when transmitted to Europe, would assist Europe to awaken from its own "Dark Ages."

[83] *Memoir of Alcohol. Written by Himself. Including Biographical Sketches of His Sons Brandy, Rum, and Whiskey. And of His Daughter Gin* (Hartford, CT: Robinson & Pratt, 1834), 8–9. See also Yale, ed., *The Temperance Reader*, 140. Another biography of alcohol linked its Arabian homeland with the lineage of Beelzebub. C. S., "The Sorcerer," *Temperance Recorder* (Albany, NY) (3 July 1832): 33.

[84] Mrs. Sarah T. Bolton, "[From the *Spectator*] The Song of Alcohol," *The Ohio Washingtonian Organ, and Sons of Temperance Record* (Cincinnati) (June 6, 1846): 337. The poem ends with these verses: "I teach the souls that God has given / To mock the oracle of heaven; / I reign, I reign, in every land, / And rule the world with a flaming brand."

poison" in their midst, producing an elaborate conspiracy theory that is worth quoting at length.

> A subtle spirit, has been found out, in a cruel and an iron age, amid the darkness of the mahommedan barbarity, . . . it is banished in the country, and the empire, which gave it existence; and the besotted mussulman, wiser than the age which are to succeed him, interdicts its use as unfit for his brethren of the CRESCENT, but pronounces it good enough for *christian dogs!*
>
> Inspired with the most deadly and diabolical hate towards the followers of the CROSS, the same besotted mussulman, palms upon *them*, the wretched delusion, which has ruined himself. – He tells them, that, imbued with this infernal spirit, their nature will be exalted, and *they* rendered perfectly happy! And the delusion has lasted for more than nine hundred years. The infernal spirit . . . imposed upon christendom by its bitterest enemies, has insinuated its way throughout the Cottages of poverty, and has even pervaded the Palaces of the great, – It is mingled with, and makes part of, the daily beverage of our lives, – we have swallowed the poison and have known it not! – Century after century has rolled away, while millions upon millions of our race have drunk their bane and died, falling unconsciously before the mighty destroyer.[85]

Part of the reason why alcohol could be viewed as emerging from a satanic conspiracy was that it was a substance not found in nature but rather one that had to be concocted by secular science. Another widely distributed temperance pamphlet voiced this logic in dialogue form.

> "Pray, in what stream of his bounty, from what mountain and hill does it flow down to man?"
>
> "O, it is in the rye, and the apple, and the sugar, and the Mussulman has taught us Christians how to distil it."
>
> " – And so the poet tells us Satan taught his legions how to make gunpowder. . . ."[86]

This infernal figuration of alcohol reflected cultural anxieties about how the narrative of religious redemption was challenged by both persistent belief in the supernatural agency of magic and the healing claims of secular medicine. For staunch temperance reformers like these, many of whom were ministers, alcohol itself seemed the embodiment of antichristian evil and

---

[85] *The First Annual Report of the Richmond Society for the Promotion of Temperance* (Richmond, VA: T. W. White, 8 January 1830), 8–9. An article twenty years later attests to the persistence of this formulation: "as if the finger of Providence pointed it out in history," *The American Temperance Magazine* finds followers of Islam to be "the unhonored instrument of evil who discovered the baleful poison, still bearing in its name its Mahometan origin – ALCOHOL." 2 (1851): 303. See also *The Temperance Text-Book: A Collection of Facts and Interesting Anecdotes, Illustrating the Evils of Intoxicating Drinks*, 3rd ed. (Philadelphia: E. L. Carey and A. Hart, 1838), 11–12.

[86] Rev. John Marsh, *Putnam and the Wolf; or, the Monster Destroyed, An Address Delivered at Pomfret, Con., October 28, 1829, before the Windham Co. Temperance Society* (Hartford, CT: D. F. Robinson, 1830), 13.

their effort to stem its tide nothing short of a new facet of the millennium-old "crusade" against Islam. Indeed several nineteenth-century temperance newspapers from different sections of the country emblazoned this "crusade" in the very titles of their publications.[87] Aligning the reign of alcohol with Islam's realm of antichristian evil enabled helped polemicists to construct an equivalence between temperance and Christian mission and helps to explain how abstinence came to be considered one of the dogmas of evangelical belief.[88]

Forging this link between alcohol and the Eastern antichrist enabled the weight of orientalist eschatology to brand alcohol as a poison manufactured by the devil. The term "mighty destroyer" was one of the more common designations for alcohol, a name that connected it with Apollyon, the "destroying angel" of Revelation's Fifth Trumpet, which was connected in eschatological thought with the rise of Islam. Alcohol was figured as a satanic plague released from the bottomless pit to pollute the morals of the world. In this vein, the *Journal of the American Temperance Union* called alcohol "one of the pestilential fruits of the apostasy... [that] will cease with all other sin."[89] John Pierpont, a Boston minister often called upon for occasional poems and hymns (and later ousted from his pulpit for "preaching *temperance* too intemperately"[90]), composed an ode in which Alcohol plays the role of the destroying angel of the bottomless pit.

> Wake! Wake! friends of your kind,
> There's a Demon, a Demon abroad!
> Ye'll scent him in every breath of the wind;
> Around him is woe, Death and Hell are behind! –
> The foe of man and of God.
> The *Prince* of the Devils is it,
> Escaped from the bottomless pit, –
> Escaped, in his wrath, or his mirth,
> To put out the lights of the earth.

The poem's remaining four stanzas depict the stealthy conquests of this scorpion fiend before calling upon its audience to forestall the coming apocalypse of inebriation by resolving to close up the "pits that yawn... [t]hat spirits

---

[87] *The Crusader* was the name of two papers from the 1850s: one from Cincinnati and another a southern New Hampshire publication that served Manchester, Nashua, Dover, and Portsmouth; also in that decade the *Temperance Crusader* was published in Warsaw, Illinois. The early 1870s also featured *The Crusader* of Chicago and of Gosport, Indiana.

[88] The fact that most Roman Catholics came from drinking cultures help to further the connection between demon rum and antichristian pollution.

[89] *Journal of the American Temperance Union* 2 (July 1838): 104. Ellen Dwyer discussed the centrality in temperance rhetoric of plague imagery and the association of alcohol as a Destroyer and a Devil, although without discussing the eschatological dimension. See "The Rhetoric of Excess," "The Rhetoric of Reform: A Study of Verbal Persuasion and Belief Systems in the Anti-Masonic and Temperance Movements, 1825–1860" (Ph.D. diss., Yale University, 1977), 183, 187–8.

[90] *Niles' National Register* 57 (7 December 1839): 240.

infernal may rise" so that they "[n]o more shall insult the skies."[91] Another speaker lecturing temperance societies in the Hudson River Valley claimed "[h]ere is one monster – one plague of plagues – one scorpion of scorpions – one curse of curses, that can single-handed, outdo them all . . . [h]is footsteps must be arrested, or the nation is undone."[92]

This orientalist genealogy portrayed thralldom under the influence of alcohol as not simply a matter of physical addiction; rather, it generated a correspondence of alcohol with the slavery of the soul under the worst form of satanic despotism. Addiction caused the individual to become unconscious of his God-given moral agency, causing him to consider "his thirst for ardent spirits, as irresistible, as the follower of the prophet of Mecca does fate."[93] Purveyors of liquor were islamicized as "a band of assassins scattering poison and death" that no moral people should permit to thrive in their midst.[94]

In the early republic, islamicism was effective in part because it evoked a common cultural enemy to both evangelical mission and republican nationalism. This dual resource helps explain why islamicism persisted as a critical strain within temperance rhetoric. While islamicism could be employed to help demonize rum, alcohol was also portrayed as an autocratic tyrant who enslaved American democrats. Using this rhetorical attack, alcohol became the most recent manifestation of the despotism that threatened American liberty. Temperance reform therefore was portrayed as a type of patriotic emancipation. Two of the earliest references to Islam in temperance literature described alcoholism as a slavery "worse than Turkish."[95] One exhorter

---

[91] "Ode" from "Order of Services" included in William Sullivan, *Discourse Delivered before the Mass. Society for the Suppression of Intemperance, May 23, 1832* (Boston: Richardson, Lord & Holbrook, 1832), 53; reprinted in John Pierpont, *Airs of Palestine and Other Poems* (Boston: James Munroe & Co., 1840), 179–80. "Philadelphus" made a similar call in 1821: "[C]ome up then, with all your forces to the help of the Lord against the mighty, gird on your armour with the sword of the Spirit, the word of God, slay this mighty Apollyon, this enemy of God and man, who is bidding defiance to the armies of the living God; let him be taken, bound, and cast into the bottomless pit, that he go no more out to deceive the nations." *The Moral Plague of Civil Society; or, The Pernicious Effect of the Love of Money on the Morals of Mankind Exemplified in the Encouragement Given to the Use of Ardent Spirits in the United States, with the Proper Remedy for the Cure of this National Evil* (Philadelphia, 1821), 15.

[92] Rev. Nathan S. S. Beman, *A Discourse Delivered in Stephentown, December 25, 1828, and in Troy, Sabbath Evening, January 11, 1829, before the Temperance Societies of those Towns* (New York: J. P. Haven, 1829), 16.

[93] Levi Loring, *The Origin, Evils, and Remedy, of Intemperance. An Address Delivered in Buxton, April 10, 1828* (Portland, ME: Shirley and Hyde, 1828), 16.

[94] Alexander Gunn, *A Sermon on the Prevailing Vice of Intemperate Drinking* (New York: Whiting and Watson, 1813), 24.

[95] William Cogswell argued that "intemperate drinking [is] the worst plague of our country, and as it declines, or prevails, our nation will rise or fall; for it injures the morals and happiness of the community, crowds our prisons, hospitals, work-houses, and alms-houses, destroys sixty-five millions of dollars annually, keeps eighty thousand persons in worse than Turkish slavery." *A Discourse Delivered before the Dedham Auxiliary Society for the Suppression of Intemperance, Feb. 2, 1816* (Dedham, MA: Abel D. Alleyne, 1818), 15. See also Abiel Abbott, *An Address Delivered before the Massachusetts Society for Suppressing Intemperance . . . June 2, 1815* (Cambridge, MA: Hilliard and Metcalf, 1815), 11.

enlisted temperance reformation against "King Alcohol" as the newest and most challenging phase of the fight for liberty by claiming "neither the heroes of America or of Greece were engaged against a more cruel or a more despotic tyrant than are the friends of temperance."[96] Indeed, after the victory of Greek independence over Turkish tyranny in the late 1820s, many Americans began to observe alcoholism as a domestic despotism sapping the strength of their own democratic vitality. Francis Gillette, addressing a Temperance Society in Connecticut during the winter of 1830, appealed to philanthropists who had long supported liberty in the Mediterranean to arm themselves against this moral danger at home: "We now invoke your aid to exterminate from our country a merciless foe, that is visiting it with tortures more excruciating than Asiatic superstition inflicts; with a captivity more cruelly inhumane than that experienced from the Algerine; and with a despotism more awfully scathful and sanguinary than that of the Ottoman Porte."[97]

The feverish islamicism of temperance polemic attempted to muster national support for its cause by figuring the cultural war against alcohol as both a Christian crusade against evil and the continuation of the American Revolution against tyranny in all its forms. Such an inflation of the American drinking problem to the levels of both a patriotic imperative of national liberty and a cosmic confrontation with evil helps to explain why some temperance advocates viewed the presence of alcohol in America with more moral horror than they saw in the involuntary human bondage of African American slavery in the Southern states.[98] Although some temperance advocates also championed the abolitionism of slavery, the field of temperance activism gave others an opportunity to advocate a form of the abolition that did not address the political problems involved with incorporating emancipated blacks into the body-politic of national citizenship. By transposing the rhetoric of slavery onto alcoholism, these reformers could fervently struggle as symbolic abolitionists without having to deal with the problem of racial equality.

To better exhort citizens to avoid the dangerous effects of drunkenness, the cultural logic of temperance required polemicists to stigmatize alcohol

---

96 Yale, ed., *The Temperance Reader*, 137; "What was the tyranny of England to the tyranny of this devouring mischief?" John Neal, *Address Delivered before the Portland Association for the Promotion of Temperance, February 11, 1829* (Portland, ME: Day & Fraser, 1829), 9.

97 Francis Gillette, *An Address, Delivered at Windsor (Wintonbury,) Con., February 10th, 1830* (Hartford, CT: Augustus Bolles, 1830), 25. See also Daniel Kimball, "The Slavery of Intemperance," *Massachusetts Temperance Standard* (15 August 1845): 2, reprinted in *The Fountain: A Temperance Gift*, eds. J. G. Adams and E. H. Chapin (Boston: George W. Briggs, 1847), 27; which was itself reprinted under the title *The Temperance Fountain: or, Jettings from a Town Pump* (New York: H. Dayton, 1859).

98 "The voluntary slavery of the mind, the voluntary slavery of the passions, is far more degrading and deplorable, than the unwilling servitude of the body." Daniel Kimball, *An Address, Delivered before the Needham Temperance Society* (Dedham, MA: H. & W. H. Mann, 1830), 9–10. See also, for example, Heman Humphrey, *Parallel between Intemperance and the Slave-Trade* (New York: John P. Haven, 1828).

itself as an enemy of American aspirations. Such a rhetorical crusade aimed to discredit alcohol by aligning its domestic consumption with the work of satanic conspiracy, demonic possession, or despotic oppression. Such discourse engaged in a form of cultural alchemy in which spirits were animated out of a material and liquid substance into an alien and transnational agent of evil. This strategy raised the specter of the genie to explain both alcohol's nefarious origins and its power to possess the soul of the inebriant. Through the same process, writers augmented the supernatural power of alcohol so that temperance reform might be perceived as a form of evangelical exorcism. By branding alcohol itself as oriental in origin and its ingestion as un-American, it was rendered into a heathen substance symbolizing the forces of oriental despotism. Such an ethnic pedigree gave ammunition to nativists who viewed the drinking habits of unassimilated immigrants (especially Irish Catholics) as a threat to national purity. Importantly, though, the islamicist rhetorics of temperance transcended domestic politics by aligning reform activism with the more global and cosmic cause of religious redemption.

"THE SAGACIOUS EYE OF MOHAMED": THE COMPARATIVE ANOMALY OF TURKISH TEMPERANCE

Even as Americans invested alcohol with the attributes of satanic intention and despotic power, increasing exposure to the cultures of the eastern Mediterranean after 1830 confounded them with examples of Turkish temperance. While alcohol may have originally been concocted in Arabia, its consumption had been prohibited by Qur'anic injunction with the result that nineteenth-century Muslims comprised a population that was predominately sober. "Turkish" temperance offered such a dramatic contrast with the tavern culture of growing American cities that it became an ironic model for American reform. The charge that Muslims had instituted moral practices that had yet to take hold in the United States was a surprising and disturbing fact that many temperance advocates employed to motivate more vigorous efforts to stop domestic drunkenness. "The Mohammedan nations present a singular anomaly," wrote one critic, "[t]he greatest antipode to Christianity, its most inveterate foe, Mohammedanism has adopted one principle, for the want of which Christian nations have been the greatest sufferers."[99]

One reason why Turkish sobriety surprised Americans was because they had long thought that Muslims of the Ottoman Empire were under the influence of opium and hashish. A powerful collective image of the Turk was of a turbaned gentleman lolling in luxury upon cushions or sofas relating supernatural tales while smoking a hookah, hubble-bubble pipe, or chibouque. The exotic construction of these pipes, combined with the

---

[99] "Mohammedan Temperance," *Journal of the American Temperance Union* 4 (September 1840): 130.

TURK.

The Turks are a grave people, and also kind to those who think as they do, but they are cruel to christians. They smoke opium.

THE END.

FIGURE 3.2. Children's literature was a vehicle for perpetuating stereotypes of Turks and their cultural practices. *People of Different Countries* (New York: Mahlon Day, 1837). Courtesy American Antiquarian Society.

imagined indolence of its users, deceived many Americans into thinking that its bowl contained opium and other smokeable substances as well as tobacco. One writer suggested a comparison of addictions as early as 1816 when he wrote that "alcohol had become the bane of the Christian world, as opium of the Mahometan."[100] Since Turkey was the source of much of the opium that American merchants transported to the Far East in the China trade (the monopoly of the British East India Company prohibited its own ships from engaging in the commerce between 1805 and 1839), American travelers expected to find much Turkish addiction to the substance. By the 1830s, however, the Turkish government had attempted to establish a state monopoly on the trade in order to increase its export revenues, decreasing the domestic use of the substance.[101] When the British resumed their traffic with China in 1839, Turkish opium was replaced by a finer quality substance cultivated in their South Indian colonies, and the image of the oriental addict began its migration further east. Chinese immigrants to the nineteenth-century United States took on the mantle of the chief ethnic stereotype of the oriental opium addict.

All types of American travelers to the Near East throughout the antebellum years attested to the fact that Islamic peoples for the most part obeyed Qur'anic prohibitions against the drinking of alcohol. For example, President Stephen Olin of Wesleyan University observed that "[a] drunken man is a rare spectacle in Egypt."[102] "Temperance in eating and drinking is a well-known characteristic of the Turk," Caroline Paine noted in her narrative *Tent and Harem*, but could still assert as late as 1859 that "few have any ideal of the extent to which it is carried."[103] As these first-hand observations were published within the reform press, more Americans learned of the phenomenon of Turkish abstinence from alcohol. One writer for a

---

[100] [Jesse Torrey] *The Intellectual Flambeau* (Washington City: Daniel Rapine, 1816), 53. See also "Tyranny," *Genius of Temperance, Philanthropist and People's Advocate* (13 June 1832): 2.

[101] See Ibrahim Ihsan Poroy, "Expansion of Opium Production in Turkey and the State Monopoly of 1828–1839," *International Journal of Middle East Studies* 13 (1981): 191–211. American participation in this trade also made opium both more familiar and available for domestic use. See "Opium Eating," *Genius of Temperance, Philanthropist and People's Advocate* (20 October 1830): 2.

[102] Stephen Olin, *Travels in Egypt, Arabia Petraea, and the Holy Land*, 2 vols. (New York: Harper & Brothers, 1842), 1: 202. The traveler Samuel Prime likewise remarked after making his way to the Levant by land in 1856, "I have seen but little drunkenness since I have left Europe." *Travels in Europe and the East*, 2 vols. (New York: Harper and Bros., 1856), 2: 293. The British keynote speaker for a "Temperance Festival" recounted his conversion to the movement after he "had spent many years in the East, in Mohammedan and Pagan countries, where he traveled over thirty thousand miles, and saw three millions of people, and not more than six drunkards." *Journal of the American Temperance Union* 2 (March 1838): 34. The missionary Horatio Southgate testified: "I have never myself seen in the East but two men overpowered by liquor, staggering through the streets"; both were English-speakers. *Narrative of a Tour through Armenia, Kurdistan, Persia and Mesopotamia*, 2 vols. (New York: D. Appleton & Co., 1840), 2: Appendix; also quoted in "Mohammedan Intemperance," *Journal of the American Temperance Union* 4 (September 1840): 131.

[103] Caroline Paine, *Tent and Harem: Notes of an Oriental Trip* (New York: D. Appleton & Co., 1859), 12.

Boston temperance newspaper expressed his amazement in 1835 that temperance societies were not needed in the Ottoman Empire because it was unlawful to taste alcoholic beverages and to make a living by its sale. "In this respect," he concluded, "the Mahometans furnish a salutary example for Christians."[104] The missionary Horatio Southgate was saddened after confronting a drunken American seaman in Constantinople and exasperated by how such scenes must be "regarded by a Turk, whose religion teaches him temperance, and who obeys the precepts of his religion!"[105]

The more broad-minded thinkers were able to distinguish between the wisdom of Turkish temperance and the purported infidelity of the religion that espoused it and counseled Americans to model themselves on Muslim practice. The temperance movement thus became one vehicle for the partial reevaluation of derogative stereotypes about Muhammad with more romantic representations of the Prophet's intelligence. "Christian pilgrim, come!" poetically exhorted Lydia Sigourney, "Thy brother of the Koran's broken creed/Shall teach thee wisdom."[106] The *American Temperance Intelligencer* reported in 1835 that "[t]he sagacious eye of Mohamed long ago discovered that if he would train a hardy and happy people, he must prohibit the use of this intoxicating liquor."[107] Speaking at his alma mater Harvard, the popular temperance novelist Lucius M. Sargent found Muhammad to be a "false prophet," but he was nevertheless a "sagacious legislator" for having prevented his followers from imbibing "the paralyzing draught."[108] Dr. James E. De Kay, himself no stranger to the bottle, went so far as to forthrightly suggest that "if our praiseworthy associations for promoting temperance should be in want of a patron saint, we know of none who comes furnished with stronger recommendations than Mohammed."[109]

---

[104] "Temperance in Turkey," *Temperance Journal* 3 (July 1835): 3.

[105] "Rev. H. Southgate's Journal, September 23, 1837," *The Spirit of Missions* 2 (May 1837): 147–8.

[106] Mrs. Sigourney, "Cold Water," *American Quarterly Temperance Magazine* 3 (August 1833): 206–7, reprinted in *The Temperance Fountain*, 115.

[107] "Address to the People of the State of New York," *American Temperance Intelligencer* 2 (August 1835): 1.

[108] L. M. Sargent, *An Address Delivered before the Temperance Society of Harvard University, November 20, 1834* (Cambridge, MA: Metcalf, Torry, and Ballou, 1834), 4. Influenced by his reading of Henri de Boulainvillier's admiring biography of Muhammad (*The Life of Mahomet* [London, 1731]), Sargent calls the Prophet an "incomparable magician" with "a keen and penetrating insight into the character of men" for having issued the "shrewd and sensible decree" against alcohol. Sargent nevertheless found it a matter of "grave reflection" that the "uncultivated and barbarous disciples of the false prophet of Mecca" had, twelve centuries earlier, abolished drunkenness when nineteenth-century American Christians desiring the same ends could not gain the support of their legislatures. *Address Delivered before the Massachusetts Society for the Suppression of Intemperance, Delivered May 27, 1833* (Boston: Temperance Press, 1833), 20–1. "The prophet of Mecca, though an impostor, was a sagacious man, and wisdom may be gathered from the Koran." Sargent, *Letter on the 'State of the Temperance Reform,' to the Rev. Caleb Stetson, of Medford, Mass* (Boston: William S. Damrell and Gould, Kendall and Lincoln, 1836), 27.

[109] James De Kay, *Sketches in Turkey in 1831 and 1832* (New York: J. & J. Harper, 1833), 360. Shortly after his return from Turkey, Dr. De Kay was sent to Quebec with another doctor named Rhinelander

Americans of a more Calvinist bent were less willing to emphasize the virtues of Turkish infidels and instead lashed out against the shameful vice of American intemperance to audiences both young and old. Drunkenness in America, accentuated by its juxtaposition with the sobriety of the Muslim world, offended their sense of national and religious pride. Employing his reluctant assertion that "the Mahommedan is wiser than the Christian who clings to his cup," one minister ended a discourse by challenging his listeners to "wipe away the foul reproach upon the Christian name, which has so long resounded from the sanctuaries of the false prophets. Let the world see, that a Christian is not a whit behind the Mahommedan in his readiness to abjure wine, if he can thereby lessen the evils of Intemperance, and save but a single soul from death."[110] Such a note of humiliation was frequently employed to shame Americans into temperance reform. In 1819, ex-President John Adams expressed his mortification that Americans led the world in the "degrading, beastly vice" of intemperance, asking, "[i]s it not humiliating that the Mahometans and Hindoos should put to shame the whole Christian world, by their superior examples of temperance?"[111] One temperance treatise designed to be used in schools even contrasted the image of a sensuous Muslim paradise, one ironically gained through abstinence, with the worldly thralldom to alcohol.

> [I]f the devout Moslem expects to share the company of the Houris in the land of spirits, he must refrain from the intoxicating bowl, which poisons while it exhilarates. Are we, then, who are justly proud of the high privileges we enjoy, are we to stand in the front rank of nations, and bend the knee the lowest to this idol of a depraved appetite?[112]

to help stem an outbreak of the plague, where they recommended port wine as an antidote. One eyewitness remembered: "[I]t soon became a standard joke with those who took advantage of every opportunity to fortify themselves against cholera by a frequent preference for either a 'Rhinelander' or a 'De Kay.'" Charles H. Haswell, *Reminiscences of an Octogenarian of the City of New York, 1816 to 1860* (New York: Harper & Bros., 1896), 267.

[110] "Rev. Mr. Hatfield's Discourse on the Wine Question (concluded)," *Journal of the American Temperance Union* 4 (April 1840): 55. "Is there not one among ye who says so fearful an enemy ought not to be hunted down – destroyed – banished – consumed with fire? The Mohammedan interdicts it, and shall he stand above the CHRISTIAN?" "The Serpent of the Distillery," *Youth's Temperance Advocate,* 17 (June 1856): 22.

[111] John Adams, "Letter of February 21, 1819," quoted in Thomas Herttell, *An Exposé of the Causes of Intemperate Drinking* (New York: E. Conrad, 1819), 56, also quoted in Andrew Nichols, *Address, Delivered in ... Danvers. April, 27, 1819* (Salem, MA: Cushing & Appleton, 1819), 18. In 1836, the practice of Westerners in India taking their daily dram of liquor led one missionary to note: "This custom, quite unnecessary and injurious, as I am sure it is, operates, without their seeming to know it, against the respect which the Christian religion might have, among Mahometans and Brahmins, who consider the use of intoxicating liquors irreligious and degrading." "Letter from Allen Graves, Missionary in Bombay, to E. C. Delavan, Esq., Dec 1, 1836," *The Journal of the American Temperance Union* 1 (June 1837): 95.

[112] Yale, ed., *The Temperance Reader,* 171.

"The Mahometans have us," Lucius Sargent sighed when he understood that the seeming accomplishment of 30,000 signers of the abstinence pledge might be ironic ammunition for a Muslim criticism of the intemperance of all those Americans who had not signed it.[113] By eliciting these blushes of cultural embarrassment through rhetorical confrontation, temperance crusaders hoped to motivate American Christians to arise to actively suppress the corrupting influence of alcohol.

No traffic in alcohol, even the spirits supplied to the Native American populations on the Western frontier, outraged prohibitionists more than the trade of New England rum in the Eastern lands that Christians were hoping to convert to Protestantism. The trade in the region that contained the Holy Land itself not only heightened the shame of the American reformers but also rendered it nearly impossible to convince Muslims of the superior morals of Christianity. "We have yet to hear of missionaries, who were not attended to the world's furthest verge, by New England Rum," complained an article in Boston's *Christian Examiner*, "[t]he missionary and New England Rum seem to be inseparably connected."[114] The exportation of rum reversed the logic that alcohol was of Arabian origin and placed the United States as a chief disseminator of the intoxicating substance. "Religion was threatening to make progress in the world," noted temperance crusader Edward Kirk, but was prevented from doing so because "we were actively engaged in shipping the bane with the antidote; invoicing together the New England Missionary and New England Rum."[115]

Notices of the presence of American rum in the Near East were often reported in travel narratives and in letters excerpted by the temperance press. To the writers and editors, such a phenomenon stank of hypocrisy and lent a stinging charge to the activists' call for temperance reform. American Board missionary Edwin Elisha Bliss wrote from Trebizond, Turkey, that it was "nothing unusual to see half a dozen porters in our streets staggering along under the weight of a huge hogshead, on which is written, 'Best New

---

[113] "Temperance Meeting," *Spirit of the Age, and Journal of Humanity* (4 July 1833): 2. See also "Letter from the Rev. L. W. Pease, Relative to the Use of Wine in the East," *American Temperance Intelligencer* 3 (February 1836): 1.

[114] "Missionaries and New England Rum," *Christian Register* 21 (6 August 1842): 125. "Rum ruins more souls annually, than there are inhabitants in New England," argued this editorial reprinted from *Africa's Luminary*, "And yet New England manufactures *all* the *New England Rum*, and continues to stand in the catalogue, for a Christian country. . . . The time has arrived, that if New England wishes to escape universal contempt, she must cease making one-third of the human family drunkards."

[115] E. N. Kirk, "Results of the Temperance Reformation," *The American Temperance Magazine, and Sons of Temperance Offering* 1 (New York: R. Van Dien, 1851): 183. "The same vessels that carry out our missionaries carry also cargoes of New England rum," bemoaned one reformer, "Life in one hand and death in the other." *The True Washingtonian and Martha Washington Advocate* 2 (6 March 1844): 4.

England Rum, Boston.'"[116] The American missionary to the Nestorian Christians of Persia, Justin Perkins, sighed with dismay that "New England Rum, is still almost the only commercial representative with which our Christian, Protestant country, has ever yet honored the markets of distant, benighted, Muhammadan Persia!"[117] Another missionary sent to explore the inland areas of the Near East, Eli Smith, was so embarrassed when his Muslim guide pointed to a group of drunk Russians with disgust, that he exclaimed: "What an unhallowed invasion of the sober customs of the country! What a false and scandalous specimen of Christianity to be exhibited among its enemies!... I felt ashamed for the moment of my Frank blood. How long shall the indulgences of the cup give us just occasion to blush before the followers of Mohammed?"[118]

Missionaries themselves viewed rum exported from their country as a shameful competition to their own evangelical enterprise. Temperance advocates made news when New England ships set off for the Levant with both rum and missionaries aboard. At such a sailing of the bark *Susan Jane* in 1845, the editors of the *Massachusetts Temperance Standard* argued that it would be better if neither had been sent, reasoning that a "cargo of rum will make more hardened and abandoned sinners, than these same missionaries, however talented and devoted, can be instrumental of reforming, should

---

[116] *Massachusetts Temperance Standard* 1 (10 October 1845): 2. After being read at a monthly concert in Boston and being published in *Niles' National Register* (69 [6 September 1845]: 2–3), Bliss's comments from a June letter spread through the temperance press, appearing in such venues as *The Journal of the American Temperance Union* and *The Ohio Washingtonian Organ, and Sons of Temperance Record* ("Temperance in Asia" [9 January 1846]: 174). Rev. George Thompson related this anecdote during a meeting onboard the temperance ship *William Penn*, when he imagined a "heathen worshipper" rejecting Christianity because its votaries appeared to worship the idol of alcohol. *The National Era* 2 (13 April 1848): 59. "Poor deluded people are often murdered by Ohio Whiskey," exclaimed two reformers when learning of this intelligence, "Oh, shame where is thy blush!" S. F. Cary and P. B. Manchester, "Our Cause in Foreign Lands," *The Ohio Washingtonian* (21 February 1846): 221. See also Samuel Prime, *Travels*, 2: 293 and De Kay, *Sketches in Turkey*, 185, 437. "I have been in the port of Smyrna, where barrels of New England rum may be seen lying on the wharf, with the Boston stamp," noted Reverend John Pierpont. "There I also learned from a traveler, that he had seen it in casks on the backs of camels, in the great desert of Arabia." Calling alcohol "distilled damnation," Pierpont chastised those liquor-sellers who put their love of money over their love of men. *Permanent Documents of the American Temperance Society*, 1: 144–5.

[117] Justin Perkins, *A Residence of Eight Years in Persia* (Andover, MA: Allen, Morrill & Wardwell, 1843), 505. Perkins's comments on temperance and Persia were reprinted in *The Christian Examiner*. "Our missionary brethren, who have just arrived, were preceded by one week by a caravan, bearing among other poisons of the kind, *eighteen barrels of New England rum*!... Well may the New England churches multiply their missionaries to this country, if it were merely to repair the evils that are sown here by *New England rum*!" "Eight Years in Persia," 34 (March 1843): 104.

[118] Eli Smith and Harrison G. O. Dwight, *Researches...in Armenia*, 2 vols. (Boston: Crocker and Brewster, 1833), 2: 122. An editorial in the *Temperance Recorder* from Albany, New York, employed the recently published comments of Smith and Dwight about being anticipated in their missionary efforts by the efforts of New England rum-sellers to suggest that rum was being sold to Georgians in exchange for their daughters. 2 (4 June 1833): 25.

they live to the age of Methusalah [sic] and labor with the zeal and industry of a Paul."[119] When Customs House records later revealed that the ship *Emma Isidore* had exported 5,213 gallons of rum along with its missionary passengers, the temperance press assured its readers that "had they known it, [the missionaries] would sooner have cut off their right hand than go in such company."[120]

The greed and power of liquor interests helps to explain the spread of alcoholism in America and abroad and why nineteenth-century temperance advocates were never able successfully to institutionalize prohibition. The New England rum trade in the Near East placed the goals of American capitalism in direct contention with reformers' vision of the United States as a beacon of temperance. The historic connection between the trade in rum and the trade in flesh further amplified the associations of their common degradation. The political power of liquor producers even led one reformer to compare their power and resistance to democratic reform to that held by the sultan himself.[121] An early temperance exponent threatened "may not the Mahometans rise up in judgment" against a country like the United States whose citizens refused to sacrifice their habit of drinking, while Muslims were able to abstain even though they "possess countries which produce grapes in the greatest perfection and abundance."[122] This use of Turkish honesty as a critique of the avarice of American capitalist practice was one of the emphases of comparative islamicism. In fact, Turkish integrity came to be known as such a reliable example that a certain promise was said to be as good as the word of a Turk. To cite but one example, *Hunts Merchants' Magazine and Commercial Review* printed an anecdote of the "Mercantile Honesty of a Turk" taken from a travel narrative that described how one

---

[119] *Massachusetts Temperance Standard* 1 (3 January 1845): 2.

[120] John Pierpont, "Missionaries and Rum," *Journal of the American Temperance Union* 4 (March 1840): 42. "The bark I came in from Boston to Smyrna had a cargo of New England rum," wrote Henry Harris Jessup in his *Fifty-Three Years in Syria*, stating that "Commerce of this kind has done its best to ruin the people of Turkey," 2 vols. (New York: Fleming H. Revell, 1910), 1: 120.

[121] "Were it not for the advantage to be derived from an appearance of activity in the cause by such a course, we might as rationally petition the Grand Turk in behalf of the Christian religion." "X.Y.," "The Way to Work It," *Journal of the American Temperance Union* 2 (January 1838): 4–5. Solomon Southwick lashed out in a sermon against the "Monied Aristocracy," before whose control "the Despotism of Turkey and Russia, will be as light clouds in the horizon, or small dark spots on the SUN of FREEDOM." *An Oration: Delivered By Invitation, at the Reformed Dutch Church, New-Scotland, July Fourth, 1838* (Albany, NY: Alfred Southwick, 1838), 34. Another critic later illustrated the ludicrousness of an effort to save drunkards without taking on the vendors of alcohol by sketching a scene of the Battle of Navarino during the Greek War of Independence when the allied fleets, after having just decimated the Turkish navy, then sent out boats to rescue the few survivors of the destroyed boats: "[W]hen the mischief is done we gather up the wrecks." Rev. Samuel Wolcott, in *Proceedings of the Sixth National Temperance Convention* (New York: National Temperance Society Publishing House, 1868), 29.

[122] William Willis, *An Address Delivered before the New Bedford Auxiliary Society for the Suppression of Intemperance . . . Jan., 4, 1819* (New Bedford, MA: Benjamin Lindsey, 1819), 17.

merchant returned a sum of money to the purchaser of an embroidered handkerchief because the buyer had failed to bargain down his excessively high first offering price. "Verily, not a few among our professing Christians might take a lesson from the believer in the Koran," the article ended.[123]

Travel accounts noted not only the presence of American rum in the Islamic world but sadly reported the damage it was causing the people of Western Asia. An article in the *American Quarterly Temperance Magazine* concluded that "the perseverance of rum-sellers and the power of evil example, have at length conquered even the followers of Mahomet."[124] A. A. Wright, a missionary to Persia, related an anecdote about how the mammoth illustrations of the stomach from *The Anatomy of Drunkenness* failed to avert the downfall of one Muslim "of high family," while for many others it only confirmed their faith in Muhammad's temperate wisdom. While Wright was concerned that more Muslims were taking up the bottle, he was more chagrined by the inebriation of the Nestorian Christians during the Christmas season. "They are oppressed by the Mussulmans," he averred, "but more by intemperance."[125] American temperance advocates even held the export of alcoholism responsible for the downfall of the Grand Seignior himself, Sultan Mahmud II, who developed a craving for liquor that purportedly contributed to his demise.[126] "What has New England done to the head of the Turkish empire?" stated an appalled John Pierpont in an account of "Rum and Missionaries" that was reprinted for over forty years, who blamed his countrymen for converting Sultan Mahmud II into a drunkard and raising a model of intemperance for all his subjects to follow. "It is known in those nations from which shore this pestilence comes – ay, and among sober Mahometans, they know on whom to charge the desolation created by it," he confessed, "Shall we make this goodly land of ours any longer to go up as such a stench in the nostrils of the nations?"[127] Clearly,

---

[123] "Mercantile Honesty of a Turk," *Hunt's Merchants' Magazine and Commercial Review* 31 (October 1854): 520; excerpted from Warington W. Smyth, *A Year with the Turks or Sketches of Travel in the European and Asiatic Dominions of the Sultan* (New York: Redfield, 1854), 180; also reprinted in "The Eastern Question," *The Living Age* 41:526 (17 June 1854): 547.

[124] "Reduction of Insurance on Temperance Vessels," *American Quarterly Temperance Magazine* 4 (November 1834): 38–9.

[125] "Letter from A. A. Wright for the Corresponding Secretary of the American Temperance Union, Oroomiah, Persia, Dec 19, 1844," *Massachusetts Temperance Standard* 1 (26 September 1845): 1. The illustrated book was Robert Macnish, *The Anatomy of Drunkenness* (New York: D. Appleton, 1835).

[126] One report blames German doctors, dismissed upon his death, "who brought on or aggravated his illness by allowing him to swallow constant and large doses of alcohol." "Affairs in the East," *Niles' National Register* 57 (31 August 1830): 14. See also "Letter from Mr. Schauffler to Rev. Dr. Edwards, January 19, 1837," *Journal of the American Temperance Union* 1 (September 1837): 140.

[127] Rev. John Pierpont, "Rum and Missionaries," *The Temperance Fountain*, 212–15. Also found in *Permanent Documents of the American Temperance Society*, 1: 386 and J. B. Wakely, ed., *The American Temperance Cyclopedia of History, Biography, Anecdote, and Illustration* (New York: National Temperance Society and Publication House, 1875), 144–5. Almost fifteen years later it was reported to American

one of the ironies of the opening of the Ottoman Empire to the influence of Western "civilization" in the 1830s was the spread of alcoholism in Near Eastern populations as a result of the importation of spirits originating in U.S. ports.

However, American rum did not have to be exported all the way to the Near East to wreak its havoc on Muslims. One of the few Muslim visitors to the United States in the antebellum period was Ahmed bin Na'aman from Oman whose ship the *Sultanah* docked in New York in 1840 with a crew of fifty after sailing from Muscat and Zanzibar. As the first Arab vessel to visit the United States, the spectacle of the *Sultanah's* crew raised a great furor among the urban throngs who overran its docking-place and followed them on their routes on shore.[128] The *Niles' National Register* told a story about how one of these lascar sailors was inveigled into a bar by sailors and served some wine. When the drunken sailor reeled back to his ship, a "grave old mussulman" confronted him, railing: "Wretch! if you go on at this rate, you will soon be as low and degraded as a Christian." The reporter added this wry retort: "Complimentary this, to the 'most civilized people on the face of the globe.'"[129]

American pretenses to superiority in civilization were punctured by other such incidents, which suggested that some Muslims equated Christianity with the license to drink alcohol. "When the Mohammedans see a man drunk," assured temperance advocate and novelist Sylvester Judd, "they say 'he has left Mohammed and gone to Christ.'"[130] A missionary noted that Armenian priests harassed Christian nondrinkers by claiming that "'Christ blessed the wine, therefore you should drink. He said, This is my blood; the more we drink the better. He is no Christian, he is a Mussulman, who does not drink."[131] Commentators noted that while the use and export of opium was decreasing in Turkey, the "Christian liquors" of rum and gin were becoming the staples of the import trade.[132] This linkage between

---

youth that the Sultan's son, Abdul-Mejid I, had learned from his father's excesses and had proclaimed anew the prohibition of alcohol, which resulted in the pouring of a million piastres worth of wine into the Bosphorus. Such an action earned the new Turkish leader the title of "A Maine Law Sultan." *Youth's Temperance Advocate*, 15 (1 March 1854): 12.

[128] For an extensive picture of this visit and its historical contexts, see Hermann Frederick Eilts, "Ahmad Bin Na'aman's Mission to the United States in 1840, the Voyage of *Al-Sultanah* to New York City," *Essex Institute Historical Collections* 98 (October 1962): 219–77.

[129] "Ahamet Ben Aman," *Niles' National Register* 58 (23 May 1840): 179. Accounts of this incident were published in the local press. See *New York Signal* (quoted in Eilts, "Ahmad Bin Na'aman's Mission," 242 and n9); *North American and Daily Advertiser* (16 May 1840); and *The Brooklyn Daily News* (22 May 1840).

[130] Sylvester Judd, *A Discourse Touching the Causes and Remedies of Intemperance. Preached February 2, 1845* (Augusta, ME: Wm. T. Johnson, 1845), 7.

[131] *Massachusetts Temperance Standard* 1 (10 October 1845): 2. See also "Mohammedan Temperance," 132.

[132] *The True Washingtonian and Martha Washington Advocate* 2 (6 March 1844): 4.

Christianity and intemperance was shown in a reprinted anecdote about the punishment of a "Mahometan Drunkard," who was tied to a mule, forced to wear a European hat, and paraded with a dog through the streets of Constantinople, and then after being shaved with the same razor used to cut a cross on the hair of the back of the dog, he was plunged into the Bosphorus.[133]

Another reason for Muslims taking up the practice of drinking alcohol was the interpretation that it was only wine that had been expressly prohibited by the Qur'an. In some mystic traditions, wine had for centuries also been sublimated into a symbol of refined spirituality.[134] The ambiguity about the status of more potent unfermented liquors that many preferred to the use of wine had the effect of "revers[ing] the natural order of criminality" according to one American observer.[135] Travelers, or "cosmopolitan" natives who interpreted the Qur'an strictly in the interest of their appetite, could be served a distilled liquor of local origin called rakee or arrak. James E. De Kay argued that the "seductive" rakee had frustrated the "wise and benevolent intentions of Muhammad" because the Turk did not always view it "with the same pious horror with which he views a glass of generous wine."[136] Other Americans who sought examples of Turkish degradation gloated over Muslim inconstancy to the dictates of their own false religion. When Warington W. Smyth penned his travel narrative *A Year with the Turks* in 1854, he argued that the presence of distilled spirits in Turkey might become an ironic "moving power" for the regeneration of Turkey by attracting Muslims to the Christians who operated dram-shops and eventually breaking down the strength of their religious prejudices.[137] Nevertheless, Turks were on the whole generally admired for being "the most temperate nation on earth," even by those who despised the religious system which taught it, and American commentators found Muslim sobriety an improvement over the problems arising from public inebriation in the beer vaults and gin palaces of emerging urban areas in the United States.

If Muslims had some problem defining the exact nature of Qu'ranic prohibition, the difficulties faced by Christians attempting to argue that alcohol was irreligious were even greater. After all, the biblical Gospels tell of Jesus Christ changing water into wine at a wedding in Cana, and temperance advocates were now trying to transform the drinking of wine back into water – or at least argue that Christ's miracle allowed no time for fermentation. One speaker argued in 1830 before an early association called the Massachusetts Society for the Suppression of Intemperance: "We taste

---

[133] "Mahometan Drunkard," *The American Temperance Cyclopedia*, 116–17.

[134] Kathryn Kueny, *The Rhetoric of Sobriety: Wine in Early Islam* (Albany, NY: SUNY Press, 2001).

[135] Horatio Southgate, *Narrative of a Tour*, 2: 344; reprinted in the *Journal of the American Temperance Union* (September 1840): 130–2.

[136] DeKay, *Sketches in Turkey*, 326.   [137] Smyth, *A Year with the Turks*, 107–8.

'the cups / That cheer but not inebriate,' and may lawfully follow the Apostolic direction to 'take a *little* wine' – And why not? We are not Musselman! We have no Alcoran of superstitious observances."[138] The movement of temperance reform away from the mere suppression of intemperance and toward the promotion of total abstinence that culminated in the passage of the "Maine Law" in 1852 represented what one historian has called "a shift from the advocacy of a Christian virtue to the insistence upon a social taboo."[139] To some American drinkers, the fact that Muslims did not drink alcohol made them indulge in surrogate stimulants and alternative appetites that not only kept them intemperate but also rendered them effeminate.[140] Many Americans drinkers resented the restriction of their civil liberties, especially since they believed imbibing alcohol was a freedom authorized by the Bible so long as moderation prevailed. The fact that the apostle Paul had counseled Christians to "take a little wine" to soothe digestive problems set off a controversy in the temperance movement. Some affirmed that this applied only to "pure wine" or unfermented grape juice, and that its use was intended only for medicinal purposes.

Others argued that such fanatical teetotalism was not only un-Christian, but also Islamic in origin. Similar to the ways in which supporters of Southern slavery counterattacked abolitionists by appropriating islamicism, opponents of teetotalism likened radical temperance reformers with followers of Islam. A controversial debate in the New York State Temperance Society dramatized the complex use of images of Turkish temperance within prohibitionary discourse.[141] Judge Samuel Miles Hopkins, a temperance gadfly from western New York opposed to the prohibition of wine, took issue with a glowing statement by a naval officer in the *American Temperance Intelligencer* that portrayed Muhammad's edict against wine as "a salutary

---

[138] James Trecothik Austin, *Address Delivered before the Massachusetts Society for the Suppression of Intemperance* (Boston: John H. Eastburn, 1830), 24. This position was taken to its extreme in an exchange on the "New Virtues of Wine," which argued that the advancement of Europe was a result of the use of wine while Muslim abstemiousness had caused their lack of progress. The editor of the *Journal of Health* roundly attacked this position and asserted that Muslim inferiority was a result of "the inherent vices of their religion, and not to their abstaining from wine," and then admitted that Muslims had once been the "most polished" people of the Mediterranean peoples. Referring to the increase in the intake of alcohol in Ottoman lands, the editorial ends by asserting: "We shall not, we suppose, find any person hardy enough to assert that the power of the Mehomatans [sic] is greater, and their intellectual manifestations of a higher order, now that the injunction of Koran against drinking wine is so often neglected and infringed." "New Virtues of Wine [from the *Journal of Health*]," *Genius of Temperance, Philanthropist and People's Advocate* (9 February 1831): 1.

[139] Fuller, *Wine and Religion*, 84–5. See, for example, "The Maine Liquor Law," *The United States Democratic Review* 30 (May 1852): 449–56.

[140] "The Use and Abuse of Stimulants," *Putnam's Monthly Magazine* 6 (November 1855): 538; "Liquor Legislation," *The United States Democratic Review* 30 (June 1852): 532.

[141] Samuel Miles Hopkins, "Review of Doctor Washington's Letter," *Correspondence on the Right Reasoning, Applicable to Temperance* (Geneva, NY: John C. Merrell, 1836), 53–64; "Letter from Dr. Washington of the United States Navy," *American Temperance Intelligencer* 1 (July 1834): 1.

code" that contributed to the prowess and probity of Muslims. Hopkins challenged this assessment in a review that he published himself after the editors refused to print the response. Hopkins's counterblast assembled evidence of the duplicity of Muslim behaviors (including their addiction to opium) and reasoned that, because Christ had sanctioned the drinking of wine – by manufacturing it and making it an element of a religious observance – while Muhammad had roundly prohibited it, the movement for total abstinence and its celebration of the Prophet's "extraordinary wisdom" was therefore motivated by the spirit of Islam.

When Hopkins raised these arguments at a meeting of the Society, his opponents retorted:

> The gentleman [Hopkins] has told us that Mohammed has been exalted above our Saviour by the arguments against wine. Now we have never believed in the sincerity of the impostor's motives; but he had the sagacity to meet certain antipathies to wine and at the same time to guard with military foresight against the use of an effeminating substance in his ecclesiastical army. And here we throw back the charge again. *They* have exalted Mohammed. –

That Hopkins's position was a minority one is evident by the fact that all present voted to postpone the debate until the following Monday out at Niagara Falls where the teetotalist Rev. Edward Kirk would argue the case with him "until he shall become tired of the sound of cold water."[142]

But even though such a position was drowned out for the moment, it was an argument that surfaced throughout the antebellum period. In 1841, the Reverend Joseph McCarrell challenged the total abstinence position by arguing that those who supported it committed the blasphemy of declaring that the Qur'an was superior to the Bible.[143] A major purpose of an article in the *American Temperance Magazine* ten years later was to counter the "monstrous absurdity" that total abstinence was "in principle opposed to the genius of CHRISTIANITY, and savors of the religion of the false prophet MAHOMET and his Alcoran." The author recited the evil "Mahometan origin" of alcohol and accused the Prophet of stealing the idea of temperance from the Proverbs of Solomon and enforcing it with "a

---

[142] "Extra: Account of Meeting of the New-York State Temperance Society in Buffalo," *American Temperance Intelligencer* 2 (August 1835): 3. (reprinted also as No. 9, September). Another antiprohibitionist from New England rejected the extremism of the Maine Law of prohibition with the converse logic that Muhammad's injunction against drinking sapped the "manly" resolve of Muslims and made them turn to "effeminate" indulgences that caused their downfall as a "race." *The Ramrod Broken; or, the Bible, History, and Common Sense in Favor of the Moderate Use of Good Spirituous Liquors* (Boston: Albert Colby, 1859), 156–7.

[143] Rev. Joseph McCarrell, *Bible Temperance: in Three Discourses* (Newburgh, NY: David L. Proudfit, 1841), 18–19, 22–3.

rigid and soul-enslaving despotism" entirely at odds with the rational free-dom of Christian temperance reformation.[144] The critics of reformers per-sisted. Proslavery Reverend Edward Josiah Stearns blasted Harriet Beecher Stowe's *Uncle Tom's Cabin* for manifesting the "anti-christian spirit... of the so-called moral reforms of the present day," adding "its sympathies are not with Christ, but with 'the false prophet.' Even the temperance movement, – the most plausible of them all, – is a Mahommedan, and not a Christian movement."[145]

Such criticism did not stem the tide of temperance reformers devoted to ridding the nation of the demon alcohol. Abstinence crusaders sought to replace the vices of dram-drinking with alternative beverages whose virtues they touted with considerable hyperbole. Indeed, some teetotalers went so far as to substitute grape juice or molasses and water for the wine of communion. One of the many reasons that urban residents in the ante-bellum United States habitually drank liquor was the relative inaccessibility of clean water in the growing congestion of the cities. Many temperance advocates celebrated the natural virtues of clean water, romanticizing such rustic symbols as the town pump and the old oaken bucket. But to better encourage Americans to adopt the practice of drinking water, temperance advocates also orientalized the oasis by celebrating the languid streams of Eden, the water rushing from the rock that Moses smote near Sinai, the well found in the desert by Ishmael and Hagar, and the models of absti-nent aquarianism provided by Near Eastern sects such as the Rechabites and Moabites.[146] Such rhetoric lionized the herculean hardiness of oriental water-drinkers as a means of challenging the manhood of occidental topers. "The Arabs of the desert are among the most hardy of the human race, enduring the greatest fatigue and exposure under a burning sun, and their habitual drink is water," argued a physician in a prize-winning temperance essay.[147] Another address claimed that "Porters in Constantinople... who drink nothing but water, are said to bear burthens, which... dram-drinking 'sons of Columbia,' could [not] sustain for a moment."[148] John Greenleaf

---

[144] "Christianity or Mahometanism," *The American Temperance Magazine* 2 (1851): 300–3.

[145] Rev. E. J. Stearns, *Notes on Uncle Tom's Cabin: Being a Logical Answer to Its Allegations and Inferences against Slavery as an Institution* (Philadelphia: Lippincott, Grambo & Co., 1853), 155–6.

[146] The banner of the *Temperance Youth's Advocate* featured an illustration of Hagar and Ishmael with a poem that celebrates how "pure cold water" preserved God's promise to Ishmael. The temperance organization called Independent Order of the Rechabites mustered its members into "tents" and "encampments."

[147] Reuben D. Mussey, M.D., *Prize Essay on Ardent Spirits, and Its Substitutes as a Means of Invigorating Health* (Washington, DC: Duff Green, 1837), 42.

[148] Thomas G. Fessenden, *Address Delivered before the Charlestown Temperance Society, January 31, 1831* (Charlestown, MA: William W. Wheildon, 1831), 15. This image about the legendary strength of Turkish porters was a persistent one. An 1858 article in a Cincinnati temperance periodical called *The Crusader* notes: "The Turkish porters at Constantinople and Smyrna are celebrated for strength" and cites a Manchester machinist who claims: "The boatmen and water-carriers of Constantinople

Whittier wrote a poem called "The Khan's Devil" that depicted alcoholism as a form of satanic possession by a fiendish genie that could only be held at bay by abstinence and persistent aquarianism. "With water quench the fire within, / And drown each day thy devilkin," advises the mystic Hamza, a lesson taken to heart by the Khan, who reiterates it on a tablet that his students read: "'Drown him O Islam's child!, the spell / To save thee lies in tank and well!'"[149] By rendering simple water into a sacred talisman of spiritual health, such rhetoric aimed to challenge the artificial enervation associated with medical materialism. This romanticization of water, combined with the high alcohol and opium content of medicines, contributed to the great popularity of the hydropathy or water-cure movement in the 1840s.[150]

For those not thrilled by rills of cold water, the drinking of coffee – another beverage and word of Arabian provenance – became an acceptable alternative.[151] The fiery rhetoric that demonized alcohol was countered by the exoticization of coffee-drinking, a shift that corresponded with the rise of romantic orientalism as a contrasting modality of viewing the Islamic world. During the same years that temperance ideology was helping to reduce the national intake of alcohol, the domestic consumption of coffee was increasing at an inverse rate, quadrupling from about 20 million pounds in 1820 and to over 90 million pounds by 1840.[152] By adopting the habit of drinking coffee, Americans were imitating a Muslim practice that had already taken hold in Europe. Temperate American travelers in the Near East were quick to comment that the hospitable custom of serving coffee in Turkey could serve as an alternative to "the more pernicious draughts of our country." The missionary Josiah Brewer, taken with this idea, thought that coffee might appeal in winter months to those who refused to convert to

---

are decidedly, in my opinion, the finest men in Europe, as regards their physical development, and they are all water-drinkers." "Can Men Be Strong without Intoxicating Drinks?" *The Crusader* 3 (June 1858): 29.

[149] John Greenleaf Whittier, "The Khan's Devil." in *The Complete Poetical Works of Whittier* (Boston: The Riverside Press, 1892), 123–4.

[150] See Jane B. Donegan, *Hydropathic Highway to Health: Women and Water-Cure in Antebellum America* (Westport, CT: Greenwood Press, 1986) and Susan E. Cayleff, *Wash and Be Healed: The Water-Cure Movement and Women's Health* (Philadelphia: Temple University Press, 1987).

[151] Coffee is derived from the Arabic word *qahvah* for berry juice. Two other common designations for coffee are derived from the Islamic lands of their cultivation: Mocha is a port in Yemen and Java an island in Indonesia.

[152] No doubt because of the difficulty of collecting reliable data, statistics about the domestic consumption of coffee varied, although its rapid growth is clear. One source claimed an increase in consumption from 21,273,659 pounds in 1821 to 93,790,507 pounds in 1836. William A. Alcott, *Tea and Coffee* (Boston: George W. Light, 1839), 131. Another charted a rise from 14 million pounds in 1822 to 79 million in 1831, the year when the duty on coffee began to be lifted (it could be imported for free in 1832). *Hunt's Merchants' Magazine* (16 January 1847): 78.

aquarianism, and made the appeal that "innholders . . . should be persuaded to offer their customers, this cheap and wholesome refreshment."[153] Coffee became an ally of the temperance movement just as alcohol had been its enemy. Sylvester Judd argued that coffee was a coconspirator with Qur'anic law in enabling the moderation of the Turks.[154] One traveler to the Levant gave coffee the sobriquet of "sober berry's juice."[155] *The North American Review* acceded to this in 1838 when it argued that "use of a single fruit, we mean the coffee berry, has served more effectively to check the use of ardent spirits, than all other causes united, previous to the formation of the Temperance Societies."[156] The drinking of coffee, and the habits of sober social leisure it fostered (including the focused productivity that continues its popularity today), were other important ways that nineteenth-century Americans sought to imitate Turkish temperance. Even liquor-sellers became aware of the cultural allure of coffee, causing many to change the name of their establishments to coffee-houses (later cafés) even while continuing the practice of dispensing alcoholic drinks.

This examination of the function of Islamic orientalism in antebellum reform rhetoric reveals the changing American perceptions of Muslim peoples in the quarter century following the Greek War of Independence. Domestic islamicism described American slave-holding as a domestic tyranny that challenged Christian morality and embodied alcoholism as an infiltration of satanic proportions. While Americans continued to frequently apply the stereotypes of the antichristianity and despotism of Islam to infidelize unwanted American behaviors, more exposure to Muslim lands – expressed through the publication of travel narratives – set some of the harshness of such views in gentler relief.

The emergence of a chastened comparative orientalism, however, revealed the embarrassing examples of the relatively humane treatment of slaves by Muslims and the anomaly of Turkish temperance. Both of these rhetorical modalities were employed by reformers who desired an end to slavery and drunkenness. American orientalism, which figured Islam as the epitome of soul-starving bondage, also generated images of Muslim slavery that served to challenge the humanity of American practices. Turks had once

---

[153] Josiah Brewer, *A Residence at Constantinople, in the Year 1827,* 2nd ed. (New Haven, CT: Durrie & Peck, 1830), 217.

[154] Judd, *A Discourse,* 24.

[155] Francis Schroeder, *Shores of the Mediterranean; with Sketches of Travel,* 2 vols. (New York: Harper & Brothers, 1846), 1: 169.

[156] "Kenrick's American Orchardist," *North American Review* 47 (October 1838): 449–50. An article on "Coffee" in the *Boston Weekly Magazine* noted: "The Turk offers coffee to his guest, as we do wine, brandy and whiskey, sherry, cobblers, juleps, &c., to ours – and of course they take the lead in the temperance way." (27 September 1838): 22.

been perceived as soulless tyrants and slaves to opium, but their collective avoidance of alcohol and their sober and leisurely hospitality of serving coffee freed them to serve more readily as romantic representatives for Americans eager to imbibe lessons of how they might attain cosmopolitan expressions of civility at once more refined and more exotic.

Chapter 4

"Turkey Is in Our Midst":
Mormonism as an American "Islam"

From the far west a voice arises claiming sovereignty; proclaiming the advent of a second Mahomet, the unsheathing of a sword as devastating as was his, backed by the same omnipotence; and calling upon all the nations of the world to give way before its might. That second Mahomet was Joseph Smith; that kingdom is the Mormon settlement.

E. Boteler Chalmer, *Mormonism. A Delusion* (1852)[1]

In 1847, the year before gold was discovered in California, the small community of Yerba Buena raised the flag of the United States and changed its name to San Francisco. An enormous influx of settlers from both the eastern seaboard of the United States and from across the Pacific soon produced a burgeoning western city that helped to spawn the mythos of the California experience. The rough image of San Francisco as a frontier city during these years was perhaps embodied most fully when its sordid and dangerous waterfront districts – known for crime, drunkenness and prostitution – became infamously known as the "Barbary Coast."[2]

This transposition of North African geography, one we have seen had been charged with despotic energies, onto a territory newly colonized by the United States registered the profound anxieties associated with national expansion. Imagining western spaces as "domestic orients" was a cultural process that marked frontier practices as deviant from the moral customs of the incorporated states. From the time of the first landings by British settlers, the territory of the western frontier had been feared as an unregenerate challenge to orthodox religious, political, and educational systems and structures. Its unformed possibilities not only attracted unmonitored adventurers but also threatened to disrupt the stability of the Christian social order attained in eastern establishments. Islamicist imagination – such as the location of a Barbary Coast in San Francisco Bay – provided a symbolic means to render suspect domestic territories into alien and outlandish space in a way that opened a variety of versatile forms of cultural work and play. By defining strange behaviors as beyond the pale of acceptable Protestant

---

[1] (London: Wertheim and Macintosh, 1852), 3.
[2] See, for example, Herbert Asbury, *The Barbary Coast: An Informal History of the San Francisco Underworld* (Garden City, NY: Garden City Pub. Co., 1933).

American values, such comparative rhetoric incorporated foreign difference in ways that universalized national territory and domestic affairs as an exotic destination of symbolic world encounter.

While the previous chapter examined drunken citizens and slave plantations as sites that a variety of nineteenth-century Americans read as irruptions of infidel Muslim practices into the nation's body-politic, this chapter explores an even more thorough domestication of islamicism: the way that the religious history and practices of the Mormons were represented as the replication of Islam as an American phenomenon. During the same months in 1846 that American ships sailed to California to lay claim to its territory, leader Brigham Young and his Mormon pioneers were trekking toward the basin of the Great Salt Lake, a less promising portion of the occidental landscape where they nevertheless hoped to establish an American Zion. An examination of the comparative archive through which Protestant Christians rendered Mormonism into a domestic Islam reveals the circuitous contours through which oriental and occidental frontiers were symbolically aligned in the settlement of the American West. An in-depth recovery of this archival imagination demonstrates how the discursive energies of expansion associated with manifest destiny incorporated a broader global trajectory and a more diverse negotiation of cultural difference than those grounded only by domestic minorities within continental territory. Transposing islamicist observations to define the moral boundaries of the community of the United States enabled a comparativist critique of the direction of domestic polity, but it also at times had the ironic effect of promoting the social prominence and worldly relevance of the fledgling Mormon church.

"Not inaptly or without logical force has Joseph Smith been designated the Mohammed of America," wrote T. B. H. Stenhouse in his history *The Rocky Mountain Saints*: "Between the prophet of Arabia and the prophet of Nauvoo (each claiming divine, prophetic powers) there is a strong family resemblance and a more than singular coincidence of experience."[3] Stenhouse's excessive identification ("more than singular") reflects the ideological strategy of discrediting both religions through the association of their mutual distance from palatable Protestant practice. While the cultural work of eschatology examined in the second chapter located its authority within the interpretation of the Bible, this comparativist discourse deployed orientalist allusions and references to the history, geography, doctrines, and practices of Islam as a means of defining the infidelity of the Mormon example and negating its claims to a Christian genealogy. It represented a revealing strain in the popular imagination of comparative religion before such an enterprise emerged as a field of social science. The publication in 1830 of the Book of Mormon by Joseph Smith, Jr., and the subsequent rise of the Church of Jesus Christ of Latter-day Saints (LDS) challenged such

---

[3] T. B. H. Stenhouse, *The Rocky Mountain Saints* (New York: D. Appleton and Company, 1873), 203.

established Protestant principles as the sufficiency of the Bible, the separation of church and state, and the sanctity of monogamy. Because many
European Americans had long viewed Islam as compromising these very
principles, nineteenth-century critics frequently attempted to discredit the
claims of Mormonism through islamicist identifications. Anti-Mormon literature regularly aligned not only the Mormon and Muslim prophets but
also compared the two religion's rise, beliefs, and practices, especially those
that confirmed orientalist notions of deception, despotism, and polygamy.[4]

The polemical strategy of declaring this "more than singular coincidence"
of the Mormon church with Islam arose coevally with the publication of the
Book of Mormon itself, and it remained a strong rhetorical alliance well into
the twentieth century.[5] The persistence of this alignment and the partisan
and denominational diversity of the critics and publications that expressed
it give ample proof of its widespread currency.[6] "The mean origin, the
astonishing spread, the shallow devices, the blind devotion, and the untiring

[4] For literature about the Mormons see the comprehensive Chad J. Flake, *A Mormon Bibliography, 1830–1930* (Salt Lake City: University of Utah Press, 1978); its *Ten Year Supplement* (1989); and its *Indexes* (1992); as well as David J. Whitaker, *Mormon Americana: A Guide to Sources and Collections within the United States* (Provo, UT: Brigham Young University Studies, 1995). For early anti-Mormon works, there are annotated bibliographies in Richard Burton, *The City of the Saints* (New York: Harper & Brothers, 1862), 203–14; and Jules Remy, *A Journey to Great-Salt-Lake City*, 2 vols. (London: W. Jeffs, 1861), 2: 561–9. See also the trade catalogue for Charles L. Woodward's collection of Mormon materials called *Bibliothica Scallawagiana* (New York: Bangs & Co., 1880).

[5] Davis Bitton argued that the earliest instance of Smith being compared with Muhammad was when Abner Cole, editor of the newspaper in Smith's hometown, claimed "it is only in their ignorance and impudence that a parallel can be found." *Palmyra Register* 1 (18 January 1831): 84, in Bitton, *Images of the Prophet Joseph Smith* (Salt Lake City, UT: Aspen Books, 1996), 23, 27. Cole, writing as Oliver Dogberry the year before, called Smith's counselor Oliver Cowdery "this second Mahomet." *Palmyra Reflector* 3 (1 June 1830): 28, in Francis W. Kirkham, *A New Witness for Christ in America: The Book of Mormon* (Salt Lake City, UT: Brigham Young University Press, 1959), 50, 67. Although this chapter emphasizes the Mormon–Muslim link in the mid-nineteenth century, the comparison was still being explicitly made at the beginning of the twentieth century, after Utah had been admitted as a state in the Union (1896). See, for example, Jennie Fowler Willing, *On American Soil, or Mormonism the Mohammedanism of the West* (Louisville, KY: Picket Pub. Co., 1906); Bruce Kinney, *Mormonism: The Islam of America* (New York: Fleming H. Revell, 1912); "The American Mohammedanism," *Missionary Review of the World* 22 (November 1899): 844–5; and Frank J. Cannon, *Under the Prophet in Utah: The National Menace of a Political Priestcraft* (Boston: C. M. Clark Pub. Co., 1911).

[6] For other discussions of this phenomenon see Hans Thimme, "Mormonism and Islam," *The Moslem World* 24 (April 1934): 155–67; Arnold H. Green and Lawrence P. Goldrup, "Joseph Smith, an American Muhammad? An Essay on the Perils of Historical Analogy," *Dialogue: A Journal of Mormon Thought* 6 (Spring 1971): 46–58; Arnold H. Green, "The Muhammad–Joseph Smith Comparison: Subjective Metaphor or a Sociology of Prophethood," in *Mormon and Muslims: Spiritual Foundations and Modern Manifestations*, ed. Spencer J. Palmer (Provo, UT: Religious Studies Center, Brigham Young University, 1983), 63–84; Marianne Perciaccante, "The Muslim–Mormon Comparison," *The Muslim World* 82 (July–October 1992): 296–314; Terryl L. Givens, *Viper on the Hearth: Mormons, Myths, and the Construction of Heresy* (New York: Oxford University Press, 1997), 130–3; and Arnold H. Green, "Mormons and Islam: From Polemics to Mutual Respect and Cooperation," *BYU Studies* 40 (2001):199–220. Garth Jones found interesting parallels and instructive comparisons between the lead-ers and situations of Mormons and the Ahmadiyyat, a messianic sect of Islam movement originated by

perseverance of the two sects, are all striking points of resemblance," asserted the *Southern Literary Messenger* in 1848.[7] Three years later, *The American Whig Review*, an organ with an opposing political readership, attested in an article called "The Yankee Mahomet" that "in its main features it [Mormonism] bears considerable resemblance to that propagated by Mahomet. Both recognize the principle of arbitrary power, and both that of forcible dissemination. There are, too, in both, indulgences for the faithful and sensual paradises reserved for the elect."[8]

A primary reason why most polemicists applied the rhetoric of islamicism to the Mormon church was to alert their readers more effectively to a phenomenon they believed to combine a theological challenge to Christian orthodoxy, a military threat to the United States, and a perverse affront to conventional morality. The titles of anti-Mormon publications were rife with the figures of "exposing," "unmasking," or "unveiling" the "mysteries," "crimes," and "horrors" of the upstart American sect. American and British polemicists of more mainstream denominations linked Mormonism with Islam to subordinate Latter-day claims by associating them with the orientalist heritage that viewed Islam as both carnal and coercive. Craig L. Foster has observed that "[t]he linking of Mormonism with Islam was the simple projection of the Eastern stereotype of treachery and gross sensuality on the despised religion."[9] "Since the cultural work of dehumanizing or at least demonizing Asians had been well accomplished by the advent of Mormonism," explained Terryl L. Givens in his study of anti-Mormon fiction, "exploiting that ready-made category was easier . . . than constituting an alien identity from scratch."[10]

A deeper examination of the topography of the Mormon–Muslim comparison in this chapter reveals more complex contours of this rhetorical identification between what was then a small group of domestic religious outcasts and a major existing global religion. While the nature of the comparison in many ways prevented serious examination of the claims of either

---

Mirza Ghulam Ahmad in the late nineteenth century. "The Ahmedis of Islam: A Mormon Encounter and Perspective," *Dialogue* 19 (Summer 1986): 40–1, 51.

[7] "Memoir of the Mormons," *Southern Literary Messenger* 14 (November 1848): 641.

[8] *The American Whig Review* 13 (June 1851): 559. The *Christian Examiner* likewise affirmed in 1855 that "Both [Joseph Smith and Muhammad] professed to be immediately inspired and heaven-directed; both treated with a secondary reverence the mission of Christ, while maintaining the superiority of their own; both took care in the end to provide for their individual elevation, and to secure by means of the religion which they promulgated, a law-protected indulgence of the lowest passions." E. Vale Smith, "Migrations, and Their Objects," *Christian Examiner* 24 (July 1855): 44–5.

[9] Craig L. Foster, "Victorian Pornographic Imagery in Anti-Mormon Literature," *Journal of Mormon History* 19 (Spring 1993): 125.

[10] Givens, *Viper on the Hearth*, 133. Givens has argued that the authors of anti-Mormon novels exploited the conventions of orientalism to both reify and caricature the alien identity of Mormonism and thereby establish its distance from accepted American and Christian identities. "Caricature as Containment: Orientalism, Bondage, and the Construction of Mormon Ethnicity in Nineteenth-Century Popular Fiction," *Nineteenth-Century Contexts* 18 (1995): 391–4.

religious group – indeed that was a major part of the usefulness of domestic islamicism – unpacking this archive reveals a process of transnational projection and association that accomplished more dynamic dimensions of cultural work than the simplicity and ultimate shallowness of the rhetorical contrast alone might suggest. The reciprocal parallels drawn between Mormonism and Islam clearly served to infidelize both Mormon and Muslim claims. However, the same figures and gestures also globalized the relevance of the nation by connecting its own far western territories and its domestic religious controversies with the planetary horizons and historical sagas of the sacred Near East. Importing islamicist comparisons as a means of transfiguring the religious challenge of Mormonism on the continent thus expanded the symbolic resonance of frontier developments onto more worldly registers. Anti-Mormon critics in this way engaged in a form of reverse typology that borrowed the broad universal perspective adopted by the Mormons as a means of countering and discrediting their claims.

Both the contentions of Mormonism and islamicist strategies of comprehending them confirmed U.S. nationals in their belief that global history and destiny were connected with continental events occurring within their own shores. This rhetorical crusade shifted the tenor of millennial dramas that remained as yet unmanifest in the orient onto the political problem of manifest destiny, namely, the appropriate incorporation of western territories into the growing nation-state. In these ways, the rise of Mormonism (and the reactions of its critics) ironically revealed important new cultural dimensions of the mythic rhetoric of national expansion. These dimensions dramatize the larger thesis of this book that the discourse of islamicism served to contain the global challenge of Islam by converting its exotic difference into a domestic resource that helped to universalize national experience as a globally relevant phenomenon.

THE AMERICAN WEST AS DOMESTIC ORIENT

The Book of Mormon contains sagas of ancient biblical tribes, among which were the descendants of Joseph who had migrated to the New World when the Jews were led into captivity in Babylon. The Church of Jesus Christ of Latter-day Saints aspired to restore Christ's authority to the early history of Israel and to reestablish the reign of Zion in the western hemisphere.[11] The novelist Albion W. Tourgée once characterized the Mormon religion as "the American orientalized by Christian tradition."[12] Propagandists, by identifying Mormonism as an American Islam, claimed the converse: that Mormonism orientalized America by

[11] Jan Shipps, *Mormonism, The Story of a New Religious Tradition* (Urbana: University of Illinois Press, 1987).

[12] Albion W. Tourgée, *Button's Inn* (Boston: Roberts Brothers, 1887), vii.

bringing Islam into its midst. Anti-Mormon polemic employed islamicism to negate Mormon connections with biblical history and to portray the native sect as a New World offspring of the imposture and fanaticism of Muhammad. Mormonism, and its purported restoration of Zion within the territory of the United States, stood for these critics as a domestic example of how the continuing corruption of Christianity upheld the symbolic hegemony of Islam over Protestant aspirations to regain and purify the Holy Land. This strategic use of domestic islamicism thus coopted the claim of the Book of Mormon that the North American landscape was central to the world's religious history and put it to critical use. If Mormons claimed to restore the early days of Israel and the gathering of the saints as an American experience, anti-Mormon polemic enabled other Americans to portray it as a replication of the rise and progress of the infidelity of Islam. By transposing orientalist conventions about the history of Islam and the character of Turks onto a domestic minority and religious phenomenon, critics insinuated a Mormon reenactment of a Muslim prototype that effectively alienated both from any affiliation with Christian identity. Safely centered between what they considered the excesses of the Mormon West and the Muslim East, transatlantic anti-Mormon writers stabilized their own beliefs by attempting to ally the religions as mutually defined heresies and thereby consign both to a common imposture.

Critics of Mormonism transfigured Utah into a domestic orient as a means of registering its physical and moral distance from the arbiters of Protestant taste along the Atlantic seaboard. Mormonism became most clearly associated in the public mind with Salt Lake City after Brigham Young led the Mormons west from Nauvoo, Illinois, during 1846–7. The basin of the Great Salt Lake, fed by a river that the Mormons named Jordan, led many to compare the rising Mormon city with Sodom near the Dead Sea, or Palmyra bordering the Syrian Desert, a clear rejection of the Mormon claim that it was the new Jerusalem or Zion.[13] The Mormon contention that the Native Americans in the west were "Lamanites" descended from biblical tribes of the ancient orient helped to link them with the Bedouin tribes of the eastern Mediterranean.[14] Best-selling author Grace

---

[13] That this strategy coincided with more mainstream Protestant notions of American millennialism is evident by the fact that the town in New York to which Joseph Smith's family had moved in 1816 when he was ten was called Palmyra, a city known in the Bible as Tadmor. Travelers to the Great Salt Lake carried out complex analyses of its water in the same way as travelers to the eastern Mediterranean tested the contents of the Dead Sea. See complete chapters on "The Dead Sea of America" in Fitzhugh Ludlow, *The Heart of the Continent* (New York: Hurd and Houghton; Cambridge, MA: Riverside Press, 1870), Chapter 8; and William Elkhanah Waters, *Life among the Mormons, and a March to their Zion* (New York: Moorhead, Simpson & Bond, 1868), Chapter 13. Immediately following the Mexican War, the U.S. Navy sent a special expedition to the Near East to explore the Dead Sea. See William Francis Lynch, *Narrative of the United States' Expedition to the River Jordan and the Dead Sea* (Philadelphia: Lea and Blanchard, 1849).

[14] Burton, *The City of the Saints*, 102; R. W. Mac, "Mormonism in Illinois," *The American Whig Review* 9 (March 1852): 221.

Greenwood acknowledged this orientalist aura in her travel narrative of Utah, noting that "[t]he whole region has a singularly foreign aspect, strange and ancient and solemn . . . it certainly, independent of Scripture nomenclature, reminds one of Palestine."[15] Other writers compared the Far West and the Near East with an even more imaginative islamicism. The introduction to the popular humorist Artemus Ward's 1864 *Travels among the Mormons* claimed that "the crescent-crowned dome and the minaret for the muezzin are all that are wanted to give Salt Lake City the respect of the Asiatic Orient."[16] "America has no other [city] like it," claimed an anti-Mormon novel from 1879: "Surveyed from a distance it wears a distinctly Oriental appearance. So we of the Far West who have only dreamed of the East, imagine how Damascus may look . . . [with] a spire that may answer for a minaret, . . . a sky of more than Oriental softness overhead." The Mormon settlement in Utah was called by the author "Orientalism in the Extreme Occident."[17]

Many propagandists branded the Mormon trek to Utah, and their earlier one to Nauvoo, as a "hegira," from the Arabic "hijrah" meaning emigration, with specific reference to Muhammad's flight to Medina from Mecca that inaugurated the beginning of the Muslim era, marked as 622 in the Christian calendar.[18] Some accounts asserted that when Mormon saints from any part of the world arrived within sight of Salt Lake City "they prostrate themselves to earth like the Mohammedans when they discover the sacred edifices of Mecca."[19] Richard Burton, in the nineteenth century's most widely read

---

[15] Grace Greenwood, *New Life in New Lands: Notes of Travel* (New York: J. B. Ford and Company, 1873), 141.

[16] Edward P. Hingston, "Introduction to Artemus Ward (His Travels) among the Mormons," *The Complete Works of Artemus Ward (Charles F. Browne)* (London, 1870), 181. Artemus Ward was unwelcome in Utah because before his journey he had used his dialect to call the Mormons "as theavin & omprincipled a set of retchis as ever drew Breth in eny spot on the Globe" (215).

[17] Charles Heber Clark, *The Tragedy of Thompson Dunbar, A Tale of Salt Lake City* (Philadelphia: J. M. Stoddart, 1879), 10, quoted in Givens, *Viper on the Hearth*, 132.

[18] Any movement of Mormons could be seen as a hegira. O. Turner mentioned the Mormon "hegira to Kirtland" in "Origin of the Mormon Imposture," *Littell's Living Age* 30 (30 August 1851): 431. John Hyde, Jr., described the 1837 flight from Kirtland: "Brigham Young accompanied this second Mohammed, in this second Hegira, and Missouri was the Medina that opened its gates to receive them." *Mormonism: Its Leaders and Designs* (New York: W. P. Fetridge and Company, 1857), 138. The title of a *New York Times* article reporting on the Mormon War reads "Important from Utah. Forty Thousand Mormons Moving Southward. Ineffectual Attempts of Gov. Cummin to Stop the Hegira" (16 June 1858): 5. This application of Islamic terms to American situations helped such words as "hegira" and "mecca" eventually to become adopted into English as predominately nonideological figures of speech.

[19] Austin N. Ward, *The Husband in Utah; or, Sights and Scenes among the Mormons*, ed. Maria Ward (New York: Derby & Jackson, 1857), 17. The description from Ward's fiction was taken from the Frenchman Jules Remy's two-volume narrative of his journey to Utah where he claims that "it is the custom of the Saints who arrive from Europe or the eastern States, to prostrate themselves with their faces to the earth as soon as they perceive the holy city, like the Mohammedan pilgrims when they discover the edifices of Mecca." *A Journey to Great-Salt-Lake City*, 1: 186. Richard Burton also observed similar reactions to seeing the Zion of the West for the first time. "At this place the pilgrim emigrants, like

travel book about the Latter-day Saints, called Utah "the Holy Land of the West," linked Salt Lake City with the Muslim holy city, and connected the mountains that overlooked both cities by twice calling Ensign Peak "the Jebel Nur of this new Meccah" − a reference to the "Mountain of Light," also known as Mount Hira, where Muhammad received his first revelation.[20] Such polemic not only aimed to disqualify Mormon attempts to reconstitute the Holy Land in North America but also rendered domestic terrain more exotic and universal in ways that attracted adventurers such as Richard Burton to the American west.

While many Americans localized their topographical transpositions on specific Mormon settlements, Europeans such as Burton sometimes viewed the entire American west in exotic terms similar to those with which Americans interpreted the Islamic orient. "Were there ANOTHER MAHOMET to arise," wrote the English author Robert Southey in March 1829 − even before the publication of the Book of Mormon − "there is no part of the world where he would find more scope, or fairer opportunity, than in THAT PART of the Anglo-American Union into which the elder States continually discharge the restless part of their population, leaving Laws and Gospels to overtake it if they can."[21] To some British critics, the rise of the LDS in the United States confirmed prejudices they held of the barbarism and incredulity of Americans, even after missionaries from the United States began to gain Mormon converts in England beginning as early as 1837. A study of Russian views of the Mormons from the mid-nineteenth century revealed likewise that "the question of Mormonism's similarity to Islam . . . appears in nearly every Russian writing on Mormon society."[22] Anti-Mormon Americans shared this discursive distancing of viewing Mormonism as an infidel expression, a strategy that suggested their desire for transatlantic legitimacy, but deployed islamicist rhetoric more often to

---

the hajjis of Mecca and Jerusalem, give vent to the emotions long pent up within their bosoms by sobs and tears, laughter and congratulations, psalms and hysterics." Burton, *City of the Saints*, 198.

[20] Burton, *City of the Saints*, 197–8, 287, 300, 359. See James B. Allen and Glen M. Leonard, *The Story of the Latter-day Saints* (Salt Lake City: Deseret Book Co., 1976), 319. Burton probably had more personal experience with both Islam and Mormonism than any other nineteenth-century individual. In 1853, he disguised himself as a Muslim dervish, Mirza Abdullah, and made the pilgrimage to Mecca. See Richard Burton, *The Personal Narrative of a Pilgrimage to Al-Madinah and Meccah* (London: Longman, Brown, Green and Longmans, 1855–6).

[21] Robert Southey, *Sir Thomas More; or Colloquies on the Progress and Prospects of Society*. 2 vols. (London: John Murray, 1829), 2: 42. This quotation was included in the frontispiece of a book by Henry Caswall who called it a "prediction" or "remarkable extract" because to him it presaged the rise of Mormonism at the same time that "the American Mahomet was busily engaged in his pretended translation." Henry Caswall, *The City of the Mormons; or, Three Days at Nauvoo, in 1842* (London: J. G. F. & J. Rivington, 1842), xiii. The quotation is also found at the beginning of Richard Burton's *The City of the Saints*.

[22] Leland Fetzer, "Russian Writers Look at Mormon Manners, 1857–72," *Dialogue: A Journal of Mormon Thought* 13 (1980): 76–7.

define American positions in global terms rather than only to relegate them to the peripherality of barbarism.

For many Protestant readers in the United States, the association of Islam and Mormonism marked this new faith as so beyond the pale of religious acceptability as to reinforce the boundaries of denominational norms. But the cultural work of the comparison was versatile and adapted to changing events in both Mormon and national history as well as the shifting valences of islamicism. Perhaps in ways that subverted the intentions of anti-Mormon critics, islamicist descriptions emphasizing the exoticism of Mormonism effectively sensationalized it, thereby presenting the religion as a strange and exciting contrast, if not alternative, to Protestant conventions of morality. Such rhetoric brought more attention to the Latter-day Saints and may have had the unintended effect of legitimizing their attractiveness. Some of the more secular writers who islamicized Mormonism were much more fascinated by the new world Mecca rising up in Salt Lake City, especially with the fantasy of its polygamous practices, than they were fearful of the threat of its theological extravagances. Writers saw the compounded exoticism of an islamicized Mormonism as a resonant means of attracting audiences to their various productions whether their motive was to communicate moral outrage or to entertain with burlesque humor. The conventions of Islamic orientalism thus enabled northern white Protestants to cope with and capitalize upon the challenges of both Islam and Mormonism, a form of cultural compensation for their inability to dissipate either contending religion.

"THE AMERICAN MAHOMET": RECOVERING THE ANTI-MORMON ARCHIVE

Muhammad and the religion of Islam clearly provided a major historical and rhetorical prototype for critics who wished to tarnish the claims of the Mormon religious experience. Such writers saw the new revelation as the reemergence of a colossal deception that had not been seen since the days of Islam's rise and elaborated an extensive archive that subjugated Mormon claims through islamicist representation. As early as 1831, the prophet of the Mormons, Joseph Smith, Jr., was labeled the "the Ontario Mahomet," after the region of western New York where he assumed his mission.[23] As the Mormons began moving west, attracting many adherents along the way, the titles themselves grew in stature to include "the Yankee Mahomet, "the

---

[23] James G. Bennett, "Mormon Religion – Clerical Ambition Western New York – The Mormonites Gone to Ohio," *New York Herald* (1 September 1831): 103, quoted in Leonard J. Arrington, "James Gordon Bennett's 1831 Report on the Mormonites," *BYU Studies* 10 (Spring 1970): 362.

American Mahomet," and "the modern Mahomet."[24] William S. West, who challenged the claims of the Mormons in 1837 while they were still centered in Kirtland, Ohio, encouraged his readers to send any authentic information damning it as a deception to his home. "For I am confident," he asserted, "that a knowledge of the truth respecting Mormonism, will place it on a par with Mahometanism."[25]

The equivalence that anti–Mormon propagandists drew between the Book of Mormon and the Qur'an was one important facet of their attempts to degrade both scriptures to the level of fantasies or delusions. Of course, Mormonism was also viewed as a return to Judaic ritual, and its leaders as Catholic pontiffs, but these criticisms were unable to dislodge Mormonism from its claimed connection with the Christian past as fully as did an alliance with Islam. This emphasis on imposture was important because it disassociated many Mormons from the similar ethnic backgrounds they shared with their detractors. "The attempt to append new revelations to the Word of God is as wicked and dangerous as the conduct of Mahomet, who corrupted it," asserted a British anti–Mormon tract. Claiming that both scriptures were "wretched compounds" in which sacred allusions had been "neutralized by wild notions," its author saw them as nothing more than romantic tales, which left their respective adherents "satisfied with sensual pleasures on earth and in heaven."[26] The president of a Virginia medical college likewise equated the "contemptible absurdities of Joe Smith's book" with the "fictions of Mahommed."[27] One minister relegated Mormon scripture to the shelf of romance by commenting that "the fictions of Mohammed, the story of Robinson Crusoe, or the 'Arabian Night's Entertainment,' are respectable volumes by the side of the Book of

---

[24] [Henry Mayhew], *History of the Mormons: or Latter-Day Saints. With Memoirs of the Life and Death of Joseph Smith, the 'American Mahomet'* (Auburn, NY: Derby and Miller, 1853). "Highly Important from the Mormon Empire. – Wonderful Progress of Joe Smith, the Modern Mahomet. – Spread of the Mormon Faith and a New Religious Revolution at Hand," *New York Herald* 8 (17 June 1842): 2. Other attributions included "this second Mohammed," Hyde, *Mormonism*, 138; "the Mormon Mahomet," John C. Bennett, *The History of the Saints; or, An Exposé of Joe Smith and Mormonism* (Boston: Leland and Whiting; New York: Bradbury, Soden, 1842), 151; and "the Mahomet of the nineteenth century," "The Mormons," *Christian Examiner* 64 (May 1858): 432.

[25] William S. West, *A Few Interesting Facts, Respecting the Rise Progress and Pretensions of the Mormons* (Braceville, OH, 1837), 15.

[26] Samuel Haining, *Mormonism Weighed in the Balances of the Sanctuary and Found Wanting* (Douglas, Isle of Man: Robert Fargher, 1840), 5, 55, 42, 64. Haining calls the Book of Mormon "a tale unlike any thing that ever occurred in the experience of any people, in any country. It . . . is scarcely surpassed by the Koran, when Mahomet assures his followers, that the angel Gabriel knocked at his door, and ordered him to mount the beast having sixteen wings, and that he flew with him quick as lightning" (42).

[27] John Thomas, M.D., *Sketch of the Rise, Progress, and Dispersion of the Mormons* (London: Arthur Hall, 1847), 2. See also Pomeroy Tucker, *Origin, Rise, and Progress of Mormonism* (New York: D. Appleton and Company, 1867), 124.

Mormon."[28] Reducing their divine claims to fictional fables and secular imaginations discredited the religious authority of both Mormons and Muslims. Yet, despite characterizing these scriptures as "wretched" and "contemptible" impostures, these attacks emphasized the imaginative power of these productions in romantic ways.

Anti-Mormon argument expanded such delegitimizing parallels between the scriptures of the two religions by drawing on historical accounts of how their respective prophets had received their inspirations through the medium of angels.[29] Apostate John Hyde accounted for Joseph Smith's revelation in 1820 by explaining that "God the Father and Jesus Christ came to him from the heavens; and like Mohammed's Gabriel, told him that his sins were forgiven; that he was the chosen of God to reinstate his kingdom and re-introduce the gospel, that none of the denominations were right, etc." An early calumniator noted in 1841, "[i]t is worth pausing to observe the similarity between this story and the account Mohammed gave of the first revelation he received; the coming of the angel Gabriel to his cave, the purification from original sin, and the promise of a future revelation to be given when he made the night-journey to heaven." The British author of several anti-Mormon tracts saw an "exact similarity" in these accounts and believed that Joseph Smith had "servilely imitated the impostor of Mecca."[30]

Critics also contrasted what they saw as the insufficient arguments offered by the Mormon and Muslim prophets in support of the authenticity of their scriptures. One of the proofs of the credibility of the Book of Mormon – that Joseph Smith was unable to write it himself – was countered early by Alexander Campbell when he said "Neither could Mahomet, who gave forth the Alcoran."[31] *A Short History of the Mormonites* debunked arguments

---

[28] Edmund Clay, *The Doctrines and Practices of "The Mormons" and the Immoral Character of Their Prophet Joseph Smith, Delineated from Authentic Sources* (London: Wertheim & Mcintosh, 1853), 31. R. Clarke, *Mormonism Unmasked: or the Latter-Day Saints in a Fix* (London: Houston & Stoneman, 1849), 3.

[29] Harold Bloom analyzed Smith's "First Vision," as expressed in his 1842 letter to John Wentworth, a Chicago editor, and found Smith to be a "remarkably apt" reader of the Bible with an "uncanny knowing [for] precisely what is needful for the inauguration of a new faith." *The American Religion: The Emergence of the Post-Christian Nation* (New York: Simon and Schuster, 1992), 82–4.

[30] Hyde, *Mormonism*, 199; *The Imposture Unmasked; or, A Complete Exposure of the Mormon Fraud.* 2nd ed. (Isle of Man: R. Fargher, 1841), 6–7; Edmund Clay, *Tracts on Mormonism, No. 1* (London: Wertheim & Macintosh, 1851), 9; Edmund Clay, *Tracts No. 2* (1851), 17. Clay's *Tracts* were reprinted as *The Doctrines and Practices of "The Mormons" and the Immoral Character of Their Prophet Joseph Smith, Delineated from Authentic Sources* (London: Wertheim and Macintosh, 1853). Two twentieth-century studies of the Mormon revelation and the rise of Islam agree that both Muhammad and Joseph Smith received the impulse for their revelations from the rivalry between religious sects in their respective environments. See D. S. Margoliouth, *Mohammed and the Rise of Islam* (1905; London and New York, 1931), 76; and George Bartholomew Arbaugh, *Revelation in Mormonism: Its Character and Changing Forms* (Chicago: University of Chicago Press, 1932), 12n.

[31] Alexander Campbell, *Delusions, an Analysis of the Book of Mormon* (Boston: Benjamin H. Greene, 1832), 5, originally published in the *Millennial Harbinger* (Bethany, VA) 2 (1831): 2.

about the miraculous creation of the Qu'ran and the Book of Mormon because their authors were illiterate by insinuating that each used claims of ignorance to mask their cunning and deception.[32] Hyppolite Taine and John Greenleaf Whittier each surmised that the worldly successes of Muhammad and Joseph Smith had deluded both into believing that the fables they had concocted were divinely ordained.[33] An early anti-Mormon history by James H. Hunt similarly argued that the reliance on the "internal evidences" of the Book of Mormon, rather than on the intellectual capacity of the prophet or his capacity to work miracles, comprised the same "wardrobe of imposture . . . under which that prince of impostors, Mohammed, took shelter, in order to carry in his train the ignorant and superstitious of his time."[34] One critic even employed islamicism to judge these internal evidences as wanting because the Book of Mormon's anachronistic accounts of warriors armed with "cimeters" ("a Turkish weapon, not known until after the time of Mohammed") seemed proof of its folly.[35]

Polemicists interjected quotations taken from histories of Islam into Mormon situations to slander the legitimacy of the Latter-day Saints. In *The Imposture Unmasked*, utterances of Joseph Smith are directly associated with those of Muhammad.

> Smith drew the sword, to take the possession of the lands in Missouri, and was defeated. When the citizens sent out a deputation to the Mormon army for the accommodation of their differences, said Smith, in answer to their proposition, 'Thus saith the Lord, *march*!!' Said Mohammed to those with whom he contended, there is no other alternative, 'Pay tribute – have the sword, or the Koran – the shadow of the sword is paradise.'[36]

The author aligns Smith's declaration so seamlessly with Muhammad's that the reader is forced to presume the commonness of their methods, if not their overlapping identities. Similar interjections were added in various books to compare the devotion of Joseph Smith's apostles with Muhammad's loyal

[32] John Frere, *A Short History of the Mormonites; of Latter Day Saints* (London: J. Masters, 1850), 13. Oliver H. Olney commented "We look at the case of Mahomet. How did he arise? Was it by his foreknowledge of events and a very wise head? No: it was by a low, mean, cunning, ambitious desire in him to become great." *The Absurdities of Mormonism Portrayed* (Hancock Co., IL, 1843), 30.

[33] "Taine's Essay on the Mormons," translated Austin E. Fife, *Pacific Historical Review* 31 (February 1962): 52 [translation of *Nouveau Essais de Critique et d'Histoire* (Paris, 1865), 271–99]. John Greenleaf Whittier, "A Mormon Conventicle," *Littell's Living Age* 15 (4 December 1847): 461.

[34] James H. Hunt, *Mormonism: Embracing the Origin, Rise, and Progress of the Sect* (St. Louis: Ustick & Davies, 1844), 26, 293.

[35] Benjamin G. Ferris, *Utah and the Mormons: The History, Government, Doctrines, Customs, and Prospects of the Latter-Day Saints* (New York: Harper & Brothers, 1854), 262. One of the props of Islamic orientalism, the scimitar (from the Persian *simsir*, spelled variously in nineteenth-century accounts) refers to a broad sword with a convex edge. References to cimeters appear in the Book of Mormon in the books of Mosiah, Alma, and Helaman.

[36] *The Imposture Unmasked*, 31.

follower Ali[37]; to link his wife, Emma, with Khadija, the first wife of Muhammad[38]; and to associate the lamentation of mourners at the death of the respective Prophets.[39] Islamicism gave critics the ability to bring Mormonism into disrepute at the same time that they displayed the worldliness of their knowledge, a strategy that assured them of their own righteousness without having to contend directly with the claims and arguments of either religion.[40]

The application of comparative islamicism to Mormon history, however, was not always used to disparage both Muslims and the Latter-day Saints. Some commentators claimed that one religion was superior to the other, and this allowed a romantic dimension to emerge that had the ironic effect of exalting one at the expense of the other. The accounts that found Mormonism to be more heinous, if only because it affronted American sensitivities closer to home, elevated Islam by highlighting some of its comparative virtues. The very act of placing Islam in a superior position raised its status, such as when critics called Mormonism "Mohammedanism without the spirit of Mohammed" or "Turks without Muhammad."[41] Such a parallel imagined Islam as superior in the purity of its theology, in the character of

[37] "'Who,' said Mohammed, 'will be my vizier, and become my brother, my vicar, and ambassador?' 'I,' said Ali, 'O Prophet, will obey your commands. Whoever dares oppose you, I will tear out his eyes, dash out his teeth, and rip open his body.' The same spirit is seen in the Mormon priesthood." *The Imposture Unmasked*, 24. This same incident in Islamic history reminded another writer of "the scanty beginnings" of the Mormon church during which Oliver Cowdery had played the role of Ali. "The Mormons," *Christian Examiner*, 428. James G. Bennett was the first to use the comparison when he called Martin Harris "the Ali of the Ontario Mahomet" in 1831. Arrington, "Bennett's 1831 Report," 362.

[38] "Mrs. [Emma] Smith had an extraordinary influence over Joseph. She was to him as Cadijah was to Mohammed . . . and he loved her as intensely as did the Arabian prophet his faithful wife." Stenhouse, *The Rocky Mountain Saints*, 21n. Stenhouse's quotation was misapplied to Joseph Smith's mother in William Alexander Linn's influential *The Story of the Mormons*, where he recognized that "The similarity between Smith's early life and visions and Mohammed's has been mentioned by more than one writer." (1902; New York: The Macmillan Co., 1923), 109–10n.

[39] "[W]hen the death of the leader became fully known," wrote Maria Ward, "[m]any of them were ready to take up the lamentation of the bereaved Mussulman: 'He cannot be dead – our Prophet, our leader, and intercessor with God!'" *Female Life among the Mormons; A Narrative of Many Years' Personal Experience* (New York: J. C. Derby, 1855), 140. See also George Sexton, *A Portraiture of Mormonism, Animadversions on the Doctrines and Pretensions of the Latter-day Saints* (London: W. Strange, 1849). "[I]f the Arabian impostor was now on the earth," Sexton argued at the close of his first lecture, "I have no doubt but here would be rivalship of prophets, and each would be jealous of the other's spiritual communications, and wicked and extravagant liberties," 51–2.

[40] Marianne Perciaccante affirmed this "widespread, though shallow, familiarity with Islam in nineteenth-century American popular culture" and argued: "The supposition that twentieth-century Americans know more about Islam than their nineteenth-century predecessors is patently false, and has resulted in a neglect among contemporary historians in one of the most striking aspects of nineteenth-century writing on the Mormons." Perciaccante, "The Muslim–Mormon Comparison," 296, 301–2.

[41] T. W. P. Taylder, *The Mormon's Own Book; or, Mormonism Tried by Its Own Standards* (London: Partridge & Co., 1857), 189–90; *À Travers les États-Unis; Notes et Impressions par le Comte d'Haussonville*

its prophet, and in the social success of its establishment. An essay published in the *Christian Examiner* in 1855 found Muhammad to be "the honest man" because, unlike Joseph Smith, he "substituted a better religion for the one he found."[42] "Mohammed was rich, and became poor; was respected, and became despised; was elevated to positions of authority and influence, and had to flee for his life," claimed John Hyde, "but Smith was miserably poor, universally despised and hopelessly degraded, and his imposture opened his prospective wealth, influence and power."[43] The *Southern Literary Messenger* argued that Muhammad might "complain of this company" because "however mortifying to our national pride, it must be admitted that the eastern impostor far excelled his western imitator, in character, in policy, and in achievement."[44]

The composition of such parallels between Mormon and Islamic history ironically expanded the relevance of Mormons by associating their experience with practices both older and more global than those expressed by the new American sect. That American pride could be mortified by Muhammad's superiority to Joseph Smith exemplifies how the Mormon–Muslim comparison had the effect of universalizing American identity on both temporal and spatial registers. National pride is most evident, however, in the accounts that found Mormonism to be superior to Islam, especially in the successful expansion of its adherents. James H. Hunt indicated that Muhammad had several advantages over Joseph Smith, including his "gigantic intellect" and "intrepidity of character," qualities augmented by the fact that his followers were abject slaves with no recourse to science or literature. And yet he still asserted that "Mahomet was not so successful in the commencement of his career as has been Joseph Smith, the Mormon Prophet."[45] The romantic element is clear in an article that, while ultimately contending that Smith was "the most . . . wicked impostor of modern times," still

---

(Paris: Calmann Lévy, 1888), 324, 353, in Wilfred Decoo, "The Image of Mormons in French Literature, Part 1," *BYU Studies* 14 (Winter 1974): 172.

[42] Smith, "Migrations," 44–5. A similar tone was taken in another article from the same journal three years later. "Thus died Joseph Smith, the Mahomet of the nineteenth century, – if the application of that name to him is not a wrong to the Arabian prophet. For the faith of Mahomet, with whatever of conscious imposture he may have proclaimed it, was at least a great advance upon the idolatry which previously existed among his country men; while the doctrine of the Western deceiver rejects what is highest and purest in the prevalent religion, and degrades its followers to a grovelling materialism and a worse than Asiatic sensuality." "The Mormons," *Christian Examiner*, 432.

[43] Hyde, *Mormonism*, 271–2. "Imitating Mohammed in polity of government, the Mormons obtain some of the results of Moslem rule," Hyde claimed. "All know that there is not so much crime among Mussulmans as among Christians, still but few Anglo-Saxons, from that cause, would be willing to become Turks" (113–14).

[44] "Memoir of the Mormons," 641. Unlike Joseph Smith, argued one writer, "Mahomet, to whom the Mormon Prophet has frequently been compared, was a reformer" and the doctrine of "the noble principle of the unity of Deity – the base of his splendid superstructure – was itself a mighty triumph over the corrupt mysteries of pantheism. "Mormonism in Illinois," 532.

[45] Hunt, *Mormonism*, 2, 4.

saw the Mormon prophet's success as "a series of supernatural incidents and brilliant conquests, more miraculous, complete, and dazzling than the rapid march of the Moslem prophet under his crescent banner."[46] A remarkable editorial in *Harper's Magazine* of 1851 went beyond demographic measures to celebrate the scripture itself as an American success story. It endowed the Qur'an with the "prestige of authority" but still exclaimed of the Book of Mormon that "we do not hesitate to say it, Joe Smith, or whoever was its author, has made a book superior to that of the Arabian prophet; deeper in its philosophy, purer in its morality, and far more original."[47] Mormonism was an American phenomenon that commentators could not only compare with Islam, but also imagine as an improvement on it, and thus celebrate as a perverse form of national achievement.

As anti-Mormons conflated Mormonism and Islam, they benefited from evidence that Joseph Smith may have likened himself to Muhammad. In an act that contributed to his excommunication from the Mormon hierarchy, Thomas B. Marsh, a President of the Quorum of Twelve, testified about hearing Smith compare himself to Muhammad in an 1838 court proceeding that sought to indict Joseph Smith as a traitor to the State of Missouri. Marsh heard Smith claim that

he would yet tread down his enemies, and walk over their dead bodies; and if he was not let alone, he would be a second Mohammed to this generation, and that it would be one gore of blood from the Rocky Mountains to the Atlantic Ocean; that like Mohammed, whose motto in treating for peace was, 'the Alcoran or the Sword,' so should it be eventually with us, 'Joseph Smith or the Sword.'[48]

---

[46] "Mormonism in Illinois," 221. This tone is continued in a later segment when the author notes: "The Moslem prophet, whose brilliant and almost superhuman achievements startled the world, and have continued in all subsequent time to excite wonder and admiration, toiled, and fasted, and prayed for twenty years in the solitary desert, before his creed was acknowledged, before his star of empire sparkled in the orient, or his crescent banner was given to the winds." He then intimates that "Smith had accomplished much in his short mission besides fasting and prayer." (June 1852): 524–5. See also Charles A. Dana, ed., *The United States Illustrated* (New York: H. J. Meyer, 1853), 37–8.

[47] "Editor's Table," *Harper's New Monthly Magazine* 3 (October 1851): 701. This editorial viewpoint resembles the boast of a Mormon proselytizer: "Mohammedanism is without either prestige or power, and the future is ours.... When the apostle of Mecca explained his first Revelation to a jeering, hooting crowd, what stretch of imagination would have reached the vast empires to be subjugated in his name... at the end of three years Mohammed had made one convert, and that one his wife; Joseph Smith has many thousand followers in that length of time. Has the world ever witnessed a parallel to our success?" Ward, *Husband in Utah*, 250.

[48] Joseph Smith, Jr., *History of the Church of Jesus Christ of Latter-day Saints.* 7 vols. (Salt Lake City: Deseret News, 1948–57), 3: 167n. James H. Hunt would paraphrase this testimony by claiming "Joe says he will be to the people of this generation what Mahommed was to the people of his day, and that he will yet make it a gore of blood from Maine to the Rocky Mountains." *A History of the Mormon War* (St. Louis: Ustick & Davies, 1844), v. A form of this quotation is also included in the popular author Mayne Reid's anti-Mormon novel: "Joseph declared publicly that he would yet 'tread down his enemies and trample on their dead bodies,' and that he 'would be a Mahomet to

Two recent scholars have discounted this statement, arguing that Orson Hyde, a recanting Mormon who seconded Marsh's testimony, later confessed that some "unspecified" portion of Marsh's deposition had been concocted.[49] Even if this portion was Smith's mention of himself as a Muhammad, Marsh and Hyde were not alone in their observations. Two other excommunicated Mormons made similar allegations. George M. Hinkle testified: "I have heard Joseph Smith, junior, say, that . . . the world believed Mahomet, as they had believed him; and he believed Mahomet a true prophet."[50] Similarly, John Corrill claimed that that "Joseph Smith, jun., said, if the people . . . came on to us to molest us, we would establish our religion by the sword, that he would become to this generation a second Mahomet."[51] Despite the vague provenance of where Smith uttered these words and the potential for bias in the testimony of excommunicants and apostates, the presence of four witnesses whose wording is similar yet distinct, renders less credible the theory of a conspiracy defaming Smith by comparing him to Muhammad, and suggests the possibility that Joseph Smith had at some point associated his mission with that of the Messenger of Allah.

Whatever the truth of these allegations, they were easily incorporated into early anti-Mormon histories of the Church to feed fears that Smith was a tyrant who intended to overthrow organized government violently, as well as a deceiver who had revolted against Christian orthodoxy. *An Authentic History of Remarkable Persons*, published in 1849, portrayed Smith as "at once a king, a chief, and a prophet; [who] threatened, in a manner, to

---

this generation.'" *The Californian Crusoe; or, the Lost Treasure Found. A Tale of Mormonism* (New York: Stanford and Swords, 1854), 127.

[49] Green and Goldrup called this assertion "quite probably a mere fabrication" in "Joseph Smith, an American Muhammad?," 47. When Vice-President of the United States Schuyler Colfax used Marsh's testimony to allude to the Mormon's violent disregard for civil law, Mormon leader John Taylor acknowledged the fact that his affadavit had been written, but compared the assertion to "the acts of Peter when he cursed and swore and denied Jesus; not the acts of Judas who betrayed him." He accounts for Marsh's claims by asserting that his "nerves" were not adequate to the "shocks" of those "troublous times" and for Hyde's accession to them as a result of his "laboring under a severe fever, and was at that time only just recovering." "Reply of John Taylor to the Honorable Vice-President Schuyler Colfax, on the Mormon Question," in *The Mormon Question* (Salt Lake City: Deseret News Office, 1870), 19.

[50] "Deposition of George M. Heckle [sic], 1838," in Hunt, *Mormonism*, 222. This quotation is also printed in the *Anti-Mormon Almanac for 1842* (New York: Health Book Store, 1841) and in W. Sparrow Simpson, *Mormonism: Its History, Doctrines, and Practices* (London: A. M. Pigott, 1853), 33, where the word "believed" in the penultimate clause is replaced in both cases by "belied." This version of the claim is also included in Sydney Ahlstrom's magisterial *A Religious History of the American People* where he acknowledges "the Prophet's infamous cry 'I will be a Second Mohammed.'" Ahlstrom also calls Salt Lake City the Mormon's "Mecca." 2 vols. (1972; Garden City, NY: Image Books, 1975), 1: 610, 613. William Wyl spoke of Smith's "intoxication with the idea of being a second Mahomet" and of his "bold Mahomet-scheme" in *Mormon Portraits or the Truth about the Mormon Leaders from 1830–1886* (Salt Lake City, UT: Tribune Printing and Publishing Co., 1886), 187, 137.

[51] "Deposition of John Corrill, 1838," in Hunt, *Mormonism*, 213–14; and Simpson, *Mormonism*, 33.

become the Mahomet of the New World."[52] Especially before the Mormon War of 1857, polemicists argued that this new religion was poised to replicate the political despotism of Islam by using violence to consolidate and expand its foothold in the American west. If the Mormons were successful, they argued, they would erase the civilizing properties of Christianity and imprison the occident in a barbarism as dark as that which Islam had installed throughout its vast Asian and African domains, including the Holy Land.

One of the dogmas of islamicism was the belief that Muhammad had gained his ascendancy by forcing his adherents to accept Islam at the point of the sword. Polemicists admonished their audiences in fiery prose that Mormon leaders intended to follow Muhammad's example by violently coercing conversion to the new religion. William Harris had become convinced by 1841 that the writings and actions of the Mormon leaders "show a design to pursue the same path, and attaining the same end by the same means, as did Mahomet."[53] Henry Caswall asserted in his 1842 book, *The City of the Mormons*, that "it remains (under God) for Christians of the present day to determine whether Mormonism shall sink to the level of those fanatical sects which, like new stars, have blazed for a little while, and then sunk into obscurity; or whether, like a second Mahometanism, it shall extend itself sword in hand, until, throughout western America, Christianity shall be levelled with the dust."[54] Another book prophesied that same year that Mormonism would be the cause of more bloodshed than America had yet witnessed, "For, what will not religious fanaticism do, when *united with the* SWORD, as in the case of Mohammed?"[55] Such a prospect was terrifying enough that the former mayor of Nauvoo, John C.

---

[52] *An Authentic History of Remarkable Persons* (New York: Wilson and Company, Brother Jonathan Press, 1849), 6. In his 1854 book, former secretary of the Utah Territory Benjamin Ferris argued that Smith was "well read in the history of Mohammed" and thrice surmises that Smith attempted to "play the part of the Arabian impostor." Ferris, *Utah and the Mormons*, 66, 89, 103. Ferris argued that Smith would have succeeded in matching Muhammad "had he possessed equal resources, and found a field of popular ignorance and delusion sufficiently extensive for his operations" (96). There are many other examples of the orientalization of Mormon violence in anti-Mormon rhetoric. See, for example, Clay, *Tracts, No. 1*, 9; Chancey Herbert, "Nauvoo and Deseret," *The National Magazine* (October 1854): 347; Edwin De Leon, "The Rise and Progress of the Mormon Faith and People," *Southern Literary Messenger* 10 (September 1844): 527.

[53] William G. Harris, *Mormonism Portrayed: Its Errors and Absurdities Exposed and the Designs of Its Authors Mode Manifest* (Warsaw, IL: Sharp & Gamble, 1841), 44.

[54] Caswall, *The City of the Mormons*, 56. Caswall asserted in his next book: "Having experimented freely on the credulity of mankind, their [Joseph Smith and other Mormon leaders'] plans assumed a wider range, and at length the prophet determined to pursue a path similar to that of Mahomet, and to attain his end by similar means." Henry Caswall, *The Prophet of the Nineteenth Century: or, The Rise, Progress, and Present State of the Mormons, or Latter-Day Saints* (London: J. G. F. & J. Rivington, 1843), 206.

[55] [La Roy Sunderland], *Mormonism Exposed and Refuted* (1838; New York: Watchman, Piercy & Reed, 1842), 48. In a similar vein, Sunderland argues: "Let the reader ponder the foregoing testimonies,

Bennett, could state: "There is no doubt that Joe Smith would, if he possessed the capacity, imitate the great Arabian impostor, even in his wars and conquests."[56] John Hyde asserted an even more intentional linkage when he argued in 1857 that Joseph Smith, "[h]aving imitated Mohammed in his pretended mission and revelations, like him, having become the chief of a second Medina . . . wished to extend the resemblance still further, and aspired to rule the continent." If this was allowed to happen, he believed: "The silk standard of Mormonism would be as firmly and furiously sustained as was the silver crescent."[57] These quotations clearly demonstrate that a major tactic of early anti-Mormon literature was to arouse fear in its readers that the success of a Mormon theocracy would lead to its eventual control over America, even as Islam had subsumed the Holy Land under its political hegemony. Reformers used the charged rhetoric of islamicism to elicit from their readers support for a cultural crusade against Mormon excesses, similar to the way that it had been employed in temperance and antislavery discourse.

POLYGAMY AND THE PULL OF EXOTIC PATRIARCHY

Fears of a Mormon military despotism were quelled during the 1850s as the federal government expanded its reach over western territory, and as Mormon attempts to establish a State of Deseret after the Mexican Cession in 1848 were ended by the establishment of Utah Territory in 1850. The national disruption over the issue of slavery eventually overshadowed concerns about Utah as sectional violence in Kansas raised more immediate

---

and then ask himself what religious fanaticism may not yet do to accomplish its designs? What has it not done for Mahommedanism?" (42).

[56] Bennett, *History of the Saints*, 306. Bennett feared that a Mormon military despotism would cause apocalyptic destruction, or at least a return to "savage barbarity," and "the best interests of the country will be sacrificed to the ambitious views of an ancient or modern Prophet – a Mahomet or a Smith!" (49). In a fascinating note in his bibliography, Richard Burton wrote: "The Mormons speak of him [J. C. Bennett] as the Musaylimat el Kazzab – Musaylimat the Liar, who tried and failed to enter into partnership with Mohammed – of their religion." *City of the Saints*, 205, n 12. If Burton is to be believed, then the early Mormons appear to be fully aware of the link between their church and Islamic history. Burton suggested that Mormonism was "[i]mitative to an extent that not a vestige of originality appears," citing as one of his examples his contention that "the titles of the apostles, *e.g.* Lion of the Lord, are literally borrowed from El-Islam" (410).

[57] Hyde, *Mormonism*, 308. Hyde argued not only that the fanaticism of the Mormons would enable them to excel in their military drills, but also that their devotion to Brigham Young will lead them to "blindly and cheerfully obey, as [had] the soldiers of Mohammed" (308, 183–4). Testimonies of the dangers of the military despotism of Mormonism alluded to the practices of contemporary Muslims as well. A long article of the Mormons ended: "If the Mormons should establish themselves in strength upon the sea coast," one writer asserted, "the commerce of that region may find in them enemies, as active and relentless as the piratical Malays of the other continent." "Memoir of the Mormons," *Southern Literary Messenger*, 654.

and proximate worries that culminated in the outbreak of the Civil War. Joseph Smith had been killed in 1844, and John Brown emerged as a new type of ultraist revolutionary whose political cause was more resonant with New England Protestants. In 1857, President Buchanan's attempt to replace Brigham Young as governor of the Utah territory with a non–Mormon leader named Alfred Cumming eventually led to U.S. military occupation of Salt Lake City the following year. Fears of the military prowess of the Mormons gradually gave way and were surpassed by attention to the sensual features of Mormon despotism as polygamy became the chief focus of attack for critics of the church. Although the Mormon practice of plural marriage was first made public in 1842, it did not become a cause célèbre until after the Church of the Latter-day Saints authorized the practice in 1852. This public recognition prompted the new Republican Party to define polygamy along with slavery in its 1856 platform as the "twin relics of barbarism" that Congress must prohibit from the territories of the west. In 1862, Congress passed the Morrill Act, which made bigamy in a federal territory a crime punishable by a fine and five years in prison.

In the minds of many Americans, polygamy was most clearly associated not with the Old Testament patriarchs, where the Mormons looked for justification, but rather with the seraglios and harems of oriental despots.[58] Its establishment raised the relevance of islamicist comparison and expanded the association to include the imitation of contemporary Turkish customs as well as the reenactment of Islamic history. Even more than religious imposture or martial fanaticism, polygamy provided an image of Mormon behavior that popularized both the Mormon–Muslim connection and anti-Mormon polemic. The perils of polygamy attracted advocates of the women's movement and supplied the dramatic plot that enabled anti-Mormon expression to expand into broader genres such as novels, dramas, confessional narratives, and visual caricature. The cultural uproar over the issue of polygamy, combined with the firm control of Mormons over the political machinery of the Territory, created a long-standing "problem" or "question," which postponed the statehood of Utah for almost half a century.

The changing uses of islamicism in anti-Mormon commentary also responded to evolving understandings of Islam within broader American culture. The alliance of Britain and France with the Ottoman Empire against the Russians during the Crimean War from 1853 to 1856 mitigated the age-old stereotypes of sultanic despotism and placed the Turks more sympathetically in the role of victims. More compellingly, biographers of Muhammad

---

[58] Benjamin G. Ferris wrote that polygamy "belongs to the indolent and opium-eating Turks and Asiatics." *Utah and the Mormons*, 247. Another critic labeled polygamy "the foul bird of Asiatic instinct." [William Dallin], *True Mormonism; or, The Horrors of Polygamy* (Chicago: W. P. Dunn & Co., 1885), 7. See also Bruce Burgett, "On the Morman Question: Race, Sex, and Polygamy in the 1850s and the 1990s," *American Quarterly* 57 (2005): 83–5, 88–90.

such as Thomas Carlyle and Washington Irving were revising the image of the Prophet into a more romantic and even heroic figure.[59] The changing and diverse views of Islam in the United States at this time were matched by shifting and complex views of the Mormon church. The establishment of Mormon polygamy elicited a broad spectrum of cultural commentary. Some found it a hideous imposition of barbaric sensuality that threatened an embarrassing regression for the nation. But others were enticed by its exotic attractions and found Mormon Utah a symbolic field for projecting fantasies of patriarchal power. Critiques of Mormon polygamy ultimately demonstrated how the multiple valences of islamicism were dynamically applied to domestic American situations both to denigrate and to titillate.

One of the ironic results of the Mormons' use of the Bible to sanction the practice of polygamy was an increased appreciation among Mormons for the role of Islam in world history. Mormon teachings on polygamy emphasized that God had not only permitted Abraham, "the father of the faithful," to take Hagar as a second wife to Sarah but had also blessed both their sons, Ishmael as well as Isaac. Accentuating God's blessing to Ishmael, widely considered to be the ancestor of Muslims, opened the door to legitimizing Islam as a rightful dominion in the Mormon worldview. This biblical validation of Islam and the sensitivity of Mormon leaders to the superficiality of "Gentile" polemic about Muslims because of their own experiences of persecution, led Mormon leaders to construct contrasting images of Islam. In a Salt Lake City lecture of 1855, Elder George A. Smith encouraged his audience to study the "useful lessons" of Islamic history to understand their own Mormon future, and even outlined a short curriculum for his hearers. Islam demonstrated, Smith argued, how religious enthusiasm contributed to the expansion and success of religion and how failure to follow the instructions of leaders caused a religion to lose its influence. Following Smith's performance, Parley P. Pratt lectured on "Mahometanism and Christianity" in which he acknowledged the prejudice of Westerners against Islam, claiming that "for my part I hardly know what to call the idolatrous side of the question, unless we consider Mahometanism Christianity, in one sense, and that which has been called Christianity, heathenism." Pratt found evidence of the blessing of Ishmael ("the hand of God") in the fact that Muslims "have better morals and better institutions than many Christian nations" and "have exceeded in righteousness and truthfulness of religion, the idolatrous and corrupt church that has borne the name of Christianity." Nevertheless, Pratt emphasized that, although blessed by the Lord, Ishmael and his descendants (like other Gentiles) were not in possession of "the keys

---

[59] Carlyle, "The Hero as Prophet," in *On Heroes, Hero-Worship and the Heroic in History* (London: Chapman and Hall; New York: White and Allen, 1840) and Washington Irving, *Mahomet and His Successors* (New York: G. P. Putnam's Sons, 1849). See also Philip Almond, *Heretic and Hero: Muhammad and the Victorians* (Weisbaden: O. Harrassowitz, 1989).

of the eternal Priesthood," and subscribed to the standard eschatological line that Islam had been raised up to scourge Christians for corrupting the teachings of the Church.[60]

While Mormons looked to the past to learn lessons from Islam, anti-Mormon critics lambasted both Mormonism and Islam for sharing a common belief in a material afterworld filled with the joys of sensual pleasures. "The idea of a temporal millennium is one of the most important principles of Mormonism, and the one most cherished by its believers," wrote the author of *Female Life among the Mormons*.[61] Critics suggested that the Latter-day Saints had adopted polygamy from Islam so that orientalist visions of the "houris" (female angels) of paradise might be manifested within earthly sexual practices. "Mormonism repudiates the celibacy imposed by the Catholic religion upon its priesthood," asserted a judge in a speech before Congress, "and takes in its stead the voluptuous impositions of the Mohammedan Church."[62] The female author of an article on "The Mahomet of the West" suggested that Mormons interpreted this injunction from Islamic history as a justification of the excesses of polygamy: "Love ye one another free . . . for each of you, in the eyes of his brother, there is heaven enough."[63] One minister was dubious of the Book of Mormon's account of the physical resurrection of bodies to a heaven where individuals would revel with pleasure and jocularly wondered how musical instruments would be transported to the afterworld, claiming: "This looks very much as if Mr. Smith had been reading the Koran, and taken a leaf out of Mahomet's book."[64]

The first public exposition of the workings of Mormon sexual politics proposed an explicit bond between Mormon and Turkish polygamy. John C. Bennett, himself a notorious adulterer while within the Mormon church, published "The Mormon Seraglio" in the *Louisville Herald*, before reprinting it in his *History of the Saints* in 1842. "The most extraordinary and infamous feature of the social and religious system established by the Mormon Prophet, and one in which he closely resembles his master and

---

[60] George A. Smith, "The History of Mahometanism" and Parley P. Pratt, "Mahometanism and Christianity," *Journal of Discourses* 3 (1855): 33–5, 38–41.

[61] Ward, *Female Life*, 90. A more recent historian of Mormonism, Ray B. West, Jr., noted in 1957: "Like the prophet of Islam, Mohammed, with whom Joseph was often to be compared, he saw paradise very much as the Moslem conceived it . . . a blissful abode / Gardens and vineyards / Damsels with swelling breasts of suitable age / And a brimming cup.'" West's quote is a poetic translation of the visions of paradise described in the Qu'ran. Three additional references by West to "Mohammed and Moslems" (including one on the first page of the preface) were evidently removed late in the editorial process, as they remain noted only in the book's index. This excision perhaps represents a moment when the popularity of comparative polygamy was no longer broadly acceptable. Ray B. West, *Kingdom of the Saints: The Story of Brigham Young and the Mormons* (New York: Viking Press, 1957), 113.

[62] John Doyle Lee, *Mormonism Unveiled* (Lewisburg, PA: S. T. Buck & Co., 1882), 22.

[63] Mrs. Thomas Fitch, "The Mahomet of the West," *Overland Monthly* 7 (September 1873): 235.

[64] Chalmer, *Mormonism*, 34.

model Mahomet," wrote Bennett, "is the secret regulations he has formed for directing the relations of the sexes." That Bennett was fully aware of the shock value of the analogy he was making is evident in his claim that "the profligacy of . . . modern Turkish and Moorish sultans, has been fully equaled by that of an American citizen in our own day."[65]

Most attacks on Mormon polygamy, however, centered on the figure of Brigham Young, largely because of the fact that Joseph Smith was killed only two years after Bennett's exposé. After ascending to power in 1844, Young was bequeathed the mantle of the polemical linkage of Mormon and Islamic leadership and himself was called a "modern Mohammed," "the New World Mohammed," a "Yankee Turk," and "the Mahomet of Salt Lake."[66] The connection between the two Mormon prophets was made clear in a letter published at the time of Young's death in 1877, which referred to Young as "This second Mohammed, of American Mohammedanism, – Joseph Smith being the first."[67] Brigham Young's leadership of both his growing state and family – he may have had as many as fifty-six wives – set him in the forefront of anti-Mormon attacks. One of his former wives, Ann Eliza Young, orientalized Brigham by calling him "the Mormon Mogul" in her account of "spiritual bondage" under the tyranny of her husband's political and familial regimes.[68]

The patriarchy of Mormonism, which asserted that the progress of a woman's soul in the next world was dependent upon the nature of her earthly conjugal relations, especially affronted non-Mormon advocates of women's rights. Women who opposed Mormonism took special care to marry islamicism to the microcosm of Mormon family practices, even after Utah became in 1869 the second territory in the Unites States to grant

---

[65] Bennett, *History of the Saints* 218.

[66] Mrs. C[atherine] V. Waite, *The Mormon Prophet and His Harem* (Cambridge, MA: Riverside Press, 1866), 4; Greenwood, *New Life*, 157; George Alfred Townsend, *The Mormon Trials at Salt Lake City* (New York: American News Company, 1871), 47; "The Mormons at Utah," *The Living Age* 33 (10 April 1852): 93–4; George W. Pine, *Beyond the West*, 4th ed. (Buffalo, NY: Baker, Jones, and Co., 1873), 323–5. In a series of articles, Albert T. Browne, contended that considering the Mormon Church "as a kind of Mahometan Sam Slick" had kept Americans from seeing it as anything more than one of the "curiosities in a popular museum." "The Utah Expedition: Its Causes and Consequences," *The Atlantic Monthly* 3 (March, April, May 1859): 361.

[67] Ballard S. Dunn, *How to Solve the Mormon Problem. Three Letters* (New York: American News Company, 1877), 3–4. See also E. M. Tullidge, "Brigham Young and Mormonism," *Galaxy* 4 (September 1867): 541. Tullidge went on to qualify his assertion: "[T]he world to-day is more impressed with the name of Brigham Young than it ever was with the exaggerated one of the 'American Mohammed'" (543). In an earlier article, Tullidge had asserted that "our mission [not] at all resembl[es] that of Mahomet and his disciples." "Views of Mormonism," *Galaxy* 2 (October 1866): 304. See also Nelson Winch Green, ed., *Mormonism: Its Rise, Progress, and Present Condition* (New York: C. Scribner, 1858; Hartford: Belknap & Bliss, 1870), v.

[68] Ann Eliza Young, *Wife No. 19, or The Story of a Life in Bondage* (Hartford, CT: Dustin, Gilman & Co., 1875); reprint, New York: Arno Press, 1972), 129, 604, 601. Wesley Bradshaw also called Young a "Mormon Mogul" in the novel *Brigham Young's Daughter* (Philadelphia: C. W. Alexander, 1870), 66.

women the right to vote. A British anti-Mormon tract argued that "[t]he Mormon principle of polygamy is the doctrine of the Koran, encircled with a spiritualistic verbiage to conceal its innate indelicacy and sensual grossness."[69] Nelson Slater concluded his assessment of Mormonism in the first book copyrighted in California by asserting that "Mormon women are degraded and subjected by the system to a state of mental and physical slavery more abject and perfect than attaches to the inmates of a Turkish harem."[70] Female critics echoed this charge that Mormonism imitated the subjugation of women, a key element of Islamic orientalism, and placed them in the position of the slaves of male despotism. President of the Woman's Christian Temperance Union Frances Willard cited illustrations of female degradation from her travels in the Islamic Near East in her introduction to *The Women of Mormonism*, and then argued

> But Americans need not go so far for illustrations. Turkey is in our midst. Modern Mohammedanism has its Mecca at Salt Lake, where Prophet Heber C. Kimball speaks of his wives as "cows." Clearly the Koran was Joseph Smith's model, so closely followed as to exclude even the poor pretension of originality in his foul "revelations."[71]

"Mark the contrast between loyal and Christian Nevada, and disloyal and Mohammedan Utah!" wrote Catherine Waite, author of *The Mormon Prophet and His Harem*, another anti-Mormon writer who asserted that Saints borrowed directly from Islam. "Mahomet is the great exemplar and proto-type whom Brigham Young aims to imitate."[72] Waite thought that Young's

---

[69] Dawson Burns, *Mormonism: Explained and Exposed* (London: Houston and Stoneman, 1853), 37.

[70] N. Slater, *Fruits of Mormonism* (Coloma, CA: Harmon & Springer, 1851), 87.

[71] Frances Willard, "Introduction," *The Women of Mormonism; or The Story of Polygamy, as Told by the Victims Themselves* ed. Jennie Anderson Froiseth (Detroit: C. G. G. Paine, 1882), xv–xvi. Such a linkage is also implied by the inclusion in the book of an illustration by G. H. Reed of "A Turkish Scene" in which female is being beckoned by a turbaned and bearded man sitting on a cushion (while out the window can be seen two laborers cruelly treating a draft animal), 163. The reference to Heber Kimball (he was the leader of the Mormons second only to Brigham Young) calling his wives "cows" was common and appeared in both humorous and political critiques of the Mormon treatment of women. See Artemus Ward, *The Complete Works*, 225; *Speech of the Hon. Thomas A. R. Nelson, of Tennessee, on Polygamy in Utah, Delivered in the House of Representatives, April 4 and 5, 1860* (Washington, DC, 1860), 15; *Utah and the Mormons, Speech of the Hon. John Cradlebaugh, of Nevada, on the Admission of Utah as a State. Delivered in the House of Representatives, February 7, 1863* (Washington, DC, 1863), 7. Richard Burton wrote that "Mr. Kimball is accused by Gentiles of calling his young wives, from the pulpit, 'little heifers'; of entering into physiological details belonging to the Dorcas Society, or the clinical lecture-room, rather than the house of worship; and of transgressing the bounds of all decorum when reproving the sex for its *penchants* and *ridicules*. At the same time, I never heard, nor heard of, any such indelicacy during my stay at Salt Lake City." Burton, *The City of the Saints*, 263.

[72] Waite, *The Mormon Prophet and His Harem*, 35. Waite asserts: "and doubtless he [Young] took from the Koran his ideas about the deity of Adam," quoting the Qu'ran as proof (57). Extending this assumption, Waite twice calls Brigham Young a "modern Mohammed" (4, 59) and later asks: "Indeed, is it not itself interesting to see and hear the Mohammed of America?"(273).

most loathsome imitation of Islam was his subordination of women and employed islamicist dogma when she asserted inaccurately that he declared that "women have no souls, – that they are not responsible beings, that they cannot save themselves, nor be saved, except through man's intervention." *A Husband in Utah*, however, saw salvation through "sealing" to a man for eternity (celestial marriage) as "a slight advance on the doctrine of Mohammedanism, that women have no souls to be saved."[73]

The Mormon practice of polygamy was amplified into a major threat because it transgressed cultural conventions of domesticity through which the monogamous home regulated the decent expression of sexuality. The fantasy of a harem of multiple wives opened the door of the imagination not only to sensuality and adultery, but also to other social transgressions such as spouse abuse, incest, jealousy, lack of privacy, and betrayal. *Polygamy: or, The Mysteries and Crimes of Mormonism* lashed out against Mormon marriage practices, finding them more vile than those practiced in Turkey because of the "universal, and worse than Moslem, jealousy" arising out of the incestuous "intermarriage of near relations."[74] Academic criticism of anti-Mormon attacks on polygamy intimated that the jealousy and tone of moral indignation directed toward the institution of polygamy may have also reflected a hidden envy with which they contemplated exotic notions of Mormon sexuality.[75] Such a position may be more apt to have validity given the facts that polygamy was always a minority practice among Mormons (Mormon historians have estimated that it was practiced by between a tenth and a third of nineteenth-century Mormon women depending on their date and location[76]) and that the ethics and specific practices of Mormon sexuality

---

[73] Waite, *The Mormon Prophet and His Harem*, 218, see also 216; Ward, *Husband in Utah*, 299.

[74] J. H. Beadle, *Polygamy, or The Mysteries and Crimes of Mormonism* (Cincinnati: W. E. Dibble & Co, 1882), 256, 262.

[75] Historian Charles A. Cannon claimed that "[t]he line between disgust and envy in the literature is sometimes difficult to draw." "The Awesome Power of Sex: The Polemical Campaign against Mormon Polygamy," *Pacific Historical Review* 43 (February 1974): 70; Foster, "Victorian Pornographic Imagery," 131–12. Leonard J. Arrington and Jon Haupt claim that "One is tempted to suggest that many 'frustrated' Victorian women, whose role was largely restricted to the sanctity and purity of hearth and home, sought to preserve that sanctity and purity by conducting campaigns against lustful Turks, lustful southern slaveholders, and lustful Mormons. This at once got them out of hearth and home and gave them a means of 'striking back,' if only indirectly and subconsciously, at husbands and fathers. Resentment for the male in this male-dominated monogamous society was thus transferred to the hated Turk, slaveholder, and Mormon." Arrington and Haupt, "Intolerable Zion: The Image of Mormonism in Nineteenth Century American Literature," *Western Humanities Review* 22 (Spring 1968): 254, n.19. Such an analysis can be seen as early as David Brion Davis's 1960 article that states that "the literature of countersubversion could thus serve the double purpose of vicariously fulfilling repressed desires, and of releasing the tension and guilt away from rapid social change and conflicting values." Davis, "Some Themes of Counter-Subversion: An Analysis of Anti-Masonic, Anti-Catholic, and Anti-Mormon Literature," *The Mississippi Valley Historical Review* 47 (September 1960): 220.

[76] Stanley S. Ivins, "Notes on Mormon Polygamy," in *The New Mormon History: Revisionist Essays on the Past*, ed. D. Michael Quinn (Salt Lake City: Signature Books, 1992), 170–1; Davis Bitton, *Historical*

was no less conventional than those found in other American populations.[77] Richard Burton, whose wide experience in Muslim lands had extinguished Western idealizations of licentious Muslim sexuality, spoke of "a Moslem gloom . . . [which] hangs over society" in Salt Lake City, "the result of austere morals and manners, of the semi-seclusion of the sex."[78]

Although Mormons believed that polygamous families would strengthen the church by increasing family ties and raising up a larger number of saints from its already converted members, anti-Mormons countered that polygamy would degrade members of the white race until they resembled Asians and Turks. Racializing Mormons as alien ethnics gave anti-Mormon critics more power to exile them metaphorically from the province of the imagined nation. J. H. Beadle reasoned that polygamy was not made to thrive in North America where, "with snow in sight the year round, they [the Mormons] pattern their domestic life after that of inter-tropical barbarians, and vainly hope to produce the vigor of hardy Northmen from the worst practices of effeminate Asians."[79] Another exposé writhed at the horrors of allowing "the libidinous Turks of Mormonism to thus degrade the sex . . . [and] to deprave our race by the intermixing of the foul polygamous brood of Mormonism with the noble stock of American manhood."[80] These arguments that polygamy would weaken northern European racial stock echoed John Hyde's argument of 1857: "Degrade the position of Anglo-Saxon women to that of Circassian slaves, and you degrade Anglo-Saxon men to the level of the Turks, those slaves' masters."[81] For critics of Mormonism, polygamy divorced Mormons from their consanguinity with white Americans and affiliated them instead with infidel Muslims. Racial thinking formed an element of domestic orientalism, which, in the words of Terryl L. Givens, "create[d] the illusion of a comforting distance and distinctness" to a religious group that was more

Dictionary of Mormonism (Metuchen, NJ: Scarecrow Press, 1994), 178; Larry M. Logue, *A Sermon in the Desert: Belief and Behavior in St. George, Utah* (Urbana and Chicago: University of Illinois Press, 1988), 47–52; Lowell Bennion, "The Incidence of Mormon Polygamy in 1880: 'Dixie' versus Davis Stake," *Journal of Mormon History* 11 (1984): 27–42.

77 Cannon, "The Awesome Power," 65–6. Of course, some Mormon women defended polygamy because it freed them from having to submit to frequent sexual relations with their husbands, as well as cleansed Utah of prostitution. Ward, *Husband in Utah*, 32. See also Edward W. Tullidge, *The Women of Mormondom* (New York: Tullidge and Crandall, 1877); and Davis Bitton, "Polygamy Defended: One Side of a Nineteenth-Century Polemic," in his *The Ritualization of Mormon History and Other Essays* (Urbana and Chicago: University of Illinois Press, 1994), 34–53.

78 Burton, *The City of Saints*, 418–19. Burton also noted: "There is a Moslem air of retirement about the Bee House; the face of woman is rarely seen at the window, and her voice is never heard from without" (248–9).

79 Beadle, *Polygamy*, 273.

80 [By a Mormon of 1831], *The Crimes of the Latter Day Saints in Utah. A Demand for a Legislative Commission. A Book of Horrors* (San Francisco: A. J. Leary, 1884), 77.

81 Hyde, *Mormonism*, 297.

indigenous to the United States than any nineteenth-century Christian denomination.[82]

The issue of polygamy, especially the imagined family script of how women were forced to submit and suffer under a Mormon patriarchal regime, formed the central theme of most nineteenth-century anti-Mormon novels and dramas. Most of them were written in a dime-novel style lacking in significant allusion, but some derided the institution of plural marriage as a barbarous practice of the Turks. As Leonard Arrington and Jon Haupt noted, "anti-Mormon novels are replete with such words as 'Western Turks,' pasha, bashaw, sultana, harem, seraglio."[83] Some popular anti-Mormon novels, all written by women in the mid-1850s, demonstrate different ways that fiction writers disparaged Mormon customs by tarring them with the exotic brush of Islamic infidelity. These novels extended sympathy for the women forced to submit to their Mormon husbands by portraying them as akin to their sisters in the orient who were sold to stock the sultan's harem. This comparison opened up a sentimental nexus for sympathy with global women trafficked to gratify the needs of men. The most popular mid-century anti-Mormon novel, *Female Life among the Mormons*, sold 40,000 copies in only a few weeks.[84] A Mormon sophist in that book justifies the practice of polygamy by arguing that because Turkish women are not "slighted or insulted" when their husbands take another wife, neither should Mormon wives.[85] One father in the book calls his two daughters "perfect houris" as he marries them both off to the same suitor so that they might propagate numerous saints, and thereby "fulfill her [woman's] vocation to the utmost."[86] *Boadicea, the Mormon Wife*, a novel in diary form, orientalizes polygamy through visual illustration. Opposite its contents page is a sketch depicting a male suitor, dressed in oriental slippers and a flowing robe, embracing a woman. The page lying underneath it (opposite the title page, two pages before it) is an illustration of Boadicea and her lover Hubert courting in Western dress (Fig. 4.1). The juxtaposition prefigures the descent of their pure love into polygamy and licentiousness as the book reveals the horrors of "Life Scenes in Utah."[87]

Other examples of anti-Mormon fiction engaged comparative islamicism to elevate the nature of Muslim marriage as a means of demonstrating the vice of Mormon polygamy. One novel called *The Prophets; or, Mormonism Unveiled*, feverishly portrays the Mormon city of Nauvoo as "a modern

---

[82] Givens, "Caricature as Containment," 393, 387.

[83] Arrington and Haupt, "Intolerable Zion," 247–8.

[84] The book was also translated into four languages and reprinted several times and under various titles as late as 1913. Cannon, "The Awesome Power," 71.

[85] Ward, *Female Life*, 227.   [86] Ward, *Female Life*, 326–7.

[87] Alfreda Eva Bell, *Boadicea; The Mormon Wife. Life Scenes in Utah* (Baltimore, Philadelphia, New York, and Buffalo: Arthur R. Orton, 1855), the illustration is on page 10.

FIGURE 4.1. Illustrations of the descent into islamicized polygamy from Alfreda Eva Bell, *Boadicea; The Mormon Wife. Life Scenes in Utah* (Baltimore, Philadelphia, New York, and Buffalo: Arthur R. Orton, 1855).

Sodom, which had no parallel, even in Turkey, where women are bought and sold, not forcibly seized and imprisoned in a harem, and where a Bashaw's passions are under more restraint than during the reign of Mormonism at Nauvoo, in civilized, Republican America."[88] Another female novelist likewise suggested in 1856 that while Ottoman reforms were limiting the widespread practice of polygamy in Turkey, in "republican America . . . the atrocity, protected by the strong arm of government . . . [is becoming] once more a power for evil."[89]

This fictional strategy of ideological juxtaposition is more deeply demonstrated in two polemical exposés of the "Mysteries of Mormonism" that dramatize Mormon sexual excesses as a worse than Turkish disgrace. Former Mormons Increase and Maria Van Deusen drew an extended contrast in their rendering of the "Spiritual Delusions" of the Mormon church in 1854.

> The Alcoran of Mohammed is still the great source and center of light and hope to the Arabian idolater, and portions of its voluptuous paradise, promised for his gratification, may still be found in the imperial harems of the modern Sultan. Such are the results of that despotic sway of a government which, acting upon ignorance and superstition, have so greatly contributed to the political and moral degradation of a powerful yet deluded portion of the posterity of Adam.
>
> But what shall we say to the reader of this narrative, when we are about to sketch the progress and establishment of certain abominable and immoral mysterious revelations connected with a large and flourishing association established in these United States, and tolerated, too, by that government founded by the wisdom and moral influence of the great fathers of our national independence?[90]

The implied answer to this rhetorical question can be nothing more than the fact that through Mormonism the corruptions associated with islamicism – superstition, tyranny, and sensuality – were made manifest within the territory of United States. An 1882 account similarly contended, in

---

[88] [Orvilla Beslisle], *The Prophets; or, Mormonism Unveiled* (Philadelphia: Wm. White Smith, 1855), 351–2. One innocent Englishwoman tells her Mormon tempter later in the book: "You are as bad as . . . the Turks, if indeed you carry out the principles you advocate. Really, it is so horrible!" (154). The principles are carried out, and the author by the end of the book bemoans the women and wives who had been "enticed, or when that failed, stolen . . . to stock some bashaw's den" (412). Beslisle's book was reprinted in London as late at 1919 under the title *In the Grip of the Mormons: By an Escaped Wife of a Mormon Elder* (London: Henry Hardingham, 1919).

[89] Metta Victoria Fuller, *Mormon Wives: A Narrative of Facts Stranger than Fiction* (New York: Derby and Jackson, 1856), xi.

[90] Increase and Maria Van Deusen, *Spiritual Delusions: Being a Key to the Mysteries of Mormonism* (New York: By the Authors, 1854), 8.

ways that acknowledged some of the fictive nature of islamicism, that Mormon polygamy was more indecent than that found in Turkey.

> The Turk preserves a certain decency in the public management of his seraglio nowadays, and the Orientally audacious flaunting of his sensual indulgence which makes the old romances of the East so unique in their naughty piquancy has vanished. . . . How different it is with the devotee of that bestial belief who covers, or essays to cover, the rottenness of his creed with the claim to Divine endorsement, thanks to which he dubs himself a Latter Day Saint! [91]

Both of these comparisons register their moral outrage by positing a Mormonism more immoral than modern-day Islam largely because it was flourishing under the aegis of both Christianity and the American nation.[92] In this vein, one critic of Brigham Young even imagined one of his "super-seded and lonely" plural wives in Salt Lake City "crying aloud in the bitterness of her heart, 'Give us polygamy as in Turkey!'"[93]

Nevertheless, some critics turned the valences of the equation around and, placing Mormons in a more civilized light than Muslims, tried to restore Mormon wives to public sympathy by rescuing them from the sexual disgrace imputed by islamicist association. Fannie Stenhouse, an avid crusader against polygamy, challenged the linking of Mormon and Turkish women, by claiming that the Mormon women she encountered in Utah "would be regarded with respect in the most moral community of any country; and are as far from resembling the Sultanas of an Eastern harem as one thing can be different from another."[94] Grace Greenwood admitted that "underlying their fanatical faith and their Mohammedan practices" the Mormons were generous and charitable.[95] These women were unwilling to extend their disfavor with the Mormon religion to those who espoused it, especially the women who married into it. Austin Ward wrote that Mormon men, unlike their Turkish counterparts (and Burton's observations), were not sensitive about their wives and "do not attempt to confine their wives, or keep them secreted from the gaze of others."[96] In these cases, the

---

91 [Alfred Trumble], By an Apostle's Wife, *The Mysteries of Mormonism: A Full Exposure of Its Secret Practices and Hidden Crimes* (New York: Richard K. Fox, 1882), 7.

92 A third example reflects British notions of American barbarism. "Even among the Turks, as far back as the days when Lady Mary Wortley Montague wrote her charming letters from their capital, she testified that to have more than one wife was not considered respectable, though it was allowed. The appearance of a community, in the centre of the Western continent, and descended from the blood of Western Europe, yet among whom men have their seven, eleven, sixteen, or eighteen companions under the abused name of wife, is a humiliating and disgusting step back into worse than Turkish barbarism." "The Mormons," 438.

93 Justin McCarthy, "Brigham Young," *Galaxy* 9 (February 1870): 186–7.

94 Fanny [Mrs. T. B. H.] Stenhouse, *Exposé of Polygamy in Utah, A Lady's Life among the Mormons,* 2nd ed. (New York: American News Company, 1872), 195.

95 Greenwood, *New Life,* 139–40.   96 Ward, *Husband in Utah,* 29, 203.

decency of the Mormons was upheld often at the price of degrading the humanity of Muslims.

The concern with the "seraglios" of Utah emerged as a theme to be exploited by several popular mid-century writers who were more interested in challenging the moral righteousness of the Protestant elite in the east than castigating the immorality of the Mormons in the west. George Thompson's *The Mysteries of Bond Street, or The Seraglios of Upper Tendom* (1857), for example, tells the bawdy tale of a medical quack who, out of lust for his female conquests, exchanges his office for "an elegant suit [sic] of rooms . . . where, with designs to match Turkish ideas of oriental splendour, he formed a harem in the very heart of civilized society." Thompson attacks the hypocrisy of those critics who lambaste the Mormons while turning their backs on "these lecherous lepers of civilized society [who practice] their orgies as openly as the half crazed fanatics of barren Utah." Thompson provides a cameo of one such man: a sanctimonious railroad contractor who both rents a pew at Grace church and "has a seraglio, fitted up in a style of oriental splendor, that would make a Mahometan envious."[97] William Hepworth Dixon, an English author who wrote two volumes after traveling through the United States just after the Civil War, employed islamicist contrasts to criticize what he saw as the immoral nature of American marital bondage.

> Even in the privacy of his harem, an Asiatic is governed by some kind of moral and religious rules; while an American is governed in his home only by legal and commercial precepts, from which every moral and religious feeling may have been utterly divorced. Thus it happens that an Oriental wife, though she may be living in a state of polygamy, has in some capital points a wider freedom in her circle than in the most highly cultured lady of New York.[98]

Works such as these by Thompson and Dixon redeployed the moral outrage of the Protestant majority by aiming it against the Eastern elite, placing them in the very harems they derided Mormons and Muslims for keeping. Ironically, this rhetorical strategy mimicked Mormon criticism of the "Babylon" of the eastern "Gentiles."[99] "God deliver us from such virtue," exclaimed Mormon leader John Taylor when attacking the eastern United States for its crimes and vice.

[97] George Thompson, *The Mysteries of Bond Street, or The Seraglios of Upper Tendom* (New York, 1857), 46, 82.

[98] William Hepworth Dixon, *New America* (Philadelphia: J. B. Lippincott, 1867), 299–300. Dixon claimed that "[a] Mohammedan mosque stands nearer to a Christian church than this Mormon temple stands. Islam broke down idols, Mormonism sets them up" (161).

[99] Taylor, *The Mormon Question*, 24–5.

The efforts of popular authors and travelers to point out the hypocrisy of Protestants epitomized the tension between the moral agenda of anti-Mormon narratives and their sensationalist devices. The employment of burlesque and caricature in domestic discourse about Mormons signaled the developing imperative of entertainment in the 1850s in which urbane humor began to subvert some of the pretenses of moralism.[100] Cartoons that caricatured Mormon polygamy and humorously exposed its foibles illustrated this emerging modality of romantic orientalism. One joked how the Utah settlers were protected from attacks of the U.S. Army by the "breastworks" of their plural wives. Another cartoonist even gave realistic depictions of Mormon family life a twist through the use of the caption "Scenes in an American Harem." Illustrations of Brigham Young at times portrayed him as horned satyr or imperious Bluebeard, and he was sometimes clothed in Muslim dress.[101]

In these ways reflections of the excesses of Mormons in the West allowed white Protestant Americans a domestic field for exotic orientalism. Such lampooning of Brigham Young took precedence over overt moralizing in nineteenth-century anti-Mormon plays that figured polygamous Utah as a domestic orient. The second act of *Deseret Deserted, or The Last Days of Brigham Young*, consists of a farcical dialogue between Brigham Young and Muhammad in an imagined oriental Paradise. The scene begins when Brigham Young, drunk at the end of Act One, awakens outside the gates of Paradise, on which hangs the nameplate "Mahomet" and a placard "Any Christian found trespassing on these premises will be persecuted." The banter centers around Young's attempt to gain access to beautiful houris – female consorts with "fairy shapes inhaling heavenly cobblers through ethereal straws" – that he spies through the shutters of the gates. After Young convinces Mahomet that he is not an American but rather a Mormon and a prophet as well, Mahomet comes out to learn about his doctrines, but only after his servants set out carpets and cushions for his luxury. The Mormon prophet proceeds to outline his system of polygamy, prompting Mahomet to retort: "By my beard! The rogue has filched my first idea." Young finally wheedles his way into Paradise, ignoring warnings about terrible genies from whom he will never

---

[100] An early example of this strategy of burlesque in an 1847 Philadelphia lecture declares that "Joe Smith... was by no means a contemptible imitation of Mohammed, camel driver to Cadijah, Prophet of Mecca, and Star of the Bottomless Pit," and went on to clarify "Joe's generalship, whatever his prophetship might be, was far from rivaling that of his more successful prototype. Joe was certainly 'born out of due time.' He doubtless belonged to the seventh century, and should have flourished in the desert. He might then have astonished the world, and lived in the remembrance of all future time as Lieutenant Commander of all faithful Moslems." Thomas, *Sketch of the Rise*, 8.

[101] Gary Bunker and Davis Bitton, *The Mormon Graphic Image, 1834–1914: Cartoons, Caricatures, and Illustrations* (Salt Lake City: University of Utah Press, 1983), 18, 21, 24, 118.

escape. Amidst its joys, Young drinks mint juleps with his Muslim master, makes veiled sexual suggestions, and eventually falls "exhausted into
the arms of the women" before awakening with a hangover in the next
act.[102] Brigham Young is again made to show admiration for Muhammad's
polygamous paradise in *Evelyn Gray; or The Victims of Our Western Turks*,
where he is called by other characters "Mr. Brigham Turk" and a "canting
sultan."[103] The mode of burlesque in these plays registered condescension
toward Mormon practices through humor rather than through moral outrage, a process that made Brigham Young more accessible to his audience
through the romance of his buffoonery.

The authors of these public entertainments employed orientalist burlesque to entertain their readers and make their viewers laugh. Anti-
Mormon exposés drew attention to such practices by endowing Mormon
ritual itself with the trappings of Islamic orientalism. Increase and Maria Van
Deusen revealed in rhetoric that mystified the morality of its message, how
Mormon rites – during which wives were "forced to become the abject
and willing slaves of the Sultan Brigham" – were "offer[ed] the degrading
pleasures and sensual delights of a true Mohammedan paradise."[104] The Van
Deusen's pamphlet ends by disclosing supposed Mormon mysteries through
which the reader learns that in the "First Degree" the initiate is questioned
about who is the most powerful prophet, learning that Brigham Young
is "gifted with [Christ's] power" and "mightier still" than Muhammad.[105]
Another description of the temple ceremonies incorporates chanting voices
in the distance mimicking the Muslim creed, "But now admit – nor dare to
scoff it – That God is God – and Smith the prophet."[106] The temple ceremonies reenact the expulsion of Eve from Eden, passing to the "Seventh

---

[102] *Deseret Deserted; or, The Last Days of Brigham Young* (New York: S. French, 1858), 12–17. Another
example of the dramatic construction of Utah as a domestic orient is from another Samuel French
play of the same year in which Brigham Young boasts: "Here in this western Circassia, I can defy
the power of my enemies; consolidate these Indian tribes under one standard; and, when the Union
crumbles to pieces, build up an independent empire, which will honor me as a ruler while living,
and canonize me when dead." Thomas Dunn English, *The Mormons; or Life at Salt Lake City. A
Drama in Three Acts* (New York: S. French, 1858), 14. The reference to Circassia, an area of the
Ottoman Empire infamous for purportedly selling its beautiful women to stock the Sultan's harem
in Istanbul.

[103] Herman Isidore Stern, *Evelyn Gray, or, The Victims of Our Western Turk* (New York: John B. Alden,
1890), 54–5, 114, 194. See also William Cook, *The Mormons, the Dream and the Reality; or, Leaves
from the Sketch Book of Experience of One Who Left England to Join the Mormons in the City of Zion, and
Awoke to a Consciousness of Its Heinous Wickedness and Abominations* (London: J. Masters, 1857), 21.

[104] Van Deusens, *Spiritual Delusions*, 39, 5.   [105] Van Deusens, *Spiritual Delusions*, 44.

[106] *An Authentic History of Remarkable Persons*, 9. Charles Mackay likewise employed the Muslim testimony of faith when claiming that freedom of religious expression enabled Mormons to "exclaim,
like their kindred Mohammedans, that 'God is great, and Joe Smith is his prophet!' and still retain
their hopes for admission into the American republic." Charles Mackay, *Life and Liberty in America:
or, Sketches of a Tour in the United States and Canada in 1857–8* (New York: Harper & Brothers, 1859),
147–8.

Degree" which takes place in "a gorgeous saloon . . . of Oriental magnifi-cence." There the women are dressed in a "loose Turkish fashion . . . highly becoming, and well-calculated to enhance the beauty and inflame the passions, for which they were doubtlessly intended." The account dares not detail the final mysteries of the Zion house, beyond intimating that it involved "an abandonment of reserve and propriety."[107] Referring to the ritual trappings of the endowments, John C. Bennett in his original exposé of the "Mormon Seraglio" testifies that "[t]he *investment*, the *oath*, the *cere-monies*, the *lectures*, and the GRAND FINALE, are all done up in such a manner, as to . . . cover Mahomet, the Oriental prophet, in the rubbish of things that were."[108] Anti-Mormon islamicism transformed the sacred endowments of the Mormon church into enactments of sexuality in such a way that the reader has difficulty distinguishing whether such actions are portrayed as crimes or as fantasies. In the islamicist rhetoric used to suggest the sensu-ality of Mormon secret ceremonies, American Mormonism lorded it over Islam.

The systematic discursive linkage that this chapter has presented provides an archival case study of how images of the Islamic world, whose religion and cultures spanned the world that was not American, circulated within varied forms of transatlantic expression as comparative commentary on the rise of the Mormon church in the United States. The major elements of American islamicism described in the prior three chapters – how Islam sig-nified despotism, antichristianity, slavery, and excessive sensuality – are all featured within in this discursive tradition. The religious and cultural chal-lenges of the Mormons could not be merely written off as a distant oppo-sition because they were originally American. Publicizing images of Joseph Smith and Brigham Young as deceivers, despots, and debauchers in the islamicist mold of Muhammad enabled detractors to counteract Mormon claims that their religion was a return to a purer form of Christianity. They hoped to make Mormonism appear repulsive to its readers as a means of rallying them to reform its renegade challenge. Instead of an unregenerate global contender to the universal claims of Protestantism's superior verity, Islam was contained through these discursive juxtapositions into a frontier commentary on the fringe phenomenon of the Latter-day Saints.

Comparative consignment, like the interpretive phantasms of eschatol-ogy, was doomed to fail as a means of measuring the divergent meanings that Mormon and Muslim belief provided for its respective adherents. The fan-tasy that Mormonism was a domestic manifestation of the heretical beliefs and behavior of Islam did not quell interest in the new church, whose potential for success was glimpsed in 1877 by Episcopal detractor Ballard S. Dunn who, finding the two religions to be "exact counterparts," argued that "Mormonism has a greater promise for future life and vigor, than any sect of

---

[107] Van Deusens, *Spiritual Delusions*, 60–3.   [108] Bennett, *The History of the Saints*, 217.

Christian corrupters has had since the beginnings of Mohammedanism."[109] As the history of media and propaganda since this polemic has revealed, attracting attention to the extremism of a domestic phenomenon serves as a sure way of perpetuating its prominence in public display. For those less committed to the strict scruples of Protestant morality, the same islamicist images conjured to discredit Mormonism may have elicited more interest by augmenting its exotic allure. The Mormons in this way thus became an ironic means of domesticating contrasting images of Islam within the United States. The growth (and difference) of the two religious groups in today's nation is only one evidence that the mutual disparagement of Mormonism and Islam failed to remove their challenge to mainstream Christian denominations.

[109] Dunn, *How to Solve the Mormon Problem*, 3–4.

Chapter 5

American Ishmael:
Herman Melville's Literary Islamicism

On the evening of August 9, 1850, Herman Melville – while in the throes of writing *Moby-Dick* and on the same day that he exultantly began "Hawthorne and His Mosses" – dressed up as a Turk. The occasion was a masquerade party thrown at Broadhall, the Pittsfield estate that had previously belonged to Melville's uncle, and the bearded Melville expanded the persona of the "ardent Virginian" he had adopted in "Mosses" by donning flowing robes, a turban, and a makeshift scimitar. Melville's most recent biographer, Hershel Parker, views his night as a Turk ("an exotic predatory infidel") as a displacement of the sexual and artistic arousal he experienced in glorifying Hawthorne, a state of excitability that had also led him that afternoon playfully to abduct a young wife from the local railroad station in what her husband thought was a "Berber fashion."[1] Other evidence of Melville's domestic behavior shows that his islamicist self-fashioning transcended the skylarking of a summer day and served as important equipment for the performance of both his cosmopolitan masculinity and his artistic privilege. Melville brought a pair of Turkish slippers back from his journey to the eastern Mediterranean in 1857 (Fig. 5.1). Their flat heels are proof of regular use, and the fact that Melville hung them above his chimney at Arrowhead (along with a tomahawk pipe) dramatizes their symbolic importance. Melville's granddaughter disapprovingly recalled his wearing of loose "Constantinople" pajamas around the house, even when the family was receiving company.[2]

These vestiges from Melville's own life demonstrate what is clear within the worlds of his literature: that he was invested in the evolving conventions of nineteenth-century Islamic orientalism, including its resources for romanticizing the privileges of patriarchy. Although such important nineteenth-century American writers as Poe and Hawthorne, as well as many other expressers of culture, employed the rhetoric of Islamic orientalism in their work, Herman Melville had the most revealing investment

---

[1] Hershel Parker, *Herman Melville: A Biography*, 2 vols. (Baltimore: The Johns Hopkins University Press, 1996, 2002), 1: 760–1; Leon Howard, an earlier biographer, refused to accept that Melville was this abductor. Howard, *Herman Melville: A Biography* (Berkeley: University of California Press, 1951), 159.

[2] Eleanor Melville Metcalf, *Herman Melville: Cycle and Epicycle* (Cambridge, MA: Harvard University Press, 1953), 217; Laurie Robertson-Lorant, *Melville: A Biography* (New York: Clarkson Potter, 1996), 571.

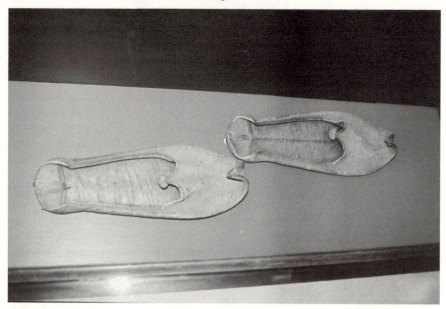

FIGURE 5.1. Herman Melville's Turkish slippers. Courtesy of Berkshire Athenaeum, Pittsfield, Massachusetts.

in the conventions of islamicism because he put them to a broader variety of critical uses and eventually grounded his orientalism through his own experience of Near Eastern travel. An analysis of the tapestry of Melville's fictive imagination offers an illuminating case study of the complex modalities of mid-nineteenth-century American islamicism. This chapter explores how Melville deployed its rhetorical patterns and symbolic geography as a powerful means of fashioning the worldly diversity of his literary characters, the transgressive privilege of his narrators, and the gendered shapes of his romantic aspirations. Islamicist positioning offered Melville the space of renegade freedom to criticize myopic cultural conventions as well as the romantic latitudes from which he could entertain his readers with the glamour of these "sea-freedoms." Deeper than exotic adornment, Melville regularly transmuted orientalist conventions through his vital artistic imagination into creative resources for both critical and contemplative symbolism. Unraveling the multivalent islamicist strands from the vast fabric of Melville's literary imagination reveals the artistry with which he used these stereotypes to launch into dimensions of the critical, the subversive, the celebratory, the symbolic, and the sublime.

Melville's engagement with islamicist rhetoric as a literary resource spanned his entire career as a writer, from his first publications while still a teenager in 1839 until the later poetry that he was still composing and assembling at his death in 1891. Scholars have long recognized the presence of Islamic orientalism in Melville's writing and emphasized his ability to approach Islam with a surprising degree of objectivity and detachment, a perspective that facilitated his capacity to use islamicist rhetoric in versatile and contrasting ways.[3] Despite the access he gained from his own travels to the eastern Mediterranean in 1856–7 and the information he gleaned from his wide reading, Melville was no expert on Islam. He drew his resources from cultural conventions rather than from personal intimacy with Muslims and their beliefs and practices. Examining the patterns of his rhetoric therefore provides a powerful means of reading the broader circulation of changing notions of the Islamic world within the regnant Protestant culture of the mid-nineteenth-century United States that Melville inhabited and so often challenged. The latitudes of Melville's islamicism provided him with a cultural resource through which he meditated on the bewildering complexity of human difference through his literary art.

In his islamicist figuration, Melville subscribed to several Muslim stereotypes of the despot, the renegade, the sensualist, and the fatalist. Yet he often played with the valences of these images to perform more vital forms of cultural work. These modalities were often varied according to racial type. On the positive side of the spectrum, Arabs and the Moors of Arab Spain were viewed as largely noble, whereas Persians, Malays, and African Moors were uniformly seen as dark and cunning. The Turk was a mixed figure for Melville: On one level his legendary cruelty and despotism was seen as all that threatened democratic systems; yet, images of Turkish patriarchy – replete with genial leisure and sensual indolence – was one of Melville's early and abiding fascinations. The five sections of this chapter explore how Melville's own rebellious authority, embodied in Ishmael and his other isolates, found congenial resources in islamicism for creating the critical vitality of his literary characters.

The first part investigates Melville's deployment of despotism to criticize cultural customs and conventions. He forcefully registered his call for reform by aligning contemporary American practices, such as the tyranny of sea captains and the materialist pretenses of Protestant propriety, with

---

[3] William Braswell first noted in 1943 that Melville "wrote of Mohammed and the Koran years before he went to the Holy Land, where he saw Mohammedanism [sic] in practice." Braswell, *Melville's Religious Thought* (1943; New York: Octagon Books, 1973), 18. In *Melville's Orienda*, Dorothee Metlitsky Finkelstein pioneered the study of "the depth and extent of Melville's concern" with what she called the "Islamic orient," uncovering in the process valuable historical and textual sources for some of his characters, images, and symbols (New Haven, CT: Yale University Press, 1961). Finkelstein argued that "Islam was the only religion that Melville was able to view with comparative detachment" (273). Jalaluddien Bakhsh's 1988 dissertation, *Melville and Islam*, acknowledged "an unusual level of objectivity on Melville's part in dealing with the religion of Islam" (Ph.D. diss., Florida State University, 1988), 9.

malignant behaviors associated with Christianity's long-term foes. While in this mode he subscribed to islamicist dispositions that emphasized Islam as a realm of dark and misguided excess. However, Melville often put these formulations to subversive uses to infidelize the moral majority of his age, whose hegemony he mocked as "King Common-Place" and "The triumph of the insincere Unanimous Mediocrity."[4]

The Cultural Roots of American Islamicism has demonstrated how the oppositional difference of Islam through which Americans frequently formulated their cultural agendas in the early republic became increasingly domesticated during the antebellum years into energizing models for glamorizing new cosmopolitan possibilities. Instead of viewing Islamic cultures solely as repulsive abodes of tyranny and infidelity, some American writers began to draw more frequently upon the romantic orientalism popularized by Lord Byron's escapades in the eastern Mediterranean to exalt the creative liberties and pleasures of authorship. Washington Irving, for example, inhabited the legendary sources of Spain's Moorish chivalry and called his residency in the Alhambra in 1828–9 "my Moslem Elysium." Irving transcended the image of Islam as antichristian despotism in his works and celebrated instead such romantic models of Muslim masculinity, such as Saladin (who was known in Irving's time "a splendid exception to most of the vices of his age, his country, and his creed"[5]) and the Prophet Muhammad (and what he called in his revisionist biography *Mahomet and His Successors* "the enigmatical career of this extraordinary man").[6] Islamicism allowed American men and women the breadth to imagine and negotiate new cultural perspectives too controversial for most to confront directly within the conventions of separate gender spheres and segregated racial economies. In this mode, islamicism evoked an expansive world less impinged upon by the duties and demands of domestic life and more a refuge of romance from which more subversive and sustaining forms of gender fashioning could be rehearsed.

Although repelled by the excesses of Islamic autocrats, Melville was equally enchanted by the imaginative reaches of the oriental sublime as well as by the leisurely gentility and sensual privileges of Muslim patriarchs. In his 1856 short story called "I and My Chimney," for example, Melville personifies the same chimney upon which he hung his slippers as a sultanic presence: a "grand seignior" so identified with his narrator's sense of

---

[4] All quotations (with the exception of his poems) are taken from the *Writings of Herman Melville*, eds. Harrison Hayford, G. Thomas Tanselle, and Hershel Parker, 15 vols. (Evanston, IL: Northwestern University Press; Chicago: Newberry Library, 1968–93). Publisher will hereafter be noted as NN. Melville, *Clarel: A Poem and Pilgrimage in the Holy Land* (NN, 1991), 12: 1.34.23 (Citations for *Clarel* reference book, canto, and verse.); "Immolated," *Poems* (London: Constable, 1924), 411. In the journal of his 1849 journey to Europe Melville sighed, "Oh Conventionalism, what a ninny, thou art, to be sure." *Journals* (NN, 1989), 14: 26.

[5] G. P. R. James, *The History of Chivalry* (New York: J. & J. Harper, 1831), 265.

[6] Washington Irving, *Mahomet and His Successors* (New York: George P. Putnam, 1850).

authority as to become the "backbone" of his domestic ego. Melville constructs in this story an inviolate den of patriarchal leisure that is comprised of he and his two "cronies" – his chimney and his pipe, "wicked old smokers" with whom he "indolently weaves [his] vapours."[7] By engaging the protean energies of Islamicist rhetoric, Melville generated the creative latitude to evoke in his literature the extravagant quest for democratic culture on a global register. Even the formation of despotism became through his invention of Ahab a means of fashioning an original romantic revolt. The second section of this chapter explores this valence in greater depth by examining how Melville gained a critical space for his early narrators – especially Omoo, Taji, and Ishmael – by frequently figuring them in islamicist guises that signified the renegade contention of their liberty.

Although Melville's romantic islamicism was manifest in his male characters and narrators, it achieved its most sublime expression in his evocation of orientalized women as embodiments of his own heterodox aspirations. The third part surveys the chivalrous yet transgressive attempts of Melville and his male renegades to embrace ideal oriental beauties. Luther S. Luedtke argued in his *Nathaniel Hawthorne and the Romance of the Orient* how Hawthorne was imbued with orientalist notions from his family's Salem past that embedded themselves in his fiction, especially in his depiction of the "oriental sunshine" of womanly beauty.[8] Melville's vision was more transgressive. By figuring females as islamicist angels called houris and peris, he transfigured mundane femininity into the ideal of a heavenly consort. This renegade dream evoked a female muse who embodied the fertile powers of creation and symbolized a sensual vision of celestial beauty.

The final sections of this chapter examine Melville's islamicist characterizations in his late poetry, especially in his long poem *Clarel* (1876). Later in life, Melville's islamicist ideal of embodying his rebellion in words was countered by the failure of his career as an author. Melville's journey to the eastern Mediterranean endowed him with a personal perspective of comparative islamicism that he employed in his poetry to suggest models of demeanor other than those accessible in Christian cultures. The islamicist characters that Melville created in *Clarel*, especially the character of the Druze guide Djalea, are the most developed Muslims in American literature up to that time. Through the fictional figures of his poetic islamicism, Melville expressed his continued search for contentment despite his critical assessments of a materialist American culture that no longer listened to his art. Like the knot called the Turk's head, which he frequently figured in his fiction, Melville tied the different strands of Islamic orientalism in his works

---

[7] Melville, "I and My Chimney," *The Piazza Tales and Other Prose Pieces, 1839–1860* (NN, 1987), 9: 367, 372.

[8] Luther S. Luedtke, *Nathaniel Hawthorne and the Romance of the Orient* (Bloomington: Indiana University Press, 1989).

into a complex clinch at once decorative and useful.[9] Unraveling that grip reveals Melville's creative use of islamicism in the intricate construction of his cosmopolitan literary characters.

"SAVAGE AT HEART": MELVILLE AND ROMANTIC DESPOTISM

An examination of Melville's depiction of his tyrannical sea captains in his fiction from the 1840s and 1850s reveals the continuing vitality of despotism as an antithetical category for admonishing American republicanism. Melville's own experience as a common sailor under several different regimes of ship discipline attuned him to the dangers of abusive authority in a democratic society. In his narrative worlds, Melville frequently portrayed his captains as possessed by an oriental despotism to illustrate the injustice of their arbitrary and absolute command. By enlisting American routines under the modus operandi of infidel autocrats, Melville deployed domestic islamicism to register more readily his clamor for democratic reform. But Melville also refigured the power of despotism as a resource for establishing the independent authority of his own narration and the power of its challenge to his reading publics. His transfiguration of Ahab into an American autocrat possessed of a power imbued with islamicist authority exemplifies how despotism during the antebellum years served not only to express the dangerous excesses of patriarchy but also to suggest the romantic power of original American manhood. An examination of Melville's shifting portrayal of the power of ship captains in his sea fiction reveals the emergence of this romantic valence of oriental male power as a resource for antebellum masculinity.

Melville's fictional captains in his early novels were invariably despots who threatened the human liberties of the sailors aboard their ships, including the narrators of his stories. The rigid rules of ship life made it difficult for Melville to find persistent conviviality on board and he was forced to represent such society in the fleeting friendships of the fringes and foretop or by abandoning ship. In *Typee*, Tommo justified his "inglorious" escape into the interior of Nukuheva because Captain Vangs had the vessel in the grip of an "unmitigated tyranny" which was "arbitrary and violent in the extreme."[10] A year later, in his March 1847 review of J. Ross Browne's *Etchings of a Whaling Cruise*, Melville again fulminated against the "brutal tyranny" and "outrageous abuse" inflicted by ship captains and claimed that "the god Janus never had two more decidedly different faces than your sea

---

[9] For Turk's head knots in Melville's fiction, see *Typee: A Peep at Polynesian Life* (NN, 1968), 1: 222; *White-Jacket: or The World in a Man-of-War* (NN, 1976), 5: 363; and *Moby-Dick; or The Whale* (NN, 1988), 6: 526.
[10] Melville, *Typee*, 1: 21.

captain." Indeed the thrust of his whole review is to affirm that – once upon the sea – all the civilized wiles of "His Nautical Highness" wash off to reveal "a heartless domineering tyrant."[11] Captain Riga of *Redburn*'s ship the *Highlander* is Melville's fictional characterization of this two-faced nature of sea captains. His appearance ashore as a sauntering, urbane gentleman with a "bland, benevolent, and bewitching merry expression" clashes completely with his shipboard demeanor as an autocrat delivering "despotic ordinances" to his crew and inflicting them "by a thousand small meannesses." Melville also draws upon cultural images associated with Turkey (as well as Russia) to suggest Riga's outlandish despotism and debauchery. He enjoys being seen indulging "in luxurious habits, costly as Oriental dissipation," one of which is being served by a profligate steward named Lavender whom Melville describes as "an elegant looking mulatto in a gorgeous turban." When *Redburn*'s narrator calls the chief mate a "Grand Vizier," he implies that Riga is a Sultan, and indeed his sailors later "salaam" before him as they receive their pay.[12]

These references to Turkish domination became an explicit theme in Melville's depiction of life aboard an American naval ship in *White-Jacket* – the book he wrote immediately after finishing *Redburn* in the summer of 1849, which was used to support antiflogging reform in the U.S. Congress. As a strategy to more effectively criticize the Navy's inhumane custom of whipping sailors for slight offenses, Melville portrays the *Neversink* as if it were under the vassalage of Muslim despots. Melville recounts the story of a seaman absurdly convicted of cowardice for jumping off a ship just before it exploded, intimating that when the sailor was flogged off the coast of Algiers, the punishers were none too different from the Barbary pirates residing nearby.[13] *White-Jacket* metaphorically links the American system of naval authority with the Ottoman political hierarchy of the Grand Porte when he labels its Articles of War "a Turkish Code." The American naval captain "with the Articles of War in one hand, and the cat-o'-nine-tails in the other," he asserts, "stands an undignified parody upon Mohammed enforcing Moslemism with the sword and the Koran." Melville explains that Captain Claret's hold over the *Neversink* is "no limited monarchy . . . but almost a despotism like the Grand Turk's . . . , he is lord and master of the sun." The Commodore of the whole fleet – that "emperor of the whole oaken archipelago" who "domineers over all" – is likewise called by Melville "magisterial and magnificent as the Sultan of the Isles of Sooloo," and his inaccessibility is compared with the aloofness of the Turkish government

---

[11] This review is included in Melville, *The Piazza Tales*, 9: 206, 210, 211.

[12] Melville, *Redburn: His First Voyage* (NN, 1969), 4: 219, 71, 263, 308, 219, 15, 18, 136, 305. During their passage, the evil sailor Jackson is able to deceive some of the female Irish emigrants into believing that Riga was plotting to sell them into slavery on the Barbary Coast (4:260).

[13] Melville, *White-Jacket*, 5: 372.

from the people.[14] ("The mightiest potentates keep the most behind the vail [sic]," claims White Jacket, explaining "you might tarry in Constantinople a month and never catch a glimpse of the Sultan."[15]) This rigid hierarchy of absolute obedience, Melville claims, "is very much like the etiquette at the Grand Porte of Constantinople, where, after washing the Sublime Sultan's feet, the Grand Vizier avenges himself on an Emir, who does the same office for him." Even the naval dress prescribed for the man-of-war seems emblematic of "Turkish trowsers." Melville describes the *Neversink's* drum-beat calling the sailors to quarters as being "as magical as the monitory sound to which every good Mussulman at sunset drops to the ground whatsoever his hands might have found to do, and, throughout all Turkey, the people in concert kneel toward their holy Mecca."[16]

Melville was disgusted by the disturbing coincidence of Christian worship aboard an American warship.[17] He argued that "war almost makes blasphemers of the best of men" and that "so long as a man-of-war exists, it must ever remain a picture of much that is tyrannical and repelling in human nature." In *White-Jacket*, Melville registers the barbaric infidelity of naval violence through the ethnic renaming of four American warships (including the *Constitution* and the *Congress*) as the *Malay*, the *Algerine*, the *Mohawk*, and the *Buccaneer*, and in *Mardi*, by barbarizing British cruisers as the "corsairs of Dominora."[18] Later, in *Israel Potter*, Melville used islamicist references to transform the American naval hero John Paul Jones into a plundering renegade, who, with "his tawny cheek, like a date," behaves like a pirate by issuing "sultanical orders" and "concealing the intent of a Turk." Melville takes Jones as emblematic of the nation-at-large when he claims "America is, or may yet be, the Paul Jones of nations," because it is "civilized in externals but a savage at heart."[19]

While Melville ostensibly used such orientalist rhetoric to infidelize the tyranny and barbarity of American naval practice, the inclusion of adjectives such as "magisterial and magnificent," "mightiest," and "magical" demonstrates that it also served to exoticize his narrative, a strategy that glamorized the Islamic world. If the American captain was an "undignified parody" of Muhammad, Melville intimated that the original model of the Prophet possessed some measure of authentic dignity. This combination of both romance and power reaches its epitome in his next book when he characterizes Ahab in *Moby-Dick* as the despotic dictator of the *Pequod*. Melville suffuses Ahab with some of the romance of the Prophet's independent revelation in order

---

[14] Melville, *White-Jacket*, 5: 297, 301, 23, 193.   [15] Melville, *White-Jacket*, 5: 285.

[16] Melville, *White-Jacket*, 5: 162; Melville, *Redburn*, 4: 101; Melville, *White-Jacket*, 5: 287.

[17] Melville, *White-Jacket*, 5: 320, 208. Melville calls the twenty-four-pound cannon aboard the *Neversink* "Thalaba the Destroyer" after the name of the islamicized oriental tale by Robert Southey (5:324). See Joyce Sparer Adler, *War in Melville's Imagination* (New York: New York University Press, 1981).

[18] Melville, *White-Jacket*, 5:253–4; Melville, *Mardi and A Voyage Thither* (NN, 1970), 3:469. Charles Roberts Anderson, *Melville and the South Seas* (New York: Columbia University Press, 1939), 62.

[19] Melville, *Israel Potter: His Fifty Years of Exile* (NN, 1982), 8: 56, 96–7, 120.

to magnify his authority and increase the register of his revolt. As with the revisionist assessments of Muhammad by Thomas Carlyle and Washington Irving, Ahab's power both threatens and attracts as Melville propels him into an earnest expression of manly rebellion against God's greater absolutism. Melville invests Ahab, who is said to be "alien" to Christendom, with a huge variety of historical allusions to autocracy to generalize and universal- ize this power. Among the most prominent of these are many references to the Islamic world that Melville diversifies by incorporating the Ottomans, Mughals, Tartars, Bedouins, as well as a succession of pre-Islamic Eastern populations. Ahab is called the "old Mogul" by five different members of the crew – an appellation that must be seen as his popular designation on board. Melville calls the three mates "Emirs," and describes the harpooners as "salt sea warriors" with "martial bones . . . like Moorish scimitars."[20] The effect of this terminology is to place Ahab in the guise of a despot with divine privilege, exemplified by Melville's comment that "the only homage he ever exacted, was implicit, instantaneous obedience." Melville grants Ahab the status of sultanship in order to display the privilege of his power – indeed, the word "sultan" means authority in Arabic. Ahab's authority, however, is experiential rather than genealogical, a "sultanism of the brain" individually assumed from within that becomes "incarnate in an irresistible dictator- ship."[21] Ahab in fact perversely mimics the *shahada*, or Muslim proclama- tion of faith, in his promulgation that "[t]here is one God that is Lord over the earth, and one Captain that is lord over the Pequod."[22] Like the comparisons of Joseph Smith and Muhammad that drew upon the Islamic dispensation to exalt the Mormon prophet's power, Melville here embodies Ahab's epic with the romantic heroism of an individual who proclaimed at all costs his vision of reality to be immutably ordained. "But not only do we look on Mohammed as honest," *The North American Review* had argued in 1846, "we regard him as one of the great souls of the world."[23] Melville drew upon contemporary revisions of Muhammad's earnest heroism to intimate the mysterious reaches of experiential authority claimed by Ahab.

Even while building up Ahab's power through romantic islamicism, Melville simultaneously portrays his mission as an arrogance that needed

---

[20] Melville, *Moby-Dick*, 6: 149, 153; Ahab is called "old Mogul" by Stubb twice (171, 432); by the Dutch sailor (174); by the St. Jago's sailor (177), by Archy (197), and by the carpenter (469).

[21] Melville, *Moby-Dick*, 6: 147–8.

[22] Melville, *Moby-Dick*, 6: 474. "La ilaha il Allah, Muhammad-ur-rasul-Allah" often translated as "There Is No God but Allah, and Muhammad Is His Messenger."

[23] "Was Mohammed an Imposter of an Enthusiast?", *The North American Review* 63 (October 1846): 513. This reassessment even reached some ministers. Rev. C. Chauncey Burr declared: "They tell me this man is an impostor. It may be so: but then his imposture (if you will commit so great a wrong upon an honest fanatic) has done more for a greater number of the human race than the truth of any other man born within these twelve centuries. His awful 'No by alla' has shook a thousand idols into dust. His holy 'ALLA ACBAR! ALLA ACBAR!' has built, in the wild waste of Arab hearts, a shrine where God is worshipped." "Introductory Essay" in George Lippard, *Washington and His Generals; or, Legends of the Revolution* (Philadephia: G. B. Zieber, 1847), ii.

to be destroyed, a fact reflected by the original Ahab's biblical role as a false prophet annihilated for his idolatry. This paradoxical venture is captured in a pair of key oxymorons with which Melville describes his captain: "infinite inferiority" and "mortal indomitableness."[24] Johann Wolfgang von Goethe and Thomas Carlyle also revised the evangelical tradition of demonizing Muhammad by recalibrating his daemonic power in romantic language that Melville read and adapted for his own purposes while composing *Moby-Dick*.[25]

In *Poetry and Truth*, Goethe contemplated the dilemma faced by "an excellent man who has something divine in him" when "[t]he celestial and eternal are lowered into the body of earthly aims and subjected to the fate of transitory things."[26] Goethe sketched the life of Muhammad, whom he "had never been able to view as a deceiver," as a dramatic representation of this tragic process of vulgar ruination. Melville likewise exalts Ahab's charismatic force as "a nameless, interior volition," "a strong, sustained, and mystic aspect," "mine own electric thing," and "that, that dazzlingly confounds."[27] But these energies are corrupted as Ahab stoops to employ "external arts . . . paltry and base," such as the posting of the doubloon and other theatrics of the deck, to maintain his control over the crew. Similar to Goethe's Muhammad, it is Ahab's need for these "entrenchments" that partly constitutes his inferiority and falseness as a prophet, however nobly he disregards their importance.[28] The same emphasis on a mighty man whose genius was corrupted by his arrogance characterized George H. Miles's tragedy *Mohammed, the Arabian Prophet,* which in 1850 won a prize of one thousand dollars from the actor Edwin Forrest for best one act play. In the fifth act, Miles attests: "A man may be a pigmy to Mohammed, / And yet o'ertop his fellows."[29]

---

[24] Melville, *Moby-Dick*, 6: 148.

[25] Merton M. Sealts, Jr., *Melville's Reading* (Madison: University of Wisconsin Press, 1966), #122, p. 163; #228, p. 179.

[26] Johann Wolfgang von Goethe, *From My Life, Poetry and Truth, Parts One to Three*, trans. Robert R. Heitner (New York: Suhrkamp Publishers, 1987), 462. The outline of this drama (which Goethe never wrote) has Muhammad converted to Monotheism in the first act. In propagating his faith among his kinsman, Muhammad is forced to use violence and cunning. As this process occurs, "the earthly element in him grows and spreads, the divine retreats and loses its clarity." By the fourth act, "his teaching becomes more of a pretext than a goal, and all imaginable means must be employed, not excluding cruelties." Although Goethe sees Muhammad as recovering his "higher ideals" in the end, this plot portrays him as becoming a slave to the need of extending his own truth (462–3).

[27] Melville, *Moby-Dick*, 6: 165–7.

[28] Goethe, *Egmont*, quoted in Luther S. Mansfield and Howard P. Vincent, "Explanatory Notes," *Moby-Dick, or, The Whale* (New York: Hendricks House, 1951), 678.

[29] George H. Miles, *Mohammed, the Arabian Prophet. A Tragedy, in Five Acts* (Boston: Phillips, Samson & Company, 1850), 134. Melville employs this same perspective of grandeur through relief when he describes a Catskill Eagle flying low in a gorge in the mountains that still is higher than any bird on the plain (Melville, *Moby-Dick*, 6: 425).

Thomas Carlyle, in his second lecture of the series *On Heroes, Hero-Worship, and the Heroic in History*, also viewed Muhammad as an "*original* man." "While others walk in formulas and hearsays, contented enough to dwell there," noted Carlyle, "this man could not screen himself in formulas; he was alone with his own soul and the reality of things."[30] Ahab's driven earnestness and courage resembles the conviction with which Carlyle invests Muhammad: "to be of *infinite* moment; all other things as no moment whatever in comparison." Carlyle imagines Muhammad's epiphanic struggle in words similar to Melville's description of Ahab's mental state in "The Chart" when "every probability [is] the next thing to a certainty":

> [A]ll kept him in a perpetual whirl, his soul knowing rest no more. In wakeful nights, as one may fancy, the wild soul of the man, tossing amid these vortices, would hail any light of a decision for them as a veritable light from Heaven; *any* making-up his mind, so blessed, indispensible for him there, would seem the inspiration of a Gabriel.[31]

Melville exalts his captain through literary islamicism by enabling Ahab to draw on primal forces similar to those granted to Muhammad in these contemporary reassessments. By rejecting Gabriel's warning in the "The Jereboam's Story" not to hunt the white whale, Ahab spurns what for Muhammad was Jibril, the messenger of God to him, earning as a result "a blasphemer's end."[32] No one on board the *Pequod* is able to counter Ahab's awesome power as he carries out his holy war. Ahab's religion is the crusading and violent absolutism that emanates from the core of religious fanaticism, epitomized for many Westerners in the religion of Islam. Yet Melville also saw fresh and universal nobility in the courageous energy and wild earnestness of Ahab's both rebellion against the petty hypocrisy of parochial conventions and the affronting dictates of divine fate.

Melville uses islamicist rhetoric in *Moby-Dick* not only to augment Ahab's authority but also to increase the mysterious grandeur of the ungraspable sperm whale. Melville metaphorically aligns Moby Dick with the nemesis of Christian civilization. The white whale that sheers off Ahab's leg evinces, in the language of *Othello* that Melville adopts, the "seeming malice" of a "turbaned Turk." Melville compares finding this white whale in the oceans of all the world to recognizing "a white-bearded Mufti in the thronged thoroughfares of Constantinople" and when he does make his majestic first appearance it is "far out on the soft Turkish-rugged waters." The whale

---

[30] Thomas Carlyle, *On Heroes, Hero-Worship, and the Heroic in History* (New York: White and Allen, 1840), 74.

[31] Melville, *Moby-Dick*, 6: 200; Carlyle, *On Heroes*, 96. Melville was taken by this quality of "wild rapt earnestness" for it was one of his own personal characteristics. (The idea of wildness permeated both their texts: It is used eighty times in *Moby-Dick*; and twenty-one times in Carlyle's short essay.)

[32] Melville, *Moby-Dick*, 6: 317.

is islamicized again as an inscrutable figure of evil fate when Ahab loses his life. As Ahab throws out his last harpoon, "the flying turn caught him round the neck, and voicelessly as Turkish mutes bowstring their victim, he was shot out of the boat, ere the crew knew he was gone." These Muslim references at the key locations of the whale's irruption into the story suggest the special resonance with which Melville invests Islam as signifying "that intangible malignity which has been from the beginning; to whose domin-ion even the modern Christians ascribe one-half of the worlds." Although the unnerving plurality of this opposing power incorporates a universal paganism, we have seen how since the early eschatology of John Cotton, American fabrications of the Antichrist had identified Islam with the biblical Leviathan.[33]

Melville's dark islamicism gains a gothic extreme in *Moby-Dick* when he embodies the shady genie Fedallah as the racial and religious symbol of the dark fate of human violence – the legacy of Cain that possesses Ahab and that he in turn projects upon the whale. The "swart" Fedallah, whose name in Arabic means "the sacrifice of God," reflects Melville's weird and unwieldy injection of melodramatic orientalist stereotypes.[34] The composite characterization of Fedallah runs the gamut of the types of the cunning Asian: he is called a Parsee (or orthodox Zoroastrian) and worships fire; he possesses a Muslim name and wears a turban; he wears a black Chinese jacket and coils his hair in braids on his head, and finally is compared, like his "tiger-yellow" crew, with "the like of whom now and then glide among the unchanging Asiatic communities, especially the Oriental isles to the east of the continent." When the *Pequod* is waylaid by Malays after it sails through the Straits of Sunda between Java and Sumatra, Ahab applauds the "inhuman atheistical devils" for encouraging him to quicken his own pursuit of the whale. Melville links the piracy of these "rascally Asiatics" with the savagery of Ahab's own monomaniacal revenge, replicated in the phantom crew that he secrets aboard.[35] But this association is most fully registered through "the muffled mystery" of Ahab's relationship with Fedallah, the pilot

---

[33] Melville, *Moby-Dick*, 6: 184, 201, 548, 572, 184. While discoursing on the natural elements of the whale earlier in *Moby-Dick*, Melville calls the whale's tongue "a rug of the softest Turkey" (6:335).

[34] Melville, *Moby-Dick*, 6: 217. For a debate about Fedallah's name, see Dorothee Grdseloff, "A Note on the Origin of Fedallah in *Moby-Dick*," *American Literature* 27 (1956): 396–403; and Mukhtar Ali Isani, "The Naming of Fedallah in *Moby-Dick*," *American Literature* 40 (1968): 380–5.

[35] Melville, *Moby-Dick*, 6: 217, 231, 383. Melville derived these images from the Malay specter in DeQuincy's *Confessions of an Opium Eater* (1821) and from accounts of East Asian violence, like the Kuala Batu incident discussed in Chapter 1 of this book. The dangerous reputation of the East Asian is testified to in "Benito Cereno" (Melville, *The Piazza Tales*, 9: 68) and *Mardi* (3: 58) where captains are wary of boarding listless ships because they fear Malay pirates may be lurking below deck. Even in his poem on the Holy Land, *Clarel*, Melville compares the monks of St. Saba surveying the desert for invading Arabs with a ship's foretopmen looking out over the sea for the "slim Malay" – whom he calls a "perilous imp" (*Clarel*, 3.21.7–9).

with whom he is linked as "a shadow is to its substance." After responding sympathetically to Starbuck's human warmth in "The Sympathy," Ahab relapses into a state of being possessed by what he calls a "cozening, hidden lord and master, and cruel, remorseless emperor," a fiend that is embodied at the end of the chapter by Fedallah's reflected eyes looking back up at Ahab's from the surface of the water. Melville describes their conspired condition: "[B]oth seemed yoked together, and an unseen tyrant driving them," and they remain in that condition in death as they plunge together attached by whale-lines to Moby Dick.[36] Melville spares some of Ahab's "humanities" by displacing the captain's perverse destiny and haunted fatalism onto Fedallah's spectral body. Through his late poetry, Melville continued to distill Asian characters as suspicious sorcerers whose uncanny influence embodied a dark and primal antagonism.[37]

Melville's varied representations of islamicist tyranny in his characterization of his captains and fatal figures suggests how useful this dimension of expression was to his literary art. Melville employed stereotypes of Muslim autocracy to criticize the undemocratic abuses of American leaders. He also islamicized characters, such as Fedallah, his white whale, and later even the Senegalese rebel Babo in "Benito Cereno" (who hails from a West African territory that is predominately Muslim) who serve as representatives of a sinister and malign fatalism that mysteriously controlled events within his literary regimes. Even when employing these negative valences of islamicist imagination, however, Melville also transfigured their power into a romantic despotism embodied most fully by the American captain Ahab, a model of his own rebellious power as author of "wicked" literary worlds.

---

[36] In his poem "The New Zealot to the Sun," Melville attributes the world's chaotic darkness to a narcotizing process of alchemical delusion arising from the "arch type of sway" of a primal Persian (Melville, *Poems*, 264–5). The lank Parsee perfumer distilling blooms into attar in the poem "The Rose Farmer" symbolizes a similar necromantic zeal (Melville, *Poems*, 343–9). In *Clarel*, Rolfe recalls drinking coffee in Constantinople with "an Asian man, / With stately cap of Astracan" (a city on the Caspian Sea) with whom he explores "themes which thrive in shade" (4.16.193–216). Also, "The Timoneer's Story" features a turbaned Moor "of visage black ... A fugitive poor Wahabee" who symbolizes a sorcerer of evil fate. The Moor brings a box of poisoned arms aboard the ship *The Peace of God*, which causes the compass's needle to wander in a storm leading to a shipwreck, which Agath, the only survivor, blames on "the black lieutenant of Lucifer" (*Clarel*, 3.12.58–130). (Melville got the idea for the Timoneer's story from Robert Taitt, the captain of the ship that took Melville from Syra to Constantinople. In his journal entry while visiting Thessaloniki on 7 December 1856, Melville writes "In the evening Captain told a story about the heap of arms affecting the compass." *Journals* [NN, 1989], 15: 56.)

[37] As Wilhelm Halbfass has shown, India (and by extension Cental Asia in general) came to illustrate "the theme of the eclipse and suppression of the 'natural light' through superstition and ritualism, a theme that enjoyed great popularity among thinkers of the Enlightenment." Halbfass, *India and Europe: An Essay in Understanding* (Albany, NY: SUNY Press, 1988), 60.

TURNING TURK: MELVILLE'S RENEGADE ISLAMICISM

The example of Ahab demonstrates how Melville employed images of islamic orientalism to register more than the negative consequences of tyrannical power and fatalistic evil. Melville also gained a release by authorizing his early narrators with orientalist privileges to lend them leeway to perform their own exotic identities. Investing his narrators in the guise of Islamicist infidels who transgressed against Protestant conventions formed another major strand of his literary characterization. Melville's boldest assumption of this figuration was the narrator of *Moby-Dick*'s proclamation to "Call me Ishmael," which announced his affiliation with an individual most widely known in the nineteenth century as the Abrahamic ancestor of the Arabs.[38] When Melville later created another character who called himself Ishmael, it was the Arab brigand-sheik of the "Clan of outcast Hagar" in *Clarel* who accosts the pilgrim entourage near the River Jordan with his band of "swart sinuous men on silvery steeds." In the Book of Genesis, God had unjustly cast Ishmael out of the family of Abraham and denied his progeny the promise of God's covenant with Israel. When Abraham interceded on behalf of Ishmael, God promised that his descendants would greatly multiply and produce twelve princes and a great nation, viewed by Christians as one of the divine sanctions for the existence of Islam. Ishmael thus remained connected with the roots of Judeo-Christian theology even though he was banished from the Mosaic and Christian dispensations which follow their ancestry through Abraham's second son, Isaac. Exclusive critical focus on the biblical Ishmael – the "wild ass of a man" whose "hand is against every man and every man's" – has led to a neglect of the islamicist perspective signified by Melville's assumption of Ishmael as his narrator's identity.[39]

By annunciating Ishmael as his narrative standpoint, Melville empowered himself to criticize Christian civilization from a position that, although biblical, was also one aligned with the traditional enemies of Christianity, one from which he could speak with the contentious power of an established outsider. In Paul's Letter to the Galatians (4:23), Ishmael is described as "the son of the slave" who was "born according to the flesh"; Melville's Ishmael shouts back: "Who ain't a slave?" Ishmael's power is represented by the fact that he replaces Fedallah as Ahab's bowsman on the third day of the chase,

---

[38] For example, an 1856 book about Islam and Christianity by Lewis Cheeseman was titled *Ishmael and the Church; or, The Fall of Mohammedanism* (Philadelphia: Parry and McMillan).

[39] Melville, *Clarel*, 2.27.44; 2.23.90. Melville did figure several of his characters as Ishmaels and the image of maternal succor afforded by Hagar to her infant was emblematic to Melville of a haven in a heartless world. See *Redburn*, 4: 62; *Pierre: or, The Ambiguities* (NN, 1971), 7: 89; *Israel Potter* (where Potter claims that "all hands are against me," ironically putting the lie to his name Israel) 8: 138; *Clarel* (4.10.189); *Mardi*, 5: 40; *The Confidence-Man: His Masquerade* (NN, 1984), 10: 138; and "The Two Temples," in *The Piazza Tales* where Melville also inverses God's covenant by figuring a painting of Madonna and Christ in an empty church as "the true Hagar and her Ishmael" (9: 308).

symbolizing a more benign face of fate, as the bow that Ishmael mans is the one whose line kills Ahab. By allowing Ishmael to be the only survivor of the events in the book, Melville cedes all authority to his perspective and brazenly indicts the enclosed nature of Christian supremacy by rendering God's covenant with humanity more open, democratic, and inclusive of the outcast. Melville's Book of Ishmael integrates the infidel renegade and sub-jugated slave into the center of his narrative, and ultimately into the national canon because of *Moby-Dick*'s later importance to American literature.[40]

Ishmael's participation in Queequeg's rituals reenacts his position as an outcast from the covenant of Israel within the literary world of *Moby-Dick*. Although Queequeg's abiding charity for others marks him as Christian in his actions, Melville ironically labels Queequeg's religious antics with various emblems of infidelity that include islamicist allusions. Queequeg is portrayed as performing ablutions, "salaming" during his evening prayers, and in a chapter bearing the name, carrying out his annual "Ramadan." By labeling Queequeg's behavior with Islamic signs, Melville solemnifies the actions of the "savage" while, ritually repaganizing Ramadan, the Muslim holy month of fasting, by reducing it to a day's apoplectic trance spent with what for Islam is a vile idolatry: a wooden idol. Melville's barbed attack on exclusive ritual is intensified even further by his triple punning about Queequeg "fast[ing] on his hams," a meat prohibited to Muslim believers even if eating were allowed during the fast. By comically pandering to traditional prejudices against Islam, Melville satirizes the exclusivity of ritual itself as the substance of religious belief, arguably the major element that Melville feels is dividing the members of "the great and everlasting First Congregation of this whole worshipping world." This example demonstrates Melville's versatility in deploying islamicist conventions, themselves an element of western literary ritual, as a means of expressing both his humorous insight and his "wicked" criticism.[41]

Melville's decision to arrogate the identity of Ishmael in the first words of "Loomings" is illumined by an examination of the evolving islamicist stances of the narrators in the books preceding *Moby-Dick*. In Melville's first two Polynesian novels, it is when Tommo fully acknowledges his renegade status that he is transformed from "Typee" into "Omoo," the wandering beachcomber who is a prototypical Ishmael. The moment of this trans-formation occurs when the narrator's encounter with a missionary family dramatizes his distance from civilized society. Outlandishly dressed in a

---

[40] Melville, *Moby-Dick*, 6: 6. The Qur'anic Ishmael also resembles Melville's in his longing for water. While tossing restlessly in the hot sands of the desert, Ishmael discovered the spring of Zam-Zam. This well, considered sacred by Muslim pilgrims, enabled Ishmael to settle in Arabia and become the father of the Arabs.

[41] Melville, *Moby-Dick*, 6: 52, 84, 88; Melville to Nathaniel Hawthorne, November 1851, *Correspondence* (NN, 1993), 14: 212.

turban and "voluminous" frock, Omoo shocks the "worthy foreigners" on their verandah with his otherwise polite address ("Good-evening, ladies, a delightful air from the sea ladies"). Melville's sly positioning of his narrator as a civilized renegade in the islamicist guise of turban and dress provided him with a critical license both to berate the incivilities done in the South Seas in the name of Christianity and to parlay his outcast exoticism to his readers. Melville turns this criticism back on his assailers when he calls the children of the missionaries "sickly exotics" and their women "a bevy of silk bonnets and parasols."[42]

The critical liminality of Omoo's islamicist identity is deepened by the names that he travels under during his excursions with his companion Dr. Long Ghost, himself a holder of a nebulous appellation. During his traipses over the Tahitian isles he pawns himself off in the guise of Paul, but Long Ghost (who pretends to be Peter) calls him "the Basha with Two Tails."[43] Melville is in reality spinning two tales here. He gives Omoo the external appearance of Christianity but more subtly reveals his vagabond nature by orientalizing his narrator with an Islamic military title. Having been pressured by his editors to expurgate critical references to missionaries in *Typee*, this islamicist positioning enabled him to deliver a more subtle and subversive attack.[44] Omoo wears his "Eastern" turban, made from a calico shirt with the sleeves drooping behind (thus forming its two tails) throughout most of the book, and twice Melville refers to one of his two nomads "sitting like a [in the fashion of a] Turk." Even when Omoo fabricates a new hat, it is ornamented by the Polynesian woman Arfretee with "a band of flame-colored ribbon; the two longs ends of which streaming behind, sailor-fashion, [that] still preserved for me the Eastern title bestowed by Long Ghost."[45]

In representing the easy companionship of Long Ghost and the "Basha with Two Tails," Melville turns to the popular Near Eastern travel narrative

---

[42] Melville, *Omoo: A Narrative of Adventures in the South Seas* (NN, 1968), 2: 166–7. Other examples of Melville's islamicist parody of female fashion are his orientalization of the island of Pimminee in *Mardi* with its ludicrous "Begum" and her "masquerade of vapidities" (398–413) and his comparison of a pod of whales both to an Ottoman harem and to a parade of fashionables in the "Schools and Schoolmasters" chapter of *Moby-Dick* (391–4).

[43] Melville, *Omoo*, 2: 236, 283. The Mustapha Rub-a-Dub Keli Khan letters in the *Salmagundi* papers, discussed in Chapter 1, mentions a "bashaw of two tails." Bruce I. Granger and Martha Hartzog, eds., *Salmaguridi, the Complete Works of Washington Irving*, Vol. 6 (Boston: Twayne, 1977), 123. For a discussion of this reference in the context of Barbary conflicts, see Warren S. Walker, "Two- and Three-Tailed Turks in *Salmagundi*," *American Literature* 53 (November 1981), 477–8. *A Pacha of Many Tales* by Frederick Marryatt, an author of sea fiction whose works Melville read, was published by E. L. Carey & A. Hunt in Philadelphia in 1834.

[44] John Sampson argues in his "Profaning the Sacred: Melville's *Omoo* and Missionary Narratives," that Omoo and Long Ghost are playing the role of parodic and profane wandering missionaries. *American Literature* 56 (December 1984): 496–509.

[45] Melville, *Omoo*, 2: 225, 257, 282–3. Arfretee's name resembles that of the Afreets who were genies from Arabic mythology.

as a literary model for accentuating his cosmopolitan identity to his readers. They even cross a beach in the hot afternoon which the narrator calls "the Sahara, or fiery desert."[46] Melville often drew upon the exoticism of the desert to evoke encounters on sea and shore. In *Redburn*, two captains of ships passing on the Atlantic are portrayed as having "drove on with all the indifference of two Arab horsemen accosting each other on an airing in the desert." In that book, Liverpool dock is compared to "a grand caravanasary inn" with "each ship . . . a floating colony of the tribe to which it belongs." Attempting to convince Captain Claret of the necessity of a Rio furlough, *White-Jacket*'s Jack Chase compares the crew to "thirsty camels of the desert" desiring the waters and grass of an oasis after journeying through "the ocean Sahara."[47] Whale pods in *Moby-Dick* are referred to twice each as "caravans," "elephants," and "dromedaries" and the canoe that transports Taji and his loquacious mates through *Mardi* is frequently referred to as an elephant with a "canopied Howdah."[48] Melville uses this Muslim motif to render the exoticism of sea experience to his readers. By imagining the sailor's life as an experience of an oriental difference, Melville's literary mirage ironically undermines the stability of conventional land identities.

That islamicist rhetoric serves more than decorative function in *Omoo* is shown when Melville calls the venture of his runaway seaman "The Hegira, or Flight." This chapter is crucial because it marks the symbolic moment (as it did for Muhammad) when Omoo and Long Ghost are driven from the land by their own kind because of the challenge of their vagrancy. The sailors' hegira fundamentally restructures both their allegiance and their sense of time. The moment becomes a touchstone referred back to three other times in the course of the narrative and measures the course of their wandering. Omoo dreams of acting out his status as Bashaw by seeking a "lieutenancy" in the court of Queen Pomare who is rallying support against the intruding Westerners in the isolated west coast of Imeeo.[49] Melville's islamicist positioning again affords a ground from which Melville launches a covert criticism of the inflated superiority of the Christian missionaries and Western imperialists.

In *Omoo*, Melville tells the tale of six rovers who bought a sailboat over which they raised "a flag of their own" and set off to find an island about which they had "heard strange and golden stories." While their journey almost ends in drunken disaster, Melville's positions them as carefree renegades singing about "sailing down, / On the coast of *Barbaree*." In his next book, *Mardi: and A Voyage Thither*, Melville sets off on an even less probable version of the same adventurous escape. The narrator of *Mardi* meets the captain of the *Arcturion*'s jibe to leave the ship if he can by jettisoning himself in the middle of the ocean. Islamicism is central to Melville's attempt

---

[46] Melville, *Omoo*, 2: 276.   [47] Melville, *Redburn*, 4: 76, 165; Melville, *White-Jaclet*, 5: 214.

[48] Melville, *Moby-Dick*, 6: 382, 461; 224, 537; 373, 386; Melville, *Mardi*, 4: 199.

[49] Melville, *Omoo*, 2: 245, 252, 271, 307, 248.

to establish the independent authority of his narrator after he decides to jump ship. Such moments range from comparing the difficulty of stealing the getaway whale boat with that of a "dashing young Janizary . . . run[ning] off with a sultana from the Grand Turk's seraglio" and his description of the narrator and his sidekick sitting down before a "bread barge" they find aboard an abandoned ship as similar to "the Grand Turk and his Vizier Mustapha sitting down before Vienna."[50]

Melville's full oriental authority, however, is not established for over fifty chapters until *Mardi*'s narrator assumes the name of Taji. In a cosmetic move symbolizing the expansion of the story into romantic allegory, the narrator "strikingly improve[s]" his costume by "making it free, flowing, and eastern" to the extent that he announces "I looked like an Emir," another title of honor referring to a military commander descended from Muhammad (and the root of the English word "admiral").[51] In creating the persona of the white demigod Taji, Melville again exalts his romantic authority through a process of islamicist allusion. Taji's name seems most clearly derived from the Arabic word meaning crown, "the assumption of which," according to Dorothee Metlitski Finkelstein, "was an essential part of the initiation ceremony of the mystic, signifying his abandonment of carnal desires and his complete devotion to Allah."[52] Taji's obsessive search for the ungraspable white maiden Yillah through the allegorical isles of Mardi (the Persian word for manhood) prefigures Ahab's monomaniacal pursuit of the white whale. Launched again at the end of the story into the midst of the "wide Pacific," Taji is a much more rebellious wanderer than Omoo had been: "Let *me* then, be the unreturning wanderer!" he exultantly shouts in a voice which, prefiguring Ishmael's to come, is the only surviving earthly presence from the book's action, since the *Arcturion* and its sailors – like the *Pequod*'s – are doomed to destruction.[53]

CIRCASSIAN LONGINGS: MELVILLE'S ORIENTALIZATION OF EVE

Melville's choice to islamicize the excesses of his ship captains empowered him with a critical voice that was able to convert literary conventions into vitally creative energies. By investing his narrators with islamicist trappings, Melville was also able to register the transgressive liberty and global expanse of his own literary authority. A third key strand of islamicism in Melville's loom was the image of Muslim paradise as a renegade realm of love that allowed everlasting access to beautiful females known as houris and peris. Melville fabricated in his fictive imagination female models whose exotic beauty enabled him to relish the natural ethos of desire without being censored by his publishers or censured by his readers. Houris are luxurious virgins awarded to the righteous in Islam's heaven. "Companions

---

[50] Melville, *Omoo*, 2: 291–2; *Mardi*, 3: 20, 64.   [51] Melville, *Mardi*, 3: 127.
[52] Finkelstein, *Melville's Orienda*, 200.   [53] Melville, *Mardi*, 3: 654.

with beautiful, big, and lustrous eyes," they are described in the Qur'an as "Reclining on green Cushions and rich Carpets of beauty."[54] Many Christians – such as some of the anti-Mormon polemicists from Chapter 4 – viewed Qur'anic metaphor as evidence of Muhammad's treachery in luring his followers with promises of sensual rewards, but more adventurous Westerners such as Melville (who wrote to Hawthorne that he refused to believe in a "Temperance Heaven"[55]) were attracted by this romantic vision of opulent consummation, seeing in its orientalized pleasures a return to the pre-lapsarian paradise of Eden. At several moments in his writing, Melville expresses admiration for the Prophet Muhammad for both the robustness of his patriarchal leisure and his attraction to perfumes and essences.[56] Peris, according to an 1847 article in *The Literary World*, lived in Peristan, located in the Caucasus and conceptually based on the Paradise of Eden. These fairies subsist on the fragrance of flowers and are "idealized as incarnations of love at its highest and purest."[57]

Edgar Allan Poe imbibed a similar islamicist vision in his arabesque attempts to intimate the idolatrous passions of earthly love. Many of Poe's angelic beauties – such as Ligeia, Eleanora, and the face in the Oval Portrait – are also etherealized as fabulous Houris, "beings either above or apart from the earth" whose beguiling glances bring with them perfume from the celestial censers of the seraphim. Poe's idea of paradise in his islamicist poems "Israfel" and "Al-Aaraaf" is evoked as "Heavens . . . of Houri glances."

> Thy world is not the dross of ours,
> Yet all the beauty – all the flowers
> That list our love, or deck our bowers
> In dreamy gardens, where do lie
> Dreamy maidens all the day,
> With the silver winds of Circassy
> On violet couches fade away.[58]

---

54 The Qur'an, trans. Abdullah Yusuf Ali, "Surah of Smoke," 44:54; "Surah of the Beneficent, the Mercy Giving," 55: 76 (see also 52: 20 and 56: 22).

55 Melville to Nathaniel Hawthorne, June 1851, *Correspondence*, 14: 189–90.

56 Melville, *White-Jacket*, 5: 268; Melville, *Pierre*, 7: 94. In a book review, Melville comments on "the pleasant spirit of the Mahometan . . . who rewards all true believers with a houri" (Melville, *The Piazza Tales*, 9: 236). The poet Botargo in *Mardi* dreams, "in merry fancies," of his poems "being trilled by the blessed houris in paradise" (5: 396).

57 S. B. H., "Of the Mythology and Superstitions of the Arabian Nights, and Other Eastern Tales," *The Literary World* 59 (18 March 1847): 123–4. The association of peris with heaven was popularized by Thomas Moore's tale "The Paradise and the Peri" in his widely read *Lalla Rookh* (1817). See Finkelstein, *Melville's Orienda*, 208–14.

58 Edgar Allan Poe, "Al Aaraaf," 1831 version, Floyd Stovall, ed., *The Poems of Edgar Allan Poe* (Charlottesville: University of Virginia Press, 1965), 190. The 1829 and 1845 versions begin "O! nothing earthly save the ray / (Thrown back from flowers) of Beauty's eye, / As in those gardens where the day / Springs from the gems of Circassy –" (25).

As had Poe, Melville's juvenile education in classical and romantic literature had equipped him to project his longings onto visions of orientalized women. This is evident in the Byronic depictions in the "Fragments from a Writing Desk," his first writings while still a teenager in 1839. The narrator of the "First Fragment" exults in "seraphic visions" of female loveliness – one of whom possesses "a little of the roseate hue of the Circassian" – that transported him "to the land of Dreams, where lay embodied, the most brilliant conceptions of the wildest fancy." Melville's narrator passionately turns Turk in the service of a more sensual vision than that offered by a Christian heaven, one motivated by some hope of achievable intimacy with an angelic embodiment of oriental beauty: "If the devout and exemplary Mussulman who dying fast in the faith of his Prophet, anticipates reclining on beds of roses, gloriously drunk through all the ages of eternity, is to be waited on by Houris such as these: waft me gentle gales beyond this lower world!"[59] This intemperate devotion is replicated in the "Second Fragment," which relates the narrator's mysterious journey to a splendid and secluded villa "as beautiful and enchanting as any described in the Arabian Nights," one filled with "delicious perfumes." The cynosure of sensual attraction is Inamorata, a voluptuous odalisque described as having "Andalusian eyes" and "Turkish sleeve," who is unable to reciprocate his voluble passion because she is dumb and deaf.[60] Thus, at the very outset of his literary career, Melville realized that despite the fact that the portrayal of female beauty posited an unattainable romantic ideal a feminized space of oriental imagination provided a powerful impetus to his own transgressive literary expression.

Throughout his literary career, Melville often figured women as spiritual symbols whose beauty and fragrance intimate celestial purity. Melville etherealizes the smoking Fayaway in his first book *Typee* as she is "languishingly giving forth light wreaths of vapor from her mouth and nostrils" to which like a peri "her rosy breath added a fresh perfume." Melville twice has his narrators fleetingly encounter beautiful women portrayed as peris. Redburn encounters three "ravishing charmers" during a Sunday excursion into the Liverpool countryside that he describes as "Peris" and "Houris." The narrator of one of his poems is accosted in his coach by a flower-girl who pins a rose on his lapel and is described as "a buoyant nymph on odorous wing" and "a flying Peri" with "titillating fingers." In an 1872 letter to his

---

[59] Melville, *The Piazza Tales*, 9: 194–5. Melville's brother Gansevoort had been similarly ravished by the Muslim heroine of Byron's "The Bride of Abydos," calling her in his journal of 1834: "the most sweetly beautiful female character that I have ever met with in Poetry . . . [who] realizes all the ideas that the Mahometan has of the beauty of the Houris, those dark eyed girls of Paradise." Jay Leyda, ed., *The Melville Log: A Documentary Life of Herman Melville, 1819–1891*, 2 vols. (New York: Gordian Press, 1969), 1: 60.

[60] Melville, *The Piazza Tales*, 9: 202–4. Melville would return to such a supercharged orientalist space, although one with more ominous metropolitan overtones, in his depiction of the London den of pleasure in *Redburn* called "Aladdin's Palace" (4: 227–36).

cousin Kate, Melville refers to a variety of angels that "leave behind them a fragrance as of violets," that he called in *Clarel* the "perfumed spell / Of Paradise-flowers invisible." It is clear even from these short examples that for Melville female beauty often brought with it the redolence of heavenly paradise that he conveyed through the vehicle of his islamicist imagination.[61]

Melville attempted to transcend the burdens of sin and guilt by symbolically abducting the white woman from her infidel earthly seraglio and resituating her in a pristine paradise of chivalrous love. Such a process is evident in the hyperbolic beginning of *Pierre*, where his youthful protagonist rhapsodizes about a natural paradise that he calls "this summer world of ours." Melville then expands beyond the cycle of the seasons into a wider temporal and spatial cosmos in which the paradise of the past is projected into the future through the rhetoric of his islamicism. "Out of some past Egypt, we have come to this new Canaan; and from this new Canaan, we shall press on to some Circassia. Though still the villains, Want and Woe, followed us out of Egypt, and now beg in Canaan's streets: yet Circassia's gates shall not admit them; they, with their sire, the demon Principle, must back to chaos, whence they came." Melville here provides a schematic view of the evolution of humanity from its origins in chaos toward a vision of a future heaven, shorn of the "demon Principle" and its offspring "Want and Woe." Melville figures the quest for paradise as a migratory pilgrimage eastward out of the earthly estate of Canaan toward Circassia, a "fairer world than this to come" that inherits the unmaterialized promise of a land of milk and honey. His transgressive vision restores the pure delight of Eden by "translating" it to Circassia, the pure matrix of human love symbolically preserved from the evil associated with the garden of Genesis.[62]

While Toni Morrison interpreted Melville's obsession with whiteness in *Moby-Dick* as his recognition that the purported superiority of white racial ideology was dangerously savage and inhuman, his longings for a Circassian paradise can be seen as an attempt to recover a pure racial identity free of the evils accomplished in its name.[63] The currency of racial exoticism in antebellum America figured an islamicized Circassian beauty as the ideal

---

[61] Melville, *Typee*, 1: 133; *Redburn*, 4: 213–15; "Naples in the Time of Bomba," *Poems* 385; Melville to Catherine Gansevoort, 9 December 1872, *Correspondence*, 14, 424; Melville, *Clarel*, 1.29.24–26.

[62] Melville, *Pierre*, 7: 32–3. Although the Marquesas might seem an earthly approximation of paradise, the valley to which Tommo flees proves not to be the hoped-for Happar. The Typee valley is stained with the "demon Principle" in the evils of cannibalism and incipient imperialism, just as Melville's own text of *Typee* is riddled with serpent imagery. In *Mardi*, Melville imagines heaven not only as a place "where want and misery come not," but a community "peopled with heretics and heathens" and "almost entirely made up of the poor and despised" (5: 428, 487). Melville wrote in the midst of his own pilgrimage to the Holy Land in 1857: "Hapless are the favorites of heaven" (*Journals*, 15: 91).

[63] Toni Morrison, "Unspeakable Things Unspoken: The Afro-American Presence in American Literature," *Michigan Quarterly Review* 28 (1989): 1–34.

female form. "No fairy tale hath yet rivaled the beauties of Constantinople, no imagination exceeded its luxuriant elegance," wrote the popular novelist Maturin Murray Ballou in his novel *The Turkish Slave*.[64] The invention of Caucasian identity effectively enabled the internationalization of sentimentality while preserving the domestic prerogatives of racial purity.

Caucasian racial identity was first established in 1795 when Johann Friedrich Blumenbach revised for the third time his work *De Generis Humani Varietate Nativa* (On the Natural Variety of Mankind). Drawing upon observations from the travel narratives of Jean Chardin and an analysis of skulls, Blumenbach construed the Caucasian as the original and most beautiful human archetype from which his other four "races" (American Indian, Asian, Malay, and Africa) had degenerated through distance and modification. Blumenbach's prototypical "Caucasian" was in fact Mahommed Jumla, a Vizier of the Mogul Emperor Aurungzeb.[65] Natural historian Alexander Kinmont believed, however, that a "race more feminine and tender-minded than the Caucasian is needed to reflect the sweetness and gentle beauty of the Christian religion."[66] The purest specimens of the Caucasian were said to abide in the territory of Circassia, which was described in the 1797 Britannica as a country long "celebrated for the extraordinary beauty of its women." James Fenimore Cooper referred to this racial narrative when he wrote of "the pure complexion of the Circassian." His missionary Parson Amen in *The Oak Openings* preaches to the Indians on the western frontier that they were descended from the lost tribes of Israel and that their red skin was once "light, like that of the fairest and handsomest of the Circassian race."[67] When the American traveler George Leighton Ditson visited Circassia in the 1840s, he brought with him the expectation that Circassians were "incomparable paradigms of all that is admirable and fascinating in feminine form and loveliness"; in fact, his own journey there exemplified how "the excess of beauty [had] drawn to these wilds many a romantic thought, and awakened curiosity in the remotest parts of the habitable globe."[68]

---

[64] Ballou, *The Turkish Slave: or, The Mahometan and His Harem. A Story of the East* (Boston: Gleason, 1850), 11. Other popular novelists to trumpet the beauties and intrigues of the Islamic orient and parlay them (often serially) into financial success were Sylvanus Cobb, J. H. Ingraham, and Samuel Atkyns.

[65] Jumla is pictured in John C. Greene, *The Death of Adam: Evolution and Its Impact on Western Thought* (Ames: Iowa State University Press, 1959), 225.

[66] Alexander Kinmont, *Twelve Lectures on the Natural History of Man* (Cincinnati: U. P. James, 1839), 281–9.

[67] James Fenimore Cooper, *The Ways of the Hour: "A Tale"* 2 vols. (New York: George P. Putnam, 1850), 107. *The Oak Openings; or, The Bee-Hunter*, 2 vols. (New York: Burgess, Stringer & Co., 1848) 2: 39–40.

[68] George Leighton Ditson, Esq., *Circassia; or, A Tour to the Caucasus* (New York: Stringer & Townsend; London: T. C. Newby, 1850), 378. For a lyrical example of a sublime Circassian beauty whose "golden trusses ... Gush from her turban o'er her slender neck," see R. H. Stoddard, "Lu-Lu: A Circassian Song," *Sartain's Union Magazine of Literature and Arts* 9 (November 1851), 355.

By locating the remote mountainous lands between the Caspian and Black Seas as the cradle of humanity, Blumenbach created a powerful *topos* of racial imagination that traced the descent of Westerners to an exotic oriental matrix. This Caucasian dislocation (which later effervesced into the parallel myth of Aryanism) was popularized partly because it resolved issues troubling to "Anglo-Saxons" who sought a deeper and more global heritage for their racial superiority. Tracing the roots of whiteness only back to the Teutonic forests of Europe left them barbarian newcomers when compared to the ancient histories of the Orient. The construction of a Caucasian cradle enabled Western Europeans to situate their origins in a remote place more contiguous to both contemporary archeological discoveries of early civilizations as well as the earthly location of Eden − "a garden eastward" that had birthed the first biblical humans.[69] By inventing a racial genealogy for whiteness rooted in the Caucasus, Westerners developed an imaginative means of subsuming the cultural resources of the Islamic orient − in this case its ancient past and its female beauty − as a foundational source of racial identity and genetic vitality.

The vagueness of Melville's description of Circassia's actual coordinates certified that it was not a land that he was able to find in his travels; like Queequeg's Kokovoko, it was "not down on any map; true places never are." Melville frequently pictured himself as gaining a symbolic paradise in the oriental lands east of the Holy Land. On board the *Southampton* during his 1849 trip to Europe, he became captivated with planning a "glorious Eastern jaunt" whose "grandness" resonated in his mind throughout the passage. In 1851, he told Hawthorne that writing *Moby-Dick* had made him feel "In my proud, humble way, − a shepherd-king, − I was lord of a little vale in the solitary Crimea." Two months later Melville explored this spiritual geography in a letter to Sophia Hawthorne by narrating a journey that leads east through the Black Sea toward "some Circassia":

> Life is a long Dardenelles. My Dear Madam, the shores whereof are bright with flowers, which we want to pluck, but the bank is too high; & so we float on & on, hoping to come to a landing-place at last − but swoop! we launch into the great sea! Yet the geographers say, even then we must not despair, because across the great sea, however desolate & vacant it may look, lie all Persia & the delicious lands roundabout Damascus.[70]

---

[69] In 1720, Samuel Croxall published in London a play that was widely reprinted called *The Fair Circassian* that set the events of the biblical Song of Solomon in a legendary Circassia. Other Eastern vales such as Kashmir were also celebrated as the source of original purity. Lucretia Maria Davidson, the prodigious U.S. poetess who died at the age of seventeen, wrote of "tall, dark beauties from the mountain recesses of Afghanistan, brilliant Georgians, delicate Circassians and young Cashmerians, snatched from their sports among the fragrant flowers of their happy valley." *Amir Khan and Other Poems, the Remains of Lucretia Maria Davidson* (New York: G. & C. & H. Carvill, 1829), 71.

[70] Melville, *Moby-Dick*, 6: 55; *Journals*, 15: 7–9; Melville to Nathaniel Hawthorne, November 1851, *Correspondence*, 14: 212; Melville to Sophia Peabody Hawthorne, 8 January 1852, *Correspondence*, 14: 220.

Melville later connects these "lands about Damascus" with the imagery of the healing waters of the streams of paradise: "grace and pleasure there, / In Abana and Pharpar's streams / (O shady haunts! O sherbet-air!) / So twine the place in odorous dreams."[71] Circassia in its various forms stood as a visionary paradise into which Melville projected the fulfillment of his desires. It formed an allusive realm of imaginative resolution where – like the vales and bowers of romantic poetry – love and leisure were the only lords.

The most fundamental basis for Melville's imagination of paradise, however, rested in his own experience of travel. Melville drew regularly upon his revealing visits to the fertile islands of the Pacific, as well as upon traditions of pagan and orientalist paradises, to gain the latitude he desired for both cultural criticism and artistic creativity. Robert Milder acknowledged that it was "Melville's particular fate . . . to have experienced a paradise that most Romantics could only theorize about." Melville's sojourn in the permissive beauty of the South Seas formed the instigating force for his literary enterprise, impressing him with powerful visions of an earthly Eden that he sustained throughout his literary career. This experience of Pacific beauty also served as an abiding memory of unencumbered freedom and a sustaining hope of ideal love amidst the many challenges of his family and professional life.[72]

Readers were attracted to Melville's Polynesian adventures by the fresh energies of encounters with unspoiled cultures, especially in the form of their beautiful women. His depictions of Fayaway in *Typee* and Yillah in *Mardi* dramatize his creative uses of orientalism to intimate the erotic liberation he experienced in his Pacific travels. Melville translated the paradise of the South Seas into Eastern metaphor as a way of celebrating its free sensuality of "naked houris." Indeed, his description of the Typeean paradise as a "heaven of bread-fruit, cocoa-nuts and young ladies" is little more than the Islamic afterworld transposed into the lush land of the South Seas. "In that happy land . . . best of all," Melville gloried, "women far lovelier than the daughters of the earth were there in abundance."[73] In the "Typee Manuscript," where Melville originally described Tommo's consummate joy at the "luxurious operation" of being massaged by a number of Marquesan maidens, he imagined himself as the amorous highwayman of John Gay's *The Beggar's Opera* relishing the sensations of an oriental paradise:

> With Macheath in the opera I could have sung "Thus I lay like a Turk
> with my doxies around." Never certainly was effeminate ottoman in the
> innermost shrine of his ser[a]glio attended by lov[e]lier houris with more

[71] Melville, *Clarel*, 4.26.119–22. "Are not Abana and Pharpar, rivers of Damascus, better than all the waters of Israel? May I not wash in them, and be clean?" (2 Kings 5:12). The waters of these "rivers of Damascus" are mentioned as sources of healing in *Omoo* 2: 27.

[72] Robert Milder, "Melville and the Avenging Dream," in *The Cambridge Companion to Herman Melville*, ed. Robert S. Levine (Cambridge: Cambridge University Press, 1998), 252; Melville, *Typee*, 1: 44.

[73] Melville, *Typee*, 1: 5, 172–3.

excess of devotion. – Sardanapalus might have experienced such sensations – but I dou[b]t whether any of the Sultans ever did.[74]

The fact that Melville chose to excise this passage before publishing *Typee* (and his feminizing of the male who experienced these pleasures) demonstrates how the sensual enjoyment of female bodies, even if they were orientalized, remained a transgressive act to antebellum American readers. When publishing his first book, Melville learned of the need to sublimate sensual desire within his literary expression. The creation of his Circassian ideal, as well as the orientalization of his narrators, gave Melville latitudes of leisure that enabled him to simultaneously etherealize and universalize female sensuality without sacrificing all of its libidinal energies.

Melville's most thorough fictional evocation of his female muse from the "land of Dreams" is the sublime white captive named Yillah whom Taji rescues in *Mardi*. The maiden is apparently a brainwashed Anglo castaway whom he releases by killing her captor, the "dusky" prince Aleema. Yillah's name connotes both the purity of the Lily and the Muslim invocation "la ilaha il Allah" (There is no God but God).[75] Yillah's beauty is more essence than substance, and Melville's progressive descriptions of her emphasize her angelic insubstantiality as houri and peri. She exemplifies the romantic paradigm of the Muslim woman that Mohja Kohf describes as "an angelic paragon of numinous feminine nothinghood, a shimmering fetish object for both the competing males within the narrative and the projected male reader."[76] She is initially portrayed as a beautiful girl cowering in her tent, but her mystery is expanded by her status as a sacrificial victim with "snow-white skin; blue, firmament eyes: Golconda locks . . . [and] gauze-like robe".[77] She is so sublimated as to become barely discernible. Her hand in Taji's "seemed no hand but a touch," and the human substance of her beauty is expressed only by allusions to fleeting flushes of nature and reducible to the rose pearl that she wears on her breast.[78] Yillah assumes for Taji, as did the seraphic maiden of Melville's first "Fragment," the status of an unearthly manifestation of heaven on earth. Taji avers, "Often I thought that Paradise had overtaken me on earth, and that Yillah was verily an angel, and hence

---

[74] This part of the "Typee Fragment" is quoted in Herman Melville, *Tales, Poems, and Other Writings.* ed. John Bryant (New York: The Modern Library, 2001), 23, and Parker, *Herman Melville*, 1: 364–5. This paragraph would have been on pages 1: 110–11 of *Typee*.

[75] Melville, *Mardi*, 3: 142; See Finkelstein, *Melville's Orienda*, 221–2, 204.

[76] Mohja Kohf, *Western Representations of the Muslim Woman: From Termagant to Odalisque* (Austin: University of Texas Press, 1999), 152.

[77] *Mardi* 3:136. "Golconda" refers to legendary diamond mines in Hyderabad, India.

[78] Melville, *Mardi*, 3: 144, 142, 152, 137–8. Melville's mystic portrayal of Yillah as houri was parodied in a lampoon in *The Man in the Moon* in May of 1849: "Yillah basks beside me – her great black eyes, lustrous and full-orbed, the doors through which angels and spirits float into her being from that heaven which is higher than the seventh heaven seen by the camel-driver [i.e., Muhammad] in his vision." Watson G. Branch, ed., *Melville: The Critical Heritage* (London and Boston: Routledge and Kegan Paul, 1974), 160.

the mysteries that hallowed her." The story that Yillah relates of her genesis tells of a peri whose essence was condensed from a flower blossom's "rosy mist" that "exhaled away in perfumes."[79]

Melville's own blasphemy, indicated by his comment in his *Journals* that "J. C. [Jesus Christ] should have appeared in Taheiti [sic]" was to be seduced like Taji by a Circassian paradise of fragrant love more passionate than that allowed by Christian sentimentality. While Melville took up the conventional romantic rhetoric of flower language and oriental maidens, he also – Ishmael-like – identified himself with its rebellious ramifications. Assuming the guise of an islamicist infidel who violated the moral constraints of the lingering Calvinism of his time, Melville tried to refabricate an enchanting Eve to whom he was the gallant and chivalrous suitor. He dreamed of their capacity to reassume their mystic regime of celestial love and demigodly wisdom together, and thereby both redeem the failure of humanity and spite the punitive God who had ousted them from paradise. As had the gnostics, Melville subversively redefined original sin to signify not the disobedience of Adam and Eve but rather the injustice of their banishment into the realm of labor and death, all because they loved each other and desired to awaken to knowledge. By authoring his own orientalized literary dominion, Melville invented a Circassian paradise where he might thrive as one of the "Dexterous tumblers eluding the Fall." Melville sought to reestablish the heavenly credentials of humanity by effacing the Fall through a redemptive transgression of love, leisure, and literature. Refusing to be condemned as "Eden's bad boy," he testified instead that "No Past pertains to Paradise."[80]

Following his evocations of female beauty in his fiction set in the South Seas, Melville continued in his attraction to his Circassian ideal of love in his literature set on land. The importance of two other major female characters, Lucy and Ruth, is symbolized by their betrothals to the protagonists, Pierre and Clarel. Melville explains when lauding Lucy in *Pierre* that "a lovely woman is not entirely of this earth" but rather "a visible semblance of the heavens," and also asserts that "heaven [has no] blessing beyond her earthly love."[81] Although these potential matches seem more lasting than Tommo's dalliance with Fayaway and Taji's mystical quest to recover Yillah, the fact these fiancées meet their end in death rather than marriage is further evidence of the unattainable ideality of Melville's Circassian vision.

Lucy Tartan is the last of Melville's pristine female idealizations in his prose, and he describes her as the "most celestial of all innocents" and "bait set in Paradise," "from whose mouth and cheek came the fresh fragrance of her violet young being."[82] Compared to "a Bird from Arabia," Lucy is described as such a prize that "the Grand Turk, and all the other majesties

---

[79] Melville, *Mardi*, 3: 158, 153, 193.　　[80] Melville, *Journals*, 15: 154; Melville, *Poems*, 428, 311, 391.
[81] Melville, *Pierre*, 7: 24, 34.　　[82] Melville, *Pierre*, 7: 57, 28, 33.

of Europe, Asia and Africa to boot, could not, in all their joint dominions, boast as sweet a girl as [she]." Pierre's paeans to female beauty are so extensive as to betray such cultural ideals as the sanctity of life and the primacy of Christ. He hyperbolically claims that a "true gentleman in Kentucky would cheerfully die for a beautiful woman in Hindostan, though he never saw her; . . . he would turn Turk before he would disown an allegiance hereditary to all gentlemen, from the hour that their Grand Master, Adam, first knelt to Eve."[83] However, Lucy's tragic death, like the disappearance of Yillah, foreshadowed by their replacement in the narrators' consciousnesses by the alluring sexuality of Isabel and Hautia, ultimately signals Melville's difficulty in representing love's capacity to counter sin in his fictional worlds.

The romantic subplot in his long poem about pilgrims in the Holy Land travels much the same road. *Clarel*'s American Jewish maiden, Ruth, is as heavenly as Lucy and Yillah: she is an "angel succorer" whose eyes are the "Pure home of all we seek and prize."[84] Ruth has "the grace of Nature's dawn: an Eve-like face," and she "looked a legate to insure / That Paradise is possible / Now as hereafter." Together, Clarel and Ruth embody the hope that "the light / Of love could redeem the trace / Of grief."[85] But this love, as well as Ruth's father's Zionist dream of the redemptive glories of Jerusalem, is shattered first by his murder by the Arabs and then by Ruth's grief, ritual seclusion, and untimely death. The expiration of Lucy and Ruth, whose names, respectively, mean light and companion, symbolize the evaporation of Melville's dream of materializing his Circassian ideal in literary characterization. With their deaths, Melville's Circassian vision of celestial companionship seems no more than a mirage.

Cast out from the Eden of his aspirations, Melville was forced to lower his standard of attainable felicity, a realization represented by the shift in his writing from prose to poetry and his change of career from professional author to Customs House Officer in New York City, a job that he worked at for almost twenty years. After he finished *Moby-Dick* in 1851, Melville had imagined himself trying on "the crown of India" that was delivered him through "the good goddess's bonus" of Hawthorne's praise, even if it did fall down on his ears.[86] By contrast, almost a quarter of a century later he declined an offer to be met when his boat docked up the Hudson, saying "When the Shah of Persia or the Great Khan of Tartary comes to Albany by the night-boat – *him* meet on the wharf and with salvoes of artillery – but not a Customs House Inspector."[87] Melville acknowledged in a poem that youthful romance had allowed him to rise upward and see the earth

---

[83] Melville, *Pierre*, 7: 24, 26.   [84] Melville, *Clarel*, 1.22.98; 1.23.67.

[85] Melville, *Clarel*, 1.16.163–6; 1.27.18–19; 1.39.5–7.

[86] Melville to Nathaniel Hawthorne, November 1851, *Correspondence*, 14: 212.

[87] Melville to Abraham Lansing, 5 August 1875, *Correspondence*, 14: 429.

as an insubstantial "Aladdin-land." But his painful wisdom had caused him to realize, as he did when he dedicated *Pierre* to Mt. Greylock and *Israel Potter* to the Bunker Hill Monument, the abiding futility of viewing earth as anything but a material tomb, confessing that "Matter in end will never abate/His ancient brutal claim."[88] Melville learned the lesson that "terra firma can deceive" during his own journey to the eastern Mediterranean in 1856–7. To Melville, the Holy Land and the romantic Orient was in reality a stony and barren landscape full of what he called the "unleavened nakedness of desolation."[89]

THE MUSLIMS OF MELVILLE'S *CLAREL*

Although Melville had originally relished a trip to the Orient in 1849, he was not able to visit the eastern Mediterranean until 1856–7, a seven-month journey at the age of thirty-seven. By then his reasons for travel were not so "glorious." Both his publishing fortunes and his physical health had declined, and the journey was financed by his father-in-law, Lemuel Shaw, as an attempt to restore Melville's vigor and balance. While the trip did not enable Melville to return to the status of successful novelist (his last full length fictional narrative, *The Confidence-Man*, was published while he was traveling), it forced him to reappraise some of the romantic notions of the Orient to which he had subscribed in his earlier fiction.[90]

The importance of Melville's Near Eastern journey can be measured by the fact that he long remained intellectually engaged in transforming the experience into poetry. *Clarel: A Poem and Pilgrimage*, one of the longest poems in the English language, was not published until nineteen years later in 1876. Melville composed this poem and many others while holding down a full-time position as a customs official on the docks of Manhattan. Through the philosophical contemplation and poetic rigor of composing *Clarel*, Melville developed an emotional endurance that enabled him to accept his loss of popularity as a writer and act out his mundane roles with some degree of resignation.

Melville's early skepticism about the superiority of Western "sniveliza-tion" was accentuated by his own journey through Muslim lands in 1856–7 as it had been during his earlier travels across the Atlantic and in the Polynesian

---

[88] "C_____'s Lament," and "Fragments of a Lost Gnostic Poem of the Twelfth Century" (Melville, *Poems*, 271, 272).

[89] Melville, *Journals*, 15: 83. Ruth's Jewish ethnicity and Clarel's failure to consummate their relationship perhaps represents Melville's inability to gain access to any embodiment of oriental female beauty during his visit, with the exception of brief glimpses of women in Turkey (Melville, *Journals*, 15: 57, 63).

[90] See Timothy Marr, "Mastheads and Minarets: Islamic Architecture in Melville's Writings," *Melville "Among the Nations"* (Kent, OH: Kent State University Press, 2001), 472–84.

Pacific. That Melville's Near Eastern trip was an experience in comparative islamicism is evident from his observations in his lecture "Traveling: Its Pleasures, Pains, and Profits," the third that Melville took onto the circuit after his return from the Levant in 1857. In discussing the liberalizing effects of travel on the perspective of the traveler, Melville claims its "legitimate tendency is to teach profound humility, while it enlarges the sphere of comprehensive benevolence until it includes the whole human race." One of the lessons of humility that Melville learned during his journey to Palestine was the insufficiency of the American pretense of superiority. "In the Levant where all nations congregate, unpretending people speak half a dozen languages," Melville acknowledges, "and a person who thought himself well educated at home is often abashed at his ignorance there." Melville explains this cosmopolitan expansion more fully:

> The Spanish matador, who devoutly believes in the proverb, "Cruel as a Turk," goes to Turkey, sees that people are kind to all animals; sees docile horses, never balky, gentle obedient, exceedingly intelligent, yet *never beaten*; and comes home to his bull-fights with a very different impression of his own humanity. The stock-broker goes to Thessalonica and finds infidels more honest than Christians.[91]

For Melville, the presence of Islam was a phenomenon enabling deeper contemplation and not a problem to be resolved by trumpeting the redemptive superiority of Christian culture. While Melville clearly and ironically saw the Ottoman Empire in danger of succumbing to the Mammon of Western materialism (indeed his own presence there demonstrated its increasing intrusion), he viewed with disdain the eschatological belief that Muslims would convert to Christianity. When Melville met the missionary families of Charles Saunders and Walter Dickson in the Holy Land, he reacted unequivocally in his journal to the "Dismal story of their experiments" by averring: "Might as well attempt to convert bricks into bride-cake as the Orientals into Christians.... It is against the will of God that the East should be Christianized."[92] Melville's most searing criticism of evangelical expectation was his representation of the babbling Nehemiah, an elderly millennialist who distributes eschatological pamphlets but whom the Muslims view as "demented or so deemed."[93] Nehemiah's ineffective faith in biblical literalism prevents any meaningful communication with the Muslims of the Holy Land. Three times his tracts are rejected by Arabs before Nehemiah, a vision of the New Jerusalem, drowns in the Dead Sea. The written word pursuing is not the medium of the desert. In the place of printed

[91] Melville, *Redburn*, 4: 101; "Traveling," *The Piazza Tales*, 9: 422–3. The ex-Confederate soldier Ungar in *Clarel* lambastes the Anglo-Saxons for inventing the phrase "as cruel as a Turk" as a cover for their own imperialist crimes (4.9.113–15).

[92] Melville, *Journals*, 15: 81.   [93] Melville, *Clarel*, 1.8.69–77.

statutes of law and religion, the Arabs obey a natural aristocracy of character. Connected with and cooperating with nature, the Arabs live in a world where the word and its idealistic dreams have been replaced by a spiritual contentment with the physical present.[94]

The inscrutability of Islamic belief and behavior posed an ongoing enigma for Melville rather than a divine scandal. An illuminating example is Melville's symbolic meditation on a group of Arab shepherds that he saw in the barren hills of Judea earnestly praying toward Mecca with their backs toward Bethlehem. Drawing upon this scene in *Clarel*, Melville makes Muslim worship a "Monument" to the way that religion had become a "monster of a million minds" and an emblem of the waning of Christ's star which can no longer attract and guide the flocks. The adventures Rolfe and the minister Derwent contemplate this scene and their dialogue reveals a spectrum of interpretations about the significance of Muslim worship ranging from either a blasphemous affront to Christian belief or an earnest practice acceptable to a "benignant" deity. Rolfe conditionally accepts Derwent's argument that Muslims are so devoted that they regularly observe their prayer times "in street or mart," claiming that "'If 'tis so,'" claims Rolfe, "'let all avow / As openly faith's loyal heart.'"[95] At earlier times in his fiction, Melville had also meditated on the comparative meaning of Muslim belief. In *Redburn*, he mused, "We talk of the Turk, and abhor the cannibals; but may not some of *them* go to heaven before some of *us*?[96] In another canto in *Clarel*, two strangers contemplate the story of a Christian creditor whose account books were destroyed in a fire and the only debtors who contined to repay were Muslims, admiring "that Koran which respects / Nor place nor person," and wondering "Are Turks our betters?"[97]

The fact that these discussions take place between Western pilgrims exemplifies the fact that Melville, like most Americans travelers to Ottoman lands, had difficulty engaging with Muslims other than through casual observation. This distance was a result of his inability to communicate in the languages of the locals, fears for his personal safety, as well as cultural preconceptions that he brought with him.[98] This situation threw Melville back on his own creative resources to try to measure the meaning of Islam. Debarred from extended intimacy with actual Arabs, he relied on various observations and encounters he had noted in his *Journals* as well as on other published travel narratives, upon which he drew heavily in the composition of *Clarel*. Ironically, a major factor that prevented Melville from engaging deeply with

---

[94] Melville, *Clarel*, 1.28 83–90; 2.13.16–43; 2.13.178–90.   [95] Melville, *Clarel*, 4.10.52–87, 111.

[96] Melville, *Redburn*, 4: 293.   [97] Melville, *Clarel*, 4.12.27–8, 64.

[98] When circumstances did allow such investigation, such as when he encountered Muslims on board the various ships he took between Mediterranean ports, Melville actively questioned Muslims about the nature of their belief. For example, Melville met the Turkish envoy to Sardinia while sailing into Leghorn: "Talked with him. His views of Mahomatism &c. Upper classes of Turkey indulge philosophical opinions upon religion &c." Melville, *Journals*, 15: 113.

Muslim thought was also the precise one that enabled him what little contact he was able to make. Melville's fear of footpads, looters, and assassins forced him to hire guides in Constantinople, Egypt, and Palestine. The locals that Melville had the most contact with during his journey were these guards and dragomen (Arabic *targuman*, meaning interpreter) that he contracted for his safety, and his Muslim characters in *Clarel* were modeled on these roles. (So may have been Fedallah in *Moby-Dick*, whose name is a homonym of Fathallah, the dragoman of Robert Curzon, who protects his charge during the same trip that Clarel makes with his Druze guide.[99]) These characters represented stereotypes of Islam, but they also provided an embodied form for Melville to contemplate creatively the cultures of Islam. The enlarged sympathy that he earned from his travel enabled him to meditate on the symbolism of Islamic worship in *Clarel* in ways that generated a vital means of evaluating the earnestness of human endeavor amidst the diversity of cultural and religious forms. Examining these characters reveals how islamicist imagery itself provided a fertile source for Melville's original artistry.

Criticism of *Clarel* has mostly focused on the Christian and Jewish pilgrims who travel to or live in the Levant. Each of them represents a position on the spectrum between struggling with faith in the tradition they espouse and the devastating realization that religion may simply be a false myth. These characters serve as models for Clarel, the lapsed divinity student, for different ways of dealing with his deep doubt. There has been little acknowledgment of the contrasting group of three characters from various parts of the Ottoman Empire who protect the pilgrims during their circuit from Jerusalem to Jericho and the Dead Sea, up to the monastery of Mar Saba, and back again through Bethlehem. Unlike the majority of the Western pilgrims, the countercorps of Belex, the Arnaut, and Djalea (a Druze whom Melville islamicizes) are unquestioning believers (if not followers) of their religion who are spared the crisis faced by the doubting or displaced Christians.

These three characters represent the most compelling creation of fictional Muslims by any major nineteenth-century American author. Melville explores through them (as well as in several other minor Muslims in *Clarel*) the value of resignation as a philosophical approach to life. Because none of them engage deeply in the intellectual colloquy of the "pilgrims" – a testament to Melville's intellectual alienation from Islamic teachings – he evaluates each by the integrity of their behavior rather than by the quality of their discourse. Judging his three Muslim guides by the fruits of their actions and the earnestness of their beliefs, Melville finds Belex and the Arnaut wanting in the balance. Djalea, however, is the strongest and most

---

[99] Robert Curzon, *A Visit to the Monasteries in the Levant* (London: John Murray, 1849), 171–4. Murray had published the London editions of Melville's first two books *Typee* and *Omoo* and released this book the same year as Melville's second journey to London.

stable leader-figure in the poem and perhaps leaves the most mysterious influence on Clarel of any of the characters he encounters. Indeed, the memorable character of Djalea embodies the personal philosophy of wise acquiescence that Melville was developing to replace his waning faith in romantic and theological verbal doctrine. Djalea's manhood is rooted in the simple virtue of natural character acting calmly in the fate of uncertainty. In Djalea, Melville confirms the most positive aspects of romantic orientalism, but he does so through a passionate pragmatism rather than through intemperate fantasy.

Melville presents the guards Belex and the Arnaut as cameos of two contrasting types of Turkish soldiers. They represent traditional stereotypes of Muslim martiality drawn from legends about the Crusades and the assassins, as well as from the Turk's contemporary struggles with Russia – most recently in the Crimean War, which ended just prior to Melville's journey. The inclusion of these Muslim characters permits Melville to infuse local color into the desert environment of Judea, comic relief into the deep abstraction of the pilgrim discourse, as well as critical commentary about romantic notions of Muslim chivalry. Possessing more will and panache than strategy or technology, they are caricatures of the misguided infidel renegade whose capacity for principled thought has been sacrificed to the vigor of the moment. Once a threat to Christendom, these soldiers are nominal allies of the European concert and serve as armed escorts to the pilgrims.

Belex (the Spahi) is the commander of the guards who escort Clarel's party in their journey around Palestine. He is an ex-janissary who symbolizes the decaying grandeur of the Sublime Porte: a "Type of the pure Osmanli breed. / But ah, equipments gone to seed –."[100] His "shabby fate" epitomizes the Ottoman rejection of progress as he wears moth-eaten garb and his twenty-year-old horse bears a second-hand ceremonial saddle stripped of its ornaments. Although "alert," "hale," and "vigilant," Belex is a belligerent opportunist whose effectiveness as a soldier is compromised by his "tyrannous spleen."[101] His ostentatious irreverence, such as when he vulgarly toasts the fast of Ramadan with wine, embodies Western notions of a weakened Turkey that condones chaos in the name of an apathetic bigotry.

Unlike Belex's ludicrous impiety, the second Muslim to join the train of tourists is a courageous veteran warrior whose power makes him a "ripe masterpiece of a man." The Arnaut, a heavily armed mercenary fighter from Albania, is a slayer who seeks to be seen as civilized. The warrior is portrayed as a giant wearing a "snow-white" kilt, a blue waistcoat with a "blood red" sash, and on his head a scorched crimson fez with a long tassel. The Arnaut's faith is in the promise of martyrdom by the sword and not in any principled morality: "An Islamite he was by creed –," Melville notes, "in act, what fortune's chances breed." Despite Clarel's attraction to

---

[100] Melville, *Clarel*, 2.7.97–9.   [101] Melville, *Clarel*, 2.9.11; 2.23.52.173.

the Arnaut's courageous willingness to sacrifice his life in military action, Melville ultimately condemns him as an ignorant fatalist whose extravagant show will never save him.[102]

Beneath the refreshing humor and exoticism of his Muslim soldiers lies little but the egoism of the "free-lance." They ultimately remain unchivalrous individuals who kill and are willing to be killed with no deeply felt purpose. Both the Arnaut and the Spahi contrast harshly with the dignity of the dying Civil War soldiers that Melville portrays in *Battle-Pieces*. In *White-Jacket*, Melville had deconstructed the glamour of Muslim martyrdom in a story related by Jack Chase, the captain of the foretopmen, who witnessed Turkish sailors dying in the naval Battle of Navarino in 1827. "'Allah! Allah! Mohammed! Mohammed!' split the air; some cried it out from the Turkish portholes; others shrieked it forth from the drowning waters, their top knots floating on their shaven skulls, like black-snakes on half-tide rocks," he observed. "By those top-knots they believed that their Prophet would drag them up to Paradise, but they sank fifty fathoms, my hearties, to the bottom of the bay."[103] Like the suicide bombers of today, Belex and the Arnaut are eager to accept rash violence as a theological dictum, a position that make them reckless candidates for guards or guides. They are unable to apply their faith in Islam to acting morally in this world. Followers of the orders of others, these soldiers confirm the stereotype of the Muslim as bellicose bigot.

In distinct contrast to the other Muslim guards, Djalea is the quintessential guide whose silent actions speak of a competence compared to which the personas of Belex and the Arnaut exhibit but shallow buffoonery. Djalea's arms are to prevent violence, not to instigate it, and they symbolize his virility and not his foolhardiness. Djalea's calm self-sufficiency is founded on a mystical attunement that embraces the physical world. The epitome of poise, Djalea is the character in *Clarel* who acts most constructively in the mundane realm without sacrificing a deeply knowing faith. Having been born an aristocrat, Djalea accepts his degradation in worldly status with serenity because

---

[102] Melville, *Clarel*, 3.11; 4.1.43–63. Though Melville draws some elements of the Arnaut's characterization from observations in his *Journals*, and from Eliot Warburton's *The Crescent and the Cross; or Romance and Realities of Eastern Travel* (New York: Wiley and Putnam, 1845), the Arnaut is largely a character (as is the monk Salvaterra) lifted from the pages of John Lloyd Stephen's *Incidents of Travel in Egypt, Arabia Petraea, and the Holy Land of 1837*. Stephen's "wild Arnaout" was "the boldest, most dashing, and martial-looking figure I ever saw; and had a frankness and openness in his countenance." Like Melville's Arnaut, "he rode his high-mettled horse, as if he were himself part of the noble animal," and his "fiery impatience to be present at a scene could not be controlled." Both warriors partake excessively in wine-bibbing in Christian convents despite Qur'anic injunctions against its use. Stephens and Clarel are both attracted to the "bold, frank bearing" of their Arnauts, although Melville's criticism of his warrior's "devil-dare" is more complete (Stephens, *Incidents*, ed. Victor Wolfgang von Hagen [Norman: University of Oklahoma Press, 1970], 325–6, 332–5); Melville, *Clarel*, 3.11.60.

[103] Melville, *Clarel*, 3.12.276–83; Melville, *White-Jacket*, 5: 326.

he obeys inner laws. As servant to the Western pilgrims, Djalea's teaching is "not by word / Indeed, but act." His power is based neither on privileged position nor intellectual argument, but rather its source is in the gravity of his character, which communicates an aura of command. Beside the figure of Djalea, the Western pilgrims are reduced to naive tourists unaware of the dangers surrounding them and incapable of protecting themselves. By preserving the pilgrims with his laconic control from the violent threats of the Bedouins, Djalea serves in the poem as a symbolic savior figure. Djalea "maintain[s] his head," which refers at once to his intellect, his autonomy, and his leadership. The character of Djalea emphasizes Melville's wisdom in knowing that it is how gracefully and effectively one acts that determines spiritual rank rather than the situation of one's birth or even the intellectual substance of one's beliefs.[104]

Djalea wears the garb of the Druze initiate: a striped woolen cloak with vest, a white linen sash, and a turban "like snow wreath." The adjectives used to describe his dress and equipment are "simple," "plain," "spare," "coarse-spun," "lean." The fact that Djalea is referred to as an "Islamite," that he is the son of an Emir, and that his faith is in Allah reflects Melville's linking of the Druzes with Islam.[105] The name Djalea might be derived from "Jahil," a term meaning ignorant, which refers to Druzes who are not initiated into the religion's secret mysteries. As an initiate with white turban, however, Djalea would instead merit the name akkal (*aqil*: intelligent). Either Melville was not aware of this discrepancy, as Dorothee Metlitsky Finkelstein points out, or he was consciously emphasizing Djalea's humility and lack of concern for external status. What is important about Djalea is that he is a mystic and his teachings cannot be imparted in words; unlike Clarel, he is full without the need for intellectual justification. Djalea is a nonideological being, who represents what Melville called the "firm, creedless faith that embraces the spheres."[106]

Djalea is the Charon of the pilgrim entourage in its journey through the underworld of Judea and the Dead Sea, which Melville calls a "land of Eblis" after the Islamic Prince of Darkness.[107] His pragmatism in accepting modernity is symbolized by the "new revolver bright" that he carries along

[104] Melville, *Clarel*, 3.15.95; 2.7.25.

[105] The fact that Djalea is a Druze isolato problematizes his consideration as a Muslim character. Melville was but dimly aware of the Druze world view; for example, Druze initiates are not permitted to smoke. Djalea probably represents the dispossessed Druzes who had been ousted from Lebanon in 1841. That their antagonists are Christians is shown by the massacre of 12,000 Christians by the Druze the same year that Melville was lecturing on traveling. Robert Brenton Betts, *The Druze* (New Haven, CT: Yale University Press, 1988), 23, 78.

[106] Melville, *Redburn*, 4: 291. Finkelstein pointed out that the name Djalea might be a derivation of the word "Djahel," used to describe the Druze leader "Emir Yousef" in C. F. de Volney's *Travels through Syria and Egypt*. Finklestein, *Melville's Orienda*, 172–3.

[107] Melville, *Clarel*, 2.10.111.

with his traditional gun and "yataghan" (sword). The absence of spurs on his boots attests both to his disdain for ostentation and his intimate control over his beloved mare.[108] During the journey, they encounter three separate groups of Turks or Bedouins, and with each Djalea is able to avert danger by his successful negotiations, which are based on natural diplomacy in which human dignity and not logical disputation ensures a calm encounter. These "parleys" function as the equivalent of the gams in *Moby-Dick* in contributing to what Newton Arvin has called *Clarel's* "crowdedness of social landscape." "Nowhere else, not even in *Moby-Dick*," claims Arvin, "does Melville fill the stage more populously, . . . or succeed more brilliantly in giving vitality to secondary and even to incidental figures."[109] All three engagements are writ large from journal notations of Melville's own experiences in Palestine, and they allow other characters to observe Djalea's noble capacity as a natural leader as well as supply additional Muslim types into *Clarel's* company of characters.

The Christian pilgrims are attracted by Djalea's "rife nature" and the quality of his "mettle and mien." The source of Djalea's "patient self-control high bred" is a mystery, but part of it is his retention of the original marrow of Adam, a primal masculinity that renders him appealing to the pilgrims and to the author who created him. To them, Djalea is full of a "virile power" and embodies "[t]he inherent vigor of man's life / Transmitted from strong Adam down."[110] Djalea's manly power is manifest in his wise repose as well as through his skillful action. Clarel portrays the guide's spiritual dignity and his statuesque contentment as he

> . . . reclined half prone,
> The long pipe resting on the stone
> And wreathes of vapors floating by —
> The man and pipe in peace as one.
> How clear the profile, clear and true;
> And he so tawny. Bust ye view,
> Antique, in alabaster brown,
> Might show like that. There all aside,
> How passionless he took for bride
> The calm — the calm, but not the dearth
> The dearth or waste; nor would he fall
> In waste of words, that waste of all.[111]

Djalea's instrument is not the pen but the pipe, which symbolized the confluence of sense and intellect in an earthly meditation. The pipe embodies the positive valence of the philosophy of fatalism, the reward of action.

---

[108] Melville, *Clarel*, 2.7.12–72.
[109] Newton Arvin, *Herman Melville* (New York: William Sloan Associates, 1950), 276.
[110] Melville, *Clarel*, 2.8.4–21.   [111] Melville, *Clarel*, 3.5.175–86.

(It was the object that Ahab tossed into the sea disdainfully growling, "What business have I with this pipe? This thing is meant for sereneness."[112]) Melville refers often in his fiction and letters to the enjoyment of smoking, a luxury that produces a "dreamy revery known only to children of the weed."[113] Babbalanja cries out in *Mardi*, in figures similar to Djalea's taking of the calm for a bride, that the pipe is "like a good wife . . . a friend and companion for life."[114] Melville even wrote a poem, "Herba Santa," which lauded tobacco as a sacrament that brings discordant peoples into earthly peace, calling it "the Truce of God."[115] Djalea's sensualism, however, does have distinct limits. He does not partake of the racka (alcohol) or the frenzy at the monastery "heedful not to dim / The escutcheon of an Emir's son / By any needless letting down."[116] His pipe is the dignified balance between spiritual contemplation and sensual enjoyment.

Limited in his capacity to explore his Muslim characters through their own words, Melville relies on their horses to elaborate their personalities, another proof of Melville's paucity of material. The pedigree of the Arabian horse had long served as a means of romanticizing the noble freedom and masculine self-sufficiency of the Arab as primordial patriarch. The horses in *Clarel* are external reflections of the souls of their owners and their descriptions are as lengthy as the portrayal of their human owners. Belex's horse, Solomon, is described as a "Don John . . . of rakish strain" and has a blood line leading back to the stables of his namesake. The Arnaut rides a "martial stud" and is so connected with his mount that the two together become a "Chiron" centaur. "A brother [the horse] seemed — as strong as he, /As brave in trappings, and with blood / As proud, and equal gravity, /Reserving latent mettle." Djalea and the sheik Ishmael, by contrast, have mares whom Melville depicts as eroticized women. Djalea's Zar has a "full eye of flame / Tempered in softness, which became / Womanly sometimes, in desire / To be caressed." She is described as a "queen" whose devotion to her patriarch at times requires of her great exertion and deprivation. Although she is sociable with other steeds, her erotic devotion is reserved for Djalea, as shown though a decorous love scene in which Zar rests "her lovesome neck" over his shoulder: "Yet lightly, as a swan might do. / An arm Djalea enfolding stretched, / While sighs the sensitive creature fetched, / As e'en that waste to sorrow moved / Instinctive." That Melville was forced to sublimate his sensual interest in Muslim women into equine representation (as well as into

---

[112] Melville, *Moby-Dick*, 6: 129. Melville noted in his *Journal* many examples of Turkish men solemnly smoking in "cheerful resignation" (15: 58, 61, 74, 77, 82, 83).

[113] Melville, *Omoo*, 2: 42.   [114] Melville, *Mardi*, 3: 376.

[115] Melville, *Poems*, 274–6. Melville's identification with Djalea is especially shown by the final verse (VI) of the poem. "Forbear, my soul! and in thine Eastern chamber / Rehearse the dream that brings the long release: / Though jasmine sweet and talismanic amber / inhaling Herba Santa in the passive Pipe of Peace."

[116] Melville, *Clarel*, 3.11.174–6.

the ethereal Jewish maiden Ruth) is a reflection of the fact that the harem, a site for erotic fantasies, remained inaccessible for male Western travelers to the Near East. It is another dimension of the challenges he faced in evoking his Circassian ideal.[117]

The clearest possible translation of the name "Djalea" is perhaps the Arabic word for clarity, and Djalea surely possesses the grounded clarity for which Clarel is seeking. Djalea's influence on Clarel is depicted most clearly through his powerful but tacit tutelage. Coincidentally, it is when Clarel is alone (during his "inner hour") that he has his only solitary encounter with Djalea. The "Emir" does not interrupt the smoking of his long pipe but regards Clarel with an "apprehending" regard. "'Twas a glance / Clarel did many a time recall, / Though its unmeant significance – / That was the last thing learned of all."[118] When Rolfe and Clarel come upon Djalea in the moonlight "on the crag at brink," Rolfe attempts to learn about his religious principles. Content, Djalea assents, but in "mute testimony" of "passive self-control," utters only the enigmatic maxims "No God there is but God . . . Allah preserve ye, Allah great!" At this Rolfe crowns him "Lord Djalea, Prince of Pith."[119]

The real silence that Melville was forced to contend with was the emptiness of his public reputation. By representing an ideal model of how silence could be both manly and wise, Melville's creation of the character of Djalea was a vital act. "There can be no question that Djalea more than any other character in *Clarel* expresses the spiritual ideal toward which Melville himself was striving in his middle years" wrote Walter Bezanson in his 1943 Yale doctoral dissertation that was instrumental in raising *Clarel* out of the oblivion into which it had fallen.[120] Interestingly, Melville's duties as a Customs House Inspector gave him the "authority to use all necessary force to board and inspect a vessel" as well as to "pursue and arrest violators" and "deputize any person within three miles." One could imagine that Melville himself had to demonstrate a similar composure that he had Djalea perform in his parleys.[121] That Melville aspired to Djalea's calm acquiescence is

---

[117] I am grateful to Dorothee Metlitzki for suggesting this meaning of Djalea.

[118] Melville, *Clarel*, 3.34.9–24.

[119] Melville, *Clarel*, 3.16.66–125; 3.17.1–5.

[120] Walter Bezanson, "Herman Melville's *Clarel*" (Ph.D diss., Yale University, 1943), 362. The personal qualities of Djalea have been noted in the small number of critical studies of *Clarel*. Vincent Kenny calls Djalea a "command presence," a representation of the "archetypal Ishmael figure" who accepts the human burden of "loneliness in calamity." Kenny, *Herman Melville's Clarel: A Spiritual Autobiography* (Hamden, CT: The Shoe String Press, 1973), 79, 127, 211, 214–15. Jalaluddien Bakhsh calls Djalea "the ultimate Ishmael" in his dissertation. William Potter finds the Druze to be the fullest incarnation of the theme of the "tempered heart" through which "the soul achieves a devout patience through its experience and endurance of the world's tribulations." Potter, *Melville's Clarel and the Intersympathy of Creeds* (Kent, OH: Kent State University Press, 2004), 97, 94, 113.

[121] Stanton Garner, "Surviving in the Gilded Ages: Herman Melville in the Customs Service," *Essays in Arts and Sciences* 15 (June 1986): 8.

apparent by the preface to *Clarel* where he states: "I here dismiss the book – content beforehand with whatever future awaits it." Only three years after *Clarel* had been published, Melville was forced to authorize the destruction of 224 copies; years later, when one of his few avid admirers admitted not knowing of its existence, he claimed it was "eminently adapted for unpopularity" and used a metaphor of disinterment when sending him a copy.[122] It was only with great reluctance that Melville had been willing to put his name on the cover of *Clarel* at all. It is Djalea's dignified stance of wise self-sufficiency, unruffled by the acclaim of world, to which Melville himself had to become resigned as he wrote *Clarel* in the evenings and weekends after returning home from his job in the Customs House.

Melville's most powerful evocation of Djalea's deeply human blending of mind, heart, and soul is his final portrayal in "The Night Ride," a canto named for the ascent that the Prophet Muhammad made to the seventh heaven while in Jerusalem.

> ...Djalea in face
> Wears an abstraction, lit by grace
> Which governed hopes of rapture lend;
> On coins *his* musings likewise bend –
> The starry sequins woven fair
> into black tresses. But an air
> considerate and prudent reigns;
> For his the love not vainly sure:
> 'Tis passion deep on man mature
> For one who half a child remains:
> Yes, underneath a look sedate,
> What throbs are known!

The word "sedate" is then rhymed by a dangling word in the next line, "But Desolate" used to describe the other pilgrims who are "eclipsed" from Djalea's private vision. This intimate account draws its power from being conducive to multivalent interpretation that blends two facets of passion: earthly love and mystical devotion. Here Djalea has just been paid for his services as guide but, unlike Belex whose coins are but "chink / in pouch of sash," he transfigures their value either into symbols of the stars in the sky or sequins in a woman's dark hair. Melville muses here again after his Circassian vision through Djalea: the "half-child" simultaneously connotes his beloved, a houri in Paradise, and his own youthful spirit. In this passage, Djalea transcends materialism by sublimating the female into a celestial infinitude where passion prefigures the felicity and reward of paradise. The

---

[122] Letter to G. P. Putnam's Sons, 27 March 1879, *Correspondence*, 14: 472; Letters to James Billson, 10 October 1884, 22 January 1885, *Correspondence*, 14: 482, 486.

fact that this rapture immediately precedes Clarel's discovery of the death of Ruth intimates a higher stage of devotion where the most merited union transcends earthly romance in a beatific at-onement. Instead of rejecting his stereotypes of Muslims, Melville transfigures them through Djalea, a man who synthesizes emotion, instinct, and belief in passionate balance while preserving his intellectual world as a private realm of active contemplation.[123]

In creating the character of the guide Djalea, Melville reaffirmed the mystery of the East. He is the mystic whose teachings cannot bear the compression and deceit of words. In the creation of his Druze, Melville transformed his incapacity to penetrate the specific secrets of Islam into a realization that the ultimate knowledge accessible to the human mind is not something that can be rendered in words. It was an act of faith that helped him to endure the obscurity of his own authorial career, and a message powerfully manifest in the empty scroll he chose as the epitaph on his own tombstone.

CELESTIAL SERAGLIOS: THE BLOOMING OF MELVILLE'S
ISLAMICISM

Unlike Djalea, however, Melville refused to submit to silence, and he continued to write to the end of his days. A short unpublished poem represents the liberation that Melville felt at being able to lay aside his daily Customs House duties and resume his own literary passions.

> My jacket old, with narrow seam –
> When the dull day's work is done
> I dust it, and of Asia dream,
> Old Asia of the sun!
> There other garbs prevail;
> Yea, lingering there, free robe and vest,
> Edenic Leisure's age attest
> Ere work, alack, came in with the Wail.[124]

The poem interlaces his sartorial symbolism, evident in the oriental guises he gave to Omoo (as turbaned "Bashaw with Two Tails") and Taji (as robed "Emir"), to dramatize his continued investment in islamicist imagination. The expansion from dust, boredom, and constriction (see Melville's

---

[123] Melville, *Clarel*, 4.29.16–29.

[124] Melville, *Poems*, 426. During his own trip to Europe in 1849, Melville wore a conspicuous green jacket, which elicited a "mysterious hint" and "play[ed] the devel [sic] with my respectability" (Melville, *Journals*, 15: 12, 40). Upon returning to New York, he exultantly donned it to promenade out to the Battery to look at the stars (Melville to Evert A. Duyckinck, 7 March 1850, *Correspondence*, 14: 159).

pun "alack" as "a 'lack'") to free and opulent expansiveness alludes to the symbolic space he was able to create for himself through his authoring of an orientalized paradise, a space where his word was made to counteract both "work" and "Wail." Melville condemned the Fall and its bitter sentence of irredeemable desire, perpetual toil, and earthly death. He explained his contempt for the Protestant work ethic in a letter to his cousin Kate: "Whoever is not in the possession of leisure can hardly be said to possess independence. They talk of the *dignity of work*. Bosh. True Work is the *necessity* of poor humanity's earthly condition. The dignity is in leisure."[125]

With his retirement from the Customs House on the last day of 1885, Melville finally found himself in possession of the leisure he had longed for. Melville realized that even if he had penetrated the illusions of youth, he had to tend its dreaming spirit against the onslaughts of hopelessness. "Grain by grain the Desert drifts / Against the Garden-Land," acknowledged Melville in the final stanza of a three-part poem called "Rosary Beads," advising, "Hedge well thy Roses, heed the stealth / Of ever-creeping Land." Melville used his pen to stave off the desert of despair. By tending his gardens of both real and figurative roses, he acknowledged the psychological necessity of "the Paradise of the Fool" and claimed that "hope [did] frequent share / The mirage when despair / Overtakes the caravan."[126]

Melville's Circassian vision survived the demise of his fictional incarnations in the collections of poetry that he assembled late in life. Melville embodied his vision, not as he had earlier by etherealizing women into untouchable houris, but rather by grounding their beauty in the "simple grace" of natural flowers.[127] Similar to how Djalea saw celestial stars and sequins in the coins in his hand, Melville figured flowers as fleeting visitations of heaven that embodied his Circassian dreams within in the cycles of nature. By conjoining flowers and women in his poetic expression, Melville found a form that attested the lasting viability of his renegade vision, one that sustained a fertile motive for his continuing literary creation and provided the reward for his past labor and his approaching death.

Melville's spiteful condemnation of the expulsion from Eden and the continuing value he bestowed upon heavenly images of women is perhaps clearest in his poem "The Devotion of the Flowers to Their Lady." The "handmaidens" who narrate the poem are the personified voices of flowers from Shushan, the Persian location of the Book of Esther, who long for the

---

[125] Melville to Catherine Gansevoort Lansing, 5 September 1877, *Correspondence*, 14: 464. Ishmael categorically rejects the punishment of work at the beginning of *Moby-Dick* when he criticizes "the universal thump" and retorts that he "abominate[s] all honorable toils, trials and tribulations of every kind whatsoever" (6: 5).

[126] Melville, "Rosary Beads," *Poems*, 336; "A Spirit Appeared to Me," *Poems*, 423; "Pausilippo," *Poems*, 282.

[127] Melville, "A Ground Vine," *Poems*, 335.

pastures of paradise of which they remain the purest trace and surest voucher. "We are natives of Eden –," they sing, "Sharing its memory with you."[128] Importantly, it is woman – the "daughter of far descent" – who remains "blessed in banishment," her Edenic allegiance affirmed and still worthy of devotion. This "secret desire for the garden of God" is also highlighted in Melville's poem "The Lover and the Syringa-Bush," in which the narrator lover is transported to "Eden's gate" where he lingers, "Love's tryst to keep with truant Eve."[129] This desire for a romantic consummation – one that elevated the lover by rendering the beloved's angelic presence accessible in nature – formed the essence of Melville's Circassian longings in his latter days.

His poem "The Rose Farmer" from *Weeds and Wildings* reflects Melville's acknowledgment that after his retirement he had "come into possession of unobstructed leisure" and now "husband(s)" his "vigor" for writing.[130] The poem attests that "down in heart youth never dies" and that he finally possessed the "silent grass-growing mood" he had longed for years before. "The Rose Farmer" relates the story of a bequest by a "corpulent grandee of the East" to the poem's narrator of a rose farm located in a "pleasure-ground" near Damascus, laved by the healing rivers of Abana and Pharpar. The substance of the poem consists of the new farmer's musings about whether he should enjoy the roses in bouquets or distill them into attar (the Arabic word for perfume). Throughout the poem the roses are personified as a harem of virgins whose fate lies in the balance. Advised by a Persian florist and a Parsee perfumist, the narrator eventually sides with the former and argues: "The flower of a subject is enough." The Persian gentleman farmer explains his logic to him in these words that flatter the roses, whom he calls his "angelic sweethearts":

> This evanescence is the charm!
> And most it wins the spirits that be
> Celestial, Sir. It comes to me
> It was this fleeting charm in show
> That lured the sons of God below,
> Tired out with perpetuity
> Of heaven's own seventh heaven aglow;
> Not Eve's fair daughters, sir; nay, nay,
> Less fugitive in charm are they:
> It was the rose.

---

[128] Melville, "The Devotion of the Flowers to Their Lady," *Poems*, 341–2. Shushan or Susa was the ancient capital of Persia. Such orientalization of Eden is also evident in *Timoleon*'s "Syra" where Melville directly links "orient finery" with Eve's sacred hands (*Poems*, 289–90).

[129] Melville, *Poems*, 341, 312.

[130] Melville to Archibald MacMechan, 5 December 1889, *Correspondence*, 14: 519.

"The Rose Farmer" conveys Melville's final reckoning of the limits of his art and the impossibility of recapturing the "fugitive" essence of paradise in prose. Yet, as humble bouquets, the short verse poems of *Weeds and Wildings* also memorialize the continuing intimation of paradise's presence amidst the dumb matter of earth. Having given up his "painstaking throes" to "crystallize the rose" through the alembic of fiction, Melville, through his jocular rose farmer, came into possession of the very paradise he desired. "There *is* nothing like the bloom," Melville would confirm in another unpublished poem that he ironically entitled "The Vial of Attar."[131]

In 1852, Melville had imagined life as "a long Dardenelles" with steep banks preventing the plucking of the beautiful flowers on its shores. By the end of his life, Melville had gathered his flowers in the delicious lands of his islamicist imagination. It was only by manifesting his renegade vision of paradise and female beauty in the evanescent spirit of the earthly flower that Melville was able to reside in a Circassia with "celestial grass that is forever tropical."[132] The humble damask roses, through the medium of the narrator's poetry, blossom into the houris of paradise and become the seraphic sweethearts of his celestial seraglio.

Melville's posthumously published poem "The Continents" confirms his faith in being able to transcend the gulf separating the dualities of earth and heaven, and ultimately life and death. Melville's transfiguring vision of Constantinople in the poem "The Continents" is based on his own enchanted entrance into the city on 12 December 1856. On drawing near, he acknowledged that the Sultan had "a sublime approach . . . to his capital. Antichambers [sic] of seas & lakes, & corridors of glorious straits." Melville describes the "magical effect" of his first glimpse of the city after a day and a half delay because of heavy fog as the "coy disclosure" of a "Sultana . . . veiled in her ashmack."[133] The poem performs a tectonic migration toward Circassia (and ultimately beyond geography) where the Bosphorus separating Europe and Asia evaporates into a new ground that links worldly delight with the solid dignity of death.

> From bright Stamboul Death crosses o'er;
> Beneath the cypress evermore
> His camp he pitches by the shore
> Of Asia old.
> Requiting this unsocial mood

---

[131] Melville, "The Rose Farmer," *Poems*, 343–9; "The Vial of Attar," *Poems*, 337–8. Interestingly, the bequest was granted because the narrator had fixed a "chowder" for the grandee during his Ramadan fast; these references look back to the trusting and playful companionship of Ishmael and Queequeg on Nantucket in "The Ramadan" and "Chowder" chapters of *Moby-Dick* and intimate that Melville's transgressive fictional labor did indeed have its symbolic rewards.

[132] Melville to Nathaniel Hawthorne, June 1851, *Correspondence*, 14: 191.

[133] Melville, *Journals*, 15: 52, 57–8.

Stamboul's inmyrtled multitude
Bless Allah and the sherbert good
And Europe hold.
Even so the cleaving Bosphorus parts
Life and Death. – Dissembling hearts!
Over the gulf the yearning starts
To meet – infold![134]

Melville's yearning to connect earthly pleasure (the myrtle, Europe) with heavenly wisdom (the cypress, Asia) here dissolves the separate continents of life and death (represented by the first two stanzas) into one lasting final embrace, one that forms a promised land freed from both want and misery by manifesting his Circassian geography in the liquid heart of the capital of Turkey.

---

[134] Howard P. Vincent, ed., *Collected Poems of Herman Melville* (Chicago: Packard and Company, Hendricks House, 1947), 409.

Chapter 6

Turning Turk: The Gendered Pageantry of Mid-Nineteenth-Century Islamicism

When John Singleton Copley painted wealthy Boston merchant Nicholas Boylston in 1767, he lavishly arrayed his subject in a blue silk gown and turban that made him appear a Sinbad or sultan rather than a merchant (Fig. 6.1).[1] John Adams had dined at Boylston's "Mansion House" the year before the portrait was painted and found it a "Seat" for a "noble Man, a Prince," replete with Turkish carpets and damask curtains that led him to call it "the most magnificent of any Thing I have ever seen."[2] In pre-revolutionary Boston, just before the heated issues of duties and nonimportation would shake the social order, the conspicuous consumption of Eastern luxuries served as emblems of the social power generated by the global reach of imperial mercantilism. But the oriental assurance of the colonial aristocracy, manifest in Copley's three portraits of Nicholas Boylston (and a similar one of his brother Thomas), would recede during the revolutionary crisis as the homespun austerity of the patriots drove out the glamorous gentility of the Georgian Tories.

Almost eighty years later in 1845, when Chester Harding – the foremost American portrait painter of his generation – painted his masterpiece of the Massachusetts philanthropist Amos Lawrence, he also portrayed him in the guise of an islamicized American nabob (Fig. 6.2). Lawrence had become one of the wealthiest and most generous antebellum Americans after establishing profitable cotton mills in Lowell in 1830, and he embodied the rising promise of American business and the successful emergence of a new mercantile elite. Lawrence's portrait, which Harding replicated three times with slight alterations, portrays him sitting confidently with crossed legs in a chair with his left arm resting on a ledger. Dressed in oriental clothes that

---

[1] Paul Staiti, "Character and Class," in *John Singleton Copley in America*, ed. Carrie Rebora (New York: The Metropolitan Museum of Art, 1995), 54. Phyllis Whitman Hunter, *Purchasing Identity in the Atlantic World: Massachusetts Merchants, 1670–1780* (Ithaca, NY: Cornell University Press, 2001), 148–53; Carol Troyen, "A Choice Gallery of Harvard Tories: John Singleton Copley's Portaits Memorialize a Vanishing Way of Life," *Harvard Magazine* (March–April 1997). Three versions of the painting were commissioned of Copley. Minor style, design, and color changes in the clothes and setting of the second version made it "more sombre and pensive. The sense of serenity and well-being has been drained from the image, just as confidence and complacency were evaporating from the painter and his society." Theodore E. Stebbins, Jr., "An American Despite Himself," *Copley in America*, 96.

[2] Lyman H. Butterfield, ed., *Diary and Autobiography of John Adams*, 4 vols. (Cambridge, MA: Belkap Press of Harvard University Press, 1961), 1: 294.

FIGURE 6.1. John Singleton Copley, *Nicholas Boylston 1716–1771* (1767). Courtesy of the Harvard University Portrait Collection. Bequest of Ward Nicholas Boylston to Harvard College, 1828.

exude an atmosphere of leisurely repose, Lawrence wears a paisley housecoat with tasseled sash, sequined slippers, and a soft velour fez on his head. The rich damask drapes and maroon tablecloth frame the red patterns in his gown and headdress, creating an image of glamorous accomplishment and assurance.

FIGURE 6.2. Chester Harding, *Amos Lawrence* (c. 1845). Given in memory of the Rt. Rev. William Lawrence by his children. © 2005 Board of Trustees, National Gallery of Art, Washington, D.C.

In the years between the portraits by Copley and Harding, American islamicism had served most fully as an oppositional resource for world-ing the political and religious aspirations of the nation and for infidelizing such suspect domestic practices as slave-holding, drunkenness, and religious innovation. By the 1840s, however, more Americans were willing to identify with islamicism's cultural repertoire to express more worldly social positions, especially in the performance of gender roles. Partly as a result of the con-comitant decline of the Ottoman Empire with the rise of the economic and cultural strength of the United States, the predominant valences of Ameri-can islamicism were shifting away from an oppositional repulsion and more toward the celebration of a romantic liberty that signified the emergent power of the nation and its citizens as global players. A dramatic exam-ple was the impresario P. T. Barnum's choice for a design for his mansion in Bridgeport, Connecticut: an airy and domed Mughal palace based upon the Brighton Pavilion in England. Completed in 1848 (and destroyed by fire nine years later), Iranistan evoked such a sultanic presence that the Swedish diva Jenny Lind is said to have trusted Barnum's invitation to come sing in the United States based solely on its nobility.[3]

The most striking examples of this shifting process were perhaps the material manifestations of domestic islamicism in popular mid-nineteenth-century American art and dress. The islamicist markers that characterized Herman Melville's literature and Chester Harding's portrait became more popular as a result of new capacities for cultural dissemination made possible by the same market revolution that had generated Amos Lawrence's wealth. The vogue of the American "howadji" – or traveler – in the Islamic ori-ent (of whom Melville was one of the most thoughtful members), reveals a deeper romance with oriental masculinity that developed among secular artists who associated the East less with the darkness of despotic antichristian-ity and more with outlandish models of male liberty and power. The cultural resumption of the orientalist privileges of patriarchy provided new critical perspectives embodied in the most famous artwork of the period, Hiram Power's nude statue called *The Greek Slave* (1847). An inspection of this white marble figure through the interpretive lens of islamicism summarizes many of the cultural dynamics that have been raised in this book. The global framework of islamicism also enables broader transnational understandings of two trendy innovations in midcentury American clothing. Analyzing the fad of the bloomer costume assumed by female reformers in 1851–2 and the colorful Zouave uniforms adopted by dozens of Civil War regiments between 1861 and 1865 reveals the vibrant role of islamicism in the expres-sive field of dress. This material dissemination of islamicist imagery within fashionable expressions of gender dramatizes the new valences made possible

[3] John Sweetman, *The Oriental Obsession: Islamic Inspiration in British and American Art and Architecture, 1500–1920* (Cambridge: Cambridge University Press, 1988), 219–20.

IRANISTAN.

FIGURE 6.3. In 1848, P. T. Barnum moved into the "oriental villa" Iranistan in Bridgeport, Connecticut, that he built from a model of the Brighton Pavilion in England. Later versions of his autobiography included a different image of Iranistan from the front with a stately horse and carriage in the foreground instead of the deer. *The Life of P. T. Barnum* (New York: Redfield, 1855), 402.

by shifting geopolitical situations and modes of cultural production. As the nineteenth century progressed, the charge of islamicism became less associated with the contentious threat of Islamic difference and more aligned with the exciting allure of commercial enterprise and burlesque performance. While some Americans still viewed the Islamic world as an alien realm of negative excess, others found in its attractive alterity a fresh cultural resource for the promotion of their own cosmopolitan power.

AMERICAN HOWADJIS AND THE EASTERN PILGRIMAGE

The combination of the rising fortunes of the U.S. market economy and the degradation of Turkish power encouraged domestic businessmen like Amos Lawrence to adopt oriental garb to express their worldliness. These developments also empowered greater numbers of Americans to travel on cultural pilgrimages to the Muslim eastern Mediterranean, especially after the area was opened for increased travel following Greek independence in 1830. Aided by advancements of new aids to tourism, more Americans visited the Levant where they hired the services of locals to provide for their comfort, especially the dragomen (translators) who, more like the Arnaut in

Melville's *Clarel* than Djalea, were often figured as gallant barbarians. Their command over the guides and guards they hired, many of whom were Arab Bedouins that some compared with native Americans on the western frontier, demonstrated how travel on the eastern frontier offered an alternative global stage for performing romantic power, one based upon an aristocratic fantasy of independent leisure. A popular term in the antebellum period for such travelers was the word "howadji," a version of the Arabic word signifying a traveler or merchant that also connoted the hajji or pilgrim to Mecca. By transforming themselves from foreign tourists into turbaned howadjis with authority over a retinue of Arab servants, Americans dramatized the fantasy of redeeming the despotic patriarch and redistributing his power as a democratic resource for upholding domestic male authority. With such resources at his command, the howadji was set to experience and appropriate such Eastern pleasures as dressing in loose oriental garb, smoking Turkish pipes, visiting public baths and slave markets, touring ruins from biblical times, and tenting with Bedouins and camels. One fertile source of imagery for Melville's rhapsodic islamicism was the many Near Eastern travel narratives that figured Americans and Europeans establishing their international credentials by assuming the privileges of oriental authority. By the time of the Civil War, over sixty travel narratives and collections of letters from a broad assortment of pilgrims had been published and offered to the public by the best editors in the country, works penned by missionaries, naval officers, vacationing professionals, and bachelor adventurers.

John Lloyd Stephens helped to establish the popularity of the genre of the Near Eastern travel narrative in 1837 with his *Incidents of Travel in Egypt, Arabia Petraea, and the Holy Land*, a book released by Harpers of New York and frequently republished over the next thirty-five years. Edgar Allan Poe wrote a glowing review of the book and Melville mentioned in *Redburn* that his first journey to Liverpool in 1839 was inspired by the adventures of Stephens, whom he called the "wonderful Arabian traveler."[4] Stephens embarked for the East with "poetical associations" of its fabled beauty and traveled through Sinai from Egypt to Jerusalem in the aliases of a Cairo merchant named Jacob-Al-Khawaja and Abdel Hasis (meaning beloved slave). "I played the Turk well...," he confessed, "There is no exaggeration in the unanimous reports of travelers of the effect which the costumes of the East give to personal appearance."[5] He describes his "unpretending and respectable costume" as comprising "a long red silk gown, with a black abbas of camel's hair over it; red tarboosh, with a green-and-yellow-striped handkerchief rolled around it as a turban; white trousers, large red shoes over yellow slippers, blue sash, sword, and a pair of large Turkish pistols."

4 Herman Melville, *Redburn* (Evanston, IL: Northwestern University Press; Chicago, IL: Newberry Library, 1969), 6.
5 John Lloyd Stephens, *Incidents of Travel in Egypt, Arabia Petraea, and the Holy Land*, ed. Victor Wolfgang von Hagen (Norman: University of Oklahoma Press, 1970), 236, 255.

Stephens testifies in a refrain whose tenor was often repeated in later narratives that his episode of oriental travel provided him with "the freedom from all restraint, and from the conventional trammels of civilized society" that he found "vastly agreeable and exciting."[6] The sense of liberation in Stephens's narrative (as well as its commercial success) was contagious and contributed to a succession of antebellum narratives of Eastern travel. Already by 1843, Wesleyan University president Stephen Olin referred to the "burdened market" for accounts of travel to the Near East but, nevertheless, viewed the "profound and general interest" with which they had been received as an "omen" for his own *Travels*.[7]

The success of Near Eastern travel narratives demonstrated to Americans that the Holy Land had more adventure to offer than its millennial role in religious redemption. Unlike Protestant missionaries like James Lyman Merrick and Horatio Southgate, male American howadjis were more inclined to adopt elements of West Asian cultures as markers of their male privilege rather than their desire to view Muslim society as a corruption to be removed. Their books helped to attract during the 1850s a steady supply of travelers that included a new breed of audacious American travel-writer, such as George William Curtis and Bayard Taylor, who added the eastern Mediterranean to their other explorations as a means of achieving a more cosmopolitan American identity. In 1851-2, George William Curtis wrote the frequently reprinted volumes *Nile Notes of a Howadji* and *The Howadji in Syria* that celebrated the eastern Mediterranean as a magical dream of Arabian Nights' mystery. Curtis relished his traveling persona as a "great American moghul" and promised to disclose the secrets of the romantic Orient to his readers. Referring both to the landscape and to his text, Curtis exclaims: "Here you shall be thrilled with that sense of lofty and primeval freedom which shall throb ever after through the limited life that we must live." The primitive sympathy that Curtis felt with the Orient even led him to dream momentarily that he had lost his birthright and become "Ishmael's brother."[8]

Another famous howadji to invest himself with an islamicized masculinity was the popular traveler and lecturer Bayard Taylor, author of *Poems of the Orient* (1854) and *The Lands of the Saracen; or, Pictures of Palestine, Asia Minor, Sicily, and Spain (1855).*[9] Taylor confessed that "pious writers have described what was expected of them, not what they found" and supplied his readers

---

[6] Stephens, *Incidents*, 146, 135, and see illustration on page 225.

[7] Stephen Olin, *Travels in Egypt, Arabia Petraea, and the Holy Land*, 2 vols. (New York: Harper & Brothers, 1843), 1: vvii.

[8] George William Curtis, *The Howadji in Syria* (New York: Harpers, 1852), 58, 62; see also *Nile Notes of a Howadji* (New York: Harpers, 1851).

[9] Bayard Taylor, *The Lands, of the Saracen; or, Pictures of Palestine, Asia Minor, Sicily, and Spain* (New York: G. P. Putnam & Co., 1855; reprinted in 1856, 1857, 1859, 1860, 1862, 1863, 1867, 1879, 1881, 1886); Taylor, *Poems of the Orient* (Boston: Ticknor and Fields, 1854).

FIGURE 6.4. Thomas Hicks, *Bayard Taylor* 1823–1890 (1855). National Portrait Gallery, Smithsonian Institution.

with new visions of the East, including an intense account of his experiences with hasheesh (which helped him to explain the supernatural imagination of the Arabian Nights). Like Stephens and Curtis, Taylor gloried in his adoption of Eastern clothing and the strange freedom it symbolized, finding "both dignity and poetry in the inertia of Oriental life."[10] He wrote from Egypt to his famous Boston editor James Ticknor Fields of the way that his islamicist transformation empowered him to transgress conventional confinements of race, religion, and gender. "If you think of me now, picture me to yourself as brown as an Arab, with a long beard, a red cap and white turban, a big shawl around my waist, and red slippers on my feet. I have quite a smattering of Arabic, and can swear by Allah with the true Moslem unction." Taylor noted in his book that "[in] painting the picture of an Oriental, the pipe and coffee-cup are indispensable accessories."[11] The artist Thomas Hicks's

[10] Taylor, *Lands*, 85; "Bayard Taylor to George H. Boker from Constantinople 7/18/1852," in *Life and Letters of Bayard Taylor*, 2 vols., eds. Maire Hansen-Taylor and Horace E. Scudder (Cambridge: The Riverside Press, 1884), 1: 236.

[11] Taylor, *Lands*, 128; "Bayard Taylor to George T. Fields from Alexandria 4/12/1852," *Life and Letters*, 1: 229.

painting of Taylor (exhibited at the National Academy of Design in 1856 and now in the National Gallery) portrays a turbaned and cross-legged howadji luxuriating with water pipe on a Damascus morning after being served by his Arab dragoman Achmet (Fig. 6.4). Taylor reinhabited his islamicist persona by donning his oriental clothes once again when lecturing on his travels on the lyceum circuit.

The attraction of the Islamic East to howadjis extended beyond exotic images of oriental opulence and chivalry – the spirit of the Arabian Nights and Saladin – to the promise of encountering the embodiments of female beauty that had inspired Melville's literary quests. The vitality of mid-nineteenth-century American figuration of Islam was heavily charged, as it had been during the earlier years of the nation, with powerful evocations of women and the symbolic status of their condition. As shown by the controversy raised by the issue of Mormon polygamy during this time, some Americans were appalled by images of the seraglio as an enigmatic space of sexual exploitation, while others could be perversely enticed by such models of vigorous male power and orientalized female bodies. While the harem provided a symbolic space that served as a locus for the regulation of excessive male authority in the early republic, it also laid out an imaginary latitude that enabled others to break free from some of the repressive pressures inherent in the ideologies of antebellum sentimental domesticity (Fig. 6.5).

Early republican fiction had imagined women revolutionizing the seraglio in ways that both glamorized and universalized the exercise of moral virtue. When male American howadjis made their way to the eastern Mediterranean, one of the sights they desired most to see was the physical manifestation of their visions of female loveliness. The male cultural fantasy of the harem as an abode of female beauty, what sailor E. C. Wines called "that Ultima Thule of European curiosity," was accentuated by the weeks of sojourning by sea to arrive in the eastern Mediterranean and the prospect of many more away from their countrywomen.[12] When John Lloyd Stephens spied a Circassian beauty with a "brilliant complexion" on the balcony across from him one morning in Cairo, he was "ready to break a lance with a Turk to rob him of his wife."[13] The indefatigable George William Curtis declared that "Eastern women dare, what the western do not dream" and found his houri in an Armenian girl named Khadra who gave him flowers and sherbet, forcing him to confess that "the Eastern Beauty is another

---

[12] E. C. Wines, *Two Years and a Half in the Navy, or Journal of the Cruise in the Mediterranean and the Levant on Board the U.S. Frigate* Constellation, *in the Years 1829, 1830, and 1831*, 2 vols. (Philadelphia: Carey and Lea, 1832), 1: 205.

[13] Stephens, *Incidents*, 96–7. His intrusive indelicacy was more evident when he actually purchased the scanty clothes of a young Nubian girl claiming that they would "make a decided sensation at a masquerade or fancy ball," revealing in the process a female nakedness that he claimed would be a "burning shame to put . . . into frock, petticoat, and the other et ceteras of a lady's dress" (158).

FIGURE 6.5. Advertisement card for the Boston-built clipper ship *Akbar*. Courtesy, American Antiquarian Society.

glory than the pale sweetness of your Blonde." In one of his most popular poems, Bayard Taylor embodied this desire by assuming the persona of a Bedouin wooing his secluded beloved: "And my kisses shall teach thy lips / The love that shall fade no more."[14]

When howadjis found themselves debarred from access to the females of the harem, most sought a substitute by magnifying the brief glimpses they gained of women into an uncivil type of voyeurism, which led either to further fantasy or, more often, to frustration. One of the experiences of comparative orientalism was the lesson that cultural constructions of oriental female beauty were Western ideals that could not be matched by experiences in the East. To the very end of his narrative, Stephens seeks for an attractive female only to discover "one of the most annoying circumstances attendant upon traveling in the East that, in spite of the poetical accounts of Eastern beauty, though I had seen Georgian and Circassian women, I had never yet met with anything that to my mind was equal to the beauty of the European and American women."[15] Upon approaching "Stamboul" (Constantinople), popular traveler J. Ross Browne expressed his sublime anticipation that his visit might "lift the soul above this earth to a realm of houris," only to discover that its fabled harems concealed lives of "absolute servitude and disgusting sensuality." Likewise, Dr. Valentine Mott arrived in the East captivated by a vision of "beautiful, fair Circassians" from "the cradle of female loveliness" but was dismayed by his encounter with covered Turkish women whom he called "wretched and misshapen hills of flesh."[16] Claims were made that fleeting glimpses between male American visitors and Muslim women confirmed their expectations, but the failure of any deep encounter more often confounded their ideals of Circassian purity. Disappointed, these travelers either discounted its romance or projected it upon more accessible ethnic examples, such as Curtis with Khadra the Armenian and Melville with his idealized Jewish maiden Ruth (and the mare Zar). In fact, the prominence of Orthodox Christian and Jewish maidens in Western representations of oriental women was a function not only of biblical, classical, and racial conditioning but also a result of the Muslim practice of secluding women from strangers' eyes, a situation that amplified the exotic elusiveness of Islamic females and forced curious Westerners to evoke more available alternatives.

---

[14] Curtis, *Howadji in Syria*, 209–19. "Bedouin Song," *The Poetical Writings of Bayard Taylor* (Cambridge: the Riverside Press, 1907), 69.

[15] Stephens, *Incidents*, 445; Stephens confessed that "it is sheer affectation or ignorance, in which a member of the civilized family sighs, or pretends to sigh, for the imagined delights of an untried freedom" (216).

[16] J. Ross Browne, *Yusef, or the Journey of the Frangi: A Crusade in the East* (New York: Harper, 1853), 141, 145; Valentine Mott, *Travels in Europe and the East* (New York: Harper & Brothers, 1842), 404, 420–1.

THE GREEK SLAVE AND THE TURKISH GAZE

One distinct way that Americans back home negotiated the gulf between romantic embodiments of oriental beauty and their comparative absence in experiential encounters was to elevate the anachronistic image of the female Greek slave and perpetuate her power as a charged cultural symbol. The complexities of antebellum American islamicism are fully exemplified by a study of the most renowned work of American art during the middle of the nineteenth century – a statue of a Greek woman held in captivity by the Turks that circulated through American society during the same years as Melville's early fiction of the sea. First conceived in Italy by Vermont sculptor Hiram Powers in 1841 (a sixth full-length version was completed twenty-five years later), *The Greek Slave* was the first American representation of female nudity to gain the wide acceptance of domestic audiences and the acclaim of European critics (Fig. 6.6).[17] Never solely a museum piece, the popularity of *The Greek Slave* was premised on its multiplication and propagation deep within a variety of domestic landscapes to the degree that it became established as a recognizable cultural icon. Its successful publicity thus signifies how advances in domestic transportation, urban development, commercial entrepreneurship, and visual reproduction fostered the expansion of popular cultural expression in the years before the Civil War. Between 1847 and 1850, two of Powers's six full-length originals toured over a dozen cities in the nation as far west as Saint Louis and as far south as New Orleans and drew over 100,000 paying viewers. Its attraction led to the fabrication of thousands of porcelain miniatures and visual representations that distributed the nude female throughout a broad spectrum of public and private venues. (Half a century after the statue's creation, Henry James reminisced about his own youthful exposure to the naked slave's "sugar-white alabaster, exposed under little domed glass covers in such American homes as could bring themselves to think such things right."[18]) Such visual saturation in turn generated a slew of printed commentary and poetry that

---

[17] The best analyses of Powers's "Greek Slave" are Joy S. Kasson, "Narratives of the Female Body: The Greek Slave," in *Marble Queens and Captives: Women in Nineteenth-Century American Sculpture* (New Haven, CT: Yale University Press, 1990), 46–72 (also in Shirley Samuels, ed., *The Culture of Sentiment: Race, Gender, and Sentimentality in Nineteenth-Century America* (New York: Oxford University Press, 1992), 172–90); Jean Fagan Yellin, *Women & Sisters: The Antislavery Feminists in American Culture* (New Haven, CT: Yale University Press, 1989), 99–124; Richard P. Wunder, *Hiram Powers: Vermont Sculptor, 1805–1873*, 2 vols. (Cranbury, NJ: Associated University Presses, 1991), 1: 207–74; Vivien M. Green, "Hiram Powers's Greek Slave: Emblem of Freedom," *The American Art Journal* 14 (1982): 31–9; Linda Hyman, "The Greek Slave by Hiram Powers: High Art as Popular Culture," *Art Journal* 35 (1976): 216–23; Samuel A. Roberson and William H. Gerdts, "The Greek Slave," *The Museum* (Newark, NJ) 17 (1965): 1–32; Nancie Clow Farrell, "The Slave That Captivated America," *Cincinnati Historical Society Bulletin* 22 (1964): 221–39.

[18] Henry James, ed., *William Wetmore Story and His Friends*, 2 vols. (Boston: Houghton, Mifflin & Co., 1903), 1: 114.

furthered the transformation of *The Greek Slave* from a dumb captive in static stone into a dynamic symbolic expression through which antebellum audiences negotiated their anxieties about female sexuality, male power, racial identity, and religious purity. An examination of its phenomenal success reveals new insights into the changing cultural work of islamicism in the mid-nineteenth-century United States as its romantic valences reemerged within gendered cultural expression.

Powers's success in rendering a nude woman morally acceptable to antebellum audiences depended upon his temporal and spatial displacement of female slavery and nudity into the Mediterranean context of the struggle between the Cross and the Crescent. Nineteenth-century news reports and fictional accounts frequently broadcasted the horrid fate of Greek maidens abducted from the shores and islands of the Aegean during the Greek War of Independence during the 1820s. To cite but one, "The Sciote Captive," published in the *Southern Literary Messenger* in 1844, portrays a "flower of the Levant," endowed with violet-blue eyes and "transparent purity of complexion," who is humiliated by public exposure and "mangled by the touch of the demon Turk."[19] The symbolic icon of *The Greek Slave* offered its viewers a vicarious opportunity to accomplish many of the cultural desires registered through the rhetorical strategies of islamicism. By monumentalizing the slave's innocence prior to her ravishment, Powers directly challenged the moral intentions of the viewer by leaving her ultimate fate to an act of interpretation. Preserving *The Greek Slave* thus gave its viewers a means of containing the challenge of oriental libidinousness by redeeming it through the sentimentalism of virtuous indignation. Her sympathetic observers could accomplish through their act of private viewing the broader goals of deposing the despot, freeing the white slave, converting the Eastern woman to Protestantism, and contemplating the ideal of oriental beauty. While Christian audiences often suspected the mythological forms of classical sculpture because they were the products of pagan Greece and Rome, Powers depicted the calm chastity of her religious resignation in ways that redeemed her transgressive nakedness without sacrificing her aesthetic nobility. Many of the published responses of those who paid to witness *The Greek Slave* reveal the great lengths to which they went to celebrate her spiritual fortitude and establish her as an emblem of virtue. Since islamicist dispositions held that "Mohammedans have ever regarded woman as a slave," such a projective imagination enabled Protestant viewers both to endow her with a soul and to fantasize her liberation.[20] Exiled from her old world idolatry – where even the sympathetic markers of the dress, locket, and cross are left behind

---

[19] [Nasus], "The Sciote Captive," *The Southern Literary Messenger* 19 (October and November 1844): 592–9, 652–61.

[20] Linus P. Bruckett, *Woman: Her Rights, Wrongs, Privileges, and Responsibilities* (Hartford, CT: L. Stebbins, 1870), 45.

FIGURE 6.6. Hiram Powers, *The Greek Slave* (1847). The Collection of The Newark Museum. Gift of Franklin Murphy, Jr., 1926.

on the post as Greek trappings symbolically aligned with the Turkish chains binding her hands – she steps forward and looks away, standing not as a slave but as an embodiment of liberty. Proper viewing thus converted the Slave from Turkish degradation to Christian nobility as well as from Byzantine idolatry to Protestant sentiment, an act that transmuted her nakedness into a symbol of sublime saintliness. The transcendent power of this sentimental liberation of the Slave was only augmented by the fact that the struggle for Greek independence from Turkish rule had been historically successful by the time of the statue's creation and circulation.

The fact that the sentimental conversion that clothed the Slave remained a fantasy in the eye of the beholder raises important questions about islamicism in the performance of mid-nineteenth-century American gender roles. The sublimity of the Slave's purity never escaped from the dialectical threat of her material form, her nakedness, and her imminent desecration – a situation that forced the onlooker to confront the implications of infidelity to the very virtue that the statue ostensibly upheld.[21] The fact that all viewers were initially placed in the vantage point of Turkish customers acknowledged the fact that the popular circulation of the statue effectively recapitulated her enslavement, a phenomenon that transformed her eager viewers into potential infidels and, far from liberating her, actually proliferated her symbolic commodification. Indeed, the commercial career of Powers's statue relocated *The Greek Slave* from a Turkish slave market to a succession of American galleries, rotundas, and parlors where she was displayed as a symbolic concubine of Western audiences who paid for the fashionable privilege of witnessing the dilemma of her possible degradation. The continuing reality of her vulnerable nakedness invited more promiscuous readings, which was one of the reasons why some clamored for separate viewing times for the two sexes. That her attractions were not always moral ones is evident by the many female model artists who successfully drew audiences by exhibiting themselves naked for money in the pose of *The Greek Slave* and other nude statues.[22]

To be sure, viewers publicly responded to their ironic identification with Turkish captors by resonantly resisting the immorality of this perspective. Yet in so doing, they were actively forced to entertain and subdue the temptations of what one poet called "sensuous vision."[23] "The Turk rolls before you his merciless tide of desolation" announced the *New York Statesman*, while another account completed her ignominy by imagining that "the iron grasp of the master is upon her ... [and] his heart is hot with lust."[24]

---

[21] "Popular Orientalism allowed Western observers to flirt with their own sensuality, still keeping it at arm's length as 'foreign' or 'exotic,'" noted Joy Kasson, who argued that "viewing is as much an act of appropriation as owning" and that the device of Turkish viewer "enabled audiences to participate in the gaze of sensuality and to distance themselves from it simultaneously." Kasson, *Marble Queens*, 54–5, 66.

[22] Wunder, *Hiram Powers*, 1: 233.

[23] Augustine Joseph Hickey Duganne, "Ode to Powers' Greek Slave," in *Duganne's Poetical Works* (Philadelphia, 1865), 320–1.

[24] *New York Statesman* (15 September 1848); *New York Express* (n.d.), both quoted in Green, "Powers's Greek Slave," 36.

One poetic rendition of *The Greek Slave* placed her beneath a minaret in Contantinople "exposed to the unhallowed gaze / And the rude jests of ev'ry passer by." Another female observer claimed that during her five-hour trance before the white marble statue she felt the freezing of the slave's blood "beneath the libidinous gaze of shameless traffickers in beauty."[25] While the tragic situation of the slave – coupled with a crystalline purity that effaced all orifices – may have elicited redemptive thoughts of her noble resignation, it was difficult to erase the sexual undertones inherent in a scenario that openly suggested that her pristine beauty was on the verge of being sacrificed to sensual appetite. Even though such a fate was interpreted in conventional discourse as a horrible and immoral degradation, it could also stimulate sexual fantasies of unbounded gendered desire.

The Greek Slave was attractive to more salacious male viewers because she embodied their desire to reappropriate an unnaturally white and beautiful femininity from its servitude to the tawny and transgressive Turk and relocate her anew under their own patriarchal authority. The political situation and aesthetic form of *The Greek Slave* ironically licensed their fantasies by displacing the transgression of such desires onto Turkish infidels acting in a distant land in a past time. Women's responses to the public display of the naked Greek slave covered a gamut that ranged from a smug satisfaction that they did not share her fate to pronounced transactive sympathy for her spiritual fortitude, but they also encompassed the transgressive imagination of female desire. Marianne Noble's provocative observation is relevant here: "The eroticism of sentimental suffering was a double-edged sword, functioning both as a discursive agent for the proliferation of oppressive ideologies and as a rhetorical tool for the exploration of female desire."[26] While *The Greek Slave* countenanced a means of fantasizing the political and religious conversion of oriental corruption for some men and women, for others it sanctioned the public opportunity to turn Turk and imagine sensual encounters ruled illicit in other forms of public expression. The popularity of *The Greek Slave* demonstrated how the Orient provided not only a model of female beauty but also a transnational field in whose latitudes a variety of sensual fantasies and anxieties could be expressed, displaced, and/or sublimated.

This fundamental irrevocability of the Turkish gaze was an essential element of the gendered and racialized cultural codes that Powers's Slave communicated to her audiences. It was also integral to the sculptor's initial attraction to his subject, for in his plans Powers imagined that that statue

---

[25] "The Greek Slave of Powers," *Southern Literary Messenger* 13 (November 1847): 645; Anna Lewis, "Art and Artists of America: Hiram Powers," *Graham's Magazine* 10 (November 1855), quoted in Hyman, "The Greek Slave," 221; and Kasson, *Marble Queens*, 63.

[26] Marianne Noble, *The Masochistic Pleasure of Sentimental Literature* (Princeton, NJ: Princeton University Press, 2000), 6.

would "relate to the practice of the Turks who often exposed their female prisoners naked for sale."[27] Later, Powers described her situation as being "among barbarian strangers" and "exposed to the gaze of the people she abhors."[28] Indeed, Powers's very act of sculpting the statue – of multiply reconfiguring her body in situations of perpetual captivity to the stone his hand knew so intimately – placed him in the promiscuous position of ultimate patriarchal privilege in which she was at once his creation and a possession to be sold. This Turkish perspective was buttressed by the ways it was presented throughout its tour in settings with oriental carpets and luxurious drapery and with other works portraying situations of oriental captivity.[29]

As a material expression of antislavery sentiments, *The Greek Slave* served as a means for projecting the issue of slavery into aesthetic and islamicist registers at a time when its domestic political import was incendiary. One might expect that the popular display of a preternaturally white slave would provoke reflection in a society whose enslavement of Africans was an issue that would soon rend the country, as the white males slaves in North Africa had done in the early years of the Republic. Certainly this was true for some African American commentators on the Slave, as shown by this ripping attack in *The North Star*, the newspaper edited by Frederick Douglass.

> Oh! how heart and brain burn with the hatred of the cruel TURK who does thus violate the sacred rights of human nature; and place his OWN diabolical SELF between GOD and his creature. And to the feeling heart and discerning eye, *all slave girls* are GREEK, and *all slave mungers* [sic] TURKS, wicked cruel and hateful; be their names HASSAM, SELIM, JAMES, JUDAS or HENRY; their country Algiers or Alabama, Congo or Carolina, the same.[30]

The Greek Slave's power as a site of repressive sublimation, however, is demonstrated more fully by how little commentary made this link explicit. Even contemporaries who admitted the connection also noted that "There were fair breasts that heaved with genuine sympathy beneath the magical power of the great artist, that never yet breathed a sigh for their sable sisters at the South!"[31] One powerful exception was an article that expressed the imagined soliloquy of a slave-holder viewing her exhibition in St. Louis soon after the passage of the Fugitive Slave Law. This spectator is initially outraged by the global traffic in white females and is gratified that such a practice does not exist in the United States. But in the midst of his contemplation of how Christianity might effect "the complete emancipation of all the white

---

[27] Quoted in Farrell, "The Slave That Captivated America," 224.

[28] Charles Edward Lester, ed., The *Artist, The Merchant, and The Statesman, or The Age of the Medici, and of Our Own Times*, 2 vols. (New York: Paine & Burgess, 1845), 1: 86–7.

[29] Wunder, *Hiram Powers*, 1: 217.   [30] S. F., "The Greek Slave," *The North Star* (3 October 1850).

[31] *The National Era* (September 1847), quoted in Yellin, *Women & Sisters*, 109.

people of the earth," he becomes disturbed by the intrusion of "black and thick-lipped images." At that moment, the slave comes alive and turns on her pedestal to rebuke his conscience: "Why limit your sympathies?" she asks. "Away henceforth, with your sophistries of the multiplied origins of the human races. . . . Cease your sympathy for a slave in Constantinople, and go show kindness and justice to those over whom you have power" – individuals that she refers to as "my sisters of another hue in the land throughout I am making my pilgrimage."[32]

Although granted a certain power to influence, this expanse of the Slave's agency was for the most part gagged by conventions of female silence, purity, and resignation rather than the bold and verbal assertion of independent prerogative. Part of the iconic power of *The Greek Slave* drew upon a tradition of classical, biblical, and historical narratives that celebrated the fortitude of captive oriental women. These models ranged broadly including the popular biblical stories of the Hebrew women Esther and Jepthah's daughter, the Quaker evangelist Mary Fisher, and the fictional women in Barbary narratives, most of whom, despite their vulnerable dependence on male despots, were able to exercise power as conservative models of moral leadership. By rendering his Slave into an ethnic Greek, Powers was successfully able to draw upon this long tradition – one that included captive Greek women, such as Helen of Troy, Iphigenia, and Irene – as well as borrow from the cultural philhellenism derived from classical education and situate this heritage within the contemporary struggle between the Crescent and the Cross.

The anachronistic domestic "pilgrimage" of *The Greek Slave* twenty years after the events associated with her capture sacrificed much of her agency by making her condition of captivity permanent, ironically preserving rather than converting the power of the Turkish gaze. By the time the statue was displayed in mid-century United States and Europe, Greek women were rarely sold in Turkey because contemporary Greece had been reabsorbed into the cartography of the West (continuing a process that would eventually lead to the disappearance of the Near East as a spatial category when Turkey and then Israel entered the western "orbit" in the twentieth century). The chains fettering the Slave's hands were never an established practice in Turkish slave markets; they function instead in the service of chastity by blocking her genitalia from onlookers.[33] The Slave was also located in a historical climate of Turkish slavery that many Americans had come to view as comparatively more benign than the racial bondage in the southern United States. During the very years that *The Greek Slave* was being transported through the states, the Bey of Tunis and the Sultan of Turkey made public proclamations outlawing the slave trade and its manifestation in urban slave markets (see Chapter 3). The spectacle of *The Greek Slave* therefore both

---

[32] "Powers' Greek Slave in St. Louis," *The National Era* (16 January 1851).

[33] Yellin, *Women & Sisters*, 122.

domesticated and universalized the Islamic slave market at the very moment when antislavery advocates were troubled by how its imminent removal challenged the speed of American abolitionism. This connection was made in a review of *The Greek Slave* that relates "the humiliating fact that while the accursed system from which it springs has well nigh ceased in Mahomedan countries, it still taints a portion of our Christian soil, and is at this very moment clamoring that it may pollute even more."[34] Indeed, paying admission to witness *The Greek Slave* most clearly domesticated the exotic – and now diminishing – visits that Western travelers had routinely made to the slave markets in Muslim lands, often in lieu of the seraglios from which they had been barred access. Broadcast back to the nation through the popular literary genre of the Near Eastern travel narrative, these encounters featured the narrator's responses to the public display of multiracial women in various stages of *dishabille*. When travelers did gain access to women in the slave markets of Turkey, the slaves that most attracted their curiosity were Muslim women from the Caucasian lands of Circassia and Georgia. The conventional narrative of these visits, during which travelers often gravitated to inspection of one female slave of fairer complexion, closely resembled the instruction in virtuous indignation with which audiences were implored to view *The Greek Slave*.[35]

What was most conspicuous about the phenomenal success of *The Greek Slave*, therefore, is not the way she furthered the agenda of the abolitionist movement but rather how she projected criticism away from domestic politics onto an alien Ottoman geography. Sympathy for the victims of slavery was transferred from black slaves within the nation to a foreign white female beauty epitomized by the Circassian Caucasian. In this way, islamicism sublimated the cultural energies of abolitionism into a more exotic desire for chivalrous rescue and romantic liberation that greatly

---

[34] *Eastport Sentinel* (23 August 1848), quoted in Green, "Powers's Greek Slave," 38.

[35] Accounts of visits to the slave market were a common feature of Near Eastern travel narratives. See, for example, Walter Colton, *Ship and Shore; or Leaves from the Journal of a Cruise to the Levant* (New York: Leavitt, Lord, & Co., 1835), 78–82; James De Kay, *Sketches in Turkey in 1831 and 1832* (New York: J. & J. Harper, 1833), 276–81; John P. Durbin, *Observations in the East*, 2 vols. (New York: Harper and Brothers, 1845), 1: 9–10; George Jones, *Excursions to Cairo, Jerusalem, Damascus, and Balbec* (New York: Van Nostrand and Dwight, 1836), 74; Stephen C. Massett, *"Drifting About"; or, What "Jeems Pipes, of Pipesville" Saw-and-Did* (New York: George Carleton, 1863), 89–90; David Millard, *A Journal of Travels in Egypt, Arabia Petraea, and the Holy Land*, 3rd edition (New York: H. Ludwig, 1847), 183–4; Valentine Mott, *Travels in Europe and the East* (New York: Harper & Brothers, 1842), 389–91; Stephen Olin, *Travels*, 1: 61; Samuel I. Prime, *Travels in Europe and the East*, 2 vols. (New York: Harper & Brothers, 1856), 2: 258–60; Francis Schroeder, *Shores of the Mediterranean*, 2 vols. (New York: Harper & Brothers, 1846), 2: 55–6; Thomas Wells, *Letters on Palestine* (Boston: B. B. Mussey, 1846), 265–9. After reprinting one depiction of the slave market in Constantinople, Frederick Douglass's paper, *The North Star*, commented that "just such scenes may be witnessed in our own free land, ten thousand times in a year" (14 September 1849).

qualified its radicalism by disassociating it from the political reforms of both women's rights and the emancipation of slaves of African descent.

However, this Caucasian identification raised new anxieties even as it resolved others. Although Circassia had gained its independence from the Ottomans at the same time as Greece (and continued to resist Russian control, especially under the rebel Shamyl who was romanticized in the popular expression of the 1850s), its inhabitants remained inaccessible Muslims who were known to willingly exploit their daughters by selling them into the service of the seraglio.[36] The symbolic apex of white beauty with its sexual and genetic energies served as a resource to uphold the sensual empire of the Sultan, which was seen by many white men of the West as a reprehensible assault on their pride and valor. Here, as in viewing *The Greek Slave*, was a symbolic cause of emancipation through which northern males could engage in the cultural discourse of abolition without confronting directly troubling issues of racial equality. Such a situation stimulated an abiding Euroamerican male fantasy of rescuing white female captives from the clutches of Islamic infidels, a vision that complemented the political and religious desire to replace Ottoman decadence and indolence with Western vigor and industry.

This romantic theme of the "abduction from the seraglio" was a central motif of Western islamicism (it was the title of an opera by Mozart) and its promethean vision of chivalrous emancipation, expressed by the quest of Melville's narrator Taji for the white captive Yillah in *Mardi*, offered an adventurous means of performing a more global American masculine identity. To liberate their imaginations from the perceived thralldom to female moral authority in the home, males sought out alternative oriental domains in ways that allowed them to reinstall their patriarchal authority and to authorize sensualized visions of female beauty. By converting the cultural power of Muslim masculinity into a fantasy of their own chivalry, adventurous white American males, at one stroke, reestablished their own racial pedigree on more exotic grounds, bolstered their own authority over both aliens and women, and dealt imaginatively with the intractable alterity of Islam. While accomplishing all this, they also disguised such power as part of the sentimental romance of reform. The transnational stance of islamicism thus empowered some American men to appropriate the global energies of oriental originality as part of the repertoire of a reinvigorated cosmopolitan manliness. This imaginative imperialism contrasts with Amy Kaplan's notion of "manifest domesticity," whose cultural work involved generating "notions of the foreign against which the nation can be imagined as

---

[36] See for example, Esther Wetherald, "The Circassian Bride," *Graham's Lady's and Gentleman's Magazine* 18 (March 1841): 107–8.

home."[37] The Eastern frontier of the Islamic Orient served also as an exotic latitude for displacing domestic pressures and romanticizing emancipation from confining ideologies well as a means of exporting the universal propriety of "home."

THE BLOOMER REVOLT: TURKISH TROUSERS AND
FEMALE LIBERTY

American men were not alone in absorbing Eastern models to express their gendered desires; women also tried to adapt islamicist cultural expressions as resources to advance their own interests. Two years after *The Greek Slave* toured in front of the American public, a new craze that responded to a different dimension of the captivity of the female body swept across the country. Some critics had viewed *The Greek Slave* as being too scantily clothed and propaganda saw the necessity of clothing her nakedness in sentiment, but many women's rights advocates began actively to protest the actual ways that reigning fashions of female dress symbolized their social restrictions. The massive "Great Pyramid" style of dress subjected the female body to ten to fifteen pounds of material made up of up to six petticoats with padded bustles made from eighteen to twenty yards of starched flannel or muslin. Tightly laced corsets, sometimes made of whalebone, necessary to keep this weight from falling off the body, further immobilized freedom of movement. (In *Moby-Dick*, Melville satirized this realm of fashion where woman and whale actually meet by figuring the male whale as "a luxurious Ottoman" and his "harem" of aristocratic females as "comparatively delicate" with their eighteen-foot waists.[38]) The fashion of wearing flounces that extended to the floor made walking in streets, much less migrating west, a challenge to both cleanliness and forward progress. The movement for dress reform sought to liberate the female body from the tyranny of this fashion for the practical reason of promoting physical health. Lucretia Mott argued – as had Mary Wollstonecraft – that women, in privileging fashion and physical beauty above other virtues as well as by submitting their lives to the authority of men, had subscribed to the degrading sensuality of the seraglio.[39]

The most prominent attempt at mid-nineteenth-century dress reform, the adoption of what came to be called the "bloomer costume," gained wide notoriety in the years 1851–2 and contributed to a broad debate about fashion and female freedom. The costume was named after Amelia Jenks Bloomer, who was one of its earliest advocates and also the editor of *The Lily* – a

---

[37] Amy Kaplan, "Manifest Domesticity," in *The Futures of American Studies*, eds. Donald Pease and Robyn Wiegman (Durham, NC: Duke University Press, 2002), 112.

[38] Herman Melville, *Moby-Dick* (Evanston, IL: Northwestern University Press; Chicago, IL: Newberry Library, 1988), 328–30.

[39] Lucretia A. Mott, "The New Costume," *The Lily* 3 (September 1851), 66–7.

temperance magazine created by and for women published in Seneca Falls, New York, where women's rights advocates had trumpeted their independence in the "Declaration of Sentiments" of 1848. The costume featured as its most controversial element a pair of draped Turkish trousers gathered at the ankle, a style probably adopted most immediately from practical clothing worn by those in health sanitariums (Fig. 6.7). Much of the furor over the bloomer centered about the idea that wearing bifurcated trousers was the province of men, and that by appropriating such a public privilege for themselves, women indecently transgressed against the separate and subordinate sphere of their sex. Part of the potential power of the bloomer was that it symbolized a release from the strictures of women's conventional activities by literally equipping them to walk on their own two feet and thereby play more active public roles.[40] Unlike *The Greek Slave* who remained immobilized in marble, women in bloomer costumes circulated in clothes that symbolized their own independence from cultural constrictions.

The costume's trousers were both celebrated as being more practical and maligned as more "masculine" than traditional women's dress. But the fact that they were also regularly noted as being Turkish adds an important islamicist dimension to the cultural challenge of the bloomer costume. When assessing this period of dress reform in their memoirs, Elizabeth Cady Stanton acknowledged that the Bloomer was "an imitation in part of the Turkish style," and Elizabeth Smith Miller, who many women's rights advocates believed had initiated the costume, noted that her first act of rebellion was to don Turkish trousers.[41] Historians of dress reform have also acknowledged the costume's oriental elements. Amy Kessleman claimed that its design was "modeled after the dress of Moslem women" and Stella Mary Newton interpreted it as being influenced by "popular engravings

---

[40] Scholarly analyses of the bloomer costume include: Gayle V. Fischer, "'Pantalets' and 'Turkish Trowsers': Designing Freedom in the Mid-Nineteenth-Century United States," *Feminist Studies* 23 (Spring 1997): 110–40; Gayle V. Fischer, "Pantaloons in Public: Woman's Rights and Freedom Dresses," in *Pantaloons and Power: A Nineteenth-Century Dress Reform in the United States* (Kent, OH: Kent State University Press, 2001), 79–101; Kate Luck, "Trouble in Eden, Trouble with Eve: Women, Trousers & Utopian Socialism in Nineteenth-Century America," in *Chic Thrills: A Fashion Reader*, eds. Juliet Ash and Elizabeth Wilson (Berkeley: University of California Press, 1993), 200–12; Kate Luck, "Trousers: Feminism in Nineteenth-Century America," in *The Gendered Object*, ed. Pat Kirkham (Manchester and New York: Manchester University Press, 1996), 141–52; Ann Kessleman, "The 'Freedom Suit': Feminism and Dress Reform in the United States, 1848–1875," *Gender & Society* 5 (December 1991): 495–510; Jeanette C. and Robert H. Lauer, "A Case Study: The Bloomer Costume," in *Fashion Power: The Meaning of Fashion in American Society* (Englewood Cliffs, NJ: Prentice-Hall, 1981), 246–59; Charles Nelson Gattey, *The Bloomer Girls* (New York: Coward-McCann, 1968); James Laver, *Clothes* (London: Burke Publishing, 1952), 153–71; Paul Fatout, "Amelia Bloomer and Bloomerism," *New York Historical Society, Quarterly* 36 (October 1952): 360–73.

[41] Elizabeth Smith Miller, "Reflections on Woman's Dress, and the Record of a Personal Experience," *Arena* (September 1892), 491–5. See "Mrs. Kemble and Her New Costume," *The Lily* 1 (1 December 1849) and "Turkish Costume," *Harper's New Monthly Magazine* 14 (July 1851): 288.

No. 1. THE AMERICAN COSTUME.

FIGURE 6.7. Amelia Bloomer in Turkish Trousers as "The American Costume." *The Water-Cure Journal* 12 (October 1851), 96. Courtesy American Antiquarian Society.

of melting beauties in Turkish trousers that followed the cult of Byron and the French conquest of Algeria."[42] Gayle V. Fischer, the scholar who has attended most fully to this dimension, has argued that the inclusion of Turkish fashion in the movement for dress reform was primarily a means of deflecting attention away from the new costume's masculine elements. That bloomers became a site of cultural contestation is shown by one song that featured the refrain "O! the devil take the one who, first / invented Turkish

---

[42] Kessleman "The 'Freedom Suit'," 38; Stella Mary Newton, *Health, Art and Reason: Dress Reformers of the Nineteenth Century* (London: John Murray, 1974), 4.

trousers."[43] The bloomer fad exhibits a material manifestation of American islamicism in antebellum reform. An important dimension of the bloomer's complex and conflicted act of gender appropriation was played out on islamicist registers in which the oppositional model of Turkey as an uncouth abode of slavery was shifting into a domestic resource for fashioning more global models of liberty.

Gayle V. Fischer's contention that the islamicist aspects of the dress appeared to mute the radicalism of taking up trousers and make the reform more conservative is valid on face value. Turkish trousers capitalized upon the existing cultural fashion of oriental female beauty and merely expanded the repertoire of already acceptable Eastern accoutrements such as shawls, veils, and robes. Moreover, the stereotype of the soulless subordination of Eastern women posed no imminent threat to male political power. The assumption of such costumes also registered the evangelical desire of American women to stand as models of liberation to their oriental sisters.[44] Indeed, Eastern dress was legitimated through its association with the garb of early Christianity. These conservative factors, however, failed to displace the more subversive connotations of the costume's symbolic innovation.

While the costume offered freedom for women both in its practical physicality and in its flouting of conventional fashion, it symbolized a more radical liberty by appropriating the emancipatory fantasies associated with islamicist imagination. By donning bloomers, women were critically adopting some of the liberatory prerogatives men had taken through their Near Eastern travel and expressed through their idealization of Muslim gender roles. The adoption of a Turkish model signalized a deeper and more transgressive form of orientalist liberation for women because it repositioned the harem as a public site of female power rather than a private province of male fantasy. Publically dressing in Turkish trousers also called attention to the ways in which the treatment of women by American men mirrored islamicist images of Turkish tyranny. Women, by wearing oriental dress, gained access to a symbolic economy that directly challenged the romantic realm of male cultural fantasy of gender power that howadjis had reserved for themselves.

The notion that Eastern forms of dress could signify liberation to Americans may seem to counter long-lasting stereotypes about the degradation of Islamic women, characterized by early national notions (see Chapter 1), as well as in the political imaginary of the early twenty-first century. There were some American travelers to the Near East, however, who confirmed the discoveries a century earlier of Lady Mary Montagu and celebrated the

---

[43] "The Bloomer Costume," sung in Georgetown, D.C., in June 1851, in Jeanette C. and Robert H. Lauer, "The Battle of the Sexes: Fashion in 19th Century America," *Journal of Popular Culture* 13 (Spring 1980): 583.

[44] Richard Martin and Harold Koda, *Orientalism: Visions of the East in Western Dress* (New York: The Metropolitan Museum of Art, 1996), 55.

freedom of mobility that Turkish women enjoyed when compared with the confining rigidity of American domestic duty. David Porter, the American minister in Constantinople for twelve years (and planner of the Tripoli Monument discussed in Chapter 1) was able to claim after his first few years there that "Turkish women are as free as any women in the world."[45] Traveler Caroline *Paine* was able to supply a female perspective and emphasized the advantages of their life style, suggesting "they would be scarcely tempted to exchange the perfect freedom and exemption from the austere duties of life, which is their acme of happiness."[46] Popular visits to the resorts in Constantinople called "Sweet Waters," where women were allowed social contact with men, frequently brought forth acclaim for the health of Turkish social relations. Dr. James De Kay was able to join a picnic of Turkish women in the countryside near Constantinople and, taken by their liberal mobility in public, stated that the middle-class women in Turkey "actually enjoy more freedom than in the other countries of Europe or in America."[47]

Many men actively resisted the costume's islamicist intrusion because it refocused their idealized notions of oriental female beauty onto the American women who most actively challenged male control. The bloomer ingeniously played into the fantasy of male possession but subversively defused its romance by making its angelic houris into recalcitrant suffragettes. Men found many ways to scorn the dress's Turkish elements as an expression of women's liberation. Some critics argued that it was unbecoming for American women to adopt the more revealing dress of uncouth infidels. One editorial ridiculed its transgressive cross-dressing by claiming that "MAHOMET warred under the Petticoat of his wife KADIGA," while "The American female Emancipist marches on her holy war under the distinguishing garment of her husband."[48] Another critic of bloomers wrote to the *Knickerbocker* in 1852: "Shall the harems of the East set the fashion for the *boudoirs* of the West? . . . Have we quit Paris, dear, delightful Paris! for the Sublime Porte, and her mantua-makers for the Blue Beards of Constantinople?"[49] One newspaper editor in an article entitled "New Dress" playfully interpreted the bloomer as an invitation to romance.

> The bloomer costume is decidedly an improvement upon the dress of the female portion of the community. It is light, graceful and seraphic, well suited to the female figure. It will be welcomed by all the lovers of taste and

---

[45] David Porter, *Constantinople and Its Environs*, 2 vols. (New York: Harper and Brothers, 1835), 1: 32.

[46] Caroline Paine, *Tent and Harem: Notes of an Oriental Trip* (New York: D. Appleton & Co., 1859), 21.

[47] James De Kay, *Sketches in Turkey in 1831 and 1832* (New York: J. & J. Harper, 1833), 125–6, 269–70, 208. This was evidence of what De Kay saw as "the profound respect which the Turks universally pay to the female sex" (208).

[48] "Ladies' Costume," *The Carpet Bag* (26 July 1851): 4.

[49] "Bloomerism: An Essay," *The Knickerbocker* 40 (September 1852): 241.

refinement in the fashionable world. The Orientals have long been celebrated for their beauty, polished manners and splendid attire. Our rivers will now be the Golden Horn; our valleys the Valley of Sweet Waters, and our seas the Bosphorus of the Turkish capitol. A voyage to Constantinople will be useless. We may now take our siesta in the gay kiosq, and glide over the moonlit waters in the light caique! Come, ladies, step forth in your gorgeous apparel, decked with rose of gold and leaves of silver, and gladden our hearts with sweet smiles![50]

Female dress reformers readily responded to the contempt that was heaped upon the bloomer. Grace Greenwood claimed that wearers "have only made free with Moslem privileges" and challenged the chivalry of its male critics who argued that bloomers had "appropriated the sign and symbol of masculine dignity and dominion" by arguing "I doubt not that the gentleman Mahomedans, more gallant Mahomedans, more gallant than trans-Atlantic Christians, will have a proper sense of the compliment."[51] Other women tried to efface the costume's oriental genealogy altogether by emphasizing that "the costume that we recommend is not Turkish nor Persian, but American; the outgrowth of our own wants, the product of our skill, and the sign of our independence."[52]

The movement for dress reform failed in the early 1850s because the bloomer costume was unmercifully caricatured in the press to the point where women wearing it were insulted in the streets. Most women who adopted the bloomer soon abandoned it because it detracted attention away from more central issues of women's rights. Elizabeth Cady Stanton confessed that "such is the tyranny of custom, that to escape constant observation, criticism, ridicule, persecution, mobs, one after another gladly went back to the old slavery and sacrificed freedom to repose."[53] This capitulation to conventional fashion sealed the failure of this mid-century attempt at dress reform. After its bloom wilted in 1853 until it was readopted during the bicycle craze of the 1890s, the bloomer dress came to be viewed more as an expression of free love rather than as a symbol of women's rights, a position that upheld traditional views of the sensuality of the Turkish harem and not the empowerment of its women.

[50] Daniel McDonald, *A Twentieth Century History of Marshall County* (Chicago: Lewis Publishing Co., 1908), 192. Samuel Cox, while traveling in the Ottoman Empire, read American papers that reported of the adoption of "Turkish" costumes similar to those he was witnessing around him. Cox, *A Buckeye Abroad; or Wanderings in Europe, and the Orient* (New York: G. P. Putnam, 1852), 231.

[51] Grace Greenwood, *The National Era* 5 (2 October 1851), 158.

[52] See the "Hope Chapel New York Resolution of 1851," in Lauers, "Battle," 584; *The Water Cure Journal* 2 (December 1851): 135.

[53] "Reminiscences By E. C. S.," in *History of Woman Suffrage*, eds. Elizabeth Cady Stanton, Susan B. Anthony, and Matilda Joslyn Gage (New York: Fowler and Wells, 1881), 469–71, 864.

THE TRANSNATIONAL PAGEANTRY OF THE ZOUAVE SOLDIER

The portraits of Amos Lawrence and Bayard Taylor signify how elite American men had invested themselves with oriental privileges in the form of dress adapted from Muslim cultures. The episode of bloomer fashion dramatizes ways that islamicism served as a symbolic site for negotiating contested American expressions of gendered liberty, specifically the desire for female freedom. The most extensive mid-nineteenth-century American investment in islamicist attire, however, occurred during the Civil War when troops on both sides of the campaigns took on Eastern costume in the phenomenon of the Zouave uniform. *The New York Times* reported in July of 1860 of a new sensation sweeping the city: "The name Zouave is just now a household word. . . . We see in the shop windows Zouave hats, caps, coats, canes, umbrellas, and shoes." The article was describing the popular response to the recent Eastern tour of the U.S. Zouave Cadets, a well-disciplined Chicago-based volunteer military company that dressed in colorful Algerian uniforms. "Their dress was picturesque in the extreme," related one account, "the fancy fez, the hollow-backed jacket, the baggy trowsers extending to the calf of the leg and tying up in folds, the slashing boots and the general devil-me-care style, was calculated to take the eye, please the sense, and impress the scene indelibly on the mind of the beholder."[54] The commander of these cadets was Colonel Elmer Ephraim Ellsworth, the man most responsible for launching the Zouave mania that caught hold in both the North and the South at the nation moved toward war in 1860. The young Ellsworth saw more romance in military exploits than in business or law and became caught up in the vogue of forming volunteer companies, a fraternal recreational outlet for aspiring young men in the 1850s. Ellsworth decided to adopt the drill and dress of the Zouaves after learning of the reputation of the French Zouaves who fought in the Crimean and Franco-Austrian Wars of the 1850s and whose exploits had been recounted in the illustrated magazines. After tirelessly disciplining his men until they were capable of astonishing their audiences with their vigorous athleticism as well as their picturesque costumes, Ellsworth toured twenty cities in the eastern United States with great fanfare, including visits to the White House and West Point. One Michigan reporter proclaimed (in an often repeated tone) that "the perfection of their drill can hardly be imagined," and called the exhibition "a surprising display of activity and endurance" that evoked "unbounded applause."[55] The exoticism of the

---

[54] "The Zouaves. Their Drill at the Academy of Music. An Immense and Enthusiastic Audience," *The New-York Times* (20 July 1860).

[55] Charles A. Ingraham, *Elmer E. Ellsworth and the Zouaves of '61* (Chicago: University of Chicago Press, 1925), 69; Meredith M. Dytch, "'Remember Ellsworth!': Chicago's First Hero of the American Civil War," *Chicago History* 11 (1982): 14–25.

Zouave uniform and drill offered a romantic view of military life that eventually helped to inspire enlistments in over fifty Zouave units in the Union and Confederate armies that fought in every campaign of the war from Bull Run to Appomattox. Ellsworth was one of the earliest casualties of the Civil War. He was killed the day after Virginia seceded after he and his Zouave Regiment pulled down a Confederate flag from atop an Alexandria hotel. Ellsworth's body lay in state in the president's White House, and he was widely celebrated as the most famous national martyr between John Brown and Abraham Lincoln.

As had the adoption of bloomers by women, the assumption of Zouave uniforms performed several important cultural functions beyond that of enabling increased physical mobility. At a time when military life and uniforms were heavily regimented, the Zouave mystique offered soldiers a glamorous vision of the skill, adventure, and community of war-making that contrasted with the stuffy gentility of military officialdom. "With his graceful dress, soldierly bearing, and vigilant attitude the Zouave at an outpost is the beau-ideal of a soldier," wrote General George B. McClellan in 1861, calling him the "most reckless, self-reliant, and complete infantry."[56] The Zouave spirit created a symbolic elite, based more on romantic performance than on class status, one whose dress and drill created a sporting combination of kinesthetic art, fraternal ritual, and public pageantry. The popularity of Zouave uniforms both domesticated and democratized access to the exotic rehabilitation of patriarchy celebrated in the popular Near Eastern travel narratives of wealthly howadjis.

The Zouave craze enabled soldiers to retain a fashionable sense of avant-garde romance at the very moment when both their bodies and their agency were being conscripted by the state. By investing themselves in clothes that signified a transgressive expression in gendered, political, and religious fields of representation and performance, the Zouave soldier also testified in powerful ways to warfare's disruption of conventional morality. By islamicizing military fervor, the fad helped to muster the spirit of enlistment in the early phases of the Civil War and expressed the new "infidel" social roles that citizens were required to play when they turned into soldiers. The "reckless" reputation of Zouaves as crack troops known for their gallantry and prowess may have also helped to fortify soldiers' sense of manly resolve in the face of violent combat, a courage that may have been needed since the gaudy colors of their uniform made them easier targets (Fig. 6.8).[57] Stereotypes of militant bellicosity offered the exotic energies of the jihad as a transcultural resource for rallying American men to kill for their respective causes.

---

[56] George B. McClellan, *The Armies of Europe* (Philadelphia: J. B. Lippincott & Co., 1861), 61.

[57] Accounts of American Zouaves that include photos and illustrations are Robin Smith, *American Civil War Zouaves* (London: Osprey, 1996); and Michael J. McAfee, *Zouaves: The First and the Bravest* (Gettysburg, PA: Thomas Publications, 1991) see Figures 6.8 and 6.9.

FIGURE 6.8. Winslow Homer gained fame as a Civil War illustrator and was fascinated by the pageantry of Zouave soldiers, as shown in this sketch *Zoauve*. Homer also painted the colorful leisure activities of Zouaves in *The Brierwood Pipe* (1864) and *Pitching Quoits* (1865). Black and white chalk on blue-green paper. Cooper-Hewitt, National Design Museum, Smithsonian Institution Gift of Charles Savage Homer, Jr., 1912-12-109.

FIGURE 6.9. Zouave Soldiers in Company G, 114th Pennsylvania Infantry, Petersburg, Virginia, August 1864. Library of Congress, Prints & Photographs Division, LC-B817-7198.

Dozens of marches and battle songs were composed to accentuate the glamour of Zouave units, and "Remember Ellsworth!" became a popular Northern battle cry in the earliest campaigns of the war (Fig. 6.9). A song called "The Gallant Zouaves" celebrates the "brave guardians of the law" for their vigilance and claims "when they *fight* there's music in that part of town."[58] Another song called "Hawkins' Zouaves at Roanoke," lauds their spirited taking of a Confederate fort, rallied by an officer who shouts "Now's the time for Zou-Zou sport!"[59] A version of the popular song "Abraham's Daughter" likewise demonstrates the attraction of the Zouaves for the enlistee, as well as some of their boisterous panache: "I am tired of city life, and I will join the zou-zous; I'm going to try and make a hit, down among the Southern foo-foos."[60]

Although not so popular as in the North, the formation of Confederate Zouave units also proved an effective way of attracting enlistment in the early years of the war. The widespread romantic appeal of the Zouave fad is expressed by the ditty "My Love He Is a Zou-Zu" in which a young Southern belle praises her nineteen-year-old Confederate lover for his brave and fierce spirit enrolling as a Zouave who wants to "show off in Washington." "His parents taught him to be a cavalier," the song narrates, "but the life of a Zou-zu he much did prefer."[61] The Zouave fervor in the Confederacy was

[58] *The Camp-Fire Songster* (New York: Dick & Fitzgerald, 1862), 66–7.
[59] *Beadle's Dime Union Song Book No. 3*. (New York: Sinclair Towsey, 1862), 9.
[60] Irwin Silber, ed., *Songs of the Civil War* (New York: Dover, 1995), 103.
[61] *The Camp-Fire Songster*, 18–9.

especially pronounced in the former French territory of Louisiana.[62] One Louisiana battalion that came to be called Coppen's Zouaves was so closely modeled on the French system that all military orders were given in French and its personnel included two female vivandières (canteen women) attired in appropriate oriental costume that drew on the style of the bloomer.[63] Enlistment in the battalion in March 1861 was stimulated by an "Operatic Buffo Spectacular and Grand Military Display" by a group of actors who toured the country as a drill team claiming to be veterans of the Crimean War patterned after the Algerian Zouaves. The *New Orleans Picayune* noted that "the red flowing breeches of the Zouaves, the fez, the pretty jacket and the leggings of the Zouaves have been a better bait than the bounty of five dollars offered to every white man who would enlist with the regulars."[64]

The cultural vogue of the Zouave uniform that cut across Union and Confederate lines was also part of a broader global genealogy. The history of this popular form of transnational cross-dressing reveals the complex dimensions of its intercultural pageantry. The invention and maintenance of Zouave troops in Western militaries was a phenomenon integrally related with the dynamics of imperialism. The French military established the first corps of Zouave troops by decree on 1 October 1830 to replace the Turkish soldiers expelled after the conquest of Algeria. Their name was derived from a group of mountain Kabyles, Berbers who never submitted to Turkish hegemony who for the most part had joined the rebellion of Abd'ul-Qadir against the French in 1830. The adoption of Algerian name and Turkish dress helped the French to claim cultural control over the populations that they were colonizing. In 1841, there were three battalions of Zouaves with a native company in each to signify the legitimacy of French authority.

---

[62] Many Southerners saw the Crimean War in its religious dimension and, viewing the end of the Ottoman Empire as a sign of Christian progress, gave their allegiance to the Russians, who also blockaded the Circassian slave trade. See the articles by Horace Perry Jones: "Southern Affinity for Russia during the Crimean War," *The Ukranian Quarterly* 39 (Autumn 1983): 240–55; "Southern Opinion on Turkey during the Crimean War," *The Ukranian Quarterly* 42 (Fall–Winter 1986): 222–38; "Louisiana Opinion on the Crimean War: As Expressed in the Newspapers," *Louisiana History* 18 (Summer 1977): 323–34; "Southern Opinion on the Crimean War," *The Journal of Mississippi History* 29 (May 1967), 95–117.

[63] *New Orleans Commercial Bulletin* (5 April 1861), in Michael D. Jones, "Jeff Davis' Pet Wolves," *Civil War Times Illustrated* 28 (March 1989): 28; see also Lee A. Wallace, "Coppen's Louisiana Zouaves," *Civil War History* 8 (September 1962), 271.

[64] Terry L. Jones, *Lee's Tigers: The Louisiana Infantry and the Army of Northern Virginia* (Baton Rouge: Louisiana State University Press, 1987), 3, 28. The popularity of the Zouaves led in one case to an abuse of its popularity in the Union army. When Lionel John D'Epineuil wanted to raise a regiment of French Americans in 1861, his gaudy uniforms helped to convince the War Department that he had years of French military service, when in fact his lack of experience eventually led to chaos and the mustering out of the unit. Gerald Wheeler, "D'Epineuil's Zouaves," *Civil War History* 11 (March 1956): 93–100.

But interethnic strife in these contingents led to the mustering out of these native troops the following year after which the French Zouaves began to establish celebrity throughout Europe for their colorful yet disciplined esprit de corps.[65] During the Crimean War, the Islamic dress of the French Zouaves signalized their alliance with the Ottoman Empire and the energies of Muslim peoples as a resource for opposing the despotism of the Russian czar.

The transnational popularity of Zouave uniforms that had initially drawn the attention of Elmer Ellsworth was not restricted to American regiments from the Union and Confederate armies. In 1859, Britain's West India Regiment, originally formed after the abolition of slavery in the British Caribbean, adopted the Zouave style as their official clothing. French troops guarding the Emperor Maximilian in Mexico were members of Zouave units. When the Pope sought a military force to protect him from Italian nationalists fired up by Giuseppe Garibaldi, a unit of Papal Zouaves was put into position, manned in part by Catholic soldiers from Canada and the United States. Both the romantic register and the intercultural circulation of Zouave fashion dramatizes how islamicist models, after being progressively disassociated from the threat of Islamic difference, were creatively mustered for the imperial work of fortifying Euroamerican cultural power. Interestingly, the earliest Arabs and Turks to migrate to the United States in fact arrived in 1857 with the camels imported by then Secretary of War Jefferson Davis, who – in the decade before the transcontinental railroad – was searching for an effective form of transportation in the dry territories annexed to the nation during the Mexican Cession.[66] The energies of Muslim military and cultural power that had threatened and entranced the West since the times of the Crusades were conscripted as a part of the symbolic arsenal of Western power.

The African origin of the Zouaves and the founding of the West Indies regiment rendered its model of military power a particularly powerful cultural resource for African Americans seeking to resist the slave system. The *Anglo-African Magazine* of New York celebrated this spirit of militancy as the nation moved into the Civil War between January 1859 and April 1861. (Indeed, the journal's own motto is a quote from Virgil that reads "et nigri Memnonis arma," "and the black Memnon in his arms.") In August of 1859, the magazine celebrated an account of the black African Zouaves known as Turcos, calling them "the most wonderful specimens of humanity . . . who walk about with a cat-like step, as if the ground were too hot for them – the

---

[65] Frank Bishop Lammons, "Operation Camel: An Experiment in Animal Transportation in Texas, 1857–1860," *Southwestern Historical Quarterly* 3 (January 1958): 20–50; Thomas L. Connelly, "The American Camel Experiment: A Reappraisal," *Southwestern Historical Quarterly* 9 (April 1956): 442–62.

[66] "The Zouaves," *New-York Daily Times* (24 May 1855): 4.

very impersonation of muscular strength."[67] The editor wondered whether "the wild Africans now being imported to our southern border are of materials such as could, in a certain event, be manufactured into a regiment of Turcos?"[68] Such racial pride was embodied in the great African American tragedian Ira Aldridge who had for thirty years played Shakespeare's Moors, Othello and Aaron, to European audiences. The second volume of the *Anglo-African Magazine* printed a powerful image of black vengeance by illustrating Aldridge on its frontispiece as the vindictive Aaron from *Titus Andronicus* with his hand on his huge scimitar (Fig. 6.10).[69] Thomas Wentworth Higginson, who captained a regiment of scarlet-panted black Union soldiers during the Civil War, viewed the devotion of his charges as "essentially Mohammedan" and his own role as similar to the interloper Haroun Alraschid in the Arabian Nights.[70] These early depictions of islamicist militancy in the Civil War period provide important historical templates for the development in the twentieth century of an African American Islam, especially Elijah Muhammad's "Lost-Found Nation of Islam in the Wilderness of North America," as a religious resource through which African Americans radically contended their subjugated status within the Christian mainstream.

The bloody horrors of the Civil War extinguished some of the romance of the Zouave craze, leading Herman Melville to write in *Battle Pieces* how "grimed War here laid aside His Orient pomp."[71] Yet, the pomp of fraternal islamicism survived the battles both in veteran's organizations and in a number of other postbellum guises. With the reestablishment of national power after the Civil War, romantic appropriations of Muslim accouterments became even more commodified and emerged more popularly as a major modality of late-nineteenth-century male pageantry. Beginning in the 1870s, a number of major fraternal organizations (such as the Order of Alhambra, the Bagmen of Bagdad, and the Ancient Arabic Order of the Nobles of the Mystic Shrine – more popularly known as the Shriners) established long-lasting recreational rites that incorporated and burlesqued islamicist dress, titles, and oaths. For men who desired to stay at home, the development of the smoking den as an element of male domestic space

---

[67] "Zouaves and Turcos," *Anglo-African Magazine* 1 (August 1859): 254–5.

[68] [Ethiop], "The Anglo-African and the African Slave Trade," *Anglo-African Magazine* 1 (September 1859): 283–4.

[69] *Anglo African Magazine* 2 (January 1860): frontispiece.

[70] Thomas Wentworth Higginson, *Army Life in a Black Regiment* (New York: W. W. Norton, 1984), 71, 46. Higginson was attracted by the exoticism of African American expressive culture, noting that while in camp he experienced "a tinge of Orientalism in all our life" (44). His first response to being offered the command of the unit was: "Had an invitation reached me to take command of a regiment of Kalmuck Tartars, it could barely have been more unexpected" (28). He compares the willingness of the American blacks to resist slavery with Maroons (235) and Turcos (236).

[71] Herman Melville, "A Utilitarian View of the Monitor's Fight," *Poems* (London: Constable, 1924), 44.

FIGURE 6.10. "Mr. Ira Aldridge as Aaron" in Shakespeare's *Titus Andronicus*. The original ornate caption includes a quotation from Act 4, Scene 2: "He dies upon my scimetar's sharp point, That touches this my first-born son and heir!" *The Anglo-African Magazine* 2 (January 1860): frontispiece. Courtesy American Antiquarian Society.

featured exotic implements of leisure such as tasseled sofas and ottomans that further domesticated oriental masculinity as a masquerade of American manhood. Even the "New World" plant of tobacco became orientalized as a means of advertising its allure in the new commodified form of cigarettes.

The entertainment industry also capitalized upon this islamicist romance in various ways. During the war, P. T. Barnum sought out a "Fair Circassian" slave for his museum, but parodied the image of inviting white beauty by displaying hired actresses with freaky, frizzled hair. In the late nineteenth century, both Zouave troops and Arab horsemen comprised an important sideshow of Buffalo Bill's Wild West extravaganza. The film industry of the early twentieth century founded a new media for expressing orientalist spectacles that saw enormous popularity in the transformation of Rudolph Valentino into "The Sheik" and in Lowell Thomas's transfiguration of T. E. Lawrence into "Lawrence of Arabia." When the Ottoman Empire and Caliphate finally fell following its alliance with Germany in World War I, its symbolic power persisted in islamicist appropriations of its exotic energies by Westerners seeking a more exciting and global cosmopolitanism.

These readings demonstrate the emergent popularity in the United States of adopting the dress and performing the perspective of Muslims as the nineteenth century progressed. While Protestant missionaries such as Horatio Southgate and Eli Smith had expediently adopted Muslim dress "to avoid unnecessary notice, expense, and trouble, if not insult," howadjis and Zouaves (and later Shriners and Sheiks) imported them as conspicuous emblems of their American worldliness.[72] The threat of Islam to the political and religious values of the early nation that had so charged early American leaders was generally subordinated to the valences of romantic islamicism by the era of the Civil War. Such a shift represented in part the changes in the respective political fortunes and religious cultures of the United States and the Ottoman Empire during the previous century. In this modality, aspects of Islam were fashioned into symbols of liberty rather than of slavery and rendered into resources for constituting transcultural cosmopolitanism rather prophesying the darkness of antichristian despotism.

AFTERWORD

Since the beginnings of the settlement of what is today the United States, the Islamic world has formed an extrahemispheric horizon that Americans have engaged to define the cultural contours of their changing sense of worldliness. The cultural discourse of islamicism dislocated Islam from its diverse everyday practices and recalibrated it into an imaginary resource for articulating local, regional, and national situations within a broader planetary perspective. Because early Americans were largely unable or unwilling to understand the religious ethos held by Muslims themselves, they imported islamicist images instead and then applied and elaborated them in attempts

---

[72] Eli Smith, *Researches of the Rev. E. Smith and Rev H. G. O. Dwight in Armenia*, 2 vols. (Boston: Crocker and Brewster, 1833), I: 73, 84.

to generate a more global relevance for their varied domestic productions. Islamicist expression therefore is ultimately an invented appropriation of the difference of Islam used to mark American boundaries rather than an intercultural means of measuring Muslim meanings.

Despite the larger trends in the shifting uses of early American islamicism explained in this book, the full spectrum of its multivalent modalities persist as an integral part of the continuing enterprise of transnational cultural definition. The fact that so few academic studies have acknowledged the role of islamicism in cultural formation, especially in the historical period this book examines, is itself evidence of the impediments that still retard a fuller understanding of Americans' relations with Muslims throughout the world. For many Americans, the Muslim world remains today a contested symbolic geography – a "mobile sign" that can either repulse or attract depending on the nature of the engagement and the conventions employed to interpret Islam's significance. The studies of early American negotiations of the Muslim world examined in this book demonstrate the elasticity of American islamicism and how its protean meanings rely upon the historical circumstances, the performative situations, and the ideological intent of the different individuals who deploy its expressive grammar. Whether the millennium that has just begun promises a peaceful future ultimately does not depend on the ways that non-Muslim Americans convert Islam into a versatile resource of their own imagination. Rather such a goal requires a fuller declaration of interdependence that joins all peoples of differing backgrounds in the intercultural dialogue that comprises the world's shared cultural and religious history.

This study's work of revision has been to reveal the heritage of replications that constituted early American islamicism. The further work of vision that must follow is less confined by the limitations that pressed on Americans from the seventeenth to the nineteenth centuries. The critical nature of comparative study that has emerged within academic disciplines in the arts, humanities, and social sciences is more acutely aware of (while not free from) the ideological dangers of intercultural comparison. Technological advances in transportation and communications – especially in translation and publication – have enabled privileged access that some individuals have used to evaluate the sufficiency of cultural presuppositions using the balance of their own educations. The mobility of bodies enabled by the global market revolution, the process that first brought the first Muslims to the United States as part of the enforced migration of slavery, has made many Muslims into U.S. citizens in ways that check superficial stereotypes with the examples of living individuals.

Index

Abana and Pharpar (streams of paradise), 242, 259
Abolition Society of Pennsylvania, The, 142
abolitionism, *see* antislavery movement,
Abraham, 6–7, 92, 204, 232
Adams, John, 172, 262
Adams, John Quincy, 66
Africa, 25, 54, 77, 97, 145–7, 201. *See also* North
    Africa and North Africans
African Americans, 6, 17–19, 134–5, 140–1,
    147–55, 157, 160, 167, 278, 281, 293–4
Africans, 41, 54, 93, 142–3, 145, 146, 148, 221,
    231, 293. *See also* African Americans
  Muslims enslaved in the Americas, 17–18
alcohol and *See also* rum; drunkenness;
    temporance
  as antibellum social problem, 159–60
  as Arabian invention and word, 162–4
  equated with Christian belief, 177, 178
  as islamicist agent of destruction, 159, 163, 168
  in Ottoman Empire, 173–8
  permitted in Bible, 178
  prohibited in Qur'an, 170–1, 178
alcoholism. *See* drunkenness
Aldridge, Ira (actor), 294–5
Aleroyla, Laurilla, 146
Algeria, 5. *See also* Algiers
  colonized by French in 1830, 12, 71, 112, 117,
    284
  Zouave troops in, 292
Algerine Captive, The (Tyler), 35, 55, 58
Algerine Spy in Pennsylvania, The (Markoe), 37,
    41, 44, 46, 61
Algiers, 22, 62. *See also* North Africa and North
    Africans
  American fiction about, 37, 42, 49–52, 55, 58,
    144, 146
  attacks by U.S. Navy on, 32
  attacks on American ships, 29–33, 39
  captives in, 30–3, 35, 41–2, 46, 49, 50–6, 141,
    143–4
  compared with Georgia by Benjamin Franklin,
    142
  defeat by British in 1816, 69
  as emblem of slavery, 141–3, 145–6, 149, 150,
    225, 278
  spies in United States from, 37
  treaty of 12 July 1796, 33

Allied Despots, The (engraving by Valentine
    Verax), 31–2
Allison, Robert, 16, 54
American Board of Commissioners for Foreign
    Missions or ABCFM, 84, 85, 117–19,
    121, 124, 130, 132
American in Algiers, The (antislavery poem), 143
Anderson, Eric, 116
antichrist (Islam figured as eastern), 91, 92, 94,
    99, 102, 165, 230
Anti-Slavery Catechism, The (1836), 149
antislavery movement, 134, 159. *See also* slavery
  and Hiram Powers's "The Greek Slave,"
    278–81
  reform of slavery in Islamic lands, 150, 152,
    159
Apollyon (destroying angel of the Book of
    Revelation), 97, 109, 165, 166
Arabia, 79, 113, 156, 244
  origin of alcohol, 162–3, 168, 174
Arabian Nights. See One Thousand and One Nights
Arabs, 2, 5, 6, 27, 37, 64, 82, 85, 110, 131, 149,
    163, 177, 181, 190, 212, 221, 227, 232,
    235, 245, 247–8, 254, 267, 270, 293
Armenia and Armenians, 117, 119, 129–30, 157,
    177, 270
Arrington, Leonard, 210
Arvin, Newton, 253
Asia, Southeast and South. *See* India; Kuala Batu;
    Malays;
attar. *See* perfumes
Aubin, Penelope, 49
Austin, Allan D., 17
Austin, David, 109

Badía y Leblich, Domingo (*Travels of Ali Bey*), 60
Baepler, Paul, 47
Baghdad, 98
Bailyn, Bernard, 26
Bainbridge, Commodore William, 33, 63
Ballou, Maturin Murray (*The Turkish Slave*), 240
Bancroft, George, 3
Barbary States. *See* North Africa and North
    Africans, Algiers, Tunis, or Tripoli
Barnby, Henry, 32
Barnum, P. T., 265–6, 296
Barrell, George, 11

bashaws, 3, 4, 22, 25, 26, 29, 38, 43, 50, 62, 64–6, 68, 76, 115, 144, 210, 212, 234
Beadle, J. H., 209
Beckford, William, 68
Bedouins. *See* Arabs
Bennett, John C., 201–2, 205–6, 217
Benton, Thomas Hart, 136
Berbers (North Africans), 219, 292
Bernard, Francis, 25
Bezanson, Walter, 255
Bible
    alcohol in, 162, 178–9
    Book of Daniel, 93, 109–13. *See also* king of the north
    Book of Esther, 258, 279
    Book of Galatians, 232
    Book of Genesis, 6–7, 71, 92, 232, 239. *See also* Eden (garden of)
    Book of Matthew, 86, 102
    Book of Revelation, 87, 93, 95–6, 101, 109, 111–12, 116. *See also* Fifth Trumpet; Sixth Trumpet; kings of the east; Sixth Vial
    distribution of, 84–5, 118, 120, 152, 247
    polygamy in, 204
    prophecies in, 7, 10, 83–7, 93–4, 97–8, 108, 110–11, 114–15, 118, 123, 133, 232. *See also* eschatology
Bickerstaffe, Isaac, 50
Bird, Isaac (missionary), 86, 95, 118
Bliss, Edwin Elisha (missionary), 173
Bloch, Ruth, 48, 109
Bloomer, Amelia Jenks, 282, 284
bloomers (female dress), 14, 265, 282, 284, 287
    as Turkish trousers, 283, 285–7
Blumenbach, Johann Friedrich, 240–1
Bodin, Jean, 23
Bohon Upas (poisonous tree), 161
Book of Mormon, 186–7, 189, 190, 192, 195, 196
    compared with Qur'an, 194, 199
    viewed as fiction, 194, 196
Bosphorus (Turkish waterway), 33, 178, 260, 261, 287
bottomless pit
    as origin of alcohol, 163, 166
    biblical metaphor for Islam, 95–7, 114, 123–4, 128, 132, 163, 215
Bourdieu, Pierre, 8
Boylston, Nicholas, 262–3
Brewer, Josiah, 182
Brightman, Thomas (biblical commentator), 95, 98, 102
Britain and British citizens, 20, 29–31, 37, 41, 50, 55, 65, 69, 76, 106, 108, 149, 192, 203, 265, 293
Brown, John (abolitionist), 203, 289
Brown, John (English playwright), 49
Browne, J. Ross, 224, 272

Browne, Martha Griffith, 150
Bryan, Edward B., 153
Buffalo Bill's Wild West, 296
Burr, Aaron, Sr., 105
Burton, Richard, 191, 192, 202, 207, 209
Bush, George (minister), 98, 113
Byron, George Gordon, 69, 222, 238, 284

Calhoun, John C., 69, 136, 154
Campbell, Alexander, 195
Campbell, Donald, 11
captivity, narratives of, 35, 36, 53–5, 61, 143
    Affective History of the Captivity and Sufferings of Mrs. Mary Velnet, An, 48
    Algerine Captive, The (Tyler), 55–8
    Authentic Narrative of the Loss of the Brig Commerce, An (Riley), 54
    Humanity in Algiers, 144–6
    Journal of the Captivity and Suffering of John Foss, A, 53–4
    Louisa, A Novel, 41–2, 44
    Narrative of the Captivity and Sufferings of Mrs. Maria Martin, 47
    Narrative of the Captivity of John Vandike, 46–7
    Noble Slaves, The, 49
    Slaves in Algiers (Rowson), 50, 52
Caramalli, Jusef (Qaramanli, Yusef) of Tripoli, 64–5
Carey, Mathew, 31
Carlyle, Thomas, 204, 227–9
Carpenter, Frederick, 15
Carroll, Charles, 78
Cass, Lewis, 163
Caswell, Henry (*The City of the Mormons*), 201
Cathcart, James Leander, 66
Catholics and Catholicism, 19, 40–1, 91–3, 102, 106–8, 165, 168, 194, 205, 293
Caucasian racial identity, 241, 280–1
    Mahommed Jumla as prototype, 240
Caucasus, 112, 237, 240–1, 280. *See also* Caucasian racial identity; Circassia
Cervantes, Miguel de, 28
Charleston, South Carolina, 121, 134
Chess Automaton, 71–8
Child, Lydia Maria, 12–13, 140
China and Chinese, 39, 170, 230
chivalry, 13, 46, 222, 250, 270, 281, 287
cholera, 114, 161, 172
Christy, Arthur, 15
Church of Jesus Christ of Latter-day Saints. *See* Mormons and Mormonism
Çirakman, Asli, 23
Circassia and circassions, 238–42, 281. *See also* caucasion, racial identity, and caucasus
    as original location of ideal female beauty, 209, 238–40, 270, 272, 280–1

as paradise in Melville's writings, 239, 243–5, 255–6, 258
Circassian, The Fair (displayed by P.T. Barnum), 261, 296
Cobbett, William, 52
coffee, 79, 162
  as alternative to alcohol, 182–3
Columbian Orator, The, 144
Columbus, Christopher, 91
Constantinople, 26, 33, 78, 85–6, 90, 99–100, 108, 114, 116–7, 119, 121, 127–30, 151, 157, 171, 178, 181, 226, 229, 231, 240, 249, 260–1, 272, 279–80, 286, 287
  "Sweet waters," 286–7
Constitution (ship), 62
Cook, James, 71–2, 74–5
Cooper, James Fenimore, 29, 240
Copley, John Singleton, 262, 263
Cornbury, Lord [Edward Hyde] (New York Governor), 29
corsairs (North African ships), 28, 30, 144, 146, 226
Cotton, John, 89, 106–7
Creole (ship), 153
Crimean War, 112, 203, 250, 288, 292–3
Cross above the Crescent, The (Southgate), 129, 131–2
Crowley, James W., 136
Crusades, 4, 60, 90–1, 98–9, 106, 250, 293
  in the form of domestic moral reform, 134, 138, 149, 155, 162, 165, 167–8, 189, 202
  Protestants eschew the physical for the spiritual, 92, 107
Cumming, Alfred, 203
Curtis, George William, 268, 270, 272

Damascus, Syria, 68, 97, 191, 241–2, 259, 270
Dardanelles (Turkish waterway), 241
Daubuz, Charles (biblical commentator), 95
Davis, James B. (owner of cotton farm in Constaninople), 157
Davis, Jefferson, 293
Decatur, Stephen, 62–4, 69, 134
Declaration of Independence, The, 20, 78, 143
Deism, 58
De Kay, James E., 12, 171, 178, 286
Derne (city in Tripoli), 64, 154
despotism, 20, 25, 34, 43
  and islamicism, 10, 20–28, 32–4, 38, 41–5, 51–3, 55, 65, 70, 76, 81, 86, 134–5, 140–3, 147, 166, 168, 181, 183, 186, 201–3, 207, 217, 221, 265
  in Herman Melville's literature, 221, 223–4, 231
  in Montesquieu's writings, 23–6, 39, 43
Deys (Algerian leaders), 22, 29–31, 33, 37–40, 51, 54, 56
Dibdin, Charles, 49

Dickson, Walter, 247
Diderot, Denis, 23
Diouf, Sylviane, 17
Ditson, George Leighton, 240
Dixon, William Hepworth, 214
domestic orients
  defined, 136
  New Orleans, 19
  plantations in U.S. South as, 141, 147, 150, 156
  San Francisco as "Barbary Coast", 185
  Utah as orientalized space, 170–93
Douglass, Frederick, 144, 278
  North Star, The, 136, 280
Downes, John, 79
dragomen (*targumen*) interpretive guides, 4, 249, 266
dramatic plays, 35, 36, 49
  Barbarossa (Brown), 49
  Bluebeard, 67
  Evelyn Gray, or the Victims of our Western Turks (Stern), 216
  Grecian Captive, The (Noah), 70
  Mohammed, the Arabian Prophet (Miles), 228
  Deseret Deserted, 215, 216
  Seraglio, The (Dibdin), 50
  Slaves in Algiers (Rowson), 50, 52
  Slaves in Barbary (Everett), 144
  Sultan, The (Bickerstaffe), 50
  Young Carolinians, The, 51, 65
drunkenness, 12, 65, 136, 160, 167, 171, 174, 176, 183, 185–6, 215, 238, 265
  associated with idolatry, 161, 174
  as domestic blight, 168, 172
  in Ottoman Empire, 176–7
  as sign of Christian belief, 177–8
  social and physiological destruction, 161

Eastern Question
  geopolitical fate of Ottoman Empire, 76, 94, 108
Eaton, William, 64–5, 69, 154
Eckford, Henry, 78
Eden (garden of), 106, 181, 216, 237, 239, 241, 242, 244–5, 257, 258–9
Edwards, Jonathan, 89, 107
Egypt and Egyptians, 27, 60, 64, 76, 82, 89, 109–10, 113, 115, 117, 135, 170, 239, 249, 267, 269
Ellsworth, Elmer Ephraim, 288–9, 293
emirs (Muslim leaders), 226–7, 236, 252, 254–5
England. See Britain
eschatology, 10, 87–109, 116–17, 120–7, 131–3, 138, 165, 186. See also Bible, prophecies; millennialism
Euphrates (as eschatological symbol), 99, 106–8, 111–14. See also Sixth Trumpet Sixth Vial
Everett, David, 144

Faber, George Stanley (biblical commentator), 95, 113
Female Life Among the Mormons, 210
Fields, James Ticknor, 269
Fifth Trumpet (Scorpion Locusts), 95–8, 101, 114–15, 122, 132, 165. *See also* Bible: Book of Revelation; locusts; Saracens
Finkelstein, Dorothee Metlitsky, 221, 236, 252
Fischer, Gayle V., 284
Fisher, Mary (Quaker missionary), 2–3, 120, 279
Fisk, Pliny (missionary), 84–5, 95, 117–19
Foreign Missions Committee of the Protestant Episcopal Church, 126
Foss, John, 53–54
Foster, Charles, 117
Foster, Craig L., 188
Foster, Hannah Webster (*The Coquette*), 43
France and French citizens, 12, 23, 31, 40, 60, 65, 71, 76, 90, 95, 108, 112, 117, 191, 203, 284, 288, 292–3
Franklin, Benjamin, 74, 141, 145
    satirizing the slave traded as "Historicus", 142–3

Gabriel (*jibril*) (angel of revelation), 194
Gale, Benjamin, 111
Gallipoli (Ottoman port), 27
Galloway, Joseph, 112
Garrison, William Lloyd, 148
Gay, John (*The Beggar's Opera*), 242
genies (*djinn*), 36, 168, 182, 216, 230, 234
George III, King of England, 4, 20, 31–2
George Washington (ship), 33, 78
Gibbon, Edward, 100, 115
Gibraltar, 26, 30, 63
Giles, Paul, 142
Gill, John (biblical commentator), 95
Gillette, Francis, 167
Givens, Terryl L., 188, 209
Goethe, Johann Wolfgang von, 228
Goldsmith, Oliver (*The Citizen of the* World), 37
Gomez, Michael, 17
Goodell, William (missionary), 82, 84, 116, 132
Grand Turk (ship), 78
Grant, Asahel (missionary), 123
Greece, 21, 90, 148, 274, 279
    war of independence, 22, 69–71, 75–6, 113, 147, 167, 175, 274, 281
Greek Slave, The (statue by Hiram Powers), 265, 273, 281
Greenwood, Grace, 191, 213, 287
Grosrichard, Alain, 38

Hagar (bondswoman in Book of Genesis), 6, 92, 181, 204, 232
hajjis (pilgrims to Mecca), 192, 267
Halliday, Fred, 15
Ham, curse of, 93

Harding, Chester, 262, 264–5
harem. *See* seraglio
Harris, William, 201
Haupt, Jon, 210
Hawes, Joel (missionary), 132
Hawthorne, Nathaniel, 219, 223, 237, 241, 245
Hawthorne, Sophia, 241
hegira (*hijrah*)
    chapter in Melville's *Omoo*, 235
    movements of Mormons called, 191
Henry, Patrick, 37
Hicks, Thomas, 269
Higginson, Thomas Wentworth, 294
Hildreth, R. (*The White Slave*), 134
Hinkle, George M., 200
Historical and Geographical Account of Algiers, An, 146
Holy Land. *See* Palestine; Israel
Homer, Winslow, 290
Homes, Henry Augustus (missionary), 85–6
Hopkins, Samuel Miles (New York Judge), 179–80
horses
    as characters in Melville's *Clarel*, 254
    gift of Mellimelli, Tunisian Ambassador, 66
    kindness toward in Turkey, 247
    Turkish cavalry in Sixth Trumpet of Book of Revelation, 96, 99–101
houris (angels in Islamic paradise), 172, 205, 210, 215, 223, 236–8, 242–3, 256, 258, 260, 272, 286
Howadji in Syria, The (Curtis), 268
howadjis (travelers), 265, 267–70, 272, 285, 289, 296
    Curtis, George William as, 268
    Stephens John Lloyd as Jacob Al-Khawaja, 267
    Taylor, Bayard, 265–70
Howe, Fisher, 70
Huit, Ephraim, 110
Humanity in Algiers; or, The Story of Azem, 144, 146
Hunt, James H., 196, 198–9
Hutchinson, Thomas, 26
Hyde, John, 195, 198, 202, 209
Hyde, Orson, 200

Ibrahim Pasha of Egypt, 113, 117
Incidents of Travel in Egypt. Arabia Petraea, and the Holy Land (Stephens), 251, 267–8
India, 11, 75, 78, 84, 125, 154, 170, 172, 231, 243, 245
Intrepid (ship), 62, 81
Iranistan (P. T. Barnum's home), 265–6
Irving, Washington, 67, 204, 222, 227
    Alhambra, The, 222
    Mahomet and His Successors, 124, 222
Irving, William, 67

Ishmael
  as Abrahamic ancestor of Arabs in the Qur'an,
    6, 204, 232
  in Book of Genesis, 6–7, 71, 92, 118, 204–5,
    232
  Mormons accept God's blessing of, 204–5
  narrator of Melville's *Moby-Dick*, 7, 223, 232–3
  preserved by fresh water, 181, 233
islamicism, 7–15, 18, 25, 135, 296
  "abduction from the seraglio" theme, 236,
    281–2
  and despotism, 20–8, 32–4, 41–5, 134–5, 140–3
  and eschatology, 87, 116, 132–3
  and material culture. *See* bloomers; Chess
    Automaton; Greek Slave, The; Tripoli
    Monument; Zouaves
  and missionary enterprise, 82–6, 117, 133, 173,
    175
  and Mormons, 186, 217
  and North Africa, 27, 28
  and slavery, 159
  and temperance discourse, 161, 183
  and the American West, 185–6, 189, 193
  as opposite of American republicanism, 21
islamicism, comparative, 10–13, 137, 139, 183. *See*
    also Muslim-Mormon comparison; spy
    narratives
  in antislavery discourse, 147, 158
  and despotism, 20, 25, 31–2
  emphasizing Turkish virtue, 138
  example of Turkish temperance, 168, 173, 178
  and Herman Melville's *Clarel*, 223, 246, 257
  images of female beauty, 272
  and Mormons, 197
  Muslim and Mormon polygamy, 203, 205, 217
  and pro-slavery argument in the U.S. South,
    152–3
  and slavery, 138–9, 144, 146–7, 155, 158. *See* also
    Greek Slave, The
  Turkish honesty as critique of capitalism, 175
islamicism, domestic, 10–11, 135, 139, 183
  alcohol as islamicist agent, 161, 168
  and despotism, 25
  and Mormons, 186
  sea captains as despots in Herman Melville, 224
  and slavery, 136–9, 143, 146–7
  comparing Sumatra with U.S. South, 134
islamicism, literary
  and the antislavery movement, 143, 146
  during the Barbary wars, 37–42, 46, 48, 50–2,
    55, 58–9. *See* also captivity narratives;
    dramatic plays; oriental tales; spy
    narratives
  and Mormons, 210–12, 214, 216
  in the works of Herman Melville, 219, 261
islamicism, romantic, 10, 13, 139, 184, 222–3
  and antislavery movement, 281–2
  coffee as exotic alternative to alcohol, 182–3

Djalea, the guide of Melville's *Clarel*, 251,
    257
  and female beauty, 270, 272–3
  and Herman Melville, 219–22, 226, 232, 245,
    256, 261
  and mid-nineteenth-century gender roles, 224,
    262, 265, 296
  Mormon polygamy, 204
  and Mormons, 193, 197–8, 215
  and slavery, 139, 140, 158
  water as healing agent, 181–2, 233
islamism, 8
Israel, 5, 189, 190, 242, 279
  as chosen community, 85, 89, 102, 107, 233.
    See also Jews, Jewish religion, and
    Palestine
  lost tribes of, 94, 240
Istanbul. *See* Constantinople

Jackson, Andrew, 59, 74, 76, 78–9, 160
Jackson, Carl T., 15
James, Henry, 273
Jamestown, Virginia (as new Algiers), 140
Jay, John, 39, 141
Jefferson, Thomas, 20, 22, 57, 66, 141
Jerusalem, 60, 82–3, 90, 98, 109, 192, 249, 256,
    267
Jerusalem, New, 89, 190, 245, 247
Jews and Jewish religion, 6, 19, 37, 89, 93, 117,
    122, 189, 272
  in Melville's *Clarel*, 249
  restoration to Jerusalem as divine sign, 83, 102,
    107–12, 133
jihad, 6, 289
Judd, Sylvester, 177, 183
Jurieu, Pierre (biblical commentator), 95

Kaplan, Amy, 281
Kempelen, Baron Wolfgang von, 75
Kesselman, Amy, 283
Khadija (wife of the Prophet Muhammad), 197,
    215
Kilco, Harne, 111
Kimball, Heber C., 207
King of the north (in Book of Daniel), 111. *See*
    also Bible: Book of Daniel
King, Jonas (missionary), 82–4, 95, 122
kings of the east (in Book of Revelation), 112,
    121, 123, 126. *See* also Bible: Book of
    Revelation
Kinmont, Alexander, 240
Kirk, Rev. Edward, 173, 180
Knapp, Samuel Lorenzo, 59, 62
Kohf, Mohja, 243
Koran. *See* Qur'an
Kuala Batu (Qualla Battoo), Sumatra, 79
  bombarded by U.S. Navy, 22, 81, 134,
    230

Lands of the Saracens, The (Taylor), 268
Langdon, Samuel, 105
Lawrence, Amos, 262–6, 288
Lawrence, T. E. ("of Arabia"), 296
Lear, Tobias, 65, 67
Leavitt, Gerald M., 74
Lewis, Bernard, 158
Lewis, Jan, 42
Liberator, The, 148
Lincoln, Abraham, 289
Lind, Jenny, 265
Litch, Josiah, 115–6
Little, Douglas, 16
locusts. *See also* Fifth Trumpet
  as biblical type of Islamic warriors, 95–7, 100, 114, 123, 133
Louis XIV, King of France, 23
Louisa, A Novel, 41–2, 44
Lowe. Lisa, 14
Luedtke, Luther S., 223
Luther, Martin (Islam in writings of), 92–3

Madison, James, 66
Maelzel, Johann, 72, 74–6
Mahomet. *See* Muhammad, Prophet
Mahometanism. *See* Islam
Malays, 6, 79, 81, 134, 221
  in Melville's literature, 226, 230
Mann, Horace, 150–1
Marana, Giovanni (*Letters from a Turkish Spy*), 37
Marine Corps., U.S., 69
Markoe, Peter, 37, 41, 44, 46, 61
Marsh, Thomas B., 199
Martyn, Henry (missionary), 119–20, 126
Mather, Cotton, 29, 89, 97, 102–4
Mather, Increase, 89, 102–4
McAlister, Melani, 16–17
McCarrell, Rev. Joseph, 180
McClellan, George B., 289
Mecca (Islamic holy city and focus of pilgrimage), 6, 57, 58, 60, 154, 192, 226, 248, 267
  compared with Salt Lake City, Utah, 191, 193, 207
Mede, Joseph (biblical commentator), 95, 97, 98, 102
Mehemet Ali of Egypt, 113, 115
Mellimelni (Mellimelli), Sidi Soliman (Tunisian Ambassador), 66–7
Melville, Herman, 14
  Arrowhead (Pittsfield home), 219
  familiarity with Islam, 220
  islamicism and female characterization, 238, 239, 242, 245, 258, 260
  literary characters
    Ahab (*Moby-Dick*), 224, 226–7, 230–1, 254
    Arnaut (*Clarel*), 249–50, 251

Babo ("Benito Cereno"), 231
Belex (*Clarel*), 249–51
Captain Claret (*White-Jacket*), 225
Captain Riga (*Redburn*), 225
Captain Vangs (*Typee*), 224
Clarel (*Clarel*), 255
Djalea (*Clarel*), 223, 249–50, 251–7
Dr. Long Ghost (*Omoo*), 234
Fayaway (*Typee*), 238, 242
Fedallah (*Moby-Dick*), 230–1, 249
Inamorata ("Fragments"), 238
Ishmael (*Clarel*), 232
Ishmael (*Moby-Dick*), 7, 223, 232–3
John Paul Jones (*Israel Potter*), 226
Lavender (*Redburn*), 225
Lucy Tartan (*Pierre*), 244–5
Moby Dick (the white whale), 229
Nehemiah (*Clarel*), 247
Omoo (*Omoo*), 223, 233–5, 257
Queequeg (*Moby-Dick*), 233, 241
Rolfe (*Clarel*), 255
Ruth (*Clarel*), 244–6, 255, 257
Taji (*Mardi*), 223, 236, 243–4, 257
Tommo (*Typee*), 233, 242
Yillah (*Mardi*), 236, 242–5, 281
Zar [Djalea's horse] (*Clarel*), 254
redefinition of original sin, 244
rejection of eschatological millennialism, 247
travel
  to eastern Mediterranean in 1856–7, 246
  in Pacific islands, 242
wore Turkish slippers and pyjamas, 219
works
  "A Ground Vine," 258
  "A Spirit Appeared to Me," 258
  Battle-Pieces, 251, 294
  "Benito Cereno," 230–1
  "C's_'s Lament," 246
  Clarel, 223, 230–2, 239, 245–57, 267
  "Continents, The," 260–1
  "Devotion of the Flowers to their Lady, The," 258–9
  "Fragments from a Writing Desk," 238
  "Fragments of a Lost Gnostic Poem of the Twelfth Century," 246
  "Grain by Grain," 258
  "Hawthorne and His Mosses," 219
  "Herba Santa," 254
  "I and My Chimney," 222–31
  Israel Potter, 226, 246
  Journals, 231, 239, 244, 246, 248, 251, 254, 257
  "Lover and the Syringa Bush, The," 259
  Mardi, 226, 230, 235–6, 242–5, 254, 281–2

Moby-Dick, 219, 226–33, 235, 241, 245, 253, 254, 260
"My Jacket Old," 257–8
"Naples in the Time of Bomba," 238
Omoo, 233, 234–5
"Pausilippo," 258
Pierre, 239, 244–5, 246
Redburn, 225, 235, 238, 248, 267
review of J. Ross Browne's *Etchings of a Whaling Cruise*, 224
"Rosary Beads," 258
"Rose Farmer, The," 259–60
"Syla," 259
The Confidence-Man, 246
"The New Zealots to the Sun," 231
"Traveling, Its Pleasures, Pains, and Profits," 247
Typee, 224, 233, 238, 242–3
"Typee Manuscript," 242
"Vial of Attar, The," 260
White-Jacket, 225–6, 235, 251
Merrick, James Lyman (missionary), 120–6, 128, 131, 157, 268
Micali, Charles, 81
Middle East. *See* Arabia; Egypt; North Africa; Ottoman Empire; Palestine; Persia
Middlekauff, Robert, 102
Mifflin, Warner, 143
Milder, Robert, 242
Miles, George, H., 228
millennialism. *See* Bible prophecies in eschatology
Miller, Elizabeth Smith, 283
Miller, William, 89, 114, 116–17
Mitchell, John Kearsley, 74
Mitchell, Weir, 76
Mocha (port), 69, 151, 156
moghuls or moguls. *See* Mughals
Mohamed. *See* Muhammad, Prophet
Mohammed. *See* Muhammad, Prophet
Mohammedanism. *See* Islam
Monroe, James, 69
Montagu, Lady Mary, 213, 285
Montesquieu, Charles de Secondat, Barón De, 23–6, 37, 39, 46, 47
Lettres Persanes, 37, 46
Spirit of the Laws, The, 23, 42
Moors, 6, 19, 27, 67, 80–1, 153, 221–2, 231
Mormons and Mormonism, 14, 185, 211, 217, 218. *See also* Muslim-Mormon comparison
as an American Islam, 186
practice of plural marriage, 203, 218
restoration of the saints in Zion, 190
sexual practices compared with urban New Yorkers, 214

understanding of Islam in world history, 204
Morocco, 26, 28, 54, 103
Morrill Act (1862), 203
Morrison, Toni, 239
Morse, Jedidiah, 111
Mott, Dr. Valentine, 272
Mott, Lucretia, 282
Mughals, 227, 268
Ahab in *Moby-Dick* as "old mogul," 227
Brigham Young as "Mormon Mogul," 206
Muhammad, Elijah, 294
Muhammad, Prophet, 1, 3, 6, 19, 75, 77, 94–5, 98, 105, 111, 114, 120, 124, 145, 176, 192, 195–7, 201, 217, 222, 227–9, 236, 243, 256, 286
as proponent of temperance, 171, 176, 178–80
Brigham Young compared with, 191, 206, 207, 215–17
called a "great soul," 227
descended from Abraham, 6
in Goethe's *Poetry and Truth*, 228
hegira to Medina, 191, 235
islamicist images of, 20–2, 68, 85, 91, 95, 97, 105, 180, 190, 196, 201, 215–16, 237
Joseph Smith compared with, 185–8, 193–202, 205–7, 216–17
Melville compares authority with captain of a ship, 225–7
in play by George H. Miles, 228
statue of in U.S. Supreme Court, 1, 2
teachings on slavery, 151, 153, 158
viewed as hero by Thomas Carlyle, 203, 227, 228–9
Washington Irving's biography of, 203, 222, 227
Muslim-Mormon comparison, 185–8
exposing sexual practices, 215–17
Islam seen as superior to Mormonism, 197–8
use of historical allusions, 196–7, 202, 205
Mormon polygamy superior to Muslim, 213
Mormonism seen as superior to Islam, 198
Muslim family life superior to Mormon polygamy, 210, 213
polygamy, 203, 205, 217
as process of transnational projection, 188
and racial difference, 209
Scriptures (Book of Mormon and Qur'an), 194–6, 205
sensual paradise, 205
Utah as "domestic Orient" 190–3
violent conquest by the sword, 201, 202
Mussulmen Humbled, The (poem), 63

Na'aman, Ahmed bin (captain of the ship *Sultanah* from Oman), 177
Napoleon, 74, 108–9

Nation of Islam, 294
Native Americans, 17, 19, 31, 84, 93–4, 173, 190, 240, 267
Navarino, Battle of, 12, 76, 78, 117, 175, 251
Navy, United States, 22, 34, 53, 62, 64, 66, 69, 70, 78–9, 81, 134
    depicted as islamicist despotism in Herman Melville's writings, 225–6
Near East. _See_ Arabia; Egypt; Greece; North Africa; Ottoman Empire; Palestine; Persia
Nestorian Christians, 117, 119, 121, 123, 174, 176
New Orleans, Louisiana, 273, 292
New York, New York, 31, 245
    African American ball in support of Greek independence, 147
    firefighters from in Constantinople, 78
    first venue of Chess Automaton, 71
    fundraiser for missionary to Persia, 127
    Tripolitan prisoners in, 66–9
    visit of _Sultanah_ from Oman, 177
Newton, Bishop Thomas (biblical commentator), 95, 99, 101
Newton, Stella Mary, 283
Nile Notes of a Howadji (Curtis), 268
Noah, Mordecai Manuel, 70
Noble, Marianne, 277
North Africa, 27.
    geography and cartography, 27, 28
    slavery in, 29. _See also_ Algiers: as emblem of slavery
North Africa and North Africans, 21, 25–31, 49, 51, 54, 56, 62, 65, 67, 87, 90, 103, 110, 140–4, 146–7, 151–2, 185. _See also_ Algiers; Egypt; Morocco; Tripoli; and Tunis
    as symbol of tyranny and darkness, 27–8

O'Bannon, Presley, 69
Olin, Stephen, 170, 268
Oman (_Sultanah_ [ship] in New York City), 177
One Thousand and One Nights, The, 13, 44–5, 67, 130, 194, 237–8, 268–9, 270, 294
opium, 27, 79, 112, 170, 182, 184
oriental tales, 13, 35, 36–7, 46, 143–5
Orientalism (Edward Said), 2
orientalism, Islamic. _See_ islamicism
Osgood, Samuel, 111
Othello (Shakespeare), 229, 294
Ottoman Empire, 9, 11–13, 20, 23, 26–7, 75–6, 90, 92, 94, 99, 102, 114, 117, 133, 153, 221, 225, 247, 249, 296.
    as antichristian curse, 82, 91–4, 106, 132. _See also_ Sixth Trumpet
    as exporter of opium, 170
    as land of temperance, 168, 171, 178
    hegemony over Palestine, 83, 87, 89, 90, 98, 109–11

in Crimean War, 203, 293
John Smith's exploits in, 2–3
Mary Fisher's travels to, 3
naval forces, 78, 251. _See also_ Navarino, Battle of
political reforms, 117, 119, 147, 212
removal as eschatological sign, 89, 92, 94–5, 100, 102–9, 111–17, 132–3, 292. _See also_ Sixth Vial
slavery in, 142, 148, 151, 155–9, 173, 279
trade in New England rum, 162, 173–9
Treaty of Commerce (1830), 71
viewed as decadent and indolent, 44, 70, 77, 114, 168–9, 178, 247, 250, 265, 281–2
war with Greece, 11, 69–71, 75–6, 148

Paine, Caroline (_Tent and Harem_), 170, 286
Paine, Thomas, 43, 100
Palestine, 6, 82–4, 87, 90–1, 93–4, 98, 109–12, 117, 133, 149, 173, 190–1, 201–2, 241, 245–7, 249–50, 253, 268, _See_ Israel
Palfrey, John Gorham, 134
Palmyra, Syria, 190
Parker, Hershel, 219
Parker, Theodore, 151–2, 156
Parker, Thomas, 110
Parsons, Levi (missionary), 82–5, 95, 107, 117–19
pasha or pashas. _See_ bashaws
Pathology of Drunkenness, The, 176
Paulding, James Kirke, 67
perfumes, 128, 231, 238–9, 244, 259–60, 296. _See also_ peris
peris (Islamic angels), 223, 236–9, 244
Perkins, Justin, 155, 174
Persia and Persians, 6, 46, 91, 107, 110–11, 113, 117, 119, 128, 154–5, 174, 176, 221, 231, 241, 245, 258–9, 287
Philadelphia (ship), 62, 64–5, 81
philhellenism, 69–70, 76, 279
Pierpont, Rev. John, 165, 176
Poe, Edgar Allan, 219
    essay on chess automaton, 74–5
    houris in works by, 237
    review of John Lloyd Stephens, 267
Poems of the Orient (Taylor), 268
Poland and Poles, 101, 147–8
polygamy
    and Mormons, 187, 203–10, 213, 215, 217, 265, 270
    and Muslims, 40, 57, 129, 203, 207, 210, 212–14
    and racial difference, 209–10, 213
Porter, David, 78, 81, 286
Post, Henry A.V., 70
Potomac (ship), 79

Powers, Hiram, 265, 273–9
Pratt, Parley P., 204
Preble, Edward, 63

Quakers, 3
  Mary Fisher, 2–3, 120, 279
  Warner Mifflin, 143
Quallah Battoo. *See* Kuala Batu, Sumatra
Qur'an, 1, 57–8, 85, 225, 248
  and missionaries, 122, 126–7
  attitudes towards slavery in, 145, 153–4, 156–9
  compared with Book of Mormon, 194–6, 205
  Ishmael in, 6, 233
  prohibition of alcohol in, 162, 168, 170–1, 176, 178, 251
  women in, 207, 237

Racknitz, Freyherr, 75
Ramadan, 66, 250, 260
  chapter in *Moby-Dick*, 233, 260
Rehnquist, William, 6
republicanism, 9–10, 20–1, 24, 35, 43, 51–3, 86, 138, 166, 224
Reynolds, David S., 36, 46
Reynolds, R. N., 79
Rhodes, Foster, 78
Rice, Stephen P., 74
Ricoeur. Paul, 14
Riley, William, 54
Rowson, Susanna Haswell, 35, 50–2
rum, New England. *See also* alcohol
  exported to the Ottoman Empire, 162, 173–8
Russia and Russians, 30, 75–6, 78, 94, 111–12, 147, 148–9, 153, 156, 174–5, 192, 203, 225, 250, 281, 292, 293

Said, Edward, 2, 4, 8, 13–14, 17, 77
Saladin, 222, 270
Sallee (port in Morocco), 28–9, 103
Salmagundi (Mustapha Rub-a-Dub Keli Khan letters), 67–8
Salt Lake City, Utah, 64, 203, 209, 213
  as domestic orient, 190–3, 207, 215
San Francisco, California (as "Barbary Coast"), 185
Saracens, 92, 95, 97–9, 101. *See also* Fifth Trumpet
Sargent, Lucius M., 160, 171, 173
Schauffler, William (missionary), 85, 122–3, 157
Scheherezade (in *The One Thousand and One Nights*), 44–5
Schlumberger, William, 74
Schöpp, Joseph, 49
Schueller, Malini Johar, 16, 56
scimitars (scimitars-swords), 51, 69, 149, 227, 294
scorpions (biblical type). *See* locusts

Seneca Falls, New York, 283
seraglio, 13, 24, 41–6, 50, 66, 132, 140, 205, 207–8, 210, 212–13, 214–17, 236, 239, 255, 259–60, 270, 272, 280–2, 285–7
  and Mormon polygamy, 203
"The Seraglio" (play by Dibdin), 50
Setton, Kenneth M., 90
Sha'ban, Fuad, 15, 29
shahada (Muslim proclamation of faith), 216, 227, 243
Shaler, William, 11
Shaw, Elijah, 65
Shaw, Lemuel, 246
Shays, Daniel, 38
simoom (destructive wind), 43, 161
Sixth Trumpet (Turkish Woe), 30, 98, 105–6, 114–15. *See also* Bible: Book of Revelation
Sixth Vial (drying up of Euphrates), 104–8, 111, 113–14. *See also* Bible: Book of Revelation
Slater, Nelson, 207
slavery, 134, 140, 159, 202–3, 217, 293. *See also* Africans; African Americans; antislavery
  The Declaration of Independence and, 20
  and despotism, 23–4
  and drunkenness, 136, 166–7
  and Hiram Powers's "The Greek Slave," 278–9
  John Smith in Tartary, 3
  Muslims in The Americas, 17–18
  and Near Eastern markets, 279–80
  in North Africa, 29. *See also* captivity narratives; despotism
  as orientalist symbol of Islam, 24, 135, 150, 198
  and *Uncle Tom's Cabin*, 140
  and women in harem, 44, 207, 216, 243. *See also* captivity narratives; Circassia, The Fair; Greek Slave, The; seraglio
Slaves in Algiers (Rowson), 35, 50, 52
Smith, Eli (missionary), 117–20, 127, 174, 296
Smith, Ethan (prophetic commentator), 107, 108, 111, 113
Smith, George A., 204
Smith, John, 22–4, 28
Smith, Joseph, 227
  compared with Muhammad, 202
  compared with the Prophet Muhammad, 185–8, 193–202, 205–7, 216–17
Smith, Sarah L. Huntington (missionary), 132
Smyrna (Ottoman port), 11, 27, 85, 174–5, 181
Smyth, Warington W. (*A Year with the Turks*), 178
Southern, R. W., 90
Southey, Robert, 68, 192
Southgate, Horatio (missionary), 118, 120, 126–32, 170–1, 268, 296

Spain, 19, 27–8, 30, 49, 67, 89, 100, 139–40, 221, 222, 247. *See also* Moors
spy narratives, 35, 36, 61–2
    Algerine Spy in Pennsylvania, The (Markoe), 37, 41
    Extracts from a Journal of Travels in North America (Knapp), 59, 61
    Salmagundi (Mustapha Rub-a-Dub Keli Khan letters), 67–8
Standage, Tom, 74
Stanton, Elizabeth Cady, 283, 287
Stearns, Rev. E. J., 181
Stenhouse, Fannie, 213
Stenhouse, T. B. H. (*The Rocky Mountain Saints*), 186
Stephens, John L., 70, 251, 267–9, 270, 272
Stowe, Harriet Beecher, 140, 147, 181
sultans, 20, 22, 26, 27, 33, 41, 60, 72, 74, 78, 89, 111–12, 115–16, 146, 148, 151, 175, 212, 216, 225, 226, 243, 260, 262, 279
    Abdel-Mejid of Turkey, 19
    Ahab in *Moby-Dick*, 227
    as epitomes of despotism, 24, 25
    Mahmud II of Turkey, 71, 176
    Mahmud IV of Turkey, 3
    Mustapha of Turkey, 31–2
    Othman, 114
Sumner, Charles, 134, 146, 151–3
Supreme Court, United States, 9, 1
Syria, 117, 132. *See also* Damascus

Taine, Hyppolite, 196
Tartary and Tartars, 3, 6, 91, 227, 245
Taylor, Bayard, 268–70, 272, 288
Taylor, John (Mormon leader), 200, 214
temperance movement, 134, 159–81. *See also* Alcohol and Alcoholism
    as popular reform, 159–60
    as symbolic abolitionism, 167
    figured as crusade, 162, 165, 167–8
    Maine Law (legal prohibition), 160, 179
    total prohibition viewed as Islamic, 179–81
Temple, Daniel, 132
Thompson, George, 214
Toon, Peter, 87
Tourgée, Albion W., 189
travel narratives, Near Eastern, 12–13, 45, 173, 183, 240, 248, 270–2, 280, 289
    depictions of slave markets, 280
Tripoli, 26, 69. *See also* North Africa and North Africans
    Treaty of Peace and Friendship (1796), 59, 62
    Tripolitan prisoners in New York City, 67–8
    Tripolitan War of 1801–5, 22, 62, 65–6, 81
Tripoli Monument, 80, 81

Tunis, 66. *See also* North Africa and North Africans
    ambassador to the United States, Sidi Soliman Mellimelni, 66–7
    Bey of Tunis (leader) prohibits slavery (1846), 150–5, 279
Turcos (African Zouaves), 293
Turkey. *See* Ottoman Empire
Turner, Bryan S., 24
Turner, James, 58
Turner, Nat, 148
Tyler, Royall, 35, 55, 58

Uncle Tom's Cabin, 140, 181
Utah Territory, 202–3, 206. *See also* Salt Lake City, Utah

Valentino, Rudolph, 15, 296
Van Deusen, Increase and Maria, 212, 216
Versluis, Arthur, 15
Vienna, Austria, 74–5, 90, 99, 236
Virginia, 3, 25, 28, 37, 66, 139, 141, 148, 156, 194, 219, 289, 291
virtue
    and republicanism, 11, 22, 24, 34, 35, 36, 41–2, 49, 52, 61, 161
    counterdespotism and female, 40–1, 44–5, 49, 50–2, 270, 274
    Muslim examples of, 11–12, 138, 145–6, 151, 175, 197, 247
    Wahabi movement, 113

Waite, Catherine (*The Mormon Prophet and His Harem*), 207
Wanderings of William, The, 46
Ward, Artemus, 191
Ward, Austin, 213
Warner, Michael, 37
Washington, D.C., 66
    Naval (Tripoli) Monument, 80–1
    return of captives from North Africa, 65
    Washington Memorial, 19
Washington, George, 31, 41, 70, 143
water (romanticized as alternative to alcohol), 181–2
Webster, Daniel, 59, 154
Webster, Noah, 35
Weinman, Adolph A., 1
West, William W., 194
Whittier, John Greenleaf, 139, 149, 153–5, 196
    "Derne" (poem), 154
    "The Christian Slave" (poem), 154
    "The Khan's Devil" (poem), 182
    "The World's Convention of The Friends Of Emancipation, Held in London in 1840" (poem), 149

Willard, Frances, 207
Wines, E. C., 270
Wollstonecraft, Mary, 43–4, 282
Woodruff, Samuel, 70
Wright, A. A. (missionary), 176

Young, Brigham, 186, 190, 203, 215–16
   and polygamy, 206, 213, 216
   compared with the Prophet Muhammad,
      206–7, 215, 217

Zouaves, 288–94, 296
   African Turcos, 293
   Britain's West India Regiment, 293
   Elmer Ellsworth's United States Zouave
      Cadets, 288–9
   French troops, 288, 292–3
   military uniform, 14, 264, 288, 290, 292–3
   Papal troops, 293
   roots in Algeria, 292
   units in Civil War armies, 289–92